CQ GUIDE TO

CURRENT AMERICAN GOVERNMENT

Fall 2004

CQ PRESS

A Division of Congressional Quarterly Inc.

Washington, D.C.

Congressional Quarterly Inc.

Congressional Quarterly Inc., an editorial research service and publishing company, serves clients in the fields of news, education, business and government. It provides comprehensive and nonpartisan reporting on Congress, government and politics.

Under the CQ Press imprint, Congressional Quarterly also publishes college political science textbooks and public affairs paperbacks on developing issues and events; information directories; and reference books on the federal government, national elections and politics. Titles include the *Guide to the Presidency*, the *Guide to Congress*, the *Guide to the U.S. Supreme Court*, the *Guide to U.S. Elections* and *Politics in America*. CQ's American Government A–Z collection is a reference series that provides essential information about Congress, the presidency, the Supreme Court and the electoral process. The *CQ Almanac*, a compendium of legislation for one session of Congress, is published each year. *Congress and the Nation*, a record of government for a presidential term, is published every four years. CQ Press also publishes *The CQ Researcher*, a weekly print periodical and online reference database covering today's most debated social and political issues.

CQ publishes *CQ Today* (formerly the *Daily Monitor*), a report on the current and future activities of congressional committees. An online information system, CQ.com on Congress, provides immediate access to CQ's databases of legislative action, votes, schedules, profiles and analyses. Visit www.cq.com for more information.

CQ Press
1255 22nd St., N.W., Suite 400
Washington, D.C. 20037

202-729-1900; toll-free, 1-866-4CQ-PRESS (1-866-427-7737)

www.cqpress.com

Printed and bound in the United States of America
08 07 06 05 04   5 4 3 2 1

♾ The paper used in this publication exceeds the requirements of the American National Standard for Information Sciences—Permanence of Paper for Printed Library Materials, ANSI Z39.48-1992.

ISBN 1-56802-901-2
ISSN 0196-612-X

Contents

Contents

Introduction

Guide to Current American Government is a collection of articles selected from the *CQ Weekly*, a trusted source for in-depth, nonpartisan reporting and analyses of congressional action, policy debates, presidential activities and other developments in Washington. The articles—selected to complement introductory American government texts through examination of current issues and controversies—are divided into four sections: foundations of American government, political participation, government institutions and politics and public policy.

Foundations of American government. This section examines issues and events that involve interpretation of the U.S. Constitution. This edition of the *Guide* provides an extensive analysis of homeland security two years after the creation of the cabinet-level Homeland Security Department, Congress's struggle over reorganizing the U.S. intelligence community and the workings of the congressional oversight process.

Political participation. The articles in this section examine current issues in electoral and party politics, including congressional focus on the 2004 elections and partisan divisions in the House and Senate.

Government institutions. This section explores the inner workings of Congress and the presidency. In this edition, the articles cover the split among Republicans over the national deficit, President George W. Bush's plan to allow private companies to compete for federal civilian jobs, the effect of presidential campaigning on congressional voting in 2003, the strains in the Bush administration's relationship with Congress and Congress's reaction to the prisoner abuse scandal in Iraq.

Politics and public policy. The articles in this section focus on major policy issues, such as trade, gay marriage and Medicare.

Foundations of American Government

The first article in this section highlights how Congress continues to grapple with combating terrorism, and the second article looks at its efforts in structuring intelligence-gathering activities. Although the federal government has spent billions of dollars on security upgrades since September 11, 2001, many experts warn that security gaps remain. As citizens, lawmakers and security experts confront the continuing threat of terrorism, they wonder whether the United States is safer today than it was before September 11, whether rescue personnel are prepared to respond to another attack and whether Congress is spending enough on homeland security.

The challenge for Congress in structuring intelligence-gathering activities is to protect the nation from domestic and international threats without trampling on civil liberties. Because the U.S. intelligence community was not created to operate as a single organization, there is no one office to logically coordinate intelligence gathering. In the wake of hearings by the independent National Commission on Terrorist Attacks Upon the United States, known better as the 9/11 Commission, some lawmakers argue that the intelligence network should be restructured.

The third article discusses one of Congress's most important responsibilities: its oversight role. In the U.S. system of checks and balances, the legislative branch acts as a watchdog that keeps the executive branch in check. Recently, however, the watchdog has gained a reputation for sometimes sleeping on the job. On such high-profile issues as Iraq, intelligence, appropriations, energy policy and the USA Patriot Act, the oversight process has faltered, in part because of an uncooperative administration, the work of independent commissions and, some critics contend, a lack of congressional effort.

John Kourtz of the U.S. Coast Guard on the bow of a new Homeland Security response boat April 2, patrolling Boston Harbor.

Safer, Yes — But Still Vulnerable

Two years later, the nation struggles to mold a strategy on homeland security

Terrorists were not behind the blackout that darkened the Northeast on Aug. 14. But the moment the lights went out, terrorism was the first thing that crossed the minds of many caught in the darkness.

The fear was understandable, given the increasing number of warnings in recent months:

On July 30, the Department of Homeland Security (DHS) warned that terrorists might be conspiring to hijack airplanes again — this time not with box cutters but by exploiting holes in the international air travel system that allow foreign visitors to pass through U.S. airports without visas.

As close to the power outage as Aug. 3, Attorney General John Ashcroft warned that the al Qaeda terrorist organization is still plotting attacks on America or its interests abroad. And in early August, an al Qaeda tape surfaced warning that Americans will be attacked if terrorist detainees in Guantanamo Bay, Cuba, are harmed.

On Aug. 12, an FBI undercover operation led to the arrest of a man in New Jersey charged with trying to buy shoulder-launched missiles that could be fired against commercial passenger jets.

In the past year, al Qaeda has been blamed for two terrorist attacks in Indonesia, as well as others in Morocco and Saudi Arabia, raising concerns that it is only a matter of time before the group turns its sights back toward the United States.

More than two years after one of the grimmest days in U.S. history, the fundamental question remains: Are we safer? Many experts and government officials contend that, yes, the United States is safer. But the nature of terrorism is to surprise the victims and exploit a security weakness, and even the most optimistic experts say that despite the efforts of the new Department of Homeland Security, America's defenses remain vulnerable.

"I think we're safer, but we're not safe enough," says Texas Rep. Jim Turner, ranking Democrat on the House Select Committee on Homeland Security. "We're still in the infant stages of developing a national strategy on homeland security. But our terrorist enemies are not waiting. We have a long way to go."

Since the Sept. 11 terrorist attacks, about $20 billion has been funneled to local police and fire "first responders," for equipment and training in responding to a terrorist attack. The training includes mock-disaster exercises nationwide involving local responders, coordinated by the DHS.

Top homeland security officials say federal, state and local agencies are ready to respond to another attack, but several security studies, including one from the New York-based Council on Foreign Relations, rate the nation's first responders as "dangerously unprepared." Other recent studies say the nation's schools and health care providers feel vulnerable and unprepared to respond to another terrorist attack.

Another lingering homeland defense question: Are the CIA, FBI and other U.S. intelligence agencies now working together effectively and able to "connect the dots" in order to avoid the massive communication failures that enabled the Sept. 11 terrorist attacks to succeed? The agencies acknowledge that the answer is still no. But in late September, the Bush administration announced it had a plan to consolidate the dozen or so different terrorist "watch lists" in the coming months.

Information-sharing has become a new priority of the Terrorist Threat Integration Center, but critics worry that the new administration initiative will not be effective because it was placed under the authority of the CIA. Opponents of the move say terrorism data analysis should be independent of the intelligence community's old guard, entrenched at the CIA.

Although firm answers to many of these fundamental security questions are elusive, the White House consistently touts its homeland security successes in the two years following the terrorist attacks.

Col. Mark Scraba of the Connecticut National Guard surveys a power plant along Long Island Sound from a Blackhawk helicopter April 15.

BLOOMBERG NEWS PHOTO / STEVEN E. FRISCHLING

"We are . . . far safer than we were," said DHS Secretary Tom Ridge in an interview broadcast Sept. 2 on PBS' "NewsHour with Jim Lehrer." Ridge cited improvements in airport security, border controls and coordination with state and local officials. "So on an incremental basis, but a steady basis day by day, we get to a new level of readiness every day," Ridge said.

Defenders of the administration and the DHS cite several victories in the war on terrorism as evidence of the success of their homeland defense policies. Domestically, they point to the detention in 2002 of an alleged terrorist ring from Lackawanna, N.Y., and the August arrest of the man accused of trying to buy shoulder-fired missile launchers. Overseas, high-ranking al Qaeda operatives have been arrested, including a top lieutenant of terrorist leader Osama bin Laden, Khalid Shaikh Mohammed, in Pakistan in March.

At the same time, some national security experts and Democrats — especially those looking to score political points — say America is unprepared for another attack. They say the administration is not spending enough money on homeland security and that its terrorism intelligence-sharing procedures are suspect.

On Sept. 5, Democrats issued a scathing, eight-page critique of the administration's war on terrorism calling for consolidation of disparate terrorist watch lists; better information-sharing with local law enforcement; more border patrols and better tracking of foreign visitors; screening of all air cargo in passenger jets, more inspections of cargo containers headed for U.S. ports; and mandatory vulnerability assessments of chemical plants.

Others are critical of President Bush's latest request for $87 billion for continuing operations in Iraq, contending that the administration sold the war in Iraq as part of the war on international terrorists, even though no clear, indisputable link has ever been made between Saddam Hussein and al Qaeda or Osama bin Laden. In making the request, however, Bush said Iraq had become "the central front" in the war against terrorism. He said $66 billion of the funds would be for military and intelligence operations over the next year in Iraq and Afghanistan. Critics have said the Iraq war has been distracting Bush from pursuing bin Laden and other terrorists in Afghanistan.

One of Bush's leading terrorism advisers, Rand Beers, made waves in March when he resigned from the White House. Beers complained in a June interview with The Washington Post that "the administration wasn't matching its deeds to its words in the war on terrorism." He contended the war in Iraq is "making us less secure, not more secure," and later joined the 2004 presidential campaign of Democratic Sen. John Kerry of Massachusetts.

Kerry wasted no time in making homeland security a political issue. "Here on the home front, every investigation, every commission, every piece of evidence we have tells us that this president has failed to make us as safe as we should be," Kerry said Sept. 2 as he formally announced his candidacy.

Critics and security experts cite several gaps in the nation's defenses. For instance, while airport security nationwide has been beefed up since the Sept. 11 hijackings, experts say other areas of air travel remain vulnerable. Air cargo on passenger jets is not screened. Jets are still vulnerable to ground-to-air missile launchers, and the airline industry is hesitant to endorse a proposal by Sen. Barbara Boxer, D-Calif., to equip all passenger airliners with missile defense shields. In one of the most recent airport alerts, the Homeland Security Department warned that terrorists have been experimenting with turning electronic devices, such as cameras or cell phones, into weapons or bombs. And on Sept. 4, the FBI warned that terrorists may be planning to hijack planes in neighboring nations, such as Canada.

In addition to the airlines, managers of other potential terrorist targets also seek to balance security needs with the desire to promote freedom of commerce and movement of people. Chemical plants, nuclear power facilities, railroads, transit systems, utilities, computer networks, seaports and even sewage systems have increased security, yet congressional legislation to mandate security upgrades for certain industries, such as chemical companies, has stalled. In other areas, including firefighter grants, advocates say less money has been appropriated for security than they had hoped for.

Meanwhile, the 180,000-employee DHS is still experiencing growing pains following the mega-merger of 22 federal agencies that created the new department.

"We're making progress, but the jury is still out on how the department is doing," said Sen. Susan Collins, R-Maine, who chairs the Senate Governmental Affairs Committee, which oversees the DHS. "We still have a lot to do to coordinate the agencies" that were consolidated, she said.

Ridge has received generally positive reviews from members of Congress on both sides of the aisle. However, the department's color-coded terror-alert system has been both ridiculed by the public and criticized as inefficient by the Congressional Research Service.

Ridge has said the department is developing more specific ways to issue terrorist threat alerts, but he nonetheless has defended the color-coded system. Ridge also has his hands full with the new Transportation Security Administration (TSA), which was created after Sept. 11 to take over airline screening. The agency has been criticized by key members of Congress, including Rep. Harold Rogers, R-Ky., chairman of the House Homeland Security Appropriations Subcommittee, who complained that the agency is overstaffed and has failed to complete background checks on all its employees, many of whom were found to have criminal records.

Meanwhile, a federal commission that is mandated to investigate the Sept. 11 attacks reportedly has run into numerous obstacles, including lack of sufficient funding and the administration's alleged reluctance to turn over intelligence about the attack and let witnesses testify freely to commission members.

The commission is run by former New Jersey Gov. Thomas Kean, a moderate Republican who has complained that witnesses have felt "intimidated" by administration officials who have insisted on sitting in on interviews. The commission is supposed to report on its findings in May 2004, but Kean says if it does not get more money and more cooperation, it may not finish the investigation on time. The 10-member commission, formally known as the National Commission on Terrorist Attacks Upon the United States, will investigate events leading up to the attacks, including aviation security, immigration and U.S. diplomacy.

As citizens, lawmakers and security experts confront the continuing threat of terrorism, here are some of the key questions they are asking:

In his State of the Union address last Jan. 28, Bush said,

QUESTION #1

Is America safer today than it was two years ago?

"we are winning" the war on terrorism. Almost eight months later, at an Aug. 13 press conference at his ranch in Crawford, Texas, he said, "We're doing everything we can to protect the homeland." Asked about the threat of missile launchers and a breach in security at John F. Kennedy International Airport in New York City, Bush responded, "America is a safe place for people to fly."

Frank Cilluffo, a consultant on national security and a former terrorism consultant for administration, said, "Un-

equivocally we are safer, but the question is how do you define safer? If you're asking, 'Are we ever going to be able to protect everything from every possible attack?' the answer is no. Defining success is difficult because the good guys have to bat a thousand, and the bad guys only have to be right once."

Most agree that airports and airplanes are indeed safer. The government will spend more than $5 billion on the TSA in fiscal 2004, largely to cover costs for 45,000 new airport screeners, as well as baggage screening equipment. However, many critics say the TSA is overstaffed and suffers from image problems due to longer security lines at airports.

"The TSA still has a big job to do in getting 100 percent of all bags screened electronically [by bomb detectors] by the end of the year," says Todd Hauptli, a lobbyist for the American Association of Airport Executives and the Airports Council International, two leading aviation associations. "Vigilance is up, security has increased, but there are still soft spots."

One of those spots is air cargo screening. About 22 percent of all air cargo flies in the cargo holds of passenger planes, instead of cargo planes, but those packages are not required to be screened. Rep. Edward J. Markey, D-Mass., in June sponsored a successful amendment to the House version of the fiscal 2004 homeland security appropriations bill (HR 2555) requiring the TSA to screen all air cargo on commercial jets. However, that language was removed in the final version of the law enacted Oct. 1 (PL 108-90).

"It's a huge, backdoor loophole," Markey says. "[But] the cargo industry is very opposed to my amendment."

Many security experts agree the country is safer than before Sept. 11, 2001, but they also note a laundry list of vulnerabilities, including the electricity grid and chemical plants. The DHS has been assessing the nation's "critical infrastructure" — such as telecommunications networks, dams and power plants — for vulnerabilities. The assessments, some of which will be completed within the year, are expected to lay the groundwork for tougher security regulations and legislation in the future.

Not surprisingly, the debate over security has reflected political agendas. In the Senate, for instance, there is an ongoing chemical plant security debate in which the Democrats, led by Jon Corzine of New Jersey, are supporting a bill (S 157) that is long on regulatory requirements. The Democrats want all chemical facilities to conduct security studies and submit them to the EPA for approval. Chemical plants would also be required to study using alternative — and potentially safer — chemicals, a move the industry says is meddlesome and has little to do with security. So far, there is little sign that the Democrats' bill will be considered in committee or brought to a floor vote.

The Republicans support a measure (S 994) that takes a lighter regulatory approach, requiring chemical plants only to keep their security plans on file, rather than submitting them for approval to the federal government. Sponsored by Sen. James M. Inhofe, R-Okla., that bill also does not require companies to consider switching to alternative chemicals. Moreover, it would shift chemical security oversight from the EPA to the DHS. Inhofe's bill is more likely to move because he is chairman of the Senate Environmental and Public Works Committee, which would consider it.

Port security is another headache for security officials.

Only about 5 percent of the millions of shipping containers that enter U.S. seaports every year are physically inspected. The rest of the cargo containers go uninspected, although homeland security officials have said they inspect 100 percent of suspicious cargo. Along with Customs agents, they try to keep tabs on all containers by using computers to monitor shipping manifests, looking for suspicious cargoes originating from ports with questionable security.

The 2002 Maritime Transportation Security Act was supposed to address the gap in port security, but the bill did not authorize any money to assess security at the country's major ports. The fiscal 2004 homeland security appropriations law provides $125 million for port security, but the Coast Guard says it would need $1 billion to carry out recommendations of the Maritime Transportation Security Act, which mandates vulnerability assessments be conducted at all the nation's major ports.

"An area of vulnerability remains in our ports," said Collins, whose home state has hundreds of miles of coastline. "We need to step up programs to put Customs inspectors in foreign ports, and identify risky cargo."

Determining whether the country is safer, Collins and other experts say, will be a day-to-day, ongoing assessment as the war against terrorism continues.

As the World Trade Center towers teetered on the brink

QUESTION #2

Are rescue personnel prepared to respond to another attack?

of collapse Sept. 11, the New York City Police Department realized it had to get all emergency personnel out of the towers. But it could not alert fire department personnel inside the towers because the two departments could not communicate over each others' radios. The city lost 343 firefighters in the collapse, while the police department lost 23 officers. Since then, police and firefighters have demanded better training, better communication and better equipment, including inter-operable radios.

The nationwide effort to improve preparations for another terrorist attack has been watched over by Michael Brown, DHS undersecretary for emergency preparedness and response. Brown has overseen major mock terrorism exercises in Seattle and Washington, D.C. In the aftermath of a terrorist attack, Brown's federal emergency responders are prepared to sweep in and help run command centers, as they did during the mid-August blackout in New York, Detroit, Cleveland and other cities.

"We're learning you have to put in a command-and-control structure, because otherwise it'll be chaos," Brown said. "First responders know how to do their jobs, but they need to be able to reach back into the federal government for resources. If we take care of first responders, we take care of the homeland."

However, funding for state and local first responders has become a major political football. Democrats have regularly attacked the Republican Congress and the administration, saying they are underfunding the people who will be on the front lines of a terrorist attack. Democrats proposed adding billions of dollars to fiscal 2004 appropriations bills in an attempt to funnel more homeland security grants to cities and states.

The Council on Foreign Relations bolstered the Democrats' argument in June when it said America's first responders were "dangerously unprepared" for another attack. "Based on our analysis, America will fall roughly $98.4 billion short of meeting critical emergency responder needs over the next five years if current overall funding levels are maintained," the report said. "Covering this shortfall using federal funds alone would require quintupling federal funding."

The report carried considerable weight because it was written by Richard A. Clarke, a former national security adviser who served in four presidential administrations and was among the first senior administration officials to raise warnings about al Qaeda before the Sept. 11 attacks.

The report also noted that on average, fire departments only have enough radios for half the firefighters on a shift and only enough breathing apparatuses for a third; police departments do not have the protective gear to safely secure a site after an attack with weapons of mass destruction; and public health labs in most states still lack basic equipment and expertise to respond adequately to a chemical or biological attack.

Two other studies, released in August, also raised doubts about whether front-line responders are prepared for another attack. A study by the federal Centers for Disease Control and Prevention said police officers and firefighters "feel vastly unprepared" for another attack and do not have the equipment and training they need to handle biological, chemical or radiological weapons. Another study, released by the National Association of School Resource Officers, showed that 76 percent of the resource officers surveyed say schools are not prepared for a terrorist attack.

Other critics say too much money is being spent on preparations in some areas while not enough is being spent in others. For example, because of the way the funds are distributed, Wyoming gets much more anti-terrorism money per capita than New York and New Jersey. Homeland security funds have reached well beyond traditional terrorism targets to places such as Springdale, Ark., where the police department received a $760,000 homeland security grant for its bomb squad. The Clearmont, Wyo., fire department, meanwhile, recently received $81,000 for firefighter safety and training. Small towns such as Clearmont receive homeland security grants because the formula for grant money guarantees every state a minimum amount of money, which is then funneled down to counties and towns.

Christopher Cox, R-Calif., chairman of the House Homeland Security Committee has proposed additional grants to local agencies that would be based on the level of threat in a particular region. These new grants would be intended to address some of the perceived imbalance.

Rep. William M. "Mac" Thornberry, R-Texas, says the sweeping reorganization that created the DHS has forced federal agencies and employees involved in terrorism response to refocus their mission away from prevention to preparedness. "One of the biggest challenges in homeland security is making up for years of neglect," Thornberry says. "We are more prepared [for an attack]. But in some areas we may not be as prepared as we were [before Sept. 11] because we shuffled the deck, and it takes time to develop relationships again."

Jamie F. Metzl, who directed the Council on Foreign Relations task force on first responder preparedness, says he and other researchers visited emergency personnel nationwide to see if they had the specific equipment and training needed to handle various terrorist events. It was not a pretty picture, Metzl says.

"We're not nearly as prepared as we need to be in multiple areas," he warns. "We came away with the conclusion that America's first responders are not prepared for another terrorist attack."

In San Francisco, for example, the two nearest federally certified search-and-rescue teams that specialize in digging through the rubble of buildings after explosions, earthquakes or other calamities, are located miles outside of the city in Menlo Park and Oakland. The Menlo Park team would have to travel as much as 40 miles to respond to a disaster in San Francisco, and the Oakland team would have to cross a bridge. If the Bay Bridge or the Golden Gate Bridge, which would require a more circuitous route, were shut down, it could take hours longer for the Oakland-based team to get to the disaster, Metzl says. Similar gaps in preparedness are repeated in firehouses and police departments around the country, he says.

Undersecretary Brown, however, defends his department's preparations. All 28 of the nation's urban search-and-rescue teams are now certified to handle the aftermath of a weapon of mass destruction, he says. And disaster response exercises are being done somewhere in the country on almost a daily basis. At the Federal Emergency Management Administration (FEMA) headquarters in southwest Washington, the command center that used to be open only during hurricanes or after other disasters is now a 24-hour operation.

"That is a quantitative leap in preparedness," Brown says. "I want it to be up 24/7, so any agency or locality can reach into DHS and start communicating [instantly]."

In September, Congress approved the first-ever appropri-

QUESTION #3

Is Congress spending enough on homeland security?

ations bill dedicated to homeland defense — a spending plan that provides increases for several components of homeland security, including the Coast Guard, terrorism intelligence and bioterrorism research. The enacted bill provides $30.4 billion to DHS for fiscal 2004.

While members of Congress, the administration and state and local officials have all shifted their spending priorities to put homeland defense at the top, the big question — both in Washington and in state capitals — remains hotly debated: How much is enough? The appropriations bill increased the Homeland Security budget by less than 2 percent over fiscal 2003.

Notably, the 2003 budget for DHS activities had already received $6.3 billion in additional funds for aviation security, first responders and an airline bailout, all of which were included in the supplemental spending bill that financed the war in Iraq. That boosted the fiscal 2003 figures to close to the levels eventually enacted for fiscal 2004.

Democrats made homeland security spending one of their top national security issues this year. They complained that the administration is shortchanging homeland defense spending, putting first responders in the position of being unprepared for another attack. Senate Democrats forced nearly a dozen votes on amendments to the Senate's homeland security appropriations bill in an effort to increase funding for ports, border security and first responders. Republicans complained that the Democrats' tactics were part of a political strategy to get the GOP on the record as voting against Homeland Security spending.

"Police and fire departments say they don't have enough money, chemical plants say they don't have enough money [for security]," Markey says. "Al Qaeda is still targeting the same objectives" as they were Sept. 11.

Republicans say it's not how much you spend but how you spend it. As evidence that the administration has its spending priorities straight, they point to major increases in critical areas, such as terrorism intelligence, which focus on preventing an attack and analyzing data that could lead to arrests of terrorists.

The National Governors' Association, however, warns that states' homeland security obligations are continuing to grow and that governors want to make sure they have a guaranteed stream of funding from the federal government to cover state and local homeland defense costs. At the outset of the Iraq war in March, the governors point out, the DHS launched "Operation Liberty Shield," a homeland security program that raised nationwide terrorist alerts to Code Orange, the second-highest threat level. During the alert, which lasted several weeks, states had to cover millions of dollars worth of overtime costs for local and state law enforcement officers. Most governors contend that when the federal government issues a nationwide alert that will cost local law enforcement extra overtime, Washington should help defray the added costs.

"In the face of possible terrorist threats, we cannot overstate the importance of . . . the need for a stable, multi-year federal funding commitment," said Delaware Gov. Ruth Ann Minner, a Democrat and the association's spokeswoman on homeland security, in a statement.

In a speech to the governors, DHS Secretary Ridge defended the administration's outreach to states and localities but said extra dollars do not equate to better security. "It's just not a matter of putting billions of dollars in this system," Ridge said. "We need to make sure at all levels of government that we are building up a national capacity, which, in my mind, means we need to rely on the governors to coordinate statewide security plans, working in collaboration with their partners at the local government."

Bush signed the homeland security appropriations bill Oct. 1. While much of the bill will fund programs and agencies that have always had a role in homeland defense, it also includes money for several programs born out of new fears of specific types of terrorism.

For example, DHS will receive at least $400 million for explosive-detection systems — the large luggage scanners that search for explosives in baggage at airports. The bill also includes money for radiation detectors for port and border security, bioterrorism and chemical weapons research, plus more than $98 million for cybersecurity.

CURRENT SITUATION

Homeland Security's growing pains: a work in progress.

Created at the beginning of 2003, the Department of Homeland Security is still a young institution. But it is already experiencing growing pains and taking flak on several fronts. In promoting his fledgling department, Ridge tries to portray homeland security as a national, rather than purely federal, obligation. So he asks states, cities, counties and even individuals to change their mindset about national security, to view it as a shared task.

In Washington, however, parts of Ridge's department have faced heat from a frustrated public and an impatient Congress. The TSA, probably because it is under the constant scrutiny of the traveling public, has been criticized since its inception immediately after Sept. 11, 2001. Many GOP lawmakers originally opposed creating the agency, and homeland security leaders on Capitol Hill, among them Rep. John L. Mica, R-Fla., have been critical of the agency.

The TSA got off to a rough start when its first director, John Magaw, was ousted July 18, 2002, after just six months on the job. He was replaced by former Coast Guard Commandant James M. Loy, who is respected both within the airline industry and on Capitol Hill.

But Loy's high standing has not immunized the agency from criticism. At a hearing on June 3, 2003, the TSA revealed it had fired more than 1,200 workers who made it onto the airport screening staffs despite having criminal records. The agency also had to admit it had not completed background checks on about half of its employees. The TSA also has come under fire for being understaffed in some major airports while being overstaffed at smaller facilities. Agency critics on Capitol Hill joke that TSA stands for "Thousands Standing Around."

More crucially, perhaps, the department's Information Analysis and Infrastructure Protection Directorate — charged with analyzing terrorism intelligence, protecting critical infrastructure and making threat assessments — also has been criticized as being unprepared. According to a July 21 report in The Washington Post, the agency was not receiving all the terrorism data it needed from the intelligence community and did not have all its computers connected to permit data-sharing. Cox called the agency "a work in progress." He said although the agency was sharing information as never before between state, local and federal agencies, "we are still constructing a robust intelligence and analytical capability."

Controversy erupted in the DHS' Customs and Border Security division in May, when Ashcroft and Ridge agreed that certain investigations undertaken by DHS' Bureau of Immigration and Customs Enforcement would be handed over to the FBI as soon as links to terrorism were established. Ridge's apparent ceding of power to Ashcroft had some veteran Customs and border security officials seething, because they opposed handing over the new department's powers to the Justice Department.

The department also has had a rocky relationship with the federal labor unions representing the nearly 200,000

DHS employees. The bill consolidating 22 agencies into the department was nearly derailed last year over a dispute about the amount of flexibility the administration wanted in hiring and firing employees and removing them from unions.

A compromise finally allowed the White House to remove employees from unions and set aside collective bargaining if it was necessary for national security. Federal unions saw the move as union busting. Bush and congressional Republicans who approved the employee language in the bill said the new department needed flexibility over employees in order to meet emerging terrorist threats. The TSA has already tried to limit unions from organizing airport screeners.

States and local governments also have attacked the way the DHS distributes state grant money to prepare and train first responders. The current formula distributes the money based not only on population but also on a guarantee that every state will get at least 0.75 percent of the total. As a result, states with low populations get more money per capita than high-density areas, which are considered the more likely terrorist targets. For instance, New York state receives about $4.60 per capita in grants; Wyoming receives $32.25.

Under legislation introduced in the Senate by Collins, homeland security grants would be distributed based more on where terrorist threats are more likely to occur. However, in acknowledgement that "all politics are local," Collins' bill would maintain a guaranteed minimum for every state, perhaps as a way to assuage small-state members of Congress who don't want to lose any funding.

Collins' bill is pending before the Governmental Affairs Committee, which she chairs. Cox has introduced similar legislation in the House, that has earned support from lawmakers representing more urban areas, and is opposed by some from more rural areas. He hopes to have the bill marked up and sent to the floor this month. Both Cox and Collins have said they believe legislation changing the grant formulas is likely to pass this year.

Changes Planned

The DHS may also adjust its much-maligned color-coded terrorist alert system. Advocates of change say that rather than blanketing the entire country with a single, massive security alert, a more complex system would take into account the specifics of the threat. Some state officials support an alert system that is more regional, and focuses more specifically with threats and what the intelligence networks are picking up in their communications channels. With such a system, smaller cities, such as Boise, Idaho, and Jackson, Miss., would not end up being on the same level of alert as New York City and Los Angeles.

The current alerts are "bound to give way to a more sophisticated system," Cox says. "All threats are not directed evenly across the entire continent, so we may need a more subtle approach."

Despite the complaints, Ridge says it is a "good system" and that "its primary purpose is to alert law enforcement and security personnel around the country that they need to enhance security at certain venues, at certain bridges, at certain tunnels, at certain chemical plants."

The organization of the department continues to be a work in progress, with employees being transferred from agency to agency in search of better synergy among the department's various security missions. At the same time, whole divisions are being shuffled to streamline operations and break down old bureaucratic barriers, forcing agencies to work together in new ways.

For example, on Sept. 2, Ridge announced that 5,000 agents in the Bureau of Immigration and Customs Enforcement would be eligible to be trained as air marshals. The air marshals currently work for the TSA, but the addition of Customs and Immigration agents would create a workforce of "cross-trained" employees who could bolster airline security if the threat alert rises. Ridge also said the air marshal division would be absorbed into the Bureau of Immigration and Customs Enforcement. The idea is to mesh the airline security expertise of the air marshals, who travel armed and undercover on passenger jets, with the law enforcement and investigative expertise of Customs and Immigration agents. Those groups have the same mission — catching terrorists — yet they have worked in separate areas. Under Ridge's order, air marshals and Customs and immigration agents will train together. Ridge also announced he would streamline the entry process for incoming foreign visitors. Rather than being interviewed separately by Customs, Immigration and agricultural inspectors, travelers would have one DHS officer to handle all three duties.

While the DHS is still undergoing its reorganizational growing pains, Congress has tried to shuffle the ground beneath its turf-conscious committee chairmen to deal with homeland security issues. In January, the House created the Select Homeland Security Committee, with Cox as chairman. The panel includes several powerful players — for example, F. James Sensenbrenner Jr., R-Wis., chairman of the Judiciary Committee, and C.W. Bill Young, R-Fla., chairman of the Appropriations Committee. Although it has held numerous hearings, it has not produced major legislation.

In fact, homeland security legislation in the 108th Congress has not automatically been handed over to Cox's committee. Bills dealing with anti-terrorism laws still get a hearing in the Judiciary Committee, while a major bioterrorism bill went through the Energy and Commerce Committee before it was passed to Cox.

In the Senate, there has been no reorganization (outside of appropriations) to handle homeland security. The Senate Judiciary Committee still handles anti-terrorism laws and investigations, while the Commerce, Science and Transportation Committee continues to oversee border security. As chairwoman of the Governmental Affairs Committee, Collins has tried to assert some power over DHS, calling Ridge to testify before her panel.

Civil Liberties Threat?

Advocacy groups from across the political spectrum recently blasted the U.S. government's proposed air-passenger screening program, charging it as a violation of privacy and civil rights.

Groups as diverse as the American Civil Liberties Union (ACLU) and the American Conservative Union criticized the Computer Assisted Passenger Prescreening System, known as CAPPS II, which was announced in July. The plan empowers the government to take basic information about airline passengers — date of birth, address and phone number — as they book their tickets and run the information through a commercial data service to confirm the passengers' identity. It is not clear how the government will collect the information from the airlines or whether the rules will apply to foreign airlines as well.

The program also will search watch lists and other national security information to determine whether passengers have any links to al Qaeda or other militant groups, or even if they are violent criminals with outstanding arrest warrants.

Critics say the plan improperly uses the national security threat to infringe on basic civil rights. "This system will affect every single person who gets on an airplane in the United States," said Laura Murphy, director of the ACLU's Washington office, who called it a "quantum leap in government surveillance."

The latest accusations of government intrusion on civil rights comes as Ashcroft continues his monthlong, nationwide tour to defend the USA Patriot Act (PL 107-56) against critics who say the sweeping anti-terrorism law violates civil rights.

Ominous Outlook?

If anything, the nation's feelings of vulnerability have intensified, rather than diminished, since the Sept. 11 terrorist attacks. New Yorkers have been especially affected. And the anxiety almost certainly will continue, as Americans are fed a steady diet of often-vague intelligence about terrorist threats and the potential vulnerability of America's infrastructure. But will the war on terrorism ever end? And what would a victory look like? Would it be defined as no acts of terrorism for years? The outlook for how the war on terrorism will unfold in the coming years is murky, according to homeland security experts.

"My biggest fear is about sustaining efforts over the long haul," says Cilluffo, the former White House terrorism adviser. "I'm concerned that too long a lull will make us complacent."

It may be easier to look at the future in terms of short-term progress vs. long-term solutions. In the short term, homeland security experts say small victories may suffice to keep Americans vigilant, whether it is arrests of top al Qaeda operatives overseas or the foiling of plots to attack U.S. cities.

"I don't think there is any question we will win the war on al Qaeda," Cox says. "The larger issue is the capability that technology gives to crazed individuals or terrorist groups. In the 20th century, our threats were from nation-states. As we proceed in the 21st century, it will be terrorists. There will be no respite from grave threats to our nation."

With the war on terrorism having no end in sight, vigilance against terrorism may become a more permanent feature of national security policy and the American psyche. I think this will go on for a long time," Collins says. "I don't see an end to it."

At the Department of Homeland Security, top officials must not only respond to the crisis of the moment — such as the Aug. 14 blackout — but also must create models for handling other kinds of disasters. In essence, they are trying to predict the future of terrorist activity, trying to stay one step ahead in preparedness. "Our responsibilities [in the next 10 years] will become more complex because we're always thinking ahead," says DHS Undersecretary Brown. "What's the next bio-agent they'll use? Ten years from now, I hope an all-hazards approach has permeated the entire federal government."

At the airports, where American travelers see the most obvious signs of homeland security efforts, procedures are unlikely to change. "Increased vigilance and increased security are here to stay," says aviation lobbyist Hauptli. "We won't go back to pre-9/11 complacency." ◆

America's Uneasy Mandate For Domestic Intelligence

The quest: Improve analysis and information-sharing without threatening civil liberties

The Justice Department's short-lived Operation TIPS, which would have enlisted thousands of mail carriers, truck drivers and meter readers to snoop around neighborhoods for suspicious activity, showed what Americans think about the collection of "domestic intelligence."

Both liberals and conservatives were outraged at what the libertarian Cato Institute called a program to build "a nation of snitches." The U.S. Postal Service flatly refused to participate. Before it was even begun, the Terrorist Information and Prevention System was quietly shelved. The country's message: Do all the spying you want on real terrorists, but do not pull the cloak-and-dagger routine on innocent citizens.

Operation TIPS pointed to a major problem for the government: how to improve the collection and collation of the domestic intelligence so vital to disrupting terrorist networks without trampling on individual liberties.

More than two and a half years after the Sept. 11 terrorist attacks, Congress is still searching for the solution.

"What Congress has done is abdicate its traditional role, which is to get very involved in privacy and national security," said Dan Gallington, a former Justice Department attorney and general counsel to the Senate Select Intelligence Committee and now a senior research fellow with the Potomac Institute, a national security think tank.

"The public is going to look to Congress to be satisfied that the right balance has been struck" between the two imperatives, Gallington said. "But none of [the lawmakers]

CQ Weekly April 24, 2004

have stepped up to the plate except to complain. . . . The issue is radioactive."

Lawmakers are divided over whether to renew critical parts of the 2001 anti-terrorism law known as the Patriot Act (PL 107-56) due to expire at the end of fiscal 2005. The law beefed up law enforcement powers after the terrorist attacks. (*2001 Almanac, p. 14-3*)

President Bush has called for the permanent renewal of the Patriot Act along with new provisions, including an expansion of the death penalty for crimes related to terrorism. "Congress must act with the Patriot Act," he told a campaign audience April 19 in Hershey, Pa. "We must continue to stay on the offense when it comes to chasing these killers down and bringing them to justice — and we will." (*2004 CQ Weekly, p. 956*)

Though everyone wants the country to be secure, some are hesitant to broaden the government's police and intelligence powers at the further cost to civil liberties. Some provisions of the Patriot Act that Bush now calls "essential law" were in fact dropped from a counterterrorism law (PL 104-132) that Congress passed in 1996 after the Oklahoma City bombing. (*1996 Almanac, p.5-18*)

Lawmakers also worry about some of the institutions charged with protecting the country from terrorists.

The Department of Homeland Security, which Congress created to prevent another attack, has not inspired broad confidence. The Bush administration, in fact, reneged on its promise to put Homeland Security in charge of assessing counterterrorism intelligence, preferring to set up its own analysis center located at the CIA. (*Threat center, p. 12*)

Consultants testifying at a House committee hearing April 22 criticized the "poor" performance of airport security personnel hired by the department's Transportation Security Administration. (*2004 CQ Weekly, p. 969*)

Above all, there has been a cry for change at the FBI, whose past faults have been on full display before the federal commission investigating the Sept. 11 attacks. (*2004 CQ Weekly, p. 902*)

Despite an internal overhaul since the attacks and a much greater commitment to counterterrorism — it is a partner in the Terrorist Threat Integration Center — the FBI is still considered a law enforcement agency biased toward field agents arresting crooks.

The mandate for better domestic intelligence-sharing is a work in progress despite the threat center and other attempts to improve analysis and communication. Local and state officials have teamed up with the FBI through counterterrorism task forces, but still complain

Tenet, left, and Mueller, shown here testifying in February about security threats, say their agencies are working more closely on intelligence related to terrorism.

9

that federal agencies do not share enough homeland security intelligence to help them in their role as "first responders" to terrorism.

As Gallington points out, the very concept of domestic intelligence has always made politicians uncomfortable. Federal agencies, such as the FBI, operate under different restrictions in gathering material than do Great Britain's near-mythical Security Service, or MI5, and Israel's Shin Bet. *(MI5, p. 954)*

While Congress awaits recommendations this summer from the National Commission on Terrorist Attacks Upon the United States, its choices for a response are few and difficult.

If lawmakers accept FBI Director Robert S. Mueller III's promise that reforms already under way at his agency need time to work, they are embracing the status quo. At a time when the terrorist threat level fluctuates between yellow and orange, lawmakers are loath to sit and wait for bureaucratic changes to sink in. Even some Republicans have become annoyed with the administration's penchant for taking action and ignoring Congress.

"The problem is that this Congress ought to assert oversight of this administration," said Virginia Republican Frank R. Wolf, chairman of the House Appropriations Subcommittee on Commerce, Justice, State and Judiciary, which deals with the FBI's budget. "To say, 'Just let them go [and do nothing]' is not acceptable. We can't be a potted plant."

Taking the strong step of creating a separate agency dedicated only to domestic intelligence is just as disconcerting to many members of Congress. Such an agency, whose only job would be collecting and analyzing intelligence, conjures up the ghosts of J. Edgar Hoover and the FBI spying on anti-war and civil rights groups in the 1960s and investigating Hollywood stars in the 1950s.

Entrenched Culture

Some members of Congress are calling for a third way — overhauling the handling of terrorism-related intelligence without taking power away from the FBI.

The idea, which Wolf has proposed but has not yet put into legislation, is to create a "service within a service" by separating the FBI's police work from its intelligence duties, in essence creating two agencies in one. Wolf's proposal might well move through House committees by the end of the summer.

But as Congress and the administration weigh the options for addressing the FBI's past problems, a likely outcome is gridlock.

Despite the president's recent campaigning to renew and expand the Patriot Act, Republicans are reluctant in an election year to reopen debate on police powers and civil liberties. Overhauling the FBI, though it may appeal to some lawmakers, would be no easy task given the bureau's deep roots in American culture and law enforcement.

Bush himself might move to make more substantive changes in the intelligence setup. He has already indicated agreement with the idea of a director of all intelligence, civilian and military.

But some experts say rearranging the bureaucracy might not be necessary if Congress and the administration concentrate instead on raising the internal standards of the agencies that exist and hiring better personnel to do the intelligence collection and analysis.

"There is no perfect organizational solution," said Steven

Former Gov. Thomas H. Kean, who chairs the Sept. 11 commission, said intelligence failures were an "indictment" of the FBI.

Aftergood, who oversees the Project on Government Secrecy at the Federation of American Scientists. "Organizational matters are not the most important thing. If you have talented people, you can get more done."

A Congressional Research Service report dated April 6 used the phrase "deeply entrenched law enforcement culture" several times in a long critique of how the FBI is handling its new domestic intelligence mandate under Mueller.

The CRS report, by Alfred Cumming, a national security and intelligence specialist, said the easy part has been reorganizing the agency's bureaucracy to make more room for intelligence and counterterrorism. The hard part has been changing a culture that for much of the bureau's history has been associated with gang busting, cracking criminal cases and winning indictments.

In the FBI's old mandate, intelligence was a means to the end of putting people in jail, whether it was bank robbers or Soviet spies. The new mandate, gathering and analyzing intelligence with the goal of understanding the threat matrix of global terrorism, has met with some resistance among senior career agents, according to the CRS report.

Other independent studies, such as a series of reports by a domestic terrorism task force headed by former Virginia Gov. James S. Gilmore III, have been equally skeptical of the FBI's ability to change its DNA.

"The FBI cannot soon be made over into an organization dedicated to detecting and preventing attacks rather than one dedicated to punishing them," the Gilmore task force wrote in November 2002.

Members of Congress, the Sept. 11 commission and intelligence experts have repeatedly criticized the FBI's information sharing before Sept. 11. The current investigative commission pointed to the now famous July 10, 2001, "Phoenix memo," in which an FBI agent in Arizona warned of Middle Eastern men who were expressing unusual interest in flying planes, as a prime example of the FBI's inability to communicate critical intelligence to others.

Former New Jersey Gov. Thomas H. Kean, a Republican and chairman of the commission, has labeled the litany of intelligence and information-sharing failures an "indict-

The Lesson of MI5

Those seeking a model for a purely domestic intelligence agency in the United States often cite Britain's fabled Security Service, or MI5. The truth is that some British agents actually envy the FBI because of its law enforcement powers. All they can do is spy.

From its London headquarters overlooking the Thames near Westminster, MI5 is the United Kingdom's defensive security intelligence agency. Its primary mission is to protect the country from foreign espionage and from terrorism.

The Security Service dates back to 1909, when two military officers — Captain Vernon Kell of the South Staffordshire Regiment and Captain Mansfield Cumming of the Royal Navy — established the Secret Service Bureau to counter German espionage in British ports. Dividing their work, Kell (known simply as "K") took charge of domestic counterespionage, while Cumming ("C") handled overseas intelligence gathering.

In 1916, during World War I, the Secret Service Bureau was absorbed by the Directorate of Military Intelligence, where the counterespionage service was designated MI5. The overseas operation was called MI6; its more formal name now is the Secret Intelligence Service.

The Security Service (MI5) has a narrow role: to collect and analyze intelligence. It cannot arrest, detain or try suspects.

"Because the MI5 doesn't directly handle law enforcement, their investigations have to be handed over to the courts and to the police, who often have to start all over again," says Harry "Skip" Brandon, a former deputy assistant director at the FBI. "As a matter of fact, people in the MI5 often express admiration for the FBI's law enforcement capabilities, which they see as superior."

Out of the Shadows

MI5 typically operated out of the headlines until 1989, when Parliament passed the Security Service Act. That law, which is the statutory basis for the modern MI5, outlined the Security Service's main tasks as protecting Britain against terrorism, sabotage and espionage, as well as safeguarding its economic well-being. The law also included a strict ban against working for or against any political party and placed the agency under the office of the Home Secretary.

More recent legislation, including the Terrorism Act of 2000 and the Anti-Terrorism, Crime and Security Act of 2001, has broadened the agency's powers in combating terrorist groups, such as radical Islamic networks.

One of the more well-known recent changes is a ban on U.K.-based fundraising for terror groups such as al Qaeda.

Other legislation laid out explicit guidelines for electronic surveillance and spying, establishing, among other things, a tribunal to hear complaints of alleged abuses.

During the Cold War, MI5 focused primarily on anti-Soviet intelligence. One of its more celebrated achievements was the expulsion in 1971 of 105 Communist spies, which substantially undercut the Soviet intelligence network in London.

Over the years, the service has had its own spy scandals. MI5 undertook an internal review and overhaul that led to the 1989 Security Service Act after one of its officials was revealed in 1983 to be an agent of the Soviet KGB.

The service's main focus and about 60 percent of its budget now goes to counterterrorism, including surveillance against al Qaeda and both sides in Northern Ireland.

The most recent major international terrorist incident in Britain was the 1994 bombing of the Israeli embassy in London.

"MI5 is a very good agency," said Brandon. "Britain may not be the kind of target that the United States is, but the MI5 does its job very well."

ment" of the FBI. The problem, commission members say, lies both in the institutional culture of the bureau and its bureaucratic structure.

The commission's final recommendations are not due until late July. But commission member John Lehman has warned that changes will have to be made within the FBI. The CIA, although fielding its fair share of the blame for the pre-Sept. 11 intelligence failures, does not appear to be vulnerable to an overhaul.

The FBI issued its own report April 14, showing that 43 percent of its workload was now devoted to counterterrorism, compared with 10 percent in 1996. The FBI also insists it is working closely with the entire intelligence community, including the CIA, in gathering intelligence.

Mueller, defending his agency, has pointed out that the FBI has 2,835 counterterrorism agents now, compared with 1,344 in 2001. The new Office of Intelligence at the FBI has 70 employees, and the bureau's overall budget has increased almost 50 percent since 2001. The CIA has only 25 analysts detailed to the FBI's counterterrorism division, but Mueller has said that is enough to "improve our ability to analyze the masses of data generated in our post-9/11 investigations."

All these actions are part of a general overhaul Mueller initiated after the 2001 attacks to orient the agency toward preventing terrorism.

The internal reorganization of the FBI clearly is not enough for some congressional critics and members of the Sept. 11 commission who have different ideas for setting up domestic intelligence operations.

Some FBI experts dispute the idea that the bureau is unable to overcome its past missions and get along with the CIA to share the right intelligence information.

"A lot of people look at the FBI as a bunch of knuckle draggers, but the FBI has run a successful counterintelligence program for years," said Harry "Skip" Brandon, a former deputy assistant director of the bureau, in an interview. "It would be tragic to take [intelligence operations] away from the FBI."

But the FBI's intelligence operations in the past were aimed primarily at stopping or at least disrupting the espionage of other nations, mainly the Soviet Union, not gathering intelligence

Can Separate, Secret

○ Members of the intelligence community

The U.S. intelligence community "was not created and does not operate as a single, tightly knit organization," a congressional commission wrote in 1996. "It has evolved over nearly 50 years and now amounts to a confederation of separate agencies and activities with distinctly different histories, missions and lines of command." As a result, there is no single place where intelligence-gathering can be coordinated and collected information can be analyzed. In the wake of hearings by the independent Sept. 11 commission, some lawmakers say the intelligence network should be restructured.

DOMESTIC INTELLIGENCE AGENCIES

○ **HOMELAND SECURITY DEPARTMENT**
Secret Service — Primary duties are protecting the president and stopping counterfeiters.
Customs Service — Inspecting cargo coming into the country by land, sea and air.
Border Patrol — Identifying and stopping illegal aliens before they enter the country.
○ **Coast Guard Intelligence** — Processing information on U.S. maritime borders and Homeland Security.

JUSTICE DEPARTMENT

○ **Federal Bureau of Investigation** — Lead agency for domestic intelligence and operations. Has offices overseas.
Drug Enforcement Administration — Collects intelligence in the course of enforcement of federal drug laws.

○ DEPARTMENT OF ENERGY
Office of Intelligence — Key player in nuclear weapons and non-proliferation, energy security, science and technology.

○ TREASURY DEPARTMENT
The Office of Intelligence Support — Collects and processes information that may affect fiscal and monetary policy.

STATE AND LOCAL POLICE AGENCIES
Coordinate with the FBI through joint counterterrorism task forces.

Trying to Pull It All Together

Several agencies were created before and after the Sept. 11 terrorist attacks primarily to analyze and integrate intelligence data. Among them:

Terrorist Threat Integration Center — Created by President Bush in 2003, this analysis center located in the CIA is designed to assess all terrorism-related information from U.S. and foreign intelligence sources.

Counterterrorist Center — CIA unit that coordinates counterterrorist efforts of the intelligence community; feeds information to the Terrorist Threat Integration Center.

Information Analysis and Infrastructure Protection Directorate — Part of the Department of Homeland Security created in 2002 to analyze terrorist-related intelligence and assess threats to critical infrastructure.

Terrorist Screening Center — A multi-agency center administered by the FBI to develop a watch-list database of suspected terrorists.

○ **The Intelligence Community**
As director of the CIA, George J. Tenet is the titular head of the U.S. intelligence community, a network of 15 departments and agencies. These agencies conduct both domestic and international intelligence-gathering.

for its own sake.

Even with the bureaucratic restructuring and a massive counterterrorism budget increase under Mueller, congressional critics are not convinced that there has been much improvement.

"The FBI continues to have a fundamental structural problem," said Sen. Judd Gregg, R-N.H., chairman of the Appropriations Subcommittee on Commerce, Justice, State and Judiciary. "They still haven't changed their culture. . . . But we've got a director who understands the need to change the culture and get it adequately focused on intelligence."

But even Gregg and other members of Congress are not willing to ask for major changes. "Right now we have to fight terrorists," Gregg said. "Reorganization is a debilitating process."

Checkered History

Domestic intelligence is essentially any information on threats to national security gathered inside the United States. Much of it represents the sort of investigative work that the CIA is not allowed to conduct on American soil. The FBI has federal procedural and legal standards when gathering intelligence that a CIA agent in Amman, Jordan, for instance, might not have to worry about as much, though the CIA operates within its own rules.

For the FBI, intelligence-gathering is also weighed down by the baggage of the J. Edgar Hoover era.

In the 1960s, the FBI's "Cointelpro" investigations — the name is short for "counterintelligence programs" — infiltrated Vietnam War protest organizations as well as civil rights groups. The Ku Klux Klan, black separatist groups and the Rev. Martin Luther King Jr. also were spied on.

In the 1970s, mistrust of the federal government's clandestine operations

Agencies Learn to Share?

INTELLIGENCE AGENCIES OPERATING OVERSEAS

CIVILIAN AGENCIES

Central Intelligence Agency (CIA) — Lead agency for collecting and analyzing foreign intelligence, including information on terrorism. Briefs the president daily.

Department of State Counterterrorism Office — Coordinates efforts to improve counterterrorism cooperation with foreign governments.

Bureau of Intelligence and Research — Analyzes and interprets intelligence on global developments for secretary of State.

MILITARY AGENCIES

National Security Agency (NSA) — Collects and processes foreign signal intelligence from eavesdropping and signal interception. Also charged with protecting critical U.S. information security systems.

Defense Intelligence Agency (DIA) — Provides intelligence to military units, policy makers and force planners. It has operatives in many U.S. embassies.

National Geospatial-Intelligence Agency (NGA) — The intelligence community's mapmakers, able to track movements of people and machines or changes in topography.

National Reconnaissance Office (NRO) — Builds and maintains the nation's spy satellites. Provides information to the Defense Department and other agencies.

Army Intelligence

Navy Intelligence

Marine Corps Intelligence

Air Force Intelligence

TAKING STEPS TO IMPROVE COORDINATION

The weakest link in the intelligence campaign against terrorism has been the analysis and sharing of millions of bits of raw data swept up by government agencies operating in the United States and abroad.

The original plan for correcting this flaw after the Sept. 11 attacks was to centralize analysis in the Department of Homeland Security, which Congress created in 2002 (PL 107-296). After the law was passed, however, President Bush changed tack. By executive fiat in early 2003 — no written executive order was issued — Bush created the Terrorism Threat Integration Center (TTIC), housed in the Central Intelligence Agency, to coordinate terrorism-related analysis.

Except for a passage in Bush's 2003 State of the Union speech and an address to FBI employees, the administration did not formally outline the roles and responsibilities of agencies participating in the center. A memorandum signed in 2003 by Attorney General John Ashcroft, Director of Central Intelligence George J. Tenet and Homeland Security Secretary Tom Ridge explained the information-sharing responsibilities of the center's participants.

It was not until an April 13, 2004, letter from Tenet, Ridge, FBI Director Robert S. Mueller III and TTIC Director John O. Brennan to several members of Congress that the administration made clear that terrorism-related intelligence would be analyzed by the threat center Bush had created.

The letter was sent in response to a series of inquiries dating to February 2003 from Susan Collins, R-Maine, chairwoman of the Senate Governmental Affairs Committee, and Carl Levin of Michigan, the panel's second-ranking Democrat.

The letter said Brennan's unit controls "terrorism analysis (except for information relating solely to purely domestic terrorism)," which is the province of the FBI. Homeland Security manages information collected by its own components, such as the Coast Guard and Secret Service, and is responsible for analyzing material "supporting decisions to raise or lower the national warning level."

---

peaked. A special Senate committee on intelligence operations, better known as the Church committee after its chairman, Frank Church, D-Idaho (1957-81), turned the tide against the CIA and FBI's secretive operations.

The committee's 1976 report detailing civil rights and human rights abuses was followed in 1978 by congressional passage of the Foreign Intelligence Surveillance Act (PL 95-511) to further restrict domestic spying. (*1976 Almanac, p. 303; 1978 Almanac, p. 186*)

The law set strict guidelines for federal government surveillance of foreign agents in the United States. The intent of the statute was to erect a wall between surveillance and criminal investigations so that intelligence gathering would target only agents of foreign states and not U.S. citizens.

The Patriot Act, passed in 2001, was designed to bring down that wall, loosening the standard for wiretapping so that a criminal case needs to be only the "significant" purpose of surveillance, not its primary purpose. The law allows wiretapping to gather intelligence about potential terrorist conspiracies even though the wiretapping might not be linked to a specific criminal case.

The Patriot Act has made both Republicans and Democrats wary of expanding the FBI's domestic intelligence powers even further in the war on terrorism. Parts of the Patriot Act expire in another year, and Bush wants the law renewed so that investigators will retain the authority to more easily carry out surveillance of suspected terrorists on U.S. soil.

An expanded version of the law, dubbed "Patriot Act II," was circulated within the Justice Department in 2003. Though it drew a negative reaction from members of Congress of both parties after details were leaked, Bush has pushed for some provisions he says are important to combating terrorism. (2003 CQ Weekly, p. 405)

He wants Congress to expand the original law by increasing the range of terrorism-related crimes subject to the death penalty and making it more difficult for those arrested for suspected terrorist activities to gain release. He also has called on Congress to include administrative subpoenas, which would allow law enforcement agencies to search records without having to gain a judge's permission.

Even though other portions of the Patriot Act still have widespread support, the current law's lower legal standard regarding subpoenas and search warrants worries some conservative Republicans as much as it does liberal Democrats because of the civil liberties implications.

"If we can define domestic terrorism [in the law] a little tighter, the intelligence can be used as long as it meets that limited definition," said Rep. C.L. "Butch" Otter, R-Idaho, who has criticized the reach of the Patriot Act on privacy grounds. "It's always going to be a concern of mine when government collects information . . . in pursuit of other government goals and policies."

Organizational Options

The concept of a U.S. version of a British MI5 agency that only gathers intelligence but has no arrest powers has been talked about frequently, but is opposed by the CIA, the FBI and members of Congress who would have the biggest say over such a proposal.

A pure intelligence agency operating inside the United States would not carry the FBI's cultural baggage. But the idea raises questions about spying on U.S. citizens and foreign visitors without a criminal investigation to justify the snooping.

Brandon, the former FBI official, says his one-time colleagues in Britain's MI5 have actually expressed envy for the FBI because it can both gather intelligence and make arrests.

"Putting up a new player [in intelligence] on the board would set up new rivalries," said Gilmore, who chaired the commission on terrorism. "My view is that the FBI should be forced" to change to make intelligence a higher priority.

A less dramatic change that would

Legislating Security: Some Ideas

As the commission investigating the Sept. 11 terrorist attacks examines what went wrong with U.S. intelligence and what should be done to fix the problem, there is no shortage of ideas coming from Capitol Hill. Most bills will never emerge from committee, however. And while Congress will debate the issue once the commission releases its report in late July, there is neither the time nor the political will to finish any of the major legislative ideas this year. Here is a sampling of introduced bills:

Intelligence overhaul

• **HR 4104.** *Sponsor:* Rep. Jane Harman of California, ranking Democrat on the Select Intelligence Committee. The bill would consolidate leadership over the intelligence community by creating a "director of national intelligence" who would be independent of the CIA and would have budget and organizational power over military and civilian intelligence agencies. The current director of central intelligence lacks such power.
Status: Referred to Intelligence Committee.
Outlook: Bill has support from Intelligence Committee Democrats, but similar proposals have been blocked by the Pentagon in the past.

• **S 1520.** *Sponsor:* Sen. Bob Graham, D-Fla., former chairman of the Senate Intelligence Committee. The bill would create a Cabinet-level director of national intelligence who would manage the overall intelligence budget and ensure that information-sharing was better coordinated. Other provisions would bolster the FBI's counterterrorism capabilities and require a review of classification policies. Sen. Dianne Feinstein, D-Calif., has introduced a similar measure.
Status: Referred to Intelligence Committee.
Outlook: Intelligence Chairman Pat Roberts, R-Kan., has said he will hold a hearing on the bill.

• **S 410.** *Sponsor:* Sen. John Edwards, D-N.C., a member of the Senate Intelligence Committee. The bill would create a homeland security intelligence agency, modeled after Britain's MI5, and remove domestic intelligence authority from the FBI.
Status: Referred to Intelligence Committee.
Outlook: CIA, Department of Justice and FBI officials oppose an MI5-style agency. It is unlikely to find much support in House or Senate.

Legal authority/Patriot Act bills:

• **S 113.** *Sponsors:* Sens. Jon Kyl, R-Ariz., and Charles E. Schumer, D-N.Y. The measure would allow the government to use powers of the Foreign Intelligence Surveillance Act (PL 95-511) to monitor a suspect if it could show probable cause that the person would commit a terrorist attack, even if the person was not linked to a specific terrorist group or foreign power. The bill is aimed at catching "lone wolf" terrorists.
Status: Passed the Senate in May 2003 but remains stuck in House committee.
Outlook: House Judiciary Chairman F. James Sensenbrenner Jr., R-Wis., has not agreed to the idea, and any law enforcement surveillance bills would have to go through his committee, in addition to Select Intelligence.

• **HR 3352.** *Sponsor:* C.L. "Butch" Otter, R-Idaho. The bill would place new limits on "roving wiretaps" and the delayed notification search warrants that were authorized in the Patriot Act (PL 107-56).
Status: Referred to Judiciary and Intelligence committees.
Outlook: There appears to be popular support in the House for Otter's idea. Similar language passed as an amendment to the fiscal 2004 Commerce, Justice and State appropriations bill, but the provision was dropped from the omnibus appropriations bill (PL 108-199).

• **S 1709.** *Sponsors:* Sens. Larry E. Craig, R-Idaho, and Richard J. Durbin, D-Ill. The measure would curb federal law enforcement authority to conduct searches without notifying suspects. It also would limit roving wiretaps and add new privacy protections for libraries and booksellers.
Status: Referred to Judiciary Committee.
Outlook: Similar to Otter's legislation in the House, this bill has some bipartisan support, but debate will probably be put off until the larger reauthorization process for the Patriot Act begins in 2005.

strengthen domestic intelligence without separating that authority from the FBI is gaining traction in Congress.

Wolf says his proposal to give FBI intelligence-gathering more respect among career FBI employees is to create a separate division within the bureau. He says he plans to introduce legislation this spring that would require such a change.

Such proposals will have to overcome an imbedded culture within the FBI that prizes law enforcement. As Rand Corp. intelligence analyst Greg Treverton puts it, the FBI has a reputation of having "two types of employees: agents and furniture."

A senior congressional aide familiar with intelligence operations, who asked not to be identified, said, "There is a strong, midlevel bureaucracy at the FBI, and they haven't been hiring people with a knack for intelligence-gathering. They have been restrained from pure intelligence-gathering."

Under Wolf's plan, intelligence would have its own career track within the bureau. The unit would have access to all counterterrorism intelligence information, and analysts would still be able to coordinate with criminal counterparts in the FBI.

"Those guys [intelligence analysts] have been treated like second-class citizens," Wolf said. "There is reluctance [to change], but there are certain things we have to do. . . . They have worked hard, but there's more to be done."

One concern about Wolf's idea is that it could isolate the FBI's intelligence functions from its criminal investigations.

"The general feeling is that we should give Mueller a chance to enact the changes" he has already made, said Jeff Lungren, a spokesman for the House Judiciary Committee, which has jurisdiction over the FBI. "They have completely changed their focus."

Other lawmakers are content to do nothing legislatively, yet strengthen the hand of congressional oversight by calling Mueller and other FBI executives to hearings to assess whether the bureau's reforms are working.

"The overall thing is to change the equation from crime solving to crime prevention," said Sen. Charles E. Grassley, R-Iowa, one of the Senate's most vocal FBI critics. "Mueller has them on track."

As Congress considers changes in the FBI's intelligence mission, there is

Gen. Patrick Hughes, assistant secretary for information analysis at the Homeland Security Department, explains the department's color-coded threat condition system on Capitol Hill in March 2004.

a web of federal, state and local agencies collecting, and in some cases analyzing, intelligence with no distinct pipeline for how the information flows and is ultimately used.

Most of the material is gathered in the course of the agencies' own missions unrelated to counterterrorism.

Who's in Charge?

The FBI houses the Terrorist Screening Center, a joint effort by the departments of Justice, State and Homeland Security that aims to better track and identify terrorist suspects using a variety of databases.

The CIA's Counterterrorist Center is still seen as the premier terrorist intelligence shop in the federal government, and it is supposed to share information with the new Terrorist Threat Integration Center.

The Energy Department has an intelligence division that deals with nuclear secrets, security and international proliferation, while the Treasury Department has intelligence offices that focus on financial crimes and fraud. The Drug Enforcement Administration plays a role in intelligence when it investigates links between terrorists and drug trafficking.

Below the federal level, the FBI considers state bureaus of investigation, state police and the thousands of county and city police departments as the eyes and ears for domestic intelligence at the local level.

However, state and local law enforcement officials have long complained

that the information flow is only one way: They send their intelligence on suspects to the FBI or other federal agencies, but little information returns.

"Periodically, there's a conversation with local [law enforcement] if there is a targeted or specific threat," said Dalen Harris, associate legislative director for the National Association of Counties. "But there's really no national system for sharing federal, local and state homeland security information."

The FBI now operates 84 localized Joint Terrorism Task Forces, up from 34 before Sept. 11. These task forces, made up of FBI, state and local law enforcement officials, act as the primary organizing unit at the local level for terrorist investigations.

In the 108th Congress, at least 30 bills have been introduced that would in some way alter the federal government's intelligence authority and its organization, particularly in how federal agencies collect data and relate to each other. *(Bills, p. 14)*

Few of the bills will ever be acted on, and even the most popular legislation may be put off until next year. In the meantime, the administration may order changes without the imprimatur of Congress.

"If I was a pure betting man, I bet the argument that allows the FBI to say 'let us finish what we're doing' will win out," said Treverton of the Rand Corp. "Congress as usual is going to be in a reacting mode, and the administration may make a move on its own." ◆

Congress as Watchdog: Asleep on the Job?

Quality of oversight worsens as lawmakers fail to guard an important power

Over the years, Congress has become known as the staging ground for televised investigations that have turned lawmakers into minor celebrities and made administration witnesses squirm.

When Defense Secretary Donald H. Rumsfeld testified on Iraqi prisoner abuses before the Senate Armed Services Committee on May 7, live on all the broadcast networks, it seemed likely to produce a classic television moment — such as when Sen. Howard Baker, R-Tenn. (1967-85), asked the most memorable question of the Watergate hearings: "What did the president know, and when did he know it?"

Much of congressional oversight does not rise to that level. But even the more common variety — the poorly attended subcommittee hearings and the quiet exchanges of letters and phone calls — has allowed Congress to act as the watchdog that keeps the executive branch in check.

Lately, though, the watchdog is gaining a reputation for sleeping on the job.

On such high-profile issues as Iraq, intelligence, appropriations, energy policy, the 2001 education overhaul law (PL 107-110) and the anti-terrorism law known as the Patriot Act (PL 107-56), there has been a growing pattern of breakdowns in congressional oversight. In some cases, Congress has been blindsided by revelations dug up by outsiders. In others it has been stalled by the administration or, its critics say, simply has not made much of an effort in the first place.

And even the Senate Armed Services Committee hearings on the abuse of Iraqi prisoners, which promised to be some of the most aggressive since the days of Watergate in 1973-74 and the impeachment of President Bill Clinton in 1998, have started to fall short of their billing. (*Lawmakers, p. 63*)

Chairman John W. Warner, R-Va., defying pressure from some of his Republican colleagues to tone down his investigation, promised to "go where the evidence leads us, no matter how embarrassing or incriminating it may be." Instead, veteran investigators who watched the committee's questioning of top generals May 19 saw unprepared and uninformed senators. Many asked questions based on accounts in newspaper articles, leading to some embarrassing moments in which the generals flat out denied the accounts and senators were forced to back down. (*2004 CQ Weekly, p. 1196*)

"Rule No. 1: You always have to know the answer before you ask the question," said Winslow T. Wheeler, a defense specialist who worked for Sen. Jacob Javits, R-N.Y. (1957-81). "In other words, your staff is working its tail off finding out what is going on and feeding it to the senator. That's not happening."

To some, it should be little surprise that oversight would fade during a period of one-party government. "Our party controls the levers of government. We're not about to go out and look beneath a bunch of rocks to try to cause heartburn," said Rep. Ray LaHood, R-Ill. "Unless they really screw up, we're not going to go after them."

Others, though, see an erosion of one of Congress' most important powers. "In this Congress, there are no checks, there are no balances. There is no oversight," said Rep. David R. Obey of Wisconsin, the ranking Democrat on the House Appropriations Committee.

And while some Republicans say the decline has been

CQ Weekly May 22, 2004

Oversight Goes Back More Than 200 Years

Indian Attack on Troops
Spring 1792

In the first congressional inquiry, a select House committee investigated an Indian attack that killed about 600 U.S. troops commanded by Maj. Gen. Arthur St. Clair. The panel absolved St. Clair and blamed the War Department. The House took no action on the committee report, and it was never published because of its reflections on the secretaries of War and Treasury.

Civil War
December 1861 to May 1865

The first joint House-Senate investigative panel was set up to examine Union defeats at Bull Run and Ball's Bluff, but it expanded into past and future battle plans, disloyal employees, navy installations, and war supplies and contracts — and spent much effort harassing generals. Considered the worst-run congressional inquiry until the McCarthy hearings of the 1950s.

Financial Trusts
February 1912 to February 1913

A House Banking and Currency subcommittee investigated the concentration of money and credit, especially the control exercised by two New York banks. Financial giants, including J.P. Morgan Sr., were called to testify. The panel's report helped lead to enactment of the Federal Reserve Act of 1913, which created a central banking system, and the Clayton Antitrust Act and Federal Trade Commission Act of 1914.

Teapot Dome
1923 and 1924

The Senate Committee on Public Lands and Surveys investigated the lease of naval oil reserves, including one called Teapot Dome under a Wyoming rock formation, by the going on for years, not just recently, they are worried that their party has not gotten a handle on it.

"I just don't think our side has ever learned those skills," former House Majority Leader Dick Armey, R-Texas (1985-2003), said of his fellow Republicans. Armey used to give awards to members who demonstrated skillful oversight in an effort to encourage them.

Some say the White House has placed obstacles before Congress that prevent it from getting information, though defenders of the administration maintain that it has cooperated with lawmakers' oversight efforts. There is nearly universal agreement, however, that congressional Republicans themselves have not made oversight a priority.

"I don't think we have been doing the job we should have been doing for several years on oversight," said Rep. Jim Kolbe, R-Ariz., chairman of the House Appropriations Subcommittee on Foreign Operations, Export Financing and Related Programs.

Former Rep. William F. Clinger, R-Pa. (1979-97), who chaired the House Government Reform Committee, said Congress "is becoming increasingly less effective in its oversight functions."

And Rep. John D. Dingell, D-Mich., who is remembered by Republicans and Democrats as one of the most aggressive investigators in Congress when Democrats ran the House, worries that the decline will make it hard for future lawmakers to return to vigorous oversight because all the expertise will have disappeared. "Congress can always come back to it," Dingell said. "The problem is that the nexus between those who know how to do oversight and those who want to do it is being broken by the Republicans' behavior."

Working Out of Sight

That does not mean congressional oversight has faded

" I think we've had a decline in congressional oversight for some time. This isn't anything that's developed over the last year or two."

— Former Rep. Lee H. Hamilton, D-Ind.
(1965-99)

away completely. Every week, committees and subcommittees hold oversight hearings of one kind or another. Most focus on run-of-the-mill issues such as ocean policy, but others tackle more urgent subjects such as the future of Iraq.

The two top Republican leaders say Congress has hardly been lax about oversight. Senate Majority Leader Bill Frist of Tennessee says the Senate has opened tough investigations of the Iraqi prison scandal. "Our committees are working aggressively in terms of oversight, taking very appropriate action," he said in a floor speech May 19. "The Defense Department is cooperating fully in these inquiries and has been responsive to all of our requests."

And House Speaker J. Dennis Hastert, R-Ill., says he has been pushing for every House panel to have an oversight subcommittee. "Are there gaps? Will there be bad things [that] happen? Yes," Hastert said May 19. "But I think we've done an extraordinary job on oversight, and we're going to continue to do that."

Furthermore, some Republican chairmen have won bipartisan praise for their willingness to take on bureaucratic waste and occasionally tackle subjects that hit political nerves with the White House. They include Senate Finance Chairman Charles E. Grassley of Iowa, House Government Reform Chairman Thomas M. Davis III of Virginia, and Rep. James C. Greenwood of Pennsylvania, chairman of the House Energy and Commerce Subcommittee on Oversight and Investigations — the subcommittee formerly headed by Dingell. *(Congressional watchdogs, p. 20)*

Analysts say the Republican majority has been particularly active in trying to root out government waste, and that agencies such as the Transportation Security Administration have been forced to take steps to respond.

Even so, former members and independent analysts say there has been a long-term erosion of Congress' oversight

Harding administration. The hearings moved from the legality of the leases to charges of bribery against Interior Secretary Albert B. Fall. As a result of the investigation, Harding moved to cancel the leases. On March 4, 1924, the Senate Select Committee to Investigate the Justice Department opened a separate inquiry. Fall was the only Cabinet member sent to prison. Attorney General Harry M. Daugherty was prosecuted but not convicted, and oil magnate Harry F. Sinclair was tried but acquitted of contempt of Congress and jury tampering charges.

Defense Programs
March 1941 to April 1948

A Special Senate Committee to Investigate the National Defense Program was created nine months before the attack on Pearl Harbor. First

chaired by Harry S Truman, D-Mo. (1935-45), the panel's mission grew from investigating the status of national defenses to a more specific review of war mobilization problems, shortages of critical materials such as aluminum, and fraud among contractors and lobbyists. Its work, which lasted three years beyond World War II's end, is often hailed as the most effective congressional investigation ever.

Kefauver Crime Hearings
May 1950 to Summer 1951

Led by Estes Kefauver, D-Tenn. (1949-63), the Senate Special Committee to Investigate Organized Crime in Interstate Commerce held the first congressional hearings to draw the rapt attention of television viewers across the nation as prominent gangsters and underworld leaders were paraded in front of the panel.

McCarthy

McCarthy Investigations
January 1953 to December 1954

In 1950, Sen. Joseph R. McCarthy, R-Wis. (1947-57), publicly charged that there were 205 known communists in the State Department. That led to a bitter inquiry by a special Foreign Relations subcommittee, chaired by Millard E. Tydings, D-Md., who lost his seat that fall after he was tarred as soft on communism. After Republicans won control of the Senate in 1952, McCarthy became chairman of the Government Operations skills, though they believe there is more to the story than one party's reluctance to investigate itself. Long-term institutional changes have contributed to the decline, such as members' shorter workweeks, packed schedules, term limits on chairmanships and eroding salaries for investigative staff members.

Moreover, the general drudgery of routine oversight, which often involves years of work with little immediate payoff, makes it a poor sell to members whose time is increasingly limited. Sen. Judd Gregg, R-N.H., who used to serve in the House and now chairs the Senate Health, Education, Labor and Pensions Committee, said oversight is harder for senators than for House members because senators have more committee responsibilities.

Former Rep. Lee H. Hamilton, D-Ind. (1965-99), one of the leaders of Congress' 1987 Iran-contra investigation and now a member of the independent Sept. 11 commission, takes the long view as well. "I think we've had a decline in congressional oversight for some time," he said. "This isn't anything that's developed over the last year or two.

"Oversight is very tedious work. It takes a lot of preparation, and it tends to be very complicated," added Hamilton, who is director of the Woodrow Wilson International Center for Scholars and author of "How Congress Works and Why You Should Care." "Members are very busy now, and they just don't make oversight that high a priority. Most of them focus on constituent services and legislative work."

Some forms of congressional oversight are less obvious than others. Congress has the "power of the purse," which gives it the authority to check on how its appropriations are being spent. It also reacts to dramatic events, such as the abuse of Iraqi prisoners or the Watergate and Iran-contra scandals.

In addition, it has the authority to monitor how laws are being implemented, to scrutinize administration policies on issues such as Iraq and energy, and to look for waste, fraud and abuse in agency programs. It also can scrutinize the private sector, sometimes in ways that are politically sensitive to the administration, such as the 2002 Enron collapse.

To a degree, oversight — a congressional responsibility that is implied, rather than stated, in the Constitution — has often been a lower priority than legislating. As far back as 1885, Woodrow Wilson wrote, "Quite as important as legislation is vigilant oversight of administration." But analysts say it took on more prominence in the 1970s and '80s, partly because of Dingell's efforts, including a 1983 probe of problems with the superfund hazardous-waste cleanup program that led to the indictment of its director, Rita M. LaVelle. Oversight work of various committees led to a series of good-government laws and high-profile investigations.

The Casualties

Now, there is mounting evidence that the oversight process has been faltering on some of the most urgent issues before Congress.

Just weeks after lawmakers demonstrated palpable outrage at the abuse of Iraqi prisoners, the momentum of the investigations has slowed. The Senate Armed Services hearing May 19 did little to advance the inquiry, and House Armed Services Chairman Duncan Hunter of California and other Republicans have urged the Senate to back off and let the military investigations proceed. Indeed, Warner himself refused to call the hearings an investigation.

The Iraqi prison abuse scandal has become part of a pattern in which lawmakers have promised to become more aggressive in overseeing the war, then have backed off under pressure from the White House and Republicans' own ranks.

Senate Select Intelligence Chairman Pat Roberts, R-Kan., promised to "let the chips fall where they may" in the panel's investigation of prewar intelligence, only to have the probe hobbled by partisan tensions. Foreign Relations Chairman Richard G. Lugar, R-Ind., vowed in April that "we need to offer answers" in hearings on the administration's plans for Iraq, then declared himself satisfied with lower-level administration witnesses after the higher-ranking ones he wanted refused to show. (*Intelligence, 2004 CQ Weekly, p. 730; hearings, 2004 CQ Weekly, p. 974*)

And when President Bush asked for an $87 billion supplemental spending bill for Iraq and Afghanistan last fall, many Republicans promised to ask tougher questions about the administration's Iraq policies, then approved his open-ended request with few changes. (*2003 CQ Weekly, p. 3105*)

Frustrated by the quality of the information the administration was providing on the war, Rep. Christopher Shays,

---

Committee and its Permanent Investigations Subcommittee. He conducted a sweeping array of probes of purported communist subversion of the U.S. government and the United Nations. The probes attracted a nationwide TV audience when McCarthy went after the Army. Ultimately, he was judged too abrasive by his colleagues, and a special Senate panel recommended that McCarthy be censured for his attacks on Army Brig. Gen. Ralph W. Zwicker. In December 1954, the Senate voted to "condemn" McCarthy for some of his actions and statements. He lost his chairmanships the next month, because the Democrats regained control of the Senate.

Watergate
January 1973 to July 1974

A Senate Select Committee on Presidential Campaign Activities was created to investigate allegations that arose from a 1972 break-in at Democratic National Committee headquarters in the Watergate office and apartment complex. With subpoena powers and a $500,000 budget, the panel, chaired by Sam J. Ervin Jr., D-N.C. (1954-74), took testimony from top Nixon administration officials in televised hearings that made celebrities out of the seven panel members and many of the witnesses. A highlight was the disclosure that Oval Office conversations were routinely tape recorded, leading to an effort by the committee and the Justice Department's special Watergate prosecutor to obtain the recordings. When Nixon fired the special prosecutor in October 1973, the House Judiciary Committee began its impeachment investigation. Ervin's committee issued 35 recommendations for preventing abuses of government power in July 1974. That same month, Judiciary approved articles of impeachment alleging obstruction of justice, abuse of power and contempt of Congress. Nixon resigned Aug. 9.

Watergate

ARCHIVE PHOTOS

Church Committee on CIA
January 1975 to April 1976

The Senate established a Select Committee to Study Government Operations with Respect to Intelligence Activities, chaired by Frank Church, D-Idaho (1957-81), after news reports that the CIA had spied on U.S. citizens during the Vietnam War. The next year the committee made 87 recommendations, one of which was for better congressional oversight of the intelligence agency. Less than a month after

R-Conn., traveled to Iraq to find out for himself what was actually happening. He was scolded by L. Paul Bremer III, chief of the Coalition Provisional Authority, for ignoring warnings not to come. In return, Shays berated Bremer for making Congress' oversight of the Iraq operations unnecessarily difficult. *(2004 CQ Weekly, p. 1004)*

"If we had been visiting these prisons in August, September, October of last year, I don't think any of this would have happened," Shays said of the scandal. "We probably would have had someone saying to us, 'You won't believe what's going on here. Some people are about to go over the edge.' "

A report in Bob Woodward's book "Plan of Attack" that the administration spent $178 million from the $40 billion emergency supplemental bill in 2001 (PL 107-38) on projects in Kuwait — months before Congress authorized the Iraq war — prompted demands for full disclosure from Democratic appropriators Obey and Sen. Robert C. Byrd of West Virginia, who said they believed Congress had been hoodwinked. *(2004 CQ Weekly, p. 1037)*

Republican appropriators did not share their concerns, and administration officials said the money was spent on the global war on terrorism, not specifically on Iraq. But the response to Obey and Byrd — the delivery of three binders full of general information on how the supplemental appropriations were spent — succeeded only in reinforcing Democrats' belief that the administration's reports are too vague to be of any real use to Congress.

Upstaged by Commissions

Adding to the injury, Congress has also been outperformed lately by the independent commissions that increasingly are taking on the work it used to do.

The Sept. 11 commission has pried out more disclosures about the 2001 terrorist attacks than the congressional joint inquiry that preceded it. And it generated enough public pressure to force national security adviser Condoleezza Rice to testify publicly, and Bush and Vice President Dick Cheney to brief the panel in private — all witnesses that the congressional panel never heard from.

On other issues, Congress has been successfully stalled by the administration. Cheney was able to defeat the General Accounting Office (GAO), the investigative arm of Congress, in its efforts to obtain the records of the energy task force he headed in 2001 to determine who advised the administration on its energy policy. *(2002 Almanac, p. 1-15)*

Despite warnings by lawmakers such as Rep. Henry A. Waxman, D-Calif., that the defeat would permanently damage the GAO's ability to obtain information from the executive branch, Comptroller General David M. Walker, who heads the GAO, said his investigators have not had any of their requests turned down since a federal judge dismissed the GAO's lawsuit in 2002. Walker warned, however, that GAO investigators are experiencing a lot of delays from federal agencies, which "undercuts our ability to provide timely information" to help lawmakers' oversight efforts.

Similar delays frustrated House Judiciary Chairman F. James Sensenbrenner Jr., R-Wis., in his early efforts to oversee the implementation of the Patriot Act, which has raised civil liberties concerns among conservatives and liberals. The Department of Justice's answers to his first set of written questions in 2002 were so incomplete that he threatened to subpoena Attorney General John Ashcroft to get better ones.

Since then, Sensenbrenner aides say, Justice has improved its response time, and its answers have gotten better. The initial problems, however, have left lingering doubts about the department's responsiveness.

"We gave the Justice Department a huge increase in power," Armey said. Congress made a point of designing key provisions to expire, he said, "on the theory that would make them more responsive to oversight."

With the education overhaul measure known as the No Child Left Behind law, oversight efforts have been more halting. The Senate Health, Education, Labor and Pensions Committee has held no oversight hearings on its implementation this year, even as complaints mount from state and local officials that the law is underfunded and too demanding.

Sen. Edward M. Kennedy of Massachusetts, the panel's ranking Democrat, said he has asked Gregg to hold oversight hearings and has been turned down. Gregg said he has held off because the Education Department has been revising its regulations implementing the law to address some of the complaints, and "I would rather let it percolate for a while

---

the report, the Senate established its permanent Select Committee on Intelligence.

Iran-Contra
November 1986 to August 1987

Following revelations that the Reagan administration had sold arms to Iran to try to gain release of hostages held in Lebanon, and that profits from the arms sales had been diverted to the contra rebels fighting the Sandinista government in Nicaragua, a multitude of White House and congressional investigations were opened. The culmination on Capitol Hill was 12 weeks of public hearings held jointly by the House and Senate Intelligence committees, which were the outgrowth of partisan disputes in Congress over how to proceed. Several White House officials were fired — the result of administration-ordered probes — and eventually two participants went to prison. The

stars of the congressional hearings were Marine Lt. Col. Oliver L. North, who ran the illegal operation in the White House, and his boss, Vice Adm. John M. Poindexter, who said he had kept the operation from Reagan while he was the president's national security adviser. Both were convicted, but the convictions were overturned by a federal judge who ruled that their testimony to Congress under a grant of immunity had influenced witnesses at the trial.

Clinton Investigations
July 1995 to February 1999

From the time Republicans took control of the House in 1995 until President Bill Clinton left office in January 2001, his administration was the target of a string of committee investigations. The subjects included the Clintons' personal financial involvement in a failed Arkansas land deal known as Whitewater,

Iran-Contra

AP PHOTO / LANA HARRIS

the firing of White House travel office employees, the request for FBI background files on former Republican administration officials, and Democratic campaign fundraising in 1996, when Clinton won his second term. These congressional investigations were separate from those conducted by Independent Counsel Kenneth W. Starr, which led the House to impeach Clinton for allegedly committing perjury and obstructing justice to hide his affair with Monica Lewinsky, then a White House intern. The inquiries subsided after Clinton was acquitted in a 1999 Senate trial.

Three Watchdogs and What They Have Done

SEN. CHARLES E. GRASSLEY
IOWA REPUBLICAN

Chairman, Senate Finance Committee

• In the 1980s, publicized excessive Pentagon expenditures such as $7,600 for a coffeemaker.
• Sponsored the 1989 Whistleblower Protection Act (PL 101-12), which strengthened job protections for federal workers who report waste, fraud and abuse, and the 1986 amendments (PL 99-562) that increased the penalties in the False Claims Act, which allows citizens to sue people or companies who are defrauding the federal government.

• As Finance Committee chairman, included provisions in this year's corporate tax bill to strengthen rewards for whistleblowers at the Internal Revenue Service and crack down on excessive tax deductions for donated vehicles.
• Held hearings on abusive tax shelters and waste in Medicare's power wheelchair program.
• Helped expose inappropriate credit card expenses by Pentagon employees in 2001.

"It may be a little less glamorous, but you can still get a fair amount done as an individual on oversight. If you're working on legislation, you need to get at least 50 other people to go along with you."

REP. THOMAS M. DAVIS III
VIRGINIA REPUBLICAN

Chairman, House Government Reform Committee

• Held hearing on Iraq reconstruction contracts and alleged overbilling by Halliburton, March 11
• Held hearing on lead contamination of District of Columbia drinking water, March 5
• Held hearing on problems with pay to National Guard troops serving in Iraq, Jan. 28

• Held Transportation Security Administration oversight hearing after Southwest Airlines security incident, Nov. 20, 2003
• Held hearing on coordinating terrorism information at Department of Homeland Security, May 8, 2003

"My position is, if the Democrats are back in power some day, we want to proceed under the same basis. We're not going to have a witch hunt, but we're going to ask tough questions."

REP. JAMES C. GREENWOOD
PENNSYLVANIA REPUBLICAN

Chairman, House Energy and Commerce Subcommittee on Oversight and Investigations

• Held Enron hearings, 2002
• Held hearings on ImClone and Martha Stewart, 2002

• Held Firestone tire recall hearings, 2001
• Held hearings on ethics at National Institutes of Health, May 12 and 18

"My response [to the leadership] was, 'Let's think this through. Either the Democrats are going to investigate the heck out of Enron and we're going to look like we're covering it up, or we're going to do it ourselves."

rather than stirring the pot.".

The House Education and the Workforce Committee has held field hearings on the law, and Chairman John A. Boehner, R-Ohio, said that beyond the partisan disputes over funding, "there's no backing away from it." However, Kennedy and Rep. George Miller of California, the ranking Democrat on the House panel, said they have tried to deal directly with the Education Department to urge leniency in complying with the regulations. Without Republicans on their side, they have gotten little response.

"Have we been doing our job? Well, it's a little late now," Miller said.

Within Congress, one-party government gets much of the blame for the breakdowns. Lawmakers from both parties, as well as outside analysts, agree that one-party government is a recipe for weaker oversight, and this Congress is no exception.

Some Democrats say that has not always been the case, and argue that they were never shy about investigating their own presidents when they were in power. Obey, for example, noted that Harry S. Truman made a national name for himself as a Democratic senator from Missouri (1935-45) by investigating President Franklin D. Roosevelt's national defense program before he became Roosevelt's vice president.

And Dingell, who became famous for his "Dingell-grams" — detailed and time-consuming document requests he would hurl at federal agencies during his investigations — says he took on every administration regardless of who was in charge. "I didn't give a damn whether it was [Jimmy] Carter or Clinton or [Ronald] Reagan or [George] Bush. It didn't make any difference to me."

However, Republicans and outside analysts say that in general, both parties have been guilty of softening their oversight when they controlled the White House. Grassley, for example, notes that he "got a lot of help from Democrats" in exposing Pentagon waste under Reagan and President George Bush, but they became less helpful during the Clinton years.

"I think that's the history of Congress. It's not a new phenomenon," said Rep. Jim Leach, R-Iowa, who helped lead one of the Whitewater investigations in the 1990s.

Oversight generally bounces back, Leach said, during major events such as foreign policy crises or scandals such as the Enron and WorldCom bankruptcies in 2002.

Grassley, who has gone from exposing Pentagon waste in the 1980s to fighting Medicare waste and tax scams today, and Davis, who has held hearings on Iraq reconstruction contracts, say they have not let one-party government stop their oversight efforts.

Davis, who has been urged by ranking Democrat Waxman to hold hearings on the role of private contractors in the Iraqi prison scandal, said he may do so despite House GOP leaders' opposition — though he has not decided whether to focus on the abuses specifically or on the role of contractors in general.

Pressure From the Top

Lawmakers have also faced active resistance from the Bush administration in their efforts to get information. And Republican leaders have not always been helpful.

In their fight against private groups seeking the energy task force records, now before the Supreme Court, Cheney's lawyers argued that the Constitution gives presidents a "zone of autonomy" from scrutiny of the legislative advice they receive. The implication if such an argument prevails, Waxman said, is that "they can operate in secrecy without the Congress or the public knowing how they reached their decisions."

More recently, Cheney led a backlash against the accelerating congressional investigations into the abuse of the Iraqi prisoners. On May 8, the day after Rumsfeld testified in back-to-back hearings of the Senate and House Armed Services committees, Cheney issued a statement declaring that Rumsfeld's critics should "get off his case."

An aide to Cheney said that while the statement may have been interpreted as a slap at Congress, it was not meant that way, and was simply "a straightforward description of the exceptional job the defense secretary is doing." But the remark prompted Lindsey Graham, R-S.C., a member of the Senate panel, to say the White House should "let us do our job." And it acted as a brake on the growing demand for congressional investigations, prompting Republican conservatives in Congress — notably House Majority Leader Tom DeLay of Texas and Sen. James M. Inhofe of Oklahoma — to prod critical members to tone down their outrage.

Not all committee and subcommittee chairmen say they have felt pressure from the leadership to soft-pedal their activities. From the accounts of those interviewed for this article, Senate chairmen feel relatively free to take on the subjects they want, while House chairmen have been more likely to encounter friction with their leaders.

Grassley, for example, says he has "never had leadership discourage anything I've been trying to do," adding that oversight is not up to the leadership anyway: "I think it's up to the individual committee chairmen to do it."

In the House, not all chairmen feel constrained. Boehner said he has never felt pressure from the leadership not to examine complaints about the No Child Left Behind law. And Kolbe says one-party government "absolutely makes no difference. What's important is for us to carry out our constitutional responsibility."

Some House chairmen, however, have gotten definite warnings that investigations are not welcome on topics hitting too close to home with the White House. Combined with the complaints they get from the administration itself, these signals can have a chilling effect, since every chairman knows that he serves at the pleasure of the leadership.

For example, Greenwood says he encountered resistance from some members of the leadership, whom he will not name, when the subcommittee was preparing to investigate

the 2002 collapse of Enron — whose chairman, Kenneth Lay, had been a top contributor to Bush.

Although that was an issue of oversight of the private sector rather than the executive branch, Greenwood said, "I kept hearing, 'What do you want to do that for? The Republican Party is associated with big business . . . and with Bush being from Texas, he's associated with Enron; it's been a big part of our fundraising and all that.' "

"My response [to the leadership] was, 'Let's think this through. Either the Democrats are going to investigate the heck out of Enron, and we're going to look like we're covering it up, or we're going to do it ourselves.' " By going ahead with it, Greenwood said, "we essentially took that issue off the plate for the '02 elections."

Muscle Loss

Overall, Congress has lost some of its ability to mount sustained investigations, according to some outside analysts.

Paul C. Light, a senior fellow in governance studies at the Brookings Institution, said that while congressional Republicans have been skilled at tackling government waste and abuse, Congress has become less successful at "deep oversight," the investigative work needed to pry out embarrassing information that is not in open view.

That is partly because staff salaries have eroded, making it harder to retain good investigators, Light said. "You need good investigative staff members who know what doors to knock on, and that's just not the case," he said.

Joel D. Aberbach, director of the Center for American Politics and Public Policy at UCLA, found an increase in congressional oversight hearings in the 1990s, the latest figures available in his research. But the numbers say nothing about the results the hearings achieved, he said, and at a time when the congressional leadership is getting stronger and committees are getting weaker, Congress is not rattling a lot of cages.

"Even though they may still be holding a decent number of oversight activities . . . you can have lots of formal activities and no real influence," Aberbach said.

In more routine activities, such as requests for GAO reports, the trend is toward more reactive oversight and less work to anticipate problems. When problems arise, such as the prison scandal, "Congress does not hesitate to get involved," Walker said. "At the same time, there's not as much ongoing, proactive oversight as there may have been in years past."

While GAO has been getting fewer requests for reports from lawmakers, Walker said, the quality of the requests has been better — a development he attributes to the agency's efforts to work with lawmakers more closely to let them know what are legitimate requests.

But some members say Congress underestimates its own powers. "The power of Congress when it comes to oversight is extraordinary. A principled member must be careful not to use it in a capricious way," Leach said. "A congressional subpoena is very powerful. Taking the oath is very powerful."

And others, such as Grassley and Kolbe, say Congress faces no real obstacles to oversight. If it is failing at that task, they say, it is only because lawmakers themselves are not taking it seriously enough.

"I think to be successful at it, you have to treat administrations equally, whether they're Republicans or Democrats," said Grassley. "You have to have a good staff. And you have to remember that even though oversight is hard work, it is our constitutional responsibility." ◆

Political Participation

With elections looming in 2004, Republicans and Democrats in Congress are acutely aware of how their legislative track records will affect voters' decisions in November. The first and second articles in this section examine how Democratic leaders have highlighted the short-comings of the Republican-led 108th Congress, while Republican leaders point to the GOP's legislative successes, including the Medicare drug benefit. Democrats maintain that on policy and process, the GOP has overreached in ways that will come back to haunt it during the 2004 elections. Republicans claimed victory with the passage of the Medicare bill, but Democrats point to several issues that remain unresolved, such as the U.S. unemployment rate and the budget deficit. The election will also likely be influenced by a number of uncertainties: the condition of the U.S. economy in the fall, whether Iraq will be stable or possible new revelations about President George W. Bush's arguments for going to war in Iraq and his handling of the post-war phase.

The third article discusses the sharp-edged rhetoric and partisan finger-pointing in the Senate in 2003. Debates over the energy bill, the overhaul of the Medicare system and judicial nominations made 2003 a particularly rancorous year on the Senate floor. Such acrimony has traditionally been found in the House, leading some Senate veterans to blame the erosion of the Senate's long history of bipartisanship on the rising number of junior senators who previously served in the House.

Returning to Congress's focus on the 2004 elections, the fourth article chronicles how, with Congress more polarized than ever, the two parties sought to highlight their differences on health care, education and other major issues—rather than to seek broad consensus—and how they have continued to do so during the campaign season. The fifth article looks at how Republicans are making election-year campaign pitches at subsets of female voters to bridge a decades-old gender gap of women favoring Democratic candidates. In doing so, the GOP emphasizes its record on public safety, economic security and empowerment.

The sixth article examines how partisan divisions in the House reached new heights, beginning in 1995, when the Republicans assumed a narrow majority. Republican Speaker Dennis Hastert and Democratic Minority Leader Nancy Pelosi barely talk to each other, and few members even bother to attend "civility" retreats. Members, former members and longtime Congress watchers view these partisan divisions as a result of the long period of near-partisan parity in the House, a faster-paced and more impersonal working environment and the election of members who are elected by polarized districts and disinclined to work with the other party.

The seventh article spotlights again how an election year affects the inner workings of Congress. Some political paralysis in Congress—especially in the Senate—is to be expected in an election year, but the closeness of the presidential race and the Republicans' narrow controlling majority have exacerbated the problem. Lawmakers and outside observers are startled by how quickly and thoroughly Congress has become an extension of the presidential campaign, to the point at which lawmakers are visibly spending their time on little else.

GOP Hones 'Can Do' Pitch To Party Base, Swing Voters

Some see big problems down the road when effects of drug bill, tax cuts kick in

With other lawmakers looking on, Bush shakes hands with Rep. Nancy L. Johnson, R-Conn., after signing the Medicare prescription drug bill on Dec. 8. The new law is a cornerstone of the GOP election-year message to voters that Republican government can get things done.

At 11:35 a.m. on Dec. 8, surrounded by a smiling throng of Republican lawmakers and the occasional centrist Democrat, President Bush sat down at a desk in DAR Constitution Hall and signed a $400 billion Medicare prescription drug benefit into law.

It was a scene Democratic leaders had talked about for years — a promise they had dangled in front of senior citizens' faces in election after election — but somehow they had never managed to make it happen. So the signing of the Medicare drug benefit, perhaps more than any other image from the first session of the 108th Congress, captured the theme that Republicans will use in 2004 to persuade voters to give them a stronger majority.

The pitch will be simple: Republicans get things done. Democrats don't.

"We've certainly shown we can govern," said George Allen of Virginia, chairman of the National Republican Senatorial Committee, the campaign arm of the Senate GOP leadership. "You compare all of this to what you got from the Democrats, and you see a record of active, positive solutions."

When they won control of the Senate and the House in the 2002 elections — putting their party in power in all three elected branches of government — Republicans were constantly reminded that they now had to deliver on their promises. They have not succeeded on all fronts, as the frustrated sponsors of the energy bill (HR 6) can attest. But they

have chalked up enough successes in the first session that Republicans are confident they already have a track record on major issues to take to the voters in 2004. (*2003 CQ Weekly, p. 3094*)

"We've done what I ran to do," said Rep. Chris Chocola, R-Ind., a freshman who won his 2nd District seat with just 50.5 percent of the vote in 2002 and will be looking to solidify his hold on it next year.

There are, of course, many uncertainties ahead. No one knows whether Iraq will be stable next fall, as the elections approach, or what new questions may arise about the validity of Bush's arguments for going to war. The economy has been growing at a rapid pace lately, but no one knows if that will continue or how long it will take for jobs to recover.

The Congressional Budget Office has projected a deficit of about $480 billion for this fiscal year, and at some point continued deficits could become a liability for Republicans at the polls. And there are so many warnings of a backlash against the Medicare bill — especially from angry seniors, if they lose their more generous retiree drug benefits — that many analysts say the warnings cannot be dismissed. (*2003 CQ Weekly, p. 3084*)

Right now, however, GOP strategists and independent analysts do not believe that any of those issues could create the kind of tidal wave of anger necessary for Republicans to lose the House and the Senate. So the real question is not whether Republicans' message will allow them to keep their majority. Instead, it is whether it will be strong enough to allow them to build a larger majority and consolidate their power.

The House is so well protected from shifts in public opinion, thanks to districts carefully drawn by both parties, that "House Republicans are about as vulnerable as Politburo members," said David Boaz, executive vice president of the libertarian Cato Institute. And while the Senate is closer in its party balance — 51 Republicans to 48 Democrats and one independent — Republicans will be defending fewer seats, with 19 Democrats up for re-election, compared with only 15 Republicans.

"All they have to do is not blow it," said Gary C. Jacobson, a political scientist at the University of California at San Diego who studies congressional elections.

The greatest risk is that Bush himself will face a close race for re-election, which could have an impact on congressional races, given how closely the Republicans' agenda and fortunes are tied to Bush. Senior adviser Karl Rove has said he expects a close presidential race, and "I think they have some reason to fear that," said Paul Weyrich, chairman of the Free Congress Foundation, a conservative group that focuses on cultural issues.

But they also see great potential in the congressional elections. Rove has talked frequently of the 2004 election as a chance to build a solid and lasting GOP majority. Now, congressional Republicans will begin trying to convince voters that they deserve it.

"This is a referendum on us," said Rep. Thomas M. Davis III, R-Va. And while Republicans appear to be in good shape at the moment, Davis said, "a year is an eternity in politics."

The Record

Already, Republicans are giving a preview of their election message to their constituents, with the aid of thick "recess packets" of talking points prepared by GOP leaders for lawmakers to use while they are at home through Jan. 20.

Republicans will point to the $350 billion tax relief package (PL 108-27) as directly responsible for the recent spike in economic growth. They will tout their national security credentials, promoting the $87.5 billion supplemental spending bill for Iraq and Afghanistan (PL 108-106) as proof that Republicans support the troops and continue the war on terrorism. (*2003 CQ Weekly, p. 1245; p. 2783*)

They will talk about the new law banning a procedure opponents call "partial birth" abortion (PL 108-105) — which they hope will excite social conservatives — and the law authorizing the "do not call" telephone registry (PL 108-82), which they believe will excite pretty much everybody. (*2003 CQ Weekly, pp. 2358, 2780*)

"We delivered good legislation for the American people," House Speaker J. Dennis Hastert of Illinois said in a Dec. 8 floor speech summing up the first session.

"We've given our candidates a lot to talk about," said Rep. Thomas M. Reynolds of New York, chairman of the National Republican Congressional Committee, which will oversee House Republicans' efforts to expand their majority.

But it is the new Medicare law that many Republicans see as the crowning achievement of the first session: a prescription drug benefit that Democrats talked about for years but were never able to turn into a reality.

"We wanted a bill, they wanted an issue, and now the American people know who took their concerns seriously," said House Majority Leader Tom DeLay, R-Texas.

Republican pollster David Winston, who advises Senate and House Republican leaders, said the theme of the election picks up where the 2002 elections left off.

At that time, Winston said, Republicans successfully argued that Senate Democrats were unable to deliver on two major issues: Medicare drugs and the creation of the Department of Homeland Security (PL 107-296). The latter charge still rankles Democrats, who say it was actually the Republicans who were filibustering the bill, but Republicans tagged Democrats as the true obstacles because they were unwilling to give Bush the flexibility he sought on personnel rules.

Since that election, Winston said, Congress has delivered on both. "The question was, 'Can you govern?' On the two issues that drove the election, the answer is yes," Winston said. "That in itself is a huge accomplishment."

Next Year

In choosing the message that they are the party that gets things done, Republicans could inadvertently draw attention to the things they have not gotten done.

They acknowledge, for example, that they will have to be more successful in passing an energy bill next year. If they are not, they say they plan to blame the Democrats for its failure, but that message could be muddied by the fact that last month's cloture vote failed because six Republicans joined the Democrats — and that DeLay himself turned down a request from Bush to remove the liability waiver that had provoked the GOP opposition. (*2003 CQ Weekly, p. 2969*)

Republicans are also heading home for the year without completing action on all fiscal 2004 spending bills. But final passage of an omnibus spending package is expected in January, and it is unclear whether voters will even remember the spending bill debate by the November elections. (*2003 CQ Weekly, p. 3080*)

In addition, Republicans say they will have to make better progress on the "jobs" agenda they set out for themselves this fall. Of the nine items on the Senate GOP agenda, only two — bills reauthorizing the Small Business Administration (S 1375) and the 1998 Workforce Investment Act (HR 1261) — were checked off.

And they will have to deal with a Democratic minority that has become increasingly combative. Democrats plan to keep attacking the GOP record on job losses, Iraq, education funding, the environment and the numerous problems they see with the Medicare bill. They are also charging that Republicans have abused their power by locking Democrats out of conference committees and holding open the Medicare roll call vote in the House for nearly three hours until they got the result they wanted. (*Democrats, p. 27*)

Republicans say they are ready for all of that. Even as Democrats warn that the new Medicare prescription drug benefit has too many coverage gaps and could strip seniors of better private coverage, House Republican Conference Chairwoman Deborah Pryce of Ohio said, "The more [Democrats] talk about it, the better we are. We won on an issue that had traditionally been theirs."

Moreover, Pryce argued that voters will not care much about Democrats' complaints that Republicans have exercised heavy-handed leadership. "We're going to take what actions are necessary to break through [obstructionism]," she said. "I think voters appreciate that we're finally getting things done in Washington."

GOP leaders may not try to do much to add to that record next year. Senate Majority Leader Bill Frist of Tennessee says he wants to finish the energy legislation, pass a highway bill

(S 1072) — another major item on the Senate GOP jobs agenda — and reauthorize the 1996 welfare overhaul (PL 104-193). He also wants to take up tort reform measures on class action lawsuits (S 1751) and asbestos litigation (S 1125). Hastert says he wants to "cut the budget deficit in half through lower spending" and "start the debate in this nation on how to reform our tax laws."

Overall, however, Republican leaders loaded their biggest tasks into the first session, predicting that progress will be impossible in the point-scoring environment of an election year.

Speaking to the Base

Hill Republicans, like Bush, have tried to keep their base happy.

For supply-siders, there was the second major tax cut in three years. For social conservatives, there was the partial-birth abortion ban and the Senate talkathon about the Democrats' filibusters of Bush's judicial nominees. And for foreign policy conservatives, the strongest backers of Bush's decision to oust Iraqi President Saddam Hussein, Republicans can say they supported Bush by approving his request for war and reconstruction funding.

There is one segment of the Republican base, however, that could present a danger: economic conservatives and libertarians. For them, the passage of the Medicare prescription drug benefit was a slap in the face.

Already incensed by the continuing growth of federal spending and the ballooning deficit, they see the $400 billion expansion of an entitlement program as proof that Republicans' talk of smaller government is meaningless. Some Republicans see a brilliant appeal to swing voters. Economic conservatives and libertarians see a betrayal.

For congressional Republicans, the risk is not that these voters will suddenly start voting for Democrats. The risk is that they will not vote at all — which, in a close election, could be almost as dangerous.

"The biggest danger is that in a close election, half a million [to] 1 million economic conservatives might say, 'big-government liberalism, big-government conservatism, I don't see the difference," said Boaz of the Cato Institute.

"It is not insignificant. . . . They'd better have some way of addressing it," said Grover Norquist, president of Americans for Tax Reform and an influential conservative activist.

Republican leaders appear to recognize the problem. Frist, in an e-mail sent from his leadership political action committee, VOLPAC, ticked off a list of reasons why conservatives should love the Medicare overhaul, including the creation of tax-preferred health savings accounts, the move to link premiums for outpatient care to beneficiaries' incomes, and "cost containment through true competition."

Still, even conservatives who warn of a backlash against the Medicare law say the damage would go only so far. For economic conservatives, Weyrich predicted, the anger over the expansion of an entitlement program would be largely canceled out by their support for the tax cuts.

Moreover, even the most bitter opponents of the Medicare overhaul say Bush and the Republicans have done enough to please conservatives on other issues that they have probably limited the damage to themselves.

"If you're a Republican and you want to protect your conservative base, you have to do two things. You have to not raise taxes, and you have to be pro-life," said Stephen Moore, president of Club for Growth, a fiscally conservative group that fought vigorously against the Medicare bill. "For those reasons, he [Bush] is in fairly good shape with the base right now."

Swing Voters

Republicans believe they now have two major accomplishments to pitch to independent voters, who currently make up 33 percent of all registered voters, according to the Pew Research Center for the People and the Press.

They have made no secret that the Medicare bill is a key to that strategy. But Republican strategists also point to the 2001 education overhaul (PL 107-110) — one of the most significant laws of the 107th Congress — as an accomplishment they can still use as an appeal to swing voters in 2004.

Like the Medicare law, the education overhaul — which requires annual testing to determine whether federal aid to public schools is achieving results — was an example of Republicans putting their stamp on what traditionally had been considered a Democratic issue, according to Rich Bond, a political consultant and former chairman of the Republican National Committee.

"We already have a huge advantage on national security, and now we're

making inroads on Medicare, and we've cut taxes," he said. "That's a pretty good day at the office."

Outside surveys, however, show signs that independents could give Republicans a more lukewarm reception.

The Pew survey, based on a poll of 2,528 adults taken July 14-Aug. 5 and a follow-up poll of 1,515 adults taken Oct. 15-19, found that 59 percent of independents believed going to war with Iraq was the right decision. But it also found that only 51 percent agreed with the more general statement that "the best way to ensure peace is through military strength," down 11 percentage points from a similar survey a year ago.

Moreover, the center found that independent voters have become less satisfied with their personal financial situation over the last four years, mirroring Democrats' views more closely than Republicans'.

What Could Go Wrong?

If there are bombshells waiting, some analysts say, Republicans have deftly engineered the situation to make sure they do not go off in 2004. Instead, some say, it is actually the 2006 election that could prove the bigger challenge for Republicans.

The two signature accomplishments of the first session of the 108th — the tax cuts and Medicare — both carry long-term risks, said Jacobson of the University of California at San Diego. The tax cuts could eventually be seen as a cause of crippling deficits, and seniors could decide the Medicare legislation is more harmful than helpful, he said.

But right now, the tax cuts are putting money in people's pockets, and the Medicare drug benefit will not begin until 2006, Jacobson said. "The unpleasant consequences that will ensue . . . are not going to take place until after the election," he said. "This is a good political position to be in, at least for 2004."

Others say that is not necessarily a reason for Republicans to celebrate. "It may be that Bush has given Republicans a Christmas present for 2004 and a time bomb for 2006," said Lewis L. Gould, professor emeritus of American history at the University of Texas at Austin and author of "Grand Old Party: A History of the Republicans."

For now, Republicans are making sure the voters know which party gets things done. Over the long run, they will have to hope voters think they got them done the right way. ◆

Democrats Still Upbeat Despite Losses on Big Bills

Pelosi's success in unifying House Democrats means no coasting for GOP majority

On the surface, anyway, congressional Democrats disappeared from Washington this month leaving barely a trace of triumph.

Their leader in the House, Nancy Pelosi of California, made it a test of party discipline to oppose the Republicans' Medicare prescription drug bill, but the GOP played even harder ball and pushed the measure into law. Democrats' leader in the Senate, Tom Daschle of South Dakota, called for loans rather than grants to rebuild Iraq and won a bipartisan vote for the idea — only to lose the final showdown with the White House. The third-deepest tax cut in American history was enacted despite nearly unified Democratic opposition. The party's efforts to limit the Bush administration's deregulatory drives on mass communications and labor policy were thwarted at the final hour.

And yet Democrats' collective attitude at the moment is determinedly upbeat. Compared with their dispirited tones at this time last year — when they had just lost the Senate, faced unified Republican government for the first time in five decades, lacked a strong political message of their own and were riven by disagreement over the party's next move — the Democrats are ending the year in a combative posture.

Democrats maintain that President Bush and the GOP congressional leadership, despite their legislative successes, have delivered ample opportunities for selling the events of 2003 to the minority party's advantage in 2004. On both policy and process, Democrats say, the Republicans have overreached in ways that will come back to haunt them next year, when polling suggests that the presidency and the makeup of Congress will once again be decided by the moderate swing voters positioned between the one-third that is clearly Republican and the one-third that is clearly Democrat.

The Medicare overhaul (HR 1 — PL 108-173) that Bush signed Dec. 8 is but one example. To be sure, it allows Republicans the opportunity to claim victory on an issue that Democrats have long viewed as their own — giving seniors relief from high drug costs — and will be cited as proof that a Republican president and a Republican-run Congress can be counted on to accomplish longstanding domestic goals. (2003 *CQ Weekly*, p. 3084)

But the Democrats say they can effectively use the same law to market three very different points to the electorate: that it is emblematic of Republicans' desire to reward their

Pelosi and Daschle close the year with a Dec. 9 news conference on Capitol Hill meant to highlight the shortcomings of the Republican-led 108th Congress.

corporate friends, in this case the pharmaceutical and insurance industries; that the GOP drive to introduce private-market competition will lead to the crumbling of a Great Society cornerstone; and that the law is yet another example of bills forced through Congress by a GOP leadership that has become increasingly arrogant, abusive of their power and too ideologically uncompromising to govern a 50-50 nation.

Pelosi, completing her first year as the first woman to head a political party in Congress, signaled her party's Trojan horse view of this year's legislative debate when she said of the Medicare law: "Beware of Republicans bearing gifts."

Beyond making their case about the varied shortcomings of Republican rule, however, congressional Democrats will seek to make the next election a referendum on their vision for the coming years — which they assume will dovetail closely enough to the platform of their presidential nominee.

Opposition Politics

As the year came to an end, Democrats were concentrating on doing what the minority in a narrowly divided Congress is able to do most readily: thwart the priorities of the majority, generally by choosing from the menu of roadblocks available for such purposes in the Senate. On the final day of the first session of the 108th Congress, for example, Democrats blocked an $820 billion bill (HR 2673) to fund 11 Cabinet departments. Angry mainly at how their handful of policy victories on spending bills earlier in the year had been buried at the White House's insistence, Democrats simply refused to allow a voice vote in the sparsely populated chamber to clear the package — delaying the completion of the budget for fiscal 2004, which started Oct. 1, at least until Congress reconvenes Jan. 20. (2003 CQ Weekly, p. 3080)

And last month, a solid majority of Democrats teamed up with a band of GOP conservatives to prevent a final vote on a comprehensive energy policy overhaul (HR 6) that has been one of Bush's top domestic priorities since he took office. (2003 CQ Weekly, p. 2969)

"This session has been a major disappointment — the result of misguided priorities and a refusal by Republicans to compromise on any of their radical agenda," declared Daschle, the South Dakotan who dropped his plan to run for president in 2004 because, he said when the year began, the Senate "is where my heart is."

Democrats say to expect more of the same next year — from both parties. They say they can be counted on to keep resisting a Republican Congress that, as a handmaiden of a GOP president, can be counted on to keep allowing too many families to be jobless, deepening a gaping deficit by pushing tax cuts for the rich, inadequately funding improvements promised by the 2001 education overhaul (PL 107-110), putting a decade of environmental quality gains at risk, packing the federal courts with far-too-conservative judges and stretching too thin the U.S. forces committed to a nation-building campaign in Iraq that is the ill-considered obligation of a war sold under false pretenses.

"Republicans have failed," said Mark Mellman, a favored pollster of congressional Democrats. They "have no plan to win the peace in Iraq, they have no plan to get the economy moving in that they are not creating new jobs," he said. "They have made things worse rather than better."

Even such a negative approach can be blamed on the GOP, say the Democrats. Bush's 2000 campaign promise to "change the tone in Washington" has became sadly true, they say: Thanks to him and his Hill allies, things are more partisan and rancorous than ever.

If the economy continues to strengthen, however, it will weaken the Democratic case for a change in leadership. And in the meantime, Bush and the Republicans will stress a theme of having delivered important improvements in areas, especially rising medical costs and sagging scholastic standards, where Democratic promises had long gone unfulfilled.

When the legislative battle resumes in six weeks, the Democrats' promised aggressive posture will most likely complicate life for the GOP. That is because in an election year, Republicans will be seeking to both bolster enthusiasm from their conservative political base and reach out to swing voters. And to accomplish the latter, they will probably promote some social policy initiatives, including a rewrite of special-education programs (HR 1350, S 1248) and a measure to update the welfare system (HR 4). But without a strong measure of Democratic support, such proposals are likely to founder — and unity in defiance of the GOP agenda is one of the minority party's core strategies for 2004.

Partisan tensions are sure to be intensified by the presidential campaign, one of the reasons Republicans pushed so hard to complete

Medicare, energy and other top-tier legislation this year. The denunciations of the Medicare bill from the candidates for the Democratic nomination harmonized with those from congressional Democrats. Congressional leaders say they will work closely with whoever secures the nomination to ensure a unified message for November.

"We of course have our own agenda, and we work with it throughout the year. But we are clearly going to try to work with our nominee, whoever that happens to be, to coordinate our message," said Richard J. Durbin of Illinois, a leading message-maker for the Senate Democrats.

The presidential candidates have already shown how aggressive attacks on Bush and Republicans can rev up the party's core voters. This has been particularly true of Howard Dean, the former Vermont governor. Although his rhetorical brickbats have occasionally been aimed at Congress, to Democratic lawmakers' annoyance, several more members have endorsed him as his front-runner standing has solidified in recent weeks. (2003 CQ Weekly, p. 2420)

'Copycat or Naysayer'

Strategically and politically, however, Democrats are in something of a box: By opposing such potentially popular bills as the Medicare revamp and other domestic legislation — including a bill (S 11) to cap medical malpractice damages and a Bush proposal to let states merge their early-childhood initiatives with the federal Head Start preschool program (HR 2210) — they provide some glue for the obstructionist label Republicans work to affix on them. (2003 CQ Weekly, p. 3094)

Daschle and other leaders say they are preparing a proactive agenda for next year in areas including veterans' benefits, health care and job growth. At a Dec. 9 news conference with Daschle to bid goodbye to the legislative year, Pelosi listed a series of proposals, many of them focused on economic and national security, including calling for more guards at the borders, more money for police and other "first responders," an increased child tax credit for low-income families and tax breaks for small businesses.

"They ought to be out there on the Capitol steps with their

Kennedy and other leading Democrats lambasted the new Medicare law at a Capitol Hill rally with seniors just hours after Bush signed the measure Dec. 8.

10-point plan," said Democratic strategist Peter Fenn.

But as the minority party, the Democrats' opportunity to drive the agenda in Congress — or even highlight their proposals — is limited. They usually find themselves arguing against the majority agenda, with their own alternatives muffled and rarely reaching the ears of the general public.

"You either get hit with being a copycat or being a naysayer," said Ross Baker, a political scientist at Rutgers University. "It's not a great position to be in, and it's a real test of legislative leadership — how you position yourself between those two perils."

At the same time, the Republicans have proven disciplined and aggressive, particularly when it comes to poaching on traditionally Democratic issues. And Democrats have a high electoral bar to clear in the 2004 election. They need to gain a net of two seats to reclaim the majority in the Senate — all the while fighting to defend at least four open seats in the largely Republican South — and pick up at least 12 seats to reclaim the House. And they will be running against a president who has high personal popularity ratings, despite questions about his handling of Iraq and other issues.

Meanwhile, their presidential candidates have been attacking one another as often as they have criticized Bush. They have disagreed over the Iraq war, how much of the tax cuts enacted under Bush to repeal or delay, and whether to renegotiate trade deals to tighten environmental and labor standards.

As the presidential field has moved the Democratic debate to the left, party moderates fear that Bush, with Medicare and education laws on his list of achievements, will be able to outmaneuver Democrats for centrist voters in swing states.

Some strategists concede that their party's pitch for why it should be handed control of the government has yet to resonate. Democratic leaders have "attacked on particular issues, but they haven't weaved it into an overall coherent message," said Jim Kessler, a party consultant. "You need to connect these dots to create some sort of picture"

Democratic leaders say they will be building a case, bill by bill and fight by fight, for giving them the reins. For example, House Democrats held a retreat Dec. 9 to shape their message on the economy and on national security, an area in which they are perceived as being weaker than the GOP.

House Democrats' internal polling shows the party having an edge with voters on the question of being most in tune with the needs of "ordinary Americans" and being strongly viewed as the party more committed to aiding the poor. They need to define themselves as the party that best looks out for middle-income families, said Robert T. Matsui of California, who chairs the Democratic Congressional Campaign Committee.

"That is going to take time," Matsui said. "This is something that needs to permeate the American mainstream."

Said Pelosi: "Never again will the Democrats go into a campaign where people don't know who we are, what we stand for, how different we are from Republicans and what we are willing to fight for."

Democratic Unity

Meanwhile, leaders are focused on strengthening the party's cohesion; they say their unity is in itself a message to voters, because it shows Democrats as strong and confident in their agenda.

It also forces GOP leaders to work harder to assemble majorities — sometimes by making concessions to Democrats, more regularly by pressuring reluctant moderates to vote for conservative-leaning plans in the absence of Democratic votes.

"There are any number of Republicans in the Congress who represent moderate districts, who had been able to vote with the Democrats on issues because their votes weren't needed," Pelosi said. "Now they are. And now they are voting with Tom DeLay and the right-wing ideological agenda in the Congress, which is no match for their districts."

In the House, in recent years, Republicans could count on picking up 35 to 40 Democratic votes on major bills, but not as much in 2003, when Pelosi took control and placed an even greater emphasis on party unity.

Not a single House Democrat voted for the final version of the fiscal 2004 budget plan (H Con Res 95) — the first time Democrats held together on a budget resolution since the Republicans started writing them in 1995. They also united in blocking major changes in Head Start, the preschool program for poor children, and they opposed funding cuts for the education program that Bush initially won with bipartisan support after promising there would be money for under-achieving schools.

In the Senate, where individual members wield considerable power and are more apt to go their own way, the party's divisions were on display at the end. Eleven Democrats backed the final Medicare bill, and the caucus split over whether to filibuster the conference agreement. Afterwards, party insiders unfavorably compared the caucus under Daschle's leadership with Pelosi's more disciplined ranks.

The energy bill fractured Democrats along regional lines, with Daschle and other corn-state lawmakers voting to move the bill toward enactment because of its benefits for ethanol. But regional concerns on the energy bill split Republicans, too.

Daschle said the fractures within his caucus were over not substance, but strategy — whether to oppose a flawed bill or support it as a first step toward improvements. Democrats share a common vision on Medicare and other issues, he said, and he is confident they can articulate that clearly to voters.

Democrats who voted for the Medicare bill "share our concerns and largely support the efforts to make this a better bill," Daschle said. "They just felt that we had to take what we could get. . . . I found myself supporting the energy bill using the same strategy."

Pelosi's determination to keep her party unified harks back to the efforts of an unlikely role model: Newt Gingrich of Georgia (1979-97), who galvanized minority House Republicans by drawing sharp philosophical contrasts between the parties and refusing to go along with the Democrats at almost every chance for compromise. Applying that approach for six years, and then writing the "Contract With America" manifesto for the 1994 elections, resulted in the GOP takeover of the House for the first time in 40 years and made Gingrich the Speaker.

"What was important about that was not the public thinking that they had a message; it was the Republicans thinking that they had a message, so they were totally unified," said Charles O. Jones, professor emeritus of political science at the University of Wisconsin. "The candidates had great confidence in the message."

Pelosi is "sharpening the differences between the parties, and she's arguably being Gingrichian," said another political scientist, William Connelly Jr. of Washington and Lee University. "And maybe that's what the Democratic Party needs to do." ◆

Senators Pack a Sharper Edge

Former House members bring bare-knuckled politics to the Senate

Almost two centuries ago, Alexis de Tocqueville remarked upon the distinct natures of the House and Senate in his famed tome, *Democracy in America*. The French historian was struck in particular by the "vulgar demeanor" of the House when compared with the more "eloquent" upper chamber.

But de Tocqueville might have had a different reaction had he observed the Senate in 2003 — an unusually rancorous year marked by the sort of nervy political stunts, sharp-edged rhetoric and partisan finger-pointing more often seen on the other side of the Capitol.

"The Senate is becoming more like the House," observed Sen. Lindsey Graham, a former House Republican from South Carolina who moved to the Senate last year. "Looking at the Senate from afar, from the House, it's a very tradition-laden body. When I actually get here I find it works more like the House than I ever imagined."

Republicans and Democrats blame each other for the well-documented erosion of the Senate's long tradition of bipartisanship. But that partisan blame-game overshadows a more subtle, but equally important, dispute that has less to do with party labels and more to do with experience.

To some Senate veterans, it is senators such as Graham responsible for those changes in the first place. Indeed, a generation gap of sorts is developing in today's Senate, with veteran senators privately placing blame on their junior colleagues who served in the House.

This band of young Turks, senior and former senators say, has imported a political philosophy that disregards time-honored Senate rules designed to counter the majoritarian House and protect the minority party as well as the individual senator.

"So many House members have come to the Senate and brought the poison with them, and we haven't found the antidote yet," said former Sen. Alan Simpson, R-Wyo. (1979-

"So many House members have come to the Senate and brought the poison with them and we haven't found the antidote yet."

— Sen. Alan Simpson, R-Wyo. (1979-97)

97). "The rancor, the dissension, the disgusting harsh level came from those House members who came to the Senate. They brought it with 'em. That's where it began."

The senior senators say members of both parties are at fault, but Republicans seem to bear the brunt of the blame. That may be partly because they have come to the Senate in greater numbers than Democrats. Since the 1994 elections, the House has sent 29 of its members to the Senate — 18 of whom were Republicans and 11 of whom were Democrats.

But another reason could be the number of new senators who served under former Speaker Newt Gingrich, R-Ga. (1979-99), and ushered in a period of bare-knuckled politics amplified by a belligerent communications strategy.

"Most of them came up in the era when the Newt Gingrich cabal was in

full force and Republicans were engineering a takeover of House control," said Thad Cochran, R-Miss., a five-term veteran of the Senate who served in the House for six years in the mid-1970s. "That was based on sharp attack politics, and so there is that influence in the Senate now."

A five-term Democratic colleague, Patrick J. Leahy of Vermont, agreed. "Some of them were there during the severe partisanship of the Gingrich time and they try to bring that here," he said. "It's kind of win at all costs today and worry about tomorrow tomorrow."

The New Senate

The Senate's sharper edge was evident earlier this year when Republicans virtually shut Democrats out of the conference committee negotiations on legislation to establish new energy policies and overhaul the Medicare system.

The practice has its roots in a similar dispute a decade ago in the House, when the majority Democrats shut Republicans out of a House-Senate conference on the 1994 crime bill. Republicans have since adopted the practice and imported it to the Senate, prompting Democrats to retaliate with procedural tactics to block the energy bill (HR 6), the Charitable Giving Act (HR 7), and, temporarily, the Healthy Forests Act (HR 1904). (*2003 CQ Weekly, p. 2761*)

But the partisanship was perhaps most evident during the heated debate over judicial nominations — an effort led in large part by junior senators who served in the House, such as Republican Rick Santorum of Pennsylvania and Democrat Charles E. Schumer of New York. (*2003 CQ Weekly, p. 2817*)

"I watch sometimes and I think that it's a new situation," said freshman Sen. George V. Voinovich, R-Ohio, a former governor who never served in the House. "We have some different traditions in the Senate."

Voinovich added that there are "too many" House members and not enough "other people" in the Senate — picking up on an often overlooked trend: the gradual rise in the number of House members who are being promoted to the Senate.

Some congressional researchers say there are more former House members in the Senate today than there have been at any time in recent memory, an observation that is borne out by a survey of the past decade. In 1993, 34 members of the Senate had House experience, a number that jumped to 39 in 1995. The number has since inched upward, and today, 49 members — or almost half of the Senate — have served in the House at one point or another.

That number will continue to grow if political headhunters continue to recruit Senate candidates from the House at the same levels. In the past five elections, 29 of the 56 freshmen came from the House. This year, nine House members — six Republicans and three Democrats — are already running for seven Senate seats; many are considered front-runners.

These junior Republicans blame outside factors, rather than their own background, for the rise in partisanship. The narrow party divisions in Congress and across the country have polarized the parties, they say. Meanwhile, incessant news coverage on talk radio, cable channels and the Internet tends to encourage senators to use inflammatory speech in oversimplified sound bites, they say.

And, thanks in part to the new campaign finance law (PL 107-155) — most of which was upheld by the Supreme Court in a Dec. 10 ruling — these senators say special interests have a greater influence, discouraging senators from reaching compromises. (*2003 CQ Weekly, p. 3076*)

The House Influence

Nevertheless, the perception exists among senior members that former House members are culpable at least in part for the rise in partisanship. Speaking of a divide between "younger, junior" senators and their senior colleagues, Cochran simply said: "It's just a matter of age. I'm not going to use the word 'maturity.'"

Leahy added that a number of former members have told him they are glad they left the Senate when they did. "I've talked to a lot of people, both Republicans and Democrats, who just shake their heads," he said.

An analysis of "party unity" scores lends some evidence to the impression that senators with more recent House

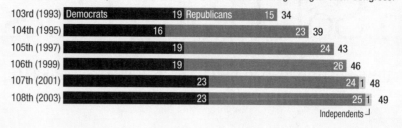

Former House Members in the Senate

Number of former Representatives in the U.S. Senate at the beginning of each Congress:

Congress	Democrats	Republicans	Independents	Total
103rd (1993)	19	15		34
104th (1995)	16	23		39
105th (1997)	19	24		43
106th (1999)	19	26		46
107th (2001)	23	24	1	48
108th (2003)	23	25	1	49

CQ GRAPHICS / YOLIE DAWSON

experience tend to be more ideological than those who did not. On ballots that pitted most Senate Democrats against most Republicans in 2003, senators who served in the House between 1990 and 2002 voted the party line an average of 94 percent of the time; those who did not voted with their party an average of 88 percent of the time.

But this group of new senators has also had a profound influence in ways that have little to do with their voting records. Two Judiciary Committee Democrats who served in the House — Richard J. Durbin, D-Ill., and Schumer — joined chairman Leahy to take leading roles in the fight to block six of the more conservative judicial nominees.

And in the judges talkathon, Santorum originally scheduled 30 hours of debate, but he granted a request by Graham and another freshman, Norm Coleman, R-Minn., to keep the Senate in session for another nine and a half hours to further drive home their point.

Since then, Graham and Saxby Chambliss, R-Ga., another former House member, have threatened to sue the Senate on the grounds that they have been denied their constitutional right to cast an up-or-down vote on executive nominations. The pair of Southerners currently are examining their legal and financial options and plan to file suit next year, Graham said.

"Lindsey, Saxby, a few others over there are trying to change the rules, change the way things operate," said Rep. Ray LaHood, an Illinois Republican. "But it's not going to happen. They've got too many of these old bulls over there."

In addition, former House members have shaped their party's communications strategy. As chairman of the Senate Republican Conference, Santorum is the architect of a more aggressive party message. His brand of attack politics was on full display during the GOP's final

press conference, when he and the other leaders devoted about half the time to attacking Democrats for "obstructing" the agenda.

Santorum, who became chairman of the conference in 2001, said he modeled it in part after the House Republican Conference. Today, he regularly coordinates his efforts with the House and the White House and speaks often with House Majority Leader Tom DeLay, R-Texas, who, along with Gingrich, helped pioneer the more combative style.

For their part, Democratic senators who served in the House have also engaged in harsher rhetoric. Democratic Policy Committee Chairman Byron L. Dorgan of North Dakota blasted the administration for establishing an online futures market designed to predict the likelihood of potential hostilities in the Middle East.

Durbin took a leading role denouncing conservative judicial nominees. And Schumer eagerly hyped allegations that senior aides leaked the name of an undercover CIA agent for political purposes.

Already an influential bunch, the force of this group of former House members will only grow if they continue to rise through the leadership ranks. Santorum and National Republican Senatorial Committee Chairman George Allen, R-Va., are considered strong leadership candidates if and when vacancies open up. On the Democratic side, the top four leaders all served in the House, and Durbin is mentioned as a likely candidate to move up in the leadership ranks.

House members throughout history have served in the Senate without fundamentally altering its nature. But if they continue to come to the Senate in such high numbers, or if they succeed in changing Senate rules or traditions, their presence may be felt for years to come. ◆

Legislative Season Drawn In Solid Party Lines

Senate takes the lead in fierce partisanship as nation remains evenly divided

Partisanship was evident throughout the year in public squabbling between Republicans and Democrats on issues from Medicare and the economy to judicial nominations and energy policy.

For the last three years, the margins of power in Congress have been so narrow that the parties have been screaming at each other, fighting over those last few seats that could tip the majority one way or another. Members of Congress and those who work with them say the atmosphere is more divided than ever.

They are right — the voting record now confirms it. In 2003, Congress as a whole was indeed more polarized than it has been in the five decades that Congressional Quarterly has been analyzing annual "party unity votes."

With both Democrats and Republicans looking ahead to the 2004 elections, the parties sought to highlight their differences on health care, education and other major issues, rather than seek broad consensus. They sharpened and intensified their conflicts in hopes of breaking the 50-50 partisan stalemate at the polls that has kept them close to parity in Congress, without a clear mandate to govern.

It was all about getting the public "off the dime," said William Connelly Jr., a political scientist at Washington and Lee University, and the polarization could be a precursor to a political realignment that tips the country in one direction or the other. It also may foreshadow a difficult and relatively unproductive legislative year ahead as the two parties continue to battle for the attention and favor of voters before the presidential and congressional elections. *(2004 CQ Weekly, p. 12)*

On roll call votes that pitted a majority of one party against a majority of the other — a party unity vote as defined by CQ — Democrats and Republicans in both chambers stuck tightly together throughout 2003.

House Democrats were more unified than at any time since 1960. On party unity votes, the average House Democrat toed the party line 87 percent of the time, according to CQ's analysis.

In the Senate, where President Bush's agenda was most in danger of being blocked by a powerful Democratic minority, it was Republicans who showed the tightest party discipline. On average, they voted with their party 94 percent of the time — their all-time high party unity score.

The Senate, historically the chamber where the parties have been most willing to cooperate, was the most polarized of all, at least statistically. Two out of every three Senate roll call votes divided the chamber down partisan lines.

Both in the raw number of party unity votes and the percentage of total roll calls that split the parties, the Senate has been more sharply divided only once in the half century that CQ has been tracking that percentage: in 1995, when the GOP took control of both sides of the Capitol for the first time in 40 years. *(1995 Almanac, p. 1-3)*

Party Unity | *Frequency of Partisan Voting by Chamber*

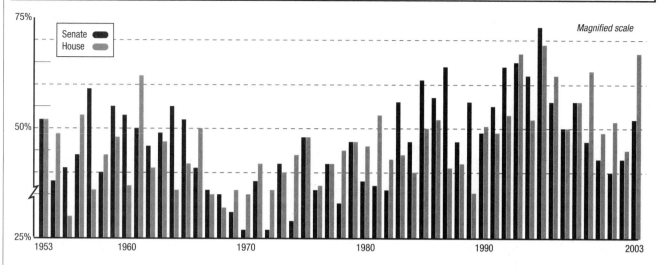

In the House, where the percentage is deflated by many routine, non-controversial votes, a little more than half of all roll calls were party unity votes. Major issues — the war in Iraq, Medicare legislation, education, the budget — most often triggered partisan votes in the House, as in the Senate.

The Great Divide

Whether the divisions between the parties are deepening because of the polarization of the electorate or vice versa is one of the great unknowns of the country's current political climate. A report released in November by the Pew Research Center for the People and the Press found that the electorate is almost evenly divided politically and, more important, further apart than ever in its political values.

"Political polarization is now as great as it was prior to the 1994 midterm elections that ended four decades of Democratic control in Congress," said the study's authors, who interviewed more than 2,500 voters about the core beliefs that shape their opinions on a range of topics. "But now, unlike then, Republicans *and* Democrats have become more intense in their political beliefs."

Over the past four years, for example, Democrats have become more critical of business and much stronger advocates of the social safety net — and their differences with Republicans on those issues have widened, the Pew report said. Differences over national security policy have grown also as Democrats become increasingly angry and disenchanted with the war in Iraq.

Sharpened rhetoric and partisan battles have often preceded a period of realignment in the body politic, Connelly said. And the combat often centers on an overarching question about the role of government.

That was true in 1932, when Republican President Herbert Hoover and Democrat Franklin Delano Roosevelt fought over whether a larger, more active federal government could help pull the nation out of the Depression, Connelly said.

Whether the debate in Washington today is building toward just such a realignment is anyone's guess. One of the biggest bills of 2003, the Medicare prescription drug measure (PL 108-173), was meant at least in part to blur the differences between the parties, to allow Bush and the GOP to claim a victory on an issue that Democrats have owned for years.

At the same time, however, both sides have worked to sharply distinguish their positions on the Medicare bill, and the arguments they make cut directly to their differing views of government.

2003 Data			
	PARTISAN VOTES	TOTAL VOTES	PERCENTAGE
Senate	306	459	66.7
House	349	675	51.7

Democrats in particular are attempting to frame the issue as just the sort of fundamental debate about the proper role of government that Roosevelt used to his advantage in 1932. They argue that the Republicans' ultimate goal is to dismantle Medicare, a program that tens of millions of seniors have come to depend on.

Republicans assert that their plan will improve Medicare by bringing market competition to the program, offering seniors more choices, not fewer.

Tipping the Electorate

Leaders of both parties in Congress spent much of the session bemoaning the heightened partisanship — and blaming the other side for it. One bad turn justified the next.

Senate Majority Leader Bill Frist, R-Tenn., complained that Democratic partisanship was holding up Bush's judicial nominees and other business even as he was enraging Democrats by shutting them out of the conference committees negotiating the Medicare drug bill and other high-profile measures. (*2003 CQ Weekly, p. 2761*)

Reviewing the year at a news conference last month, the two top Democrats — House Minority Leader Nancy Pelosi of California and Senate Minority Leader Tom Daschle of South Dakota — presented their list of "Republican failures" on a chart headlined, "Too much partisanship, too little progress." (*p. 27*)

But when a reporter asked Daschle what he expected could get accomplished in the second session of the 108th Congress, his quick first response was this: "Realistically, the most important thing we can get done next year is elect a Democratic majority in November."

Both the Republican and Democratic parties have been losing their moderate wings over time. Democrats have lost their Southern conservatives as the South trends increasingly Republican. The GOP has lost many of its Northeastern moderates.

But the more immediate factor driving the dynamics last year was the tighter margins, Connelly and other congressional observers say. When the parties are so closely balanced in Congress — and in the country as a whole — the imperative for political leaders on both sides is to play up differences, not find commonalities, in hope of tipping the closely balanced electorate their way, they said.

Final victory is so close for both parties that they are more reluctant to back down or settle for half measures.

Narrow margins also produce a rationale for the rank and file to stay in line. Republicans, who control both houses of Congress and the White House, are driven together by loyalty to their president, pressure to produce legislation and the prospect of strengthening their hold on power.

Democrats, meanwhile, have been tantalizingly close, at least in the Senate, to claiming the majority and all that goes with it — the right to claim

choice committee spots, to control what legislation comes to a vote, to direct federal spending. That provides a powerful incentive for members to subsume their individual differences and stick together behind the party. (*2004 CQ Weekly, p. 41*)

There is less willingness, too, to give the other party a share of the credit on major policy, like Medicare drugs, said Michael Malbin, a political scientist at the State University of New York in Albany. The narrow margins of power have "made both parties pay more attention to their bases and to developing a national message" in hope of winning a clear majority, Malbin said.

Unity as a Message

Pelosi, for one, has been aiming to highlight the differences between the parties in the starkest possible terms. She fought hard all year to persuade her caucus to stand together against the GOP, and she succeeded to a considerable degree.

She argued that unity is in itself a message, showing the public that Democrats are confident and excited about their agenda.

On the Nov. 22 vote to pass Medicare drug legislation, for example, all

but 16 Democrats voted against the bill. Even members of the Blue Dog Coalition, moderate Democrats who often vote with Republicans, largely stayed with Pelosi on that vote. (*2003 CQ Weekly, p. 2960*)

In the Senate, where individual members wield considerable power and are more likely to go their own way, Daschle was somewhat less successful holding his membership together on Medicare and other big votes. Still, the average party unity score for Senate Democrats — how often they vote with the majority of their party against a majority of the other party — was 85 percent, close to their all-time high since 1960 of 89 percent, reached in 2001 and 1999.

Meanwhile, House Republicans tied their own top unity score of 91 percent, hit in 2001 and 1995.

House Speaker J. Dennis Hastert, R-Ill., and his lieutenants put a premium on keeping the party together, and they leaned hard on their members to stay behind the party's agenda.

The most dramatic display of GOP command and control came with the Medicare vote: With Pelosi pushing to hold on to her own rank and file, Hastert kept the vote open for almost three hours just before dawn while he pushed enough votes into line to get the legislation through. (*2003 CQ Weekly, p. 2962*)

In the Senate, both Democrats and Republicans ginned up votes and amendments designed at least partly to highlight differences between the parties — on abortion, education, drug pricing and other issues.

With Democrats holding up a handful of Bush nominees to the federal bench, Frist worked to call attention to the standoff by holding vote after vote to try to break the filibusters.

On one nominee alone — Miguel A. Estrada, one of Bush's picks for the U.S. Court of Appeals for the D.C. Circuit — Frist held seven separate "cloture" votes through the spring and summer to try to cut off the debate. (*2003 CQ Weekly, p. 2140*)

Such efforts were aimed in large part at the motivated base of each party. Interest groups on both sides were pushing senators to be confrontational.

The Sensitive Senate

Indeed, the recent political dynamic has led some political scientists to speculate that it is the Senate today that may be

CQ Vote Study Guide

Congressional Quarterly has conducted studies analyzing the voting behavior of members of Congress since 1945. This is how the studies are carried out:

- **Selecting votes.** CQ bases its vote studies on all roll call votes on which members were asked to vote "yea" or "nay." In 2003, there were 675 such votes in the House and 459 in the Senate. The totals exclude quorum calls (there were two in the House in 2003), because they require only that members vote "present."

    The totals do include House votes to approve the Journal (12 in 2003) and Senate votes to instruct the sergeant at arms to request members' presence in the chamber (two in 2003).

    The party unity and presidential support studies are based on votes selected from the total according to the criteria described on pages 48 and 53.

- **Individual scores.** Members' scores in the accompanying charts are based only on the votes each member actually cast. That has the effect of making individual support and opposition scores add to 100 percent. The same method is used for identifying the leading scorers on pages 16 and 21.

- **Overall scores.** For consistency with previous years, calculations of average scores by chamber, party and region are based on all yea-or-nay votes. As a result, a member's failure to vote reduces average support and opposition scores. (*Methodology, 1987 Almanac, p. 22-C*)

- **Rounding.** Scores are rounded to the nearest percentage point, although rounding is not used to increase any score to 100 percent or to reduce any score to zero.

Party Unity | *Parties Set Record for Partisanship*

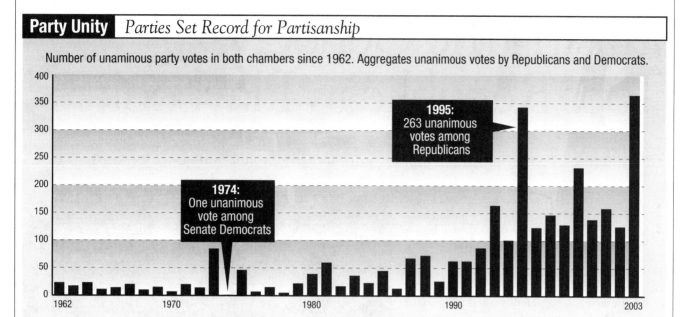

Number of unaminous party votes in both chambers since 1962. Aggregates unanimous votes by Republicans and Democrats.

1974:
One unanimous vote among Senate Democrats

1995:
263 unanimous votes among Republicans

most responsive to shifts in public mood.

The House, designed by the Founding Fathers to turn over frequently and be more sensitive to the popular will, has been made stable by partisan redistricting aimed at keeping districts safe for one party or the other. Statewide Senate races cannot be so gerrymandered thus a greater share are contested. Nearly a third of the Senate seats up for election in 2004 — 10 out of 34 — are rated highly competitive by CQ. By contrast, less than a tenth of House races — 30 out of 435 — are now considered competitive.

Some congressional observers are worried about the partisanship in the Senate, traditionally the slow-moving and deliberative chamber famously described as the place where the nation's passions are meant to cool, as hot tea cools in a saucer.

"It may be that the saucer is broken," said Ross Baker, a former Senate aide who is now a political scientist at Rutgers University. "If the saucer is in trouble, than we're in trouble. We've counted on the Senate to exert a moderating force."

Senators from both parties have observed that the chamber is becoming more like the House has traditionally been — fractious, partisan, quick-tem-

pered — and they decry the change. Some old hands blame the change in part on former House members who moved to the Senate and brought hardball tactics and sharp rhetoric with them. *(Senators, p. 30)*

Former Sen. Dale Bumpers, D-Ark. (1975-99), was distressed by the decisions of the Republican leadership last year to lock Democrats out of important conference committees. The Senate "is less collegial" today than when he first arrived, Bumpers said.

"And I'm not just talking about the legislation," he said. "I'm talking about the whole aura. There aren't as many close friendships between members of the parties."

David Hoppe, who was chief of staff to Sen. Trent Lott of Mississippi when Lott was Republican leader, also said the Senate has grown less collegial, less willing to debate issues in good faith across party lines. He ascribes this partly to a tendency to play to the edges of each party, passing over a middle viewed as apathetic and uninvolved.

He offers one remedy: force senators who want to block legislation to put up or shut up by making them filibuster the old-fashioned way. Today's quiet filibuster — with cloture votes but no "talkathon" — makes obstructionism

too easy, Hoppe said. If filibusters were difficult, senators would be more likely to try to work across party lines to make progress, he said.

"I'm convinced it will lessen the number of filibusters and force the Senate to find ground where you can get things done," he said.

But others see something largely positive at work. Rather than unhealthy partisanship, political scientists see vigorous debate and participation, with both sides working hard to present clear policy alternatives to sway a closely balanced electorate.

That is good for voters, they said. It gives them clear choices, something substantive to chew over as they consider their choices at the polls.

If 2004 is not the year that hands one party or the other the wider majority it seeks, the virtual deadlock will surely be broken eventually, Connelly and other political scientists said.

"I do not think the nation is comfortable where it is," said Gary Copeland, director of the Carl Albert Congressional Research and Studies Center at the University of Oklahoma. "In terms of public policy, every thing seems to hang in the balance by a few thousand votes every election." ◆

Erasing the Gender Gap Tops Republican Playbook

Party hopes tailored messages can turn around traditional deficit in women's vote

It was clear that election-year politics had taken hold when Senate Republicans stopped pushing the "Patients First Act of 2003" and began lobbying for the "Healthy Mothers and Healthy Babies Access to Care Act."

Both pieces of legislation were tort reform measures with the same goal: to cap the size of awards in medical malpractice suits. But Senate GOP leaders in February narrowed the scope of the legislation to obstetricians and gynecologists, casting the bill as one designed to improve women's access to health care.

The narrower bill has stalled in the Senate, blocked by Democrats who say it would hurt the very patients it is designed to protect. (*2004 CQ Weekly, p. 535*)

But the debate is not expected to end there, and the message is one that will be repeated from now until Election Day. "This is about women," said Republican Sen. Judd Gregg of New Hampshire, a sponsor of the bill. "This is about a woman's right to access health care."

The theme is one Republicans plan to talk about a lot this year in an effort to erase a gender gap that has plagued the GOP since Ronald Reagan defeated Jimmy Carter to capture the White House in 1980. Emphasizing public safety, economic security and empowerment, President Bush and Republican leaders are trying to tailor their campaign message to women voters.

While they face long odds of capturing the majority of the women's vote, Republican strategists are looking for ways to peel away enough support from the Democrats to supplement the GOP's traditional advantage with middle-class male voters. Such a shift could provide the margin of victory in an election cycle in which results will probably hinge on slight changes in voting patterns.

"The gender gap is eight to 12 points in just about every election," said Larry J. Sabato, director of the Center for Politics at the University of Virginia. In tight elections, campaigns work to chip away at the opponents' core support, he added. "You don't win any single group over in a large sense. Rather, you gain two or three [percent] with each subgroup," he said.

Republicans are first and foremost determined to get Bush re-elected, banking that his personal popularity can bolster their majorities in the House and Senate, as it did in the midterm elections of 2002.

Like his father and Reagan, Bush has struggled with the gender gap. But there are times when the gap narrows, and Republican strategists have sought to identify those times

Bush's first television ads of the 2004 campaign depict him as a strong leader in a time of crisis, a theme that polls suggest resonates with women voters.

and capitalize on the themes that appear to help them with women.

For example, in the weeks following the Sept. 11 terrorist attacks, Bush's approval rating among women surged from 47 percent to 84 percent. Many women, polling showed, came to view Bush in a new light — as a leader who could be trusted to keep American families safe. (*Chart, p. 37*)

Political operatives seized on this development, even christening the group "security moms." The moniker refers to women who traditionally oppose U.S. military intervention in other countries, yet respond positively when they perceive steady leadership in a time of domestic crisis.

Now, with Bush trailing probable Democratic presidential nominee Sen. John Kerry, D-Mass., in surveys of women voters, Republicans are trying to recapture the bump in favorable ratings they received after Sept. 11.

Bush and Republicans already are softening their tough march-to-war rhetoric and depicting the military conflict in Iraq as a defensive action to protect the nation against terrorism. They also are touting the law that created the Department of Homeland Security (PL 107-296), an effort the president maintains has strengthened the nation against possible terrorist attacks. (*2002 Almanac, p. 7-3*)

They can be expected to strike similar chords with groups that have other distinct concerns, along the way making references to domestic policy initiatives as a way of burnishing Bush's "compassionate conservative" message that had some appeal to women swing voters in 2000.

For mothers of school-age children, for example, Republicans will promote his 2001 education plan (PL 107-110) and 2001 and 2003 tax cuts that included increasing the child tax credit from $600 to $1,000 (PL 107-16, PL

President Bush and the Gender Gap

Like other recent Republican presidents, most of the time President Bush scores higher with men voters than with women. One exception was immediately after the Sept. 11 terrorist attacks, when the gender gap narrowed for several months, and many women reacted positively to what they viewed as strong and steady leadership in a time of crisis.

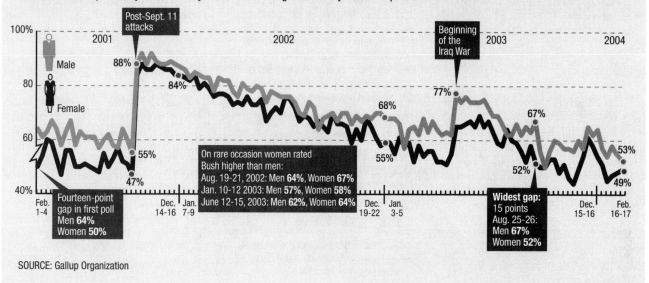

SOURCE: Gallup Organization

108-27). (*2004 CQ Weekly, p. 569; 2003 CQ Weekly, p. 1245; 2001 Almanac, p. 8-3*)

Because women purchase most of the health care goods and services in their households and worry about the cost of prescription drugs for older dependents, Bush will promote last year's overhaul of the federal Medicare program (PL 108-173). The president constantly reminds audiences that Medicare legislation — which created a first-time prescription drug benefit and new options for senior health care — was debated in Congress for years but was not completed until he came to office. (*2004 CQ Weekly, p. 408*)

Republicans also will turn to First Lady Laura Bush to act as a surrogate in campaign events highlighting education, health care and other issues that are priorities for women voters. She appears next to the president in the first set of campaign television ads that began running March 4 in 17 states.

'A Real Battleground'

The Republicans' efforts have not gone unnoticed by Democrats, who plan to protect their base by trying to increase voter registration and turnout among certain single women who have been identified as being politically apathetic. (*2004 CQ Weekly, p. 567*)

"This is a real battleground. This administration has understood targeting women better than any other [Republican] administration has," said Democratic pollster Celinda Lake, who specializes in identifying and targeting swing voters, including women, for her party. "The Bush administration understands that if you can block Democrats from women . . . they cannot put it together with men, and they lose," she added.

Democrats will try to blunt Republican efforts by arguing that the president and his congressional allies have come up short on virtually all fronts. They contend that the administration and the GOP-controlled Congress have underfunded Bush's signature education initiative, squandered the federal

budget surplus by pursuing deep tax cuts, and imposed more homeland security responsibilities on local police and fire departments without corresponding increases in federal aid.

Pollsters and analysts say Republicans are particularly focused on growing support among married women, a subset of the female vote that polling in 2000 identified as more likely to vote with the GOP than their unmarried counterparts. Married women also tend to be more religious and more likely to embrace traditional cultural values — characteristics that could mesh with the GOP's family values agenda. Single women, especially single heads of households, are viewed as being more economically insecure. They may, therefore, be inclined to view the federal government as a source of aid and to embrace traditionally Democratic social policy initiatives.

"If I were a Democratic leader, I would want to get that [unmarried women] demographic out there" to vote, said John Hibbing, a political scientist at the University of Nebraska, who has studied the gender gap in national politics. Bush, he added, should "encourage them all to get married and stay married."

A More Somber Mood

The tactical maneuvering for the women's vote is a marked contrast to the 2000 campaign, when the Republican and Democratic presidential candidates wooed the voting block in competing appearances on "The Oprah Winfrey Show," the syndicated national television talk show.

Democrat Al Gore sat on host Oprah Winfrey's easy chair one September afternoon, high-fived her when talk turned to her dark red stiletto boots and chatted about why he planted a big kiss on his wife Tipper at the Democratic Convention.

A week later, Bush one-upped Gore on Winfrey's stage. He did not just high-five Winfrey but kissed her on the cheek, drawing an "Oh, yes!" from the talk show queen. The result: a Gallup Poll a few days later showed that Bush had virtually erased Gore's 17-point advantage with women voters, though the gap widened again in Gore's favor by Election Day. Gore outpolled Bush among women 54 percent to 43 percent, according to the Center for American Women and Politics at Rutgers University.

In the tight presidential race that year, there was nothing trivial about competing on "Oprah" for the support of women — especially those who were married with children — who as a proportion of eligible voters by gender have voted in larger numbers than men in every presidential election since 1980. Winfrey, the empress of empathy, gave Gore and Bush an outlet to connect with millions of women trying to make ends meet while juggling the obligations of work and family and fretting over their retirement security.

This year, with worries about unemployment, expensive health care and the administration's management of the war in Iraq running especially high among women, the mood is more somber. Women, analysts say, are demanding more specific answers to questions about issues that matter to them.

"Not that they shouldn't do that," said Hibbing. "It's a start. If they [candidates] can go on shows like that and show they are warm and caring individuals, that's fine. But there are deep concerns about the economic situation and the war overseas."

Recent polls put Bush further behind in matchups with Kerry among women.

A CNN/USA Today Gallup Poll of 568 adults conducted February 16 and 17 showed Kerry holding a sizable 55-43 percent lead over Bush. Among likely women voters, Kerry's margin over Bush was significant: 57-42 percent. Meanwhile, male voters have shown swings in their presidential preference in recent polling. In the same mid-February survey, Kerry had an unusual 53-44 percent advantage over Bush among men.

What Women Want

Women voters are heavily courted because they vote in larger numbers than men. In 2000, 56 percent of the voting age female population cast ballots, compared with 53 percent of men, according to Rutgers' Center for American Women and Politics.

Women tend to be more concerned than men about education policy and escalating health care costs, according

Health Care Issues Concern Women Voters

A January 2004 survey conducted for the American Hospital Association showed that all voters regard health care as their No. 2 issue for Congress and the president to address, after the economy and jobs. A third of the time, women ranked health care as one of their top two concerns. For some subgroups of women voters, health care was an even more prominent issue.

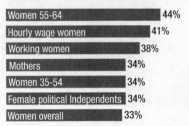

Women 55-64	44%
Hourly wage women	41%
Working women	38%
Mothers	34%
Women 35-54	34%
Female political Independents	34%
Women overall	33%

SOURCE: Public Opinion Strategies and Greenberg Quinlan Rosner Research survey for the American Hospital Association

CQ GRAPHICS / YOLIE DAWSON

to recent studies. They favor a more activist role for government, yet are slightly more likely than men to oppose a constitutional amendment banning same-sex marriage. Since the Vietnam War, most have opposed U.S. decisions to wage war in other countries.

The subsets of female voters who could vote for either party include married professionals who are likely to live in the suburbs. They are less inclined to be Republican, but are not easily pinned down on their political preferences, analysts said.

Democratic pollster Lake said her party has benefited recently from the erosion of support for Bush and congressional Republicans among older women who are upset about Iraq, the economy, and a Medicare prescription drug law they fear will not provide them with sufficiently generous benefits.

Gallup Poll Editor-in-Chief Frank Newport said that when 1,006 voters were asked in a poll conducted Feb. 6-8 to rate the importance of certain issues, women were more likely than men to cite the economy, health care, education, the situation in Iraq, terrorism and abortion. They are most at odds with men on national security-related issues, he added.

The Republicans' pitch to the secu-

rity moms will make the case that military intervention in Iraq and Afghanistan is justified, arguing that fighting terrorism overseas will keep it from entering the United States.

"Women want us to fight that war on terror in Baghdad, not Boston; in Kabul, not Kansas City," said Scott Stanzel, a spokesman for the Bush campaign committee.

The GOP pitch also portrays Bush as a strong, decisive leader. Included in the campaign's first four television ads — three in English and one in Spanish — are images of the Sept. 11 attacks. The ads, which have drawn criticism from Democrats and others for their use of images from the attacks, stress Bush's "steady leadership in times of change."

The president's highest ratings among women during his presidency have come when the nation was focused on domestic security. Some of his lowest points have come when questions about the conduct of the war in Iraq have peaked. For example, his lowest job approval rating among women last year — 44 percent — came after Congress in November cleared the $87.5 billion spending package (PL 108-106) for occupation and reconstruction of Iraq and Afghanistan. (*2003 CQ Weekly, p. 3105*)

"Those women may come back to Bush when you remind them of the 9/11 issue closer to the campaign," said Karlyn H. Bowman, a scholar at the conservative American Enterprise Institute.

Economic Concerns

On economic matters, Republicans intend to show that in a time of war, Bush and the Congress have built a record of accomplishment that will appeal to women and men voters alike. They emphasize that the nation's economic problems took root during the Clinton administration.

Despite the loss of some 2.2 million jobs since he took office, Bush maintains that the nation's economic health is improving. Republicans say the tax cuts they promoted have generated more capital that is being recirculated into the economy. The cuts have been so effective, the GOP argues, that Congress needs to make them permanent in order to further strengthen the economy. Most Democrats opposed the cuts, saying they disproportionately benefited the wealthy.

The Republican tax message is partly designed to appeal to married women, who would benefit from a permanent repeal of the so-called "marriage penalty," and to women owners of small businesses who, like their male counterparts, would gain from the expanded use of expensing of investment income by small businesses. The Bush tax plan also would extend the 15 percent tax rate for dividends and capital gains, which was temporarily reduced last year.

The child tax credit and the marriage penalty fix had strong bipartisan support in Congress.

For women concerned about retirement security, Bush and the Republicans are highlighting congressional action Republicans spearheaded in 2001 to boost the contribution limit on individual retirement accounts. The limit had remained at $2,000 for 20 years. By 2008, the contribution limits will be $5,000 for workers younger than 50, and $6,000 for those 50 and older. (*2001 Almanac, p. 18-3*)

"This president is so good at touching women," said Ann Wagner, co-chairwoman of the Republican National Committee, who also heads the Missouri Republican Party and is heavily involved in increasing the number of women activists in the party. "We want solutions, we want someone who is going to follow through, do what they say they are going to do. We want to know what the bottom line is and how whatever policy or issue is out there is going to make my life more manageable."

Spending on Health Needs

Republicans also are playing for the women's vote using issues long associated with the Democratic Party. The calls for overhauling education laws that Bush made during the 2000 campaign were part of the compassionate conservative appeal that drew critical swing voters, political scientists agreed.

This year, Republicans are trying to repeat that with health care, an issue on which polling suggests a majority of voters trust Democrats more than Republicans.

Central to that strategy is the new Medicare law. Though most of the changes to the entitlement program will not go into effect until 2006, the GOP plan calls for depicting the law as a means of promoting economic security. Republicans are mindful that elderly

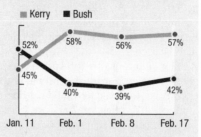

Gender Gap Favoring Kerry

In the latest polls of likely women voters, most supported Sen. John Kerry, the presumed Democratic nominee, over President Bush:

Kerry: 52%, 58%, 56%, 57%
Bush: 45%, 40%, 39%, 42%

Jan. 11 — Feb. 1 — Feb. 8 — Feb. 17

Gap Has Been Steady Since 1980
Since the 1980 Reagan-Carter presidential election, women have been more likely than men to vote Democratic. Democratic votes by gender since 1980:

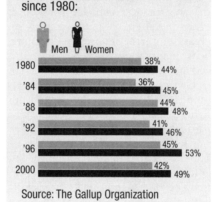

Men · Women

Year	Men	Women
1980	38%	44%
'84	36%	45%
'88	44%	48%
'92	41%	46%
'96	45%	53%
2000	42%	49%

Source: The Gallup Organization

women often live longer than men, and that care for older parents often falls on women.

Republicans tout the way the law will help seniors cope with drug costs and give them the flexibility to set up new care options that resemble those available to current workers.

"Women are very focused on [health care] issues. There's no question you can use this as a connection," said GOP pollster Bill McInturff, a partner at Public Opinion Strategies.

Women tend to make most health care purchasing decisions, and the issue is always at or near the top of their list of concerns.

"The cost of health care is an economic issue for so many women," said Karen White, national political director for EMILY's List, a group that favors Democratic candidates. "They pay the bills, they're taking care of their par-

ents, they're taking care of their kids. They want to save for college education, for retirement . . . and health care is so expensive it precludes them from doing all of those things."

The health care pitch is not limited to Medicare. Republicans are depicting other initiatives as favorable to women and blaming Democrats for the failure to enact them.

Last year's failed tort reform legislation (S 11) that would have limited the payouts in medical malpractice cases has been recast in a scaled-back measure (S 2061) that would limit liability in lawsuits against obstetricians and gynecologists.

The GOP's focus on those medical specialties, in which physicians pay some of the nation's highest medical malpractice rates, represented a play for support of rural women voters. Republicans argued that large courtroom judgments were driving up the cost of insurance premiums and forcing some doctors out of business. When obstetricians stop delivering babies, communities — especially in rural areas — may be left uncovered, the GOP lawmakers argued.

Republicans were unable to end debate on the scaled-back obstetricians and gynecologists bill but are vowing to revive it later this year.

The GOP leaders also have proposed a series of tax initiatives to help provide health care to the more than 43 million Americans who do not have coverage.

Splitting Off Votes

Republican strategists concede that such programs will not completely erode Democrats' advantage with the electorate in health care, but they are confident they can eat away at that margin and possibly make a difference in close races.

"If it makes a two-point difference or a three-point difference in close races, that could make the difference in a lot of [congressional] seats, as well as the presidency," said GOP pollster Whit Ayres.

"You only need to do that by a little bit to affect the result," said McInturff. "Democrats can't win unless they reduce our margins on taxes and terrorism or moral values."

The focus on health care is becoming a political imperative for Bush and congressional Republicans, who are not faring as well with voters in other areas, such as the economy and the war, said Robert J. Blendon, professor of health policy and management at Harvard University's School of Public Health.

"The original presumption was the president would have this big lead on the economy, terrorism and Iraq," Blendon said. "People are negative on Iraq; [Republicans] are ahead on terrorism; the economy is divided. That has forced them to look at the other issues that are likely to be prominent so you can narrow the gap" between Republican and Democratic candidates, Blendon said.

But the focus on health care carries a risk for Republicans, Blendon added. "They're going to be attacked all throughout the campaign. . . . 'You could have given [seniors] a better plan.' "

Democrats Counterattack

Democrats who opposed the Medicare bill are criticizing it on several fronts, from gaps in drug coverage to reliance on private health insurers to provide the new drug coverage.

On Feb. 25, Senate Minority Leader Tom Daschle of South Dakota and Debbie Stabenow of Michigan, along with other Senate Democrats unveiled legislation that would prevent a provision in the drug bill requiring Medicare's traditional fee-for-service program to compete with private insurers for beneficiaries' business in six areas of the country beginning in 2010 from occurring in their states.

Democrats have also persuaded the General Accounting Office to make a legal inquiry into a series of Department of Health and Human Services advertisements to promote the new benefit, which Democrats deemed political in nature.

Stabenow and other Democrats are doubtful that Republicans, no matter how hard they try, will cut into the Democrats' traditional edge on health care issues.

"I'm confident the women of the country are very smart and understand who's been on their side and fighting for their opportunities and interests," Stabenow said.

Kerry has proposed a broad array of health care initiatives, such as guaranteeing health care coverage for all children and allowing Americans to purchase their health care insurance through the Federal Employees Health Benefits Program, which covers members of Congress and federal workers.

In addition to health care, Democrats are taking apart, point by point, Bush's claims of success in other areas.

They argue, for example, that the president's plans for homeland security, education and other needs have been underfunded, placing additional burdens on financially strapped local and state governments. Any tax benefits that voters might have received are being offset by local tax increases to meet the federal mandates created by the new programs.

"If we just took one-third of what we're giving to the top wealthiest people in the country . . . we could fully fund our homeland security obligation," Stabenow said. "They're concerned about tax cuts for a very few people and risking security and opportunity for everyone else."

Democrats also note that Republicans were unable to enact many security issues. The list of bills currently gridlocked in Congress includes legislation that was meant to enhance aviation, air cargo and chemical plant security, increase bioterrorism preparedness and boost grants to firefighters, police officers and emergency workers.

Critics of the GOP also frequently point to White House efforts to limit rights that are important to women. One particular target is anti-terrorism legislation known as the USA Patriot Act (PL 107-56), which made it easier for law enforcement to track suspected terrorists. The law has come under attack from both liberals and libertarians, who contend that it gives the government too much power to pry into people's personal affairs.

Another is a new law that bans a medical procedure opponents refer to as "partial birth" abortion. (PL 108-105) (*2003 CQ Weekly, p. 3107; 2001 Almanac, p. 14-3*)

Recently, the Justice Department issued subpoenas to at least six hospitals and six Planned Parenthood affiliates, seeking private medical records of women who have undergone the procedure.

Attorney General John Ashcroft said the records are needed to determine whether the procedures are medically necessary, as plaintiffs claim. The law is the first federal statute to restrict an abortion procedure since the U.S. Supreme Court legalized abortions in its 1973 *Roe v. Wade* decision.

"What they are saying is that you will give all these private medical records to John Ashcroft — the anti-choice zealot, who is known in the United States Senate for his many efforts to reverse *Roe* — and his Justice Department, and they will, in turn, remove identifying information?" asked Ann F. Lewis, chairwoman of the Democratic National Committee's Women's Votes Center and a former communications director in the Clinton White House.

"What possible purpose could this serve except to intimidate doctors and hospitals at the expense of shredding women's privacy?" Lewis added.

Republicans say their health care agenda addresses many voters' concerns. But some believe the party must do a better job communicating its message.

"I think we have spoken to pension reform, that helps women; health care, which is their major concern; education, which is No. 2 generally for women; and we are the leaders in that effort," said Republican Sen. Kay Bailey Hutchison of Texas. "But I don't think we have made the case to women that we are doing so much."

First Lady's Role

Helping make the case is the first lady, whose popularity is "a mile wide and an inch deep" because she is not held personally responsible for driving the legislative agenda, said the University of Virginia's Sabato.

Recently, Laura Bush traveled to Bentonville, Ark., to talk about teacher recruitment at a local high school. In early February, she visited Baptist Hospital in Miami, where she discussed heart disease prevention for women.

Sabato argued that a high-profile role for Laura Bush, including a well-crafted television ad featuring her, would help the campaign. Such a role may not have worked well for less popular or more polarizing former first ladies, such as Roslyn Carter, Nancy Reagan or Hillary Rodham Clinton.

"On the theory that this election will be decided by marginal changes in a fixed vote, she might be able to make some difference," Sabato said.

But ultimately, it will be up to Bush, as the party's standard-bearer, to convince voters he has done enough to warrant a second term — and that the GOP deserves to continue leading a unified government.

"I don't think that much will change," Sabato said. "The election map will basically be the same. A few states will switch, and how they switch will determine the winner." ◆

Partisan Divisions Since 1971

The tensions in the House have reached new heights since a time of narrow Republican majorities began in 1995. But the roots of the partisan friction date back to earlier events, from the post-Watergate Democratic sweep of 1974 to the bitterly disputed Indiana House election of 1984, in which a Democrat ultimately was seated. Some of the highlights:

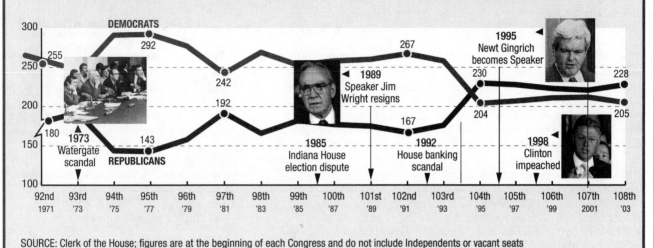

SOURCE: Clerk of the House; figures are at the beginning of each Congress and do not include Independents or vacant seats

Disorder in the House — And No End in Sight

Some call it the death of civility, while others say such partisanship is nothing new

Just a decade ago, the top party leaders in the House talked regularly. Several times a week, in fact. That is the way it was in the days when Thomas S. Foley, D-Wash., was the Speaker and Robert H. Michel, R-Ill., was the minority leader.

Sometimes in Foley's office and sometimes in Michel's, they chewed over the business before them: bills on the way to the floor, amendments to be offered, schedules and conflicts — any trouble ahead that might complicate both their lives. Those conversations were essential to the smooth running of the House, the men say.

Today, however Republican Speaker J. Dennis Hastert of Illinois and Democratic Minority Leader Nancy Pelosi of California do not talk with any regularity — nor do they have much of a relationship at all. Pelosi says she does not hesitate to call Hastert when she has something to tell him, but she sees no use in trying to confer regularly with him about the business of the House at a time when, she says, the Republican majority has made very clear its intention to trample on the rights of the Democratic minority.

"What would be the point?" Pelosi asked. "So they can tell us that they're not going to play fair on the floor?"

There is, in fact, a dearth of meaningful cross-party dialogue in the House, from the leaders on down. And that, longtime and former members say, is one big reason for the mounting incivility they say undermines the legislative process, erodes public faith in Congress as an institution and makes the House more difficult than ever to govern.

Many say they cannot remember a time when the parties were more estranged.

A series of messy standoffs and blow-ups on the floor or in committee rooms have added to the appearance that something is badly out of whack in the House. In the past year alone there have been floor votes extended for long stretches so GOP leaders could reverse the apparent outcome by twisting a few rank-and-file arms, allegations of one member bribing another for his vote, and a committee meeting that dissolved in so much acrimony the Capitol Police were summoned. The most recent biannual "civility" retreat drew just one-quarter of the House last year — the worst attendance ever.

"We have deteriorated to a level of negativity and nastiness that I haven't seen in my 10 years" as a member of the House, said Ray LaHood of Illinois, who was previously Michel's chief of staff and who has organized those retreats since 1995. "And there's plenty of blame to go around."

So what is behind the breakdown in civility? Members, former members and longtime Congress watchers point to several causes.

First, they cite the long period of near-partisan parity in the House. Republicans hold 52 percent of the House seats, its strongest hand in eight years, but still just 23 more seats than the Democrats. That tight balance of power makes the minority party an ever-present threat to the ruling Republicans, something that was never the case during the seven

Congresses when Michel (1957-95) was minority leader.

It also encourages the two parties to sharpen their differences — rather than seek consensus — in hopes of galvanizing enough like-minded voters to win a clear governing majority. That is a technique Republican Rep. Newt Gingrich of Georgia (1979-99) perfected in breaking the Democrats' four-decade hold on power 10 years ago. And it is the technique that Pelosi and her Democratic minority are employing today. (*Congress, p. 32*)

Second, the House has become faster-paced and more impersonal. It is harder than ever for lawmakers to develop the genuine friendships that can help bridge partisan divisions. Members fly back to their districts regularly, sometimes spending less than 60 hours a week in Washington. When they are in the Capitol, fewer members socialize regularly with their colleagues. Where lawmakers once learned about bills directly from one another, these days they usually send their aides to do the talking.

Third, over the past three decades, the two parties have essentially drawn the vast majority of the nation's House districts so they are politically safe bets for one party or another. These polarized districts then elect members who often are disinclined to work with the other side.

The result, say members and former members, is a vicious circle in which 20 years or more of grievances mount up. Each bad turn is built on the last.

And the current standoff, with neither side giving quarter to the other, is politically expedient for both. That, perhaps more than any other single factor, helps explain why neither caucus shows an interest in ratcheting down the tension.

Republicans can tar Democrats as obstructionists, cut them out of the process of writing legislation and then claim sole credit for whatever passes. On the other side, Democrats have no fingerprints on bills coming out of the House, which frees them to take shots at what passes and to beat up on Republicans for leaving them out of the process.

"Both view the conflict as playing to their party interests," said former Rep. Leon E. Panetta (1977-93), a California Democrat who later was White House chief of staff under President Bill Clinton. "That's the dangerous part. Both sides have lost sight of what governing is about."

'A Good Thing'

To be sure, conflict between the parties, even bare-knuckled partisanship, is the essential yin to the yang of consensus in the American political system. Particularly when the country is as evenly divided as it is today, conflict helps define and sharpen competing ideas and keeps the legislative process moving forward, said William Connelly Jr., a political scientist at Washington and Lee University.

The House has always been a politically contentious place, and "that's a good thing," Connelly said.

"That's how we work out our differences," he said. "Remember, they're not shooting each other. They're not even caning each other. As long as the weapon of choice is words, I think we're in good shape."

It is also true that civility has frayed in the Senate, and the tone there is sure to get worse as the election season continues and the parties use the floor to highlight their agendas and score points on the opposition. But in the Senate, where individual members wield considerable power, some measure of cross-party dialogue is essential for getting any business done. That is not true in the House, where the majority rule

Friendship Across The Aisle

While many longtime House members say there are fewer cross-party friendships today than in the past, there are some who still cross party lines, and say the benefits are worthwhile.

Rangel

Majority Whip Roy Blunt of Missouri lunches once a month with his Democratic counterpart, Minority Whip Steny H. Hoyer of Maryland.

Blunt says relations are "actually better under the surface than it would appear if all you do is just watch C-SPAN. I have a number of good friends who are Democrats, and I think I'm not unique in that situation."

Hoyer said he likes and respects Blunt and that he does find their lunches useful. They use them in part to hammer out ideas on issues where they can agree. Lately they have been working on legislation to ensure the continuity of Congress in the wake of a terrorist attack or other disaster.

"I think the fact that we have respect for one another helps us to work together on issues where we agree," he said.

Hoyer also worked with Administration Committee Chairman Bob Ney, R-Ohio, on the 2002 election overhaul law. Hoyer found common ground with Speaker J. Dennis Hastert, R-Ill., on that issue as well.

Crane

There are other examples. Charles B. Rangel, a 17-term Democrat from New York, has partnered with Philip M. Crane, R-Ill., on trade and tax legislation. And they are friends as well, both men said.

But the friendships only go so far in bridging partisan divisions. Hoyer is quick to add that he has deep objections that the Republican leadership is systematically shutting out Democrats on critical issues where they disagree, such as Medicare.

"Unfortunately, the relationships I have with Mr. Blunt and Mr. Hastert do not translate to working together on substantive issues where we disagree," he said.

And suspicion between the parties run deep. Many freshmen still arrive at the House primed to see the other side as the enemy, rather than colleagues with whom they have policy differences, Rangel said.

When Crane wanders to Rangel's side of the House to chat, it sends a ripple of surprise through the Democrats around them. Most of the time, Rangel said, the two men are just talking about their grandchildren.

is nearly absolute.

Among longtime and former lawmakers, there is a deep sense that the conflict in the House has crossed the line from a healthy contest of ideas to trench warfare that puts real, lasting consensus on the issues facing the country even further out of reach. And with less constructive debate, less real give-and-take between the parties, the quality of the legislation suffers, many say.

Members and former members worry, too, that the bickering is turning off voters and eroding confidence in the institution. People who do not disengage entirely are likely to be left soured on both parties, members say.

"When the people see government at any level as negative, both parties lose, and the institution loses," said Charles B. Rangel of New York, the fourth most-senior House Democrat. Voters, he said, "want to get answers to the problems of the day. If in the debate, instead of clarification and edification, they find negativism and animosity, they say, 'The hell with both of them.' "

Winning at All Costs

Nonetheless, many people close to life in the House say its culture is becoming one of "win at all costs." The GOP majority can succeed by that paradigm far more often. On March 30, to cite the most recent example, GOP leaders held open the balloting for an extra 23 minutes so they could reverse enough of their own members' votes to sink a symbolic Democratic proposal on the fiscal 2005 budget resolution (S Con Res 95). After the Republicans succeeded in killing the language on a 209-209 tie, Pelosi and other Democrats then angrily accused them of stealing the vote. Leading editorial pages also denounced the tactic. (*2004 CQ Weekly, p. 799*)

There also was last summer's fracas in the Ways and Means Committee, when a debate over a pension bill (HR 1776) devolved into name-calling, and Chairman Bill Thomas, R-Calif., summoned the police on the panel's Democrats — for which he was compelled by his own leaders to apologize. (*2003 CQ Weekly, p. 1885*)

GOP leaders have shut Democrats out of conference committees convened to write the final compromises on major legislation — saying that the minority does nothing in such meetings but sow obstruction and delay.

This was particularly irritating to Democrats during last fall's negotiations on the overhaul of Medicare (PL 108-173). Republican conferees, led by Thomas, overtly kept all but two Democrats — Sens. Max Baucus of Montana and John B. Breaux of Louisiana — away from the negotiating table. (*2003 CQ Weekly, p. 3121*)

Both times a Medicare overhaul came before the House in 2003, Republicans extended pre-dawn roll calls until they could persuade enough members of their own party to switch their votes and support the measure. Leaders on each side muscled their troops into starkly opposing camps.

In the first instance, to pass the original House bill in June, it took almost an hour for GOP leaders to find the votes for a 216-215 victory. The second vote, on the conference report in November, was a three-hour spectacle of arm-twisting where Republicans turned a 215-219 defeat into a 220-215 victory.

One member claimed that the legislation's supporters had tried to bribe him on the floor, an allegation that is now the subject of the first official investigation by the Committee on Standards of Official Conduct in two years. (*2004 CQ Weekly, p. 697*)

About two weeks before the second Medicare vote, Hastert said at a Washington symposium that as Speaker it is his job to be fair, but also to carry out the will of the majority. "Sometimes, we have a hard time convincing the majority of the House to vote like a majority of the House," he said, "so sometimes you will see votes stay open longer than usual."

Atmosphere of Distrust

The drawn-out roll calls and other tactics — which critics describe as stretching the bounds of the traditional rules of engagement, at a minimum — also exacerbate the tension, making the minority party even less willing to accommodate the majority. And that, in turn, makes it all the more necessary for the majority to stretch the rules and lean hard on its own members to squeeze out needed votes.

And as relations between the parties deteriorate, members on both sides find it more and more difficult to argue for any accommodation and detente, said Foley, who served in the House 1965-95. "It leads to such bitter feelings that they don't hear one another," he said.

Paradoxically, the breakdown in

J. Dennis Hastert, R-Ill.
Speaker

A former high school wrestling coach given to delivering pep talks, Hastert brings a soft touch to the job that is a direct contrast to the demeanor of his predecessor, Newt Gingrich, R-Ga., (1979-99) and of his majority leader, Tom DeLay, R-Texas.

At the same time, though, Hastert presides over a bitterly divided House. At the very least, he condones the pressure tactics and partisan warfare waged by DeLay, with whom he has had few public disagreements. And Hastert publicly endorses the concept of win at all costs, even if it means holding a roll call vote open for three hours — as he did with the Medicare bill in November — to secure the victory.

Hastert unexpectedly became a savior for the GOP in late 1998, when Speaker-designate Robert L. Livingston of Louisiana stepped aside after admitting to an extramarital affair. Having narrowed their margin in the 1998 elections — and with the polarizing Gingrich on his way out — Republicans turned to Hastert, then chief deputy in DeLay's whip operation, to steady the ship.

Hastert has done just that, pursuing partisan goals without engendering the level of disdain Democrats have aimed at Gingrich and DeLay.

"The two most powerful emotions in the world are fear and love," said Rep. Zach Wamp, R-Tenn. "Denny Hastert is loved."

When Hastert asked Republican C.L. "Butch" Otter of Idaho to switch his vote to "yea" the night of the marathon Medicare vote, the Speaker made a pretty simple appeal. "Give us a shot to try to reform something," Hastert said. "That's all I'm asking."

That is consistent with what Otter's home-state colleague, Mike Simpson, heard in his pre-vote meetings with Hastert.

"Not once when I sat in his office two different times did he say, 'The Conference needs this, the president needs this, I helped you get on the appropriations committee.' Not one of those things was brought up," Simpson said.

Rather, he said, the conversation boiled down to "Is this good policy? Is this bad policy?"

Both Simpson and Otter voted for the Medicare bill.

Tom DeLay, R-Texas
Majority Leader

DeLay is well known for advancing the GOP's goals without regard for whom he has to muscle to make sure his side wins.

That single-minded approach has made him invaluable to his party and the most reviled figure in the Capitol among Democrats, who often accuse him of abusing process and power to achieve his ends.

In recent years, DeLay and other Republican leaders have repeatedly kept roll calls running long past their allotted time so they could pressure defecting Republicans to switch their votes and prevent the Democrats from winning on a close vote with GOP help.

He was admonished in 1999 by the House ethics committee for threatening to seek retribution against a trade association that had hired a Democrat as its president.

Outside the Capitol, DeLay has been a relentless campaigner for Republican candidates and causes, raising millions of dollars to help elect his colleagues. One of his boldest undertakings was an effort to elect Republicans to the Texas legislature in 2002 so the map of the state's congressional districts could, in unprecedented fashion, be redrawn in the middle of a decade to elect as many as seven more Republicans in 2004. If this November's elections go as expected in Texas, that could add to the GOP's majority and that will enhance DeLay's power.

In addition, a political action committee DeLay set up to raise money for state legislative races is being investigated by a Texas prosecutor.

Inside the Capitol, DeLay was widely credited for his effectiveness as whip during his eight years as the third-ranking Republican, when he counted votes, took care of members' needs and doled out favors.

Since becoming majority leader at the start of the 108th Congress, he has won praise from colleagues for his swift transition to that post.

The bottom line for many Republicans is DeLay's seemingly innate ability to find a way to get things done.

"Tom came to this world a legislative strategist," Rep. Roger Wicker, R-Miss., said recently.

comity also may help explain the strikingly muted response from the House to mounting concerns about ethical lapses among its members — and the widespread talk of an "ethics truce" between the parties.

While there are those in the ranks of both parties who may be champing at the bit to take down the leader of the other caucus for an ethical failing, they are held back by a stronger countervailing force: They need to have faith that the other side will put the good of the institution above partisan interests — and keep the ethics process from collapsing into a partisan free-for-all that could soil the already shaky reputation of Congress for years.

The will of lawmakers to police their own crumbles when members are reluctant to start something that may engulf their own party and perhaps shift the balance of power in unpredictable ways, said former Rep. David E. Skaggs, D-Colo. (1987-99), executive director of the Center for Democracy and Citizenship at the Council for Excellence in Government, a nonpartisan group aimed at attracting new talent to public service.

Pressure to Investigate

Only after intense pressure from outside public interest groups and the media did Republicans and Democrats on the House ethics committee agree to investigate allegations by Nick Smith, R-Mich., that lawmakers or groups offered financial help to his son's congressional campaign in return for his Medicare vote. There is no telling how long Democrats in particular may hold their fire on other ethics allegations against Republicans, including Majority Leader Tom DeLay of Texas, but so far they have refrained from filing formal charges. (2004 *CQ Weekly*, p. 792)

"The business of that place depends on compromise, depends on trust, depends on people knowing each other in non-confrontational ways to engender trust," Skaggs said. "There's not enough of that glue in place to withstand the risk inherent in moving ahead with an ethics investigation."

Democrats concede that they ruled arrogantly at times when they were in the majority. They closed Republicans out of negotiations and bullied them. One senior Democrat, who asked not to be named out of concern that he would appear to be criticizing his own party in an election year, recalled a

Democratic chairman once throwing a ranking Republican out of a meeting with lobbyists, almost reducing him to tears.

Generation of Grievances

In the mid-1970s, Democrats decided to maintain a ratio of roughly 2-to-1 on important committees, even though they no longer held such a lopsided majority. That left a generation of Republican "committee orphans" who were denied a chance to legislate and whose only recourse was to rail against the majority from the floor.

"I can understand why some Republicans would bridle under that kind of treatment," said former Rep. Matthew F. McHugh, D-N.Y. (1975-93). "Democrats had given the impression of being there by divine right."

GOP anger boiled over in 1985, when Democrats refused to seat Republican Richard D. McIntyre after a close and contested House race, even though Indiana officials had certified McIntyre the winner. At one point, Republicans walked out of the House in protest. (*1985 Almanac, p. 28*)

At the same time, Gingrich and his allies were calling for an end to cooperation with the Democratic majority and criticizing their own leadership, especially Michel, the minority leader, for settling for crumbs from the Democratic table.

Gingrich and his allies said it was time for Republicans to stop being "good little cogs in a machine that is set up by the Democrats," as then Rep. Vin Weber, R-Minn., put it at the time.

"When I came here, there had been 24 years of Democratic rule," said Thomas, who arrived with Gingrich in 1979. "It was a very genteelly run plantation. They owned the place. They told you what to do and how to do it."

The battle sharpened further in the late 1980s when the House ethics committee — based on a complaint filed by Gingrich — found evidence of two sorts of inappropriate financial dealings that forced the resignation of Speaker Jim Wright of Texas (1955-89). (*1989 Almanac, p. 36*)

The year the Republicans took the House majority, 1995, was the big turning point in relations between the parties. They were aggrieved about their treatment under Democratic rule, and some were intent on payback. Democrats, meanwhile, were embittered by their unexpected loss and chafed under GOP rule.

"I haven't seen a coming together since," said Sherwood Boehlert of New York, one of the relatively few GOP moderates from that time still in the House.

Michel chastises some of the Republicans elected in 1994 for running against Congress — derogating the very institution in which they were elected to serve. Their rhetoric was partly to blame for poisoning the atmosphere, he said.

"There were a number of real hotheaded Republicans who came to trash the government," he said, "rather than come here to make it work better."

Little Face-Time

Relations between the top leaders have also been strained since, though their shared trauma at the Sept. 11 attacks and the subsequent congressional anthrax scare warmed Hastert's relationship with Rep. Richard A. Gephardt of Missouri, who was then minority leader.

Today, both Hastert and Pelosi say they do, indeed, value civility and want good communication.

"I think we have a responsibility to set an example on how a legislature should work," Pelosi said. "I have joined the Speaker on many occasions in the past year, greeting heads of state or parliamentarians from other countries, and we sit there in a bipartisan way and talk to them about our country, hear about theirs, and talk about issues before us."

But they do not actually talk to each other regularly, one on one.

"Mrs. Pelosi tends to write letters," Hastert said. "And if that's how she wants to communicate, that's fine with me. We write letters back."

Asked whether she could see the two of them developing a working relationship such as the one Foley and Michel describe, Pelosi said, "When Mr. Gingrich came in, all of that changed.

"I'd be open to that, but . . . I don't sit around and worry about when the Speaker is going to call me and invite me to coffee."

In an April 1 news conference, she redirected the discussion to what she views as Republican abuses of the legislative process and the failure of the GOP to put the "needs of the American people" first — and to include Democrats in the legislative process.

"How we chit-chat amongst ourselves is not important if we do not share the values of America's working families," Pelosi said.

Out of the Trenches

Former members say they are distressed by what they see.

"I'm glad I served my time when I did," said Michel, who came to the House in 1957, two years into the 40-year run of Democratic House control. "I hate to say it, but I'd be reluctant to return to the institution now. The well has been poisoned."

Panetta said the same. "I go back to the Hill now when I'm in Washington, and I can't wait to get out of there," he said. "Because the mood of the place has changed so dramatically."

Some Democrats and Republicans place the blame squarely on the other party. When asked late last month to explain the decline in civility in the House, Thomas pointed to the Democrats — who, he maintains, have never been able to come to terms with their status as the minority caucus after such a long run in power.

Asked if the GOP majority had done anything to worsen partisan tensions, Thomas said, "Yes, not recognize the Democrats as an equal controlling power, allowing them to define what occurs."

"We actually think they're the minority," Thomas said, with mock surprise. "And the Democrats find that unacceptable and don't believe they should be in the minority. And they will not work with us on any bill."

DeLay said much the same. Democrats "haven't laid out a vision or an agenda," he said. "They've laid out nothing but politics and destroying people. That's their agenda to win the House back."

Feelings are just as bitter on the other side, particularly toward DeLay, whom the Democrats have come to deeply dislike and resent.

"Do people really believe that Tom DeLay is interested in working out anything with anybody?" said David R. Obey of Wisconsin, the third most-senior House Democrat, who in 1997 got into a shoving match with DeLay on the floor. "There's not an ounce of trust in this place, and there will not be as long as Tom DeLay is running this place. He's a savage partisan without peer."

The most immediate way to ease the tensions would probably be for one side or the other to win a wide majority. That would give both sides more

---

Nancy Pelosi, D-Calif.
Minority Leader

Pelosi lacks the power of the majority. But through sheer determination and persuasiveness she has managed to push the Democrats' agenda, even though her party is outnumbered by more than 20 votes.

Since her election as minority leader in 2002, Pelosi has unified the Democrats to the point that on several issues — including the budget resolution for fiscal 2005 (H Con Res 393), the 2004 appropriations bill for the Labor, Health and Human Services and Education departments and a reauthorization of Head Start (HR 2210) — her caucus voted unanimously against the majority.

"From the day she took office, she has made it very clear that we're not going to be able to take back the House if Democrats run around as independent operators," said Rep. George Miller, D-Calif., a friend of Pelosi. "The respect for her leadership continues to grow."

Pelosi, 64, has been known for her impassioned, liberal stance on issues since she was elected to the House in 1987. Democratic members say that interest has made it easier for her to motivate colleagues to stay behind her, particularly during key votes.

"She's very involved in the issues," said Rep. José E. Serrano, D-N.Y. "That's the way she leads the party, by staying close, staying up front."

Pelosi was front and center for her party on March 30, when it appeared the Democrats were going to win a vote on a motion to instruct House negotiators to agree to the Senate's pay-as-you-go provision on the 2005 budget resolution (S Con Res 95). The measure would have been non-binding, but for Pelosi, it would have represented an important victory for Democrats who were aiming to prove Republicans really had not lined up all their members behind a budget resolution.

The motion failed 209-209, but only after Republicans spent more than 20 minutes calling back several GOP members to switch their vote to "nay."

Pelosi stayed in the chamber for the 28-minute vote, armed with a list of members and how they voted. "They lost today," Pelosi said, ticking off the names of the GOP members who switched the vote to 'nay.' "They may not know it but they just lost in there."

Roy Blunt
Missouri Republican — Majority Whip

In trying to keep House Republicans in line, Blunt has chosen not to emulate the style of Tom DeLay of Texas, Blunt's predecessor as majority whip.

While DeLay, now majority leader of the House, was legendary for his sometimes forceful tactics, Blunt has quiet discussions with members or holds closed-door meetings with lawmakers at odds over legislation.

"Roy doesn't twist arms," said Thomas M. Davis III, R-Va. Blunt prefers to approach dissident members and ask "what can we do outside the resolution" in exchange for their support.

Such was the case March 25, when Blunt corralled reluctant Republicans to adopt the fiscal 2005 budget resolution (H Con Res 393). Davis, chairman of the Government Reform Committee, and Rep. Frank R. Wolf, R-Va., both holdouts on the budget measure, wanted to schedule a vote to put the House on record in support of equal pay raises for federal civilian employees and the military. Davis' and Wolf's districts are home to thousands of federal workers. *(Budget resolution, p. 799)*

Blunt agreed to their request, and in return he got their votes on the budget resolution.

His more gentle tactics have not cost the Republicans any major votes so far, but there have been a few close calls. Republicans had to hold open the Nov. 22 vote on legislation creating the new Medicare law (PL 108-173) for three hours to persuade enough members to switch their votes to adopt the conference report on the measure. *(2003 CQ Weekly, p. 2962)*

And Democrats on March 30 came close to winning on a motion to instruct House negotiators to agree to a provision in the Senate budget resolution (S Con Res 95) that would impose pay-as-you-go limits on some future spending increases. Enough deficit-wary Republicans backed the Democrats' motion that the GOP had to hold open the roll call for an extra 23 minutes to get members to return to the chamber and switch their votes.

Davis said those situations do not point out a weakness in Blunt, but rather highlight his strength as whip during tough votes. "In a close game, the better team wins," Davis said.

breathing room to reach out to the other — and could compel whichever party ends up on the losing side to try to win some legislative scraps by being nice toward the winners.

But ultimately nothing will change unless the parties come out of their trenches and talk, Panetta and others say, and that begins with the leadership. "The kind of behavior that is modeled by the leaders is paid attention to," said Skaggs. "It's a powerful signal to the rank and file of what is acceptable and desirable behavior on their part."

Rep. Doug Bereuter, a veteran Nebraska Republican retiring this summer, said the leaders do not "have to like each other, but they do have to communicate, so you can avoid misunderstandings, so you can avoid complications, so you don't believe necessarily what you read in the media, which thrives on conflict."

But the responsibility is even broader than that, former members and others say. "Some of it has to come from the top, our elected leaders," LaHood said. "But it has to come from the members as well."

Risk of Reaching Out

The leaders themselves are boxed in to a great degree by their own troops. Hastert and Pelosi would be putting their credibility on the line in their own caucuses were they to reach out to the other side and try to foster consensus, Panetta said. "When you're locked in battle," he said, "suddenly your loyalty is questioned if you make any move to compromise."

Indeed, when coordinating the most recent bipartisan House retreat, in early 2003, LaHood said organizers cut top leaders out of the planning because the rank and file in both caucuses were giving them too much grief for urging them to attend.

That retreat, an all-expenses-paid getaway for members and their families at the Greenbrier resort in West Virginia, drew only about 100 members, the worst attendance of the four retreats LaHood has organized with Democrat Charles W. Stenholm of Texas.

And in the months since, LaHood and Stenholm both have grown increasingly pessimistic. It is an open question now whether there will even be a retreat next year, because there may not be enough interest among members to justify it. "It's demoralizing," LaHood said.

"Some people don't want to get

along with members of the other party," he said. "They view them as the enemy."

Hastert's spokesman, John Feehery, maintains that the partisan relations today are not as bad as they were in the 1990s, when members, including leaders, were openly trading ethics charges and smearing each other personally.

"To say it's the worst it's ever been is just inaccurate," Feehery said.

But others say the two sides are no longer talking as they once did, and it is eating away at the tradition of rich, open-minded debate in Congress that makes for a healthy, vigorous democracy.

"I've always operated under the assumption that I haven't been to the mountaintop and seen the promised land — the other guy may have some ideas worth listening to," said Boehlert. "But I think there are a whole bunch of people who wouldn't cosponsor a bill with a member of the other party."

Democrat Jim Cooper, who represented Tennessee from 1983 until 1995 and returned to Congress last year, says the House has changed during his eight years away. "We're training a whole generation of congressmen who don't know what it's like to have a real debate, a real discussion, a real hearing, a real vote. We're in danger of losing the most precious heritage of our country, which is a free and open debate.

Redistricting — customarily a once-a-decade redrawing of the congressional map to reflect shifts in population — has contributed to the growing estrangement, members and other observers say. The parties have now configured about three-quarters of the House's 435 districts to strongly favor one side or the other. Last year, DeLay orchestrated a rare mid-decade remapping of Texas to take several of the arguably competitive districts there and make them solidly Republican — one of the many things he has done to earn Democratic enmity. *(2004 CQ Weekly, p. 94)*

With little chance of serious opposition from the other party, members must worry primarily about getting challenged from the right or left, which tends to drive them toward their base and away from the center.

That has spawned a generation of lawmakers who see little need to reach toward the other party to find consensus in the middle.

A recent study by political scientists

at Emory University maintains that redistricting is not to blame for polarized House districts. Those researchers theorize it has more to do with immigration and population shifts. Democrats and Republicans, in short, are less likely today than a generation ago to live side-by-side.

But the result is the same: Less bipartisanship.

"There's no risk in being as big of a partisan blankety-blank as you want to be," said Lewis L. Gould, a professor emeritus of American history at the University of Texas and author of the recently published book, "Grand Old Party: A History of the Republicans."

The gerrymandering has also thinned the ranks of moderates, who tend to straddle the line between the parties in their voting. Two such Republicans, for example, departed after the redistricting for this decade. Constance A. Morella lost in Maryland, while Steve Horn retired when his California constituency was carved up to bolster the political safety of other Democrats.

Faster Pace, Fewer Friends

Other smaller, more prosaic changes have diminished the chances for interparty discourse.

Faster, cheaper transportation means many more members are capable of returning home whenever the House is out of session. Most members once moved their families to Washington. That is rarer today, and it means lawmakers have few chances to get to know each other socially — the grease that once helped make the House run more smoothly, members of both parties said. *(Friends, p. 42)*

(Friends, p. 42)

Congressional spouses once gathered to commiserate about life in Washington. "Now wives will be as cantankerous as members, because all they've heard are bad things about the other side," Rangel said.

More professional staff today than in generations past also has made a difference in atmosphere, by insulating lawmakers from one another, members say. Where they used to go to one another to discuss legislation, now their staffs are more likely to handle it and brief their bosses later.

And life just moves faster on the Hill today. Boehlert pointed to electronic voting as an example. In days past, a clerk called the roll — as is

still done in the Senate — which kept members milling on the floor for as long as 40 minutes, and there was time then to talk about legislation, or even baseball and children. Now, votes are sometimes conducted in as few as five minutes.

Taking the Leap

Some Democrats say the Republicans, as the majority party, are going to have to make the first move toward detente in the House. LaHood says Democrats are in large measure to blame for going negative in their zeal to win back the House and the White House. "The message has gone out: Whatever it takes, we're going to do," he said. "That tone has been sent by the Democratic leader, the Democratic whip and their lieutenants."

But whoever is to blame, someone is going to have to take the risk of reaching out to the other party, Panetta and others said.

Both sides, as well as outside observers, worry that a dysfunctional House undermines the nation's ability to come together to solve its most pressing problems.

"Legislative bodies by their very nature have to be mediating institutions," said Jerry F. Climer, a former House aide and now president of the Public Governance Institute of Alexandria, Va., which helps organize the bipartisan retreats. "They have to be places where common ground is found, where hard distinctions are worked out."

That is essential to a functioning democracy, Climer said. And it is one of the things that has made this huge melting pot of a nation so uniquely strong and successful.

But at the same time, each party points to the other as the one who must make the first move.

"Larger majorities might improve the atmosphere, but we'd be foolish to think that would be the way to fix things," Bereuter said. "I think it really takes public understanding of what is gradually happening to the Congress and demonstration of public demand that we have restraint on our partisan activities when it's counterproductive for the country."

Said Foley, "I don't see a quick resolution. I fear a country increasingly divided politically. And I think that's a bad prescription for moving forward in a dangerous time." ◆

Steny H. Hoyer, D-Md.
Minority Whip

At 64, Hoyer is, in the main, the model of civility, a legislative veteran of almost four decades whose fierce advocacy and party loyalty are tempered by a respectful manner and a rare drive to work with all of his congressional colleagues.

"Steny is not one who looks for a compromise," said former Rep. Steve Bartlett, R-Texas (1983-91), a longtime friend who heads The Financial Services Roundtable. "He looks for common ground."

With little of that to be found these days, Hoyer is building within the Democratic Caucus what he calls "the psychology of the consensus," the notion that Democrats should feel like they are part of a team and should have to be convinced to break ranks.

Last Nov. 22, in his first year as the person in charge of corralling Democrats on floor votes, Hoyer used his team-building prowess to help orchestrate a near defeat of the Republicans' Medicare overhaul bill (PL 108-173).

He persuaded party members, even a few who would eventually switch to support the measure, to vote "no" early. His was a strategy that allowed opponents of the bill to claim a temporary majority of as many as 219 and forced Republicans to hold the roll call open for almost three hours until they could get enough members to change their votes to "yes," securing passage. *(2003 CQ Weekly, p. 2958)*

Rep. Barney Frank, D-Mass., says Hoyer's determination and experience — he was first elected to the Maryland Senate in 1966 and later became its youngest president — prepared him for his current job, in which he has helped meld the most unified group of House Democrats in at least 41 years. "He's smart and he understands human nature and he works at it," Frank said.

In holding Democrats together, however, Hoyer has also contributed to the deepening partisan rift that runs against his nature. But that has not stopped him from maintaining good relations with some Republicans.

"His word is good," said Virginia Rep. Thomas M. Davis III, whose district is separated from Hoyer's by the Potomac River. "That's what makes it easy to deal with him."

Stumping From Senate Floor Starting Early This Season

Quick Contents

Political paralysis is to be expected in an election year, but the closeness of the presidential race and the narrow majority margin in the Senate have exacerbated the problem.

Senate Majority Whip Mitch McConnell gave a lengthy floor statement April 21 about why Congress needs to renew the anti-terrorism law known as the Patriot Act, parts of which expire next year. If his words sounded familiar, there was a reason. Just the day before, President Bush had said the very same thing in a highly publicized speech.

In one way, though, the Kentucky Republican went further than the president: He attacked by name his Senate colleague, Democrat John Kerry of Massachusetts, who has criticized the law (PL 107-56) as part of his campaign to oust Bush from the White House in November.

But did the Bush campaign ask McConnell to make the speech? Not at all, the senator said. He simply read about Bush's speech in the newspapers and decided to make one of his own — because he, too, feels strongly about the need to renew the Patriot Act. "Nobody had to ask me," he said.

It is not a surprise that the nature of the debates in Congress in 2004 would be influenced by the race for the White House. That happens in every presidential election year. What has startled lawmakers and outside observers this time is how quickly and thoroughly in this election year Congress has be-

CQ Weekly April 24, 2004

come an extension of the presidential campaign — to the point where lawmakers are visibly spending their time on little else.

This is particularly so in the Senate. Majority Leader Bill Frist, R-Tenn., uses floor time to give speeches attacking Kerry, as does McConnell. Minority Leader Tom Daschle, D-S.D., gave a series of floor speeches the week of April 19 on sacrifices of the troops in Iraq — working in a few digs against Bush's handling of the war in the process.

Democrats Edward M. Kennedy of Massachusetts and Tom Harkin of Iowa held a news conference April 20 to announce their opposition to Bush's proposed changes in overtime regulations. About two hours later, Kerry issued a statement that he does not like the new rules either. (*2004 CQ Weekly, p. 966*)

Off Capitol Hill, lawmakers are active in the campaign as well. The Bush campaign has tapped Frist and other GOP leaders, such as House Majority Whip Roy Blunt of Missouri and Rep. Rob Portman of Ohio, to host telephone conference calls and issue statements offering rapid-response criticisms of Kerry's proposals. Rank-and-file Republicans such as freshman Sens. Norm Coleman of Minnesota, Jim Talent of Missouri and John Cornyn of Texas have joined in the act.

The Surrogates

Kerry, who already received vital help from Kennedy during the primary campaign, now is enlisting help from other congressional Democrats. On April 15, he named Sen. Richard J. Durbin of Illinois and Rep. Stephanie Tubbs Jones of Ohio as co-chairmen of the Democratic National Committee (DNC) to work on message strategy. And on April 19, he campaigned in Florida with his former rival for the nomination, Sen. Joseph I. Lieberman of Connecticut.

Minority Whip Harry Reid of Nevada has played an active surrogate role as well. He gave a floor speech defending Kerry's views on the Patriot Act the day after McConnell's speech. Senate Democrats such as Bob Graham of Florida — another rival during the primaries — and Democratic Senatorial Campaign Committee chairman Jon Corzine of New Jersey have run conference calls responding to Bush campaign statements.

If the Senate were passing more legislation, the presidential campaign activities of its members might get less attention. But it is

REUTERS PHOTO / LARRY DOWNING

Senate Majority Leader Bill Frist, left, is breaking tradition by traveling to South Dakota to campaign against the re-election efforts of Minority Leader Tom Daschle.

not. That sets it apart from the House, which still passes bills with relative ease no matter how much its members get involved in the White House race.

The Senate passed one bill the week of April 19, to protect victims' rights (S 2329). The near-unanimous vote made it the election-year equivalent of endorsing Mom, apple pie and baseball. But a measure to curtail asbestos litigation (S 2290) stalled in the face of opposition by Democrats and some Republicans, and a long-delayed corporate tax bill (S 1637) that was under intense negotiations just before the spring recess will not return to the Senate floor until the week of April 26 at the earliest. (*Victims' rights*, 2004 CQ *Weekly*, p. 967; *asbestos*, p. 964; *taxes*, p. 854)

Senate gridlock in presidential election years is not unusual in itself. Indeed, Democrats brought the Senate to a standstill in 1996, the last time a senator headed a presidential ticket. They tried to attach a minimum wage increase to every bill moving through the Senate, forcing Majority Leader Bob Dole (1969-96), the Kansan who had just clinched the GOP nomination, to resort to embarrassing maneuvers to avoid a vote. (*1996 Almanac*, p. 7-3)

This time, however, some lawmakers and outside analysts say the presidential election has overwhelmed the Senate even more than in 1996.

"Ask any historian. This place is more paralyzed than at any time" in its history, Kennedy said. But he laid the blame squarely on the GOP, saying "they have a responsibility to govern."

Naturally, neither side thinks it has anything to do with the political paralysis. Not Kennedy, who blames Republicans for avoiding votes on proposals such as his minimum wage increase. Not Durbin, who sees his new role with the DNC as a natural one to play in an election year. And not the Republicans, who say Democrats are blocking bills and nominations so they can keep issues alive and thereby draw attention to Kerry's campaign themes.

Presidential politics will dominate the Senate "as long as it looks like Kerry has a chance," said Finance Chairman Charles E. Grassley, R-Iowa. "Otherwise, what's going to drive this is whether the Democrats have a chance to take back the Senate."

Dan Danner, a senior vice president at the National Federation of Independent Business, who lobbies Congress

Kerry-McCain Bond Lingers

On March 2, the day of the Super Tuesday primaries, John Kerry made a quick stop on Capitol Hill. The Massachusetts senator had been called back to cast votes on two amendments to a bill (S 1805) that would have limited liability for gun manufacturers and dealers.

Kerry had seen little of his Senate colleagues for weeks as he campaigned for the Democratic nomination. But the moment he set foot on the Senate floor, Kerry made a beeline to a Republican — John McCain of Arizona, recounted Ross K. Baker, a political scientist on leave from Rutgers University, who had been at the Senate that day. The two senators embraced and then chatted for "a good five minutes," Baker said, before Kerry walked across the aisle to greet fellow Democrats.

Since then, Kerry's best political weapon in the Senate has in many ways been McCain, who is probably his closest personal friend there.

Once adversaries representing views at opposing ends of the political spectrum, the pair of Navy combat veterans in Vietnam bonded in 1991, when Kerry became chairman of and McCain joined the Senate's Select Committee on POW-MIA Affairs. Later, Kerry, a reserved liberal, and McCain, a maverick conservative, developed a professional alliance as they worked to normalize diplomatic relations with Vietnam. (*1991 Almanac*, p. 491; *1995 Almanac*, p. 10-18)

They have became fast friends, even spiritual brothers, in the years since.

McCain has pledged his support for the re-election of President Bush — with whom he competed fiercely for the GOP nomination in 2000 — but his alliance with Kerry has at times appeared to belie his words. On several occasions, McCain has either defended Kerry and the Democratic Party or criticized Bush and the Republican Party. And those actions, the Democrats hope, could help send independent-minded vot-

ers — who remain fond of the independent-minded McCain — in Kerry's direction.

"John McCain may not be the most popular Republican in the Senate, but he clearly has a constituency who admires him," Baker said. "He has an appeal to swing voters and, in that sense, something that he says could have an effect on the campaign."

McCain took that gamble on April 1, when he addressed an audience in Washington at a forum hosted by Democratic Rep. Martin T. Meehan of Massachusetts. McCain said his party had "gone astray" and that Bush had failed to adequately prepare the American public for a protracted war in Iraq, according to a report in the Boston Herald.

McCain acknowledged the statements but said they were taken out of context. "I admire the Democratic Party, but I am a committed Republican," he said in an April 21 interview. Still, the comments were portrayed in the press as the latest example of his perceived apostasy.

He put himself in a similar position on March 18, when he defended Kerry's record on national security in back-to-back appearances on network morning news shows — openly undercutting a main line of attack against Kerry advanced by the Bush team. A week before that, in another television interview, he left open the possibility that he would consider an offer to be Kerry's vice presidential running mate.

McCain has since ruled out the prospect and has reiterated his support for Bush. But that has not stopped talk about a Kerry-McCain ticket, and the option of a historic bipartisan pairing has continued to be mentioned by Kerry campaign aides.

"I've been on 10 talk shows in the last two days, and always the same question comes up: 'Will you run for vice president, will you run with Kerry?' " McCain said April 21. "And I say, I am a proud Republican."

for small businesses, says there is more to it. "It's not just the presidential race," he said. "It's the competitive Senate races, and with a 51-49 Senate, that makes things very partisan," especially with the prospect that retirements and lackluster candidate recruiting by Republicans could give the Democrats an outside chance of retaking the Senate.

Still, Danner said, the role of the presidential campaign in the Senate seems to have "started sooner and with much more intensity than it did in the past," and as a result the window for enacting legislation "became much smaller and is closing much sooner than would otherwise be the case."

But so long as the presidential and Senate contests remain close, lawmakers say, no one should be surprised that senators and House members are taking such active roles in the Bush and Kerry campaigns. "It's inevitable," Durbin said. "This town is driven by politics, and this is the World Series of politics."

Frist's Role Draws Scrutiny

It is Frist, however, who has drawn the most attention lately by his political statements and actions.

He raised eyebrows with a floor speech March 30 that accused Kerry of "supporting policies that drive the price of gasoline higher and higher" — remarks that struck some Democrats as little more than a presidential campaign speech in disguise.

That statement came a few days after Frist delivered an uncharacteristically harsh floor speech criticizing former White House counterterrorism adviser Richard A. Clarke, who was also being attacked by the administration for suggesting the president and his advisers did not take terrorism seriously before Sept. 11, 2001. Frist charged that Clarke "told two entirely different stories under oath," and he sought to declassify 2002 testimony Clarke gave to the congressional inquiry on the Sept. 11 attacks.

Frist has become unusually involved in GOP efforts to thwart Daschle's bid for a fourth term this year. Although the two leaders get along well personally, Frist is scheduled to travel to South Dakota to campaign for Daschle's opponent, former Republican Rep. John Thune (1997-2003), breaking a tradition that Senate leaders do not campaign against one another.

The role of the presidential campaign in the Senate seems to have "started sooner and with much more intensity than it did in the past."

— Dan Danner,
National Federation of Independent Business

In addition, Frist's political action committee, Volunteer PAC, has been a conduit for large amounts of individual contributions to Thune's campaign, raising more than $165,000 for Thune between January and March.

Frist has been raising his profile in party politics for several years, long before he became majority leader. In 2000, he was the liaison between Senate Republicans and the Bush campaign. And, as chairman of the National Republican Senatorial Committee in 2002, he had a big hand in the campaign strategies that allowed his party to win back the Senate.

But some Democrats say Frist's actions this time have helped encourage the hyperpolitical atmosphere in the Senate. "The majority leader has taken on a very aggressive role, and he's using the floor for some very aggressive speeches," said Byron L. Dorgan of North Dakota, chairman of the Senate Democratic Policy Committee.

As for campaigning against the other Senate leader, Dorgan said, "it's certainly the first time in a long time that it's been done, and I'm surprised he's doing it."

Frist rejects the idea that he shares responsibility for stoking the partisan fires. The reason presidential politics have taken over the Senate so early this year, he says, is that the Democrats settled on a nominee so early — and their choice was a sitting senator.

"That tends to politicize things earlier, and we're seeing it in the statements that he is making every day," Frist said of Kerry.

Over the long run, Democrats plan to coordinate more tightly between the Kerry campaign and Capitol Hill. For the moment, though, Kerry's Senate aides say they are not trying to coordi-

nate on specific events, such as the overtime press conference.

And while Republican aides say Bush campaign officials have not asked Senate Republicans to make floor statements on the campaign's messages of the week, they predict they will start to get such requests in the fall as the campaign becomes more intense.

Is It Necessary?

Some historians say long-term trends help explain why this year's election activity in Congress is more intense than in past presidential years.

In 1972, when Democratic Sen. George McGovern of South Dakota (1963-81) challenged President Richard M. Nixon's re-election, voting trends in Congress were not as polarized as they are now. That is because conservative Southern Democrats and moderate Republicans acted as balancing influences on both parties, and their ranks have largely disappeared today, according to Allan J. Lichtman, a historian at American University.

Still, not everyone says the political overload this year is worse than in 1996. "The Senate was completely balled up" that spring in a partisan standoff on legislation, said Trent Lott R-Miss., who took over as majority leader when Dole resigned that June to concentrate on his campaign against President Bill Clinton.

"I had to make a decision," Lott recalled. "Were we going to govern and pass legislation, even though Clinton would be the one signing the bills and might take credit for it, or would we just mark time and hold our breaths?"

Lott decided on the first option, and that summer Congress produced not only the minimum wage increase but also the welfare overhaul (PL 104-193) and a law allowing workers to change jobs without losing their eligibility for medical insurance (PL 104-191).

That year, Lott noted, the GOP gained two Senate seats. By contrast, in 2000, "we tried to mark time and avoid the votes and hope that would keep us safe. And we failed. We lost four seats."

If the way Lott tells that story sounds like advice to his successor about how best to work through this year's presidential election politics, it is not an accident. "I've had some thoughts on that, and I've conveyed them to Sen. Frist," Lott said with a grin. "We'll see if he takes them." ◆

Government Institutions

The articles in this section provide insight into the workings of the major institutions of the U.S. government, focusing in turn on Congress (five articles) and the presidency (six articles). President George W. Bush's plan to let private companies compete for as much as half of all federal civilian jobs has outraged government workers and their unions, prompting appeals to Capitol Hill. As the first article focusing on Congress details, Republicans are joining Democrats to deny Bush the money and the authority to implement his privatization plan.

The second article discusses the impact that presidential campaigning had on voting in Congress in 2003. During the first session of the 108th Congress, members participated more than 95 percent of the time in the year's roll call votes; in stark contrast, the six Democrats seeking the presidential nomination had a 51.6 percent participation rate, which affected key legislation.

The third article examines how the national deficit has provoked the most serious split in Republican ranks since Bush took office. GOP fiscal conservatives—dismayed over the shift from surplus to deep deficit—fear that their party has moved away from its long-held principle of small government and budgetary discipline.

The fourth and fifth articles assess Congress's reaction to the prisoner abuse scandal in Iraq. Senate leaders pledged open investigations and bipartisan cooperation, while some members of the House argued that too many facts about the abuses had been made public through open-door hearings.

The six articles in the presidency section examine the strains in the Bush administration's relationship with Congress and Bush's approach to the 2004 elections. As illustrated in the first article, Bush had solid support in Congress for most of 2003, but by the fall, some Republicans had begun to raise concerns about his supplemental spending request for Iraq and Afghanistan, the unemployment rate and the deepening deficit.

As the second article notes, despite these strains, when Bush took a position, lawmakers sided with him in more than 75 percent of their recorded votes in 2003. Although this rate was down almost 10 percentage points from 2002, Bush still had the highest success rate in his third year of any president since Lyndon B. Johnson.

The third article discusses how Bush will use the campaign year to clarify his domestic vision, revealing his plans for an "ownership society" that would give individuals more control over decisions concerning their health and retirement savings.

The fourth article analyzes how Bush used the 2004 State of the Union address not only to catalog his plans for the country, but also to deliver a point-by-point rebuttal of the criticisms of his administration by the Democratic challengers who hoped to gain their party's nomination.

The fifth article returns to the issue of declining support for Bush in the GOP. Some Republicans had begun to display less confidence in Bush's ability to help them—and himself—in the 2004 elections. As Bush's approval ratings dipped in the polls, Republicans in Congress took steps to demonstrate to constituents that they were addressing their concerns about the economy, the deficit and Iraq even if the White House appeared to be complacent.

The final article discusses the importance of the swing vote in the 2004 elections. In the current polarized political climate, many voters define themselves as decidedly for or against President Bush and his policies. With the electorate almost evenly divided, the votes of millions of independents and others without strong party affiliation will likely determine the outcome of the 2004 presidential and congressional races.

Congress Builds a Barrier To Bush Privatization Plan

Republicans join Democrats to thwart president's vision for federal workforce

> *"Morale is at an all-time low about this. They're passionate about their jobs. Every single position in the park would be affected, not just maintenance."*
>
> — Dave Uberuaga, Mount Rainier National Park superintendent

NATIONAL PARK SERVICE

When Harvard MBA George W. Bush took office in 2001, it made perfect sense to start turning over as much of the federal government as possible to private contractors if they could deliver the services more efficiently and for less money.

Shrinking government to its bare essentials is an article of faith for most Republicans, and Bush set about it in a determined, methodical campaign that dwarfed similar efforts by his predecessors. In its first year, the Bush administration identified more than 800,000 federal jobs it considered essentially commercial in nature — almost half of the entire civilian workforce. Last spring, the Office of Management and Budget (OMB), which is in charge of Bush's management agenda, issued new regulations designed to streamline and accelerate the competition between government workers and private companies to provide federal services.

Then the howling began.

From airport control towers in Texas to office cubicles in Foggy Bottom, outraged federal workers and labor unions made it clear what they thought of Bush's plan, and a fusillade of messages of worry and anger rattled the mailboxes of Congress.

Now, in a series of stunning rebukes to the White House over the past month, a number of Republicans have joined Democrats to deny Bush the money or authority to study further job privatization.

In the Senate, conservative Georgia Republican Saxby Chambliss and liberal Massachusetts Democrat Edward M. Kennedy teamed up on a provision in the defense appropriations bill (HR 2658) that would make it more difficult to turn over Defense Department civilian jobs to competitors without going through a lengthy bidding process. Chambliss has several large military bases in his state.

In the Interior spending bill (HR 2691), House Republicans have backed language that would block privatization of Interior Department jobs. The Senate bill includes no outright prohibition, meaning tough conference negotiations on the issue. (*2003 CQ Weekly, p. 2364*)

Also in the House, freshman Democrat Chris Van Hollen of Maryland, whose suburban Washington district is home to thousands of federal workers, successfully sponsored an amendment to the Transportation-Treasury appropriations bill (HR 2989) that would block the administration from implementing the streamlined job competition plan it announced in May. Van Hollen's amendment was adopted 220-198, with the backing of 26 Republicans. (*2003 CQ Weekly, p. 2224*)

One major piece of legislation, a reauthorization of the Federal Aviation Administration (HR 2115 — H Rept 108-240), was stopped in its tracks last month because the conference agreement on the bill would allow the privatization of 69 airport control towers across the country, some of them in busy urban areas. Facing a revolt on the floor, House leaders decided to send the measure back to conference until the issue could be worked out. (*2003 CQ Weekly, p. 2447*)

"The White House is asking us to carry a lot with the war,

the tax cuts," said Rep. Steven C. LaTourette, R-Ohio, who represents the Cleveland area. "It begins to push people like me, from labor-intensive districts, into a corner where you can't support the president."

Bush will very likely win the battle this fall, though perhaps not the campaign. He has threatened to veto the two appropriations bills that would limit or block his privatization program, and GOP leaders probably will remove the provisions before the legislation reaches his desk.

But Congress has forced the administration onto the defensive in one of its major initiatives to overhaul the government, and sent Bush a clear message that he should proceed carefully where federal jobs are at stake.

"There's such a thing as being too aggressive," said Republican Rep. Jack Quinn, who represents Buffalo, N.Y. "There are some things with labor that are core issues." Privatization of public union jobs is one of those core issues, Quinn said.

Going to the Source

President Bush's attempt to reduce the size of government is the most ambitious since President Ronald Reagan, in his 1981 inaugural address, declared that government was not the solution, but the problem.

But while Reagan's efforts were dramatic, such as when he fired 12,000 striking air traffic controllers in his first year in office, the Bush administration's campaign is more organized and painstaking — examining every function of the federal government, from forecasting weather at airports to mowing lawns at military hospitals, to see whether it could be done better by private companies.

"It's much more aggressive in the Bush administration," said George Nesterczuk, a visiting fellow at the conservative Heritage Foundation who served in the Office of Personnel Management and the U.S. Information Agency in the Reagan administration. "But the most difficult part of outsourcing is the political pressure of members trying to save federal jobs in their district."

The overhaul of the competitive bidding process, proposed by the administration this past spring, comes after a decade in which the federal workforce has shrunk by more than 400,000 civilian jobs. That decline, credited to the Clinton administration's "reinventing government" program, came mostly at the expense of Defense Department civilian jobs following the end of the Cold War.

The Bush administration's effort is different. It is aimed at changing the definition of what is "inherently governmental" and what is "commercial." Under the new definition proposed by Bush, almost half of all federal civilian jobs could be deemed commercial and open to "competitive sourcing."

In essentially every civilian agency, from Agriculture to Energy to Veterans Affairs, managers are being told to look at their structure and figure out which divisions should face competition from private contractors.

"Virtually none of these jobs [has] ever undergone the pressure of competition," said Angela B. Styles, former administrator of the Office of Federal Procurement Policy, the division of OMB directing the administration's effort in this area. "I think we're at a turning point. People know we're serious."

Styles left the administration to return to a private law practice in mid-September, but she did not stray far from the privatization fight. Her law firm, Miller and Chevalier, specializes in helping contractors bid for government jobs.

Jobs Ticketed for Competition

The Defense Department might privatize more than a quarter-million jobs. A sample of federal positions in all agencies that would commonly be selected for private competition under the Bush administration plan:

- Administrative support
- Information technology services
- Human resources services
- Facility operation and maintenance
- Equipment operators
- Road maintenance
- Construction
- Vehicle maintenance
- Telecommunications services
- Mailroom operations

DOD PHOTO / TECH. SGT. ANDY DUNAWAY

This push for more outsourcing of federal services and jobs is endearing Bush to Republicans who have a fundamental distrust of the bureaucracy, while putting him at odds with the powerful federal employee unions and members of Congress who vociferously protect their turf when it comes to federal jobs or programs in their districts.

"This is a way to hit public-sector unions, hit programs they don't like and outsource them," said John Threlkeld, lobbyist for the American Federation of Government Employees, the largest federal employee union with 600,000 members. "I think the agenda has accelerated dramatically. Bush is taking it to a new level. It's going to be devastating to the federal workforce."

The ultimate goal for this process, if Bush has his way, is a federal workforce that performs only duties that are inherently governmental — meaning to make policy if it is a federal agency, fly planes if it is the Air Force or protect the homeland if it is Homeland Security.

The intransigence of the bureaucracy and members of Congress with local concerns comes as no surprise to members of the administration.

"When you're trying to embrace fundamental management change, this is to be expected," said OMB spokesman Trent Duffy. "These are the toughest challenges in the [president's] management agenda."

Staying In House

The tool that the White House is using for its privatization campaign is an OMB regulation called Circular A-76. First issued in 1966 and revised several times since, the rule's purpose is to guide government commercial activities, helping managers decide whether to contract for goods and services from private companies, perform the services with their own agencies or contract with other government agencies. (*Circular A-76, p. 2491*)

From fiscal 1997 to 2001, Defense Department employees won 60 percent of the bids under the A-76 process, keeping the work in house, according to the Commercial Activities Panel, a group created by Congress in the fiscal 2001 Defense

Authorization Act (PL 106-398). (*2000 Almanac, p. 8-3*)

For example, a National Institutes of Health division of 677 workers that provides support work for the agency's huge grants program recently won a public-private competition, keeping the jobs from being turned over to contractors.

In-house bargaining units have won jobs competitions by producing documents that prove they are a "most efficient organization."

One example of this was at the Offutt Air Force Base in Nebraska in 2002. Faced with a public-private competition, the civilian support staff cut personnel costs by more than 50 percent and reduced jet engine overhaul times from an average of 68 days to 28 days, saving $46 million, according to an OMB report in September on competitive sourcing.

Several government agencies that have faced competition have fought back. Take, for example, the Veterans Affairs Canteen Service.

Veterans from at least four foreign wars can walk into the Veterans Affairs Canteen in places such as Iron Mountain, Mich., and get a $4.25 haircut, a $29 pair of Dockers and a portable Sony CD player for $52, all below market price.

The small operation in Michigan's Upper Peninsula is one of 172 shops in a network of all-purpose stores run by the Department of Veterans Affairs. The stores are operated by the agency and run mostly by unionized federal workers. Customers pay no taxes on their purchases, and the prices run as much as 20 percent less than a J.C. Penney or Target store. The VA Canteen service also runs food courts nationwide, many of which are affiliated with veterans' hospitals.

The unsubsidized network of VA stores has been in business for 57 years, growing into a $250 million a year operation.

This year, Bush's fiscal 2004 budget request put the VA Canteens on the chopping block, but the VA decided in July to suspend public-private competitions in several areas.

James B. Donahoe, who directs the VA Canteen Service from its headquarters in St. Louis, proudly points out that his agency is a break-even operation, not taking any direct appropriation. But selling televisions and khakis is not seen by OMB as an inher-

Where Competition for Jobs Would Have a Major Impact

Percentage of Workforce

Government agencies that could have the largest and smallest percentages of their total workforces available for private competition:

Largest percentage

- Small Business Administration — 69%
- Education — 62%
- Corps of Engineers — 59%
- Defense — 45%
- Housing and Urban Development — 39%

Smallest percentage

- Smithsonian — 0%
- EPA — 2%
- Justice — 3%
- Veterans Affairs — 3%
- Social Security — 6%

Agency-by-Agency Look at Jobs Competition

According to provisions in the 2001 President's Management Agenda, nearly 435,000 civilian government jobs could be placed in competition for outsourcing to private companies. Following is an Office of Management and Budget estimate of jobs available for competition by agency:

AGENCY	TOTAL EMPLOYEES	AVAILABLE FOR COMPETITION	PERCENTAGE OF WORKFORCE
Agriculture	98,500	35,600	36%
Commerce	26,500	4,800	18%
Defense	596,600	270,600	45%
Education	4,700	2,900	62%
Energy	15,100	4,700	31%
EPA	17,400	400	2%
HHS	64,900	11,200	17%
HUD	9,200	3,600	39%
Interior	70,200	23,000	33%
Justice	132,100	3,400	3%
Labor	16,400	2,600	16%
State	10,400	1,000	10%
Transportation	64,600	11,900	18%
Treasury	148,100	18,400	12%
Veterans Affairs	221,500	7,600	3%
AID	2,000	300	15%
Corps of Engineers	27,900	16,500	59%
GSA	14,100	5,200	37%
NASA	19,000	3,400	18%
NSF	1,200	200	17%
OPM	3,000	600	20%
SBA	4,200	2,900	69%
Smithsonian	4,500	0	0%
Social Security	63,900	4,000	6%
	1,636,000	434,800	27%

CQ GRAPHIC / MARILYN GATES-DAVIS

Privatizing vs. Jobs Protection

While Congress has moved on several fronts to limit or block President Bush's campaign to privatize government jobs, some lawmakers have focused on preserving individual jobs close to home.

During debate on its fiscal 2004 Interior spending bill (HR 2691) in July, the House accepted an amendment by Rep. Doug Bereuter, R-Neb., that would protect from privatization — at least for now — the federal workers at two archaeological centers, one in Lincoln, Neb., and the other in Tallahassee, Fla., the district represented by Democrat Allen Boyd.

The 12 employees of the Midwest Archaeological Center have done forensic research at the battle site of Little Big Horn, worked to preserve long-abandoned copper mines and investigated Great Lakes shipwrecks.

Like many members of Congress, Bereuter said he has no problem with federal employees competing with private industry to keep their jobs, but he said the archaeological jobs are unique and should remain in government hands.

"The center has developed an excellent reputation," Bereuter said on the House floor. "I am rather certain that the persons in [the Office of Management and Budget] . . . were not fully aware of the center's mission and history."

Don Young, R-Alaska, chairman of the House Transportation and Infrastructure Committee, feels similarly protective of his state. He put language in the aviation bill conference report (HR 2115 — H Rept 108-240) removing airports in Anchorage and Juneau from a list of control towers eligible for privatization.

A spokesman for Young said it was the "unique conditions to Alaska aviation" that made such an exemption necessary.

mile park that straddles the North Carolina-Tennessee border, according to park spokesman Bob Miller.

"We want to give the public the best bang for its buck," Miller said. "But I don't know if there's a private firm that could compete."

Across the country at Mount Rainier National Park in Washington State, maintenance workers also may face a jobs competition in the coming years. The problem, park superintendent Dave Uberuaga said, is that it is almost impossible to quantify in a contract that your maintenance people not only need to be able to patch roads and remove fallen trees, but that they may also be pressed into fighting wildfires or rescuing lost campers in the treacherous back country of the 235,000-acre park.

"Morale is at an all-time low about this," said Uberuaga. "They're passionate about their jobs. Their concern has taken [away] from their enthusiasm to serve the public. Every single position in the park would be affected, not just maintenance."

GOP Rep. Charles H. Taylor, whose western North Carolina district includes a big chunk of the Smokies, is trying to save such park jobs from facing competition.

Taylor, chairman of the House Interior Appropriations Subcommittee, backed the provision that would block privatization of Interior Department jobs. The Senate has a softer provision, which would require only annual reports on outsourcing. The anti-privatization language has drawn a veto threat from Bush.

ently governmental operation.

"We are the poster boy" for outsourcing, Donahoe said. "We operate at break-even prices, and if you change to market pricing [with contractors], some of our veterans won't be able to eat. They only way they will make a profit is to raise prices, and that'll hurt the veterans."

The administration in May proposed an overhaul of A-76, issuing guidelines that may open as many as 425,000 jobs, of the more than 800,000 designated commercial in nature, to competition. The administration also wants to streamline the A-76 process, forcing the competitions to be completed and awarded within 12 months, instead of the two to three years it often takes under the current system.

Though private contractors applauded the changes, saying they would make for more even competition, federal employee unions say the new rules put their members at a disadvantage.

"This is the top issue in the minds of federal employees," Van Hollen said. "They are very nervous that this is driven by an ideological agenda.

They're not afraid of competition, they just want a level playing field."

While the Pentagon has for decades been trying to outsource more and more of its non-military functions, ranging from building complex software to digging latrines, the civilian federal workforce has never faced an A-76 mandate as broad as the one being pushed by the Bush administration.

"We're not just trying to reduce the size of government or get rid of people," Styles said. "We want to open the government to competition. We want to use competition as a tool for better management."

Defining Terms

There is a strong belief among federal employees, however, that some functions should remain under the federal government.

Deep in the Great Smoky Mountains, maintenance workers of the U.S. Park Service do not just paint cabins and fix toilets, functions that could easily be contracted out. They also help build trails and pitch in on search-and-rescue missions in the 815-square

Congressional Divisions

In general, the government reform agenda has divided Congress along party lines. Republicans such as Rep. Pete Sessions of Texas are among the most outspoken proponents of limiting the government to functions that are inherently governmental while letting private contractors do everything else, whether it is mowing the lawn at a Social Security field office or integrating agency computer systems.

"Government employees often do not have the tools, the training, the direction or the focus to do their jobs effectively," Sessions said. "The government has an obligation to perform inherently governmental duties. Government has a lack of desire to achieve efficiency, and we're after every single manager in government to take care of their core mission."

On the other side of the table are members such as Rep. Albert R. Wynn, a pro-labor Democrat who represents thousands of federal employees in his suburban Maryland district.

"They want to outsource half the federal workforce based on the assumption that outsourcing is cheaper," said Wynn, who has in the past introduced legislation that would slow down the A-76 process. "There's no evidence that [assumption] is true. We're not only concerned about people losing their jobs, but losing their jobs unfairly."

However, this partisan split over the role of government becomes more nuanced when it comes to the nitty-gritty details of legislation, as evidenced in Republican support for blocking privatization in the Interior, Defense and FAA bills.

Some members of Congress, especially Republicans who represent large numbers of government workers, feel caught in the middle.

GOP Rep. Thomas M. Davis III, who is chairman of the House Government Reform Committee and represents a northern Virginia district with thousands of federal employees and some of the biggest government contractors, says that whatever course he takes on the A-76 issue, he is going to make someone angry.

"I'm not driven by a desire to outsource more," Davis said in an interview. "What I care about is whether it's a good value for my tax money."

He is trying to take a middle path, but that is difficult.

"I don't like quotas," Davis said. "We try not to frame it as contractors vs. [government] employees, but more about what is best for the government."

A Private Government?

One of the startling facts that came out of the investigation of the space shuttle *Columbia* disaster was that $9 of every $10 appropriated for the shuttle goes to private contractors.

That made some critics wonder whether there was enough accountability when the life-or-death decisions of the U.S. space program are being left in the hands of contractors. Even if federal services are contracted out, someone must be on hand to make sure the work is performed and goods are supplied as agreed. The Defense Department, for instance, spends millions each year monitoring

all of its private contractors.

The question of whether sensitive security and safety functions should be performed by government employees or contractors has also been raised within the Federal Aviation Administration.

The reauthorization of the FAA has been stalled, with the conference report expected to be sent back to committee the week of Oct. 13 over a dispute about whether to outsource some air traffic control jobs.

The bill has language that would prohibit further privatization until Oct. 1, 2007, except for 69 airports on a list compiled by the Transportation Department inspector general in 2000. The list actually has 71 airports as potential choices for privatization, but the chairman of the House Transportation and Infrastructure Committee, Don Young, R-Alaska, included language in the FAA bill conference report that would exempt two airports in his home state. (*Saving local jobs*, p. 55)

The government now contracts out air traffic control at 219 small airports across the country, and the administration has declared air traffic control a commercial rather than inherently governmental function, meaning that the FAA can privatize the jobs at its discretion.

Republicans and Democrats on the Transportation committees were concerned about outsourcing jobs involving aviation security and safety, and conferees may produce another version of the bill that blocks privatization or drops the language altogether.

Cloudy Weather

Some FAA workers, meanwhile, are already involved in a jobs competition. The National Association of Air Traffic Specialists, which represents FAA workers who issue pilot weather reports, conduct search-and-rescue missions and enforce flight restrictions nationwide, is bidding against giants like Raytheon and Boeing to save its 2,500 jobs across the country.

"They're determined that we are commercial," said Wally Pike, president of the union. "This is by far the most threatening thing we've faced. They [Bush administration officials] have been more successful in privatizing the federal workforce than any other administration."

These jobs, however, are not necessarily in jeopardy with this public-private competition. Indeed, the internal

bargaining unit of federal employees often ends up submitting a lower-cost, more efficient bid to keep the work federalized.

The Pentagon is by far the biggest outsourcing agency in the federal government, but Chambliss and Kennedy, in the defense appropriations bill, decided to tighten the reins on efforts to hasten bids for smaller bargaining units within the government.

The two senators teamed up on an amendment that would force the Department of Defense to allow in-house Pentagon employees to prove that they could be more efficient than a contractor when it came to job competitions. The language also would force contractors to prove they could save 10 percent — or $10 million, whichever is less — compared with the cost of keeping the job with federal employees.

Chambliss echoed the concerns of many in the bureaucracy in saying that he believes Bush's proposed changes to the A-76 process are unfair because they would not give government workers a chance to prove they would cost less than a contractor. Also, government employee benefits, when counted in the overall cost of the bid, often inflate the in-house workers' bids compared with contractor costs.

"I support competition, but A-76 is not a level playing field," said Chambliss. Asked if he was worried about being a freshman senator bucking a major White House initiative, Chambliss said, "I've got to do what I think is right."

Contractors have often been just as critical of the A-76 process as government employees, at least until the rules were changed in May. They have complained that job competitions take too long — sometimes as long as three years — and they have criticized the rules as outdated, especially when it comes to bids that involve cutting-edge technologies. A software contractor who is used to business decisions being made in real time, for example, may find a two-year-long bidding process to be inefficient and unprofitable, and in the end the technology could be obsolete by the time it was deployed.

Even though they plunge enormous resources into winning contracts that displace government workers, the companies hate to see the equation as contractors vs. federal employees.

"It's not an outsourcing agenda it's a

A-76 Defines Government

Ever since George Washington commissioned French architect Pierre L'Enfant to design an urban landscape that would transform a swampy backwater into the Capital of the new nation, government leaders have relied on the private sector to perform services.

The current rule regulating government outsourcing is Circular A-76, one of more than a hundred sets of instructions that the Office of Management and Budget has issued to federal departments over the years on such matters as financial management and the rental and construction of government quarters.

Known simply as "A-76" within the bureaucracy, it was first issued in 1966 and has served as the guideline for what work should be bid out to private companies and what work should remain within the ranks of federal workers.

Detailed Regulations

The regulations, which have been revised several times and supplemented with thick books of instruction for each department, form the basis for whether Forest Service workers in New Mexico should keep their jobs and whether fixing Air Force jet engines in Nebraska is a job that should be done by a business or military employees.

The Bush administration's proposed revisions to A-76 have become the most controversial part of his presidential management agenda. The difference between the Bush version of A-76 and previous revisions of the regulation is that Bush's definition of jobs that are "inherently governmental" is more limited.

For example, national defense, intelligence and some research functions remain inherently governmental, which means those duties would never be turned over to a private firm. However, almost anything else government employees do could be considered a "commercial activity" and be contracted out.

The proposed revisions would require that A-76 public-private competitions be completed within 12 months, instead of the more typical two- to three-year time frame now. And even if an in-house government unit wins a competition, those same employees might face another A-76 review within five years.

The proposed revisions, while potentially opening up more jobs to competition, would also require performance standards not only for government contractors but also the federal employees who win the jobs.

force."

Mark Jaffe, a union member and air traffic specialist at Fort Worth Meacham International Airport in Texas, says that an ongoing competitive bidding process for his unit's services has had a negative impact on employee morale. Jaffe and his co-workers make between $60,000 and $75,000 a year providing weather reports for pilots and informing them about flight restrictions.

"The workers are in a state of limbo," said Jaffe, whose FAA unit also does search-and-rescue missions. "They don't know if they'll have a job in 18 months. Bush has tasked this administration with contracting out so many jobs, and the FAA picked us. . . . They're doing this on the backs of 2,500 people."

As chairman of the Government Reform Committee, Tom Davis says that Congress and the administration need to get beyond the ideological divisions over privatizing government functions and focus on reforming the process. Davis says the federal government should spend more on employee training, so federal workers will have the expertise to compete with the innovations of the private sector.

"We have failed to let people learn to perform the jobs to keep them in-house," Davis said. "That's why we need civil service reform."

Others are worried that too much outsourcing will demoralize the federal workforce.

"We ought to be ensuring the work force that we need them," said Del. Eleanor Holmes Norton, D-D.C., who sits on House Government Reform. "We're going to be left behind with an inexperienced workforce."

There also is evidence that the federal workforce will contract all by itself in the decade ahead, and perhaps more dramatically than the administration would like. Nearly 50 percent of senior federal workers will be eligible to retire in the next four to five years, and the loss of so many experienced personnel is creating what many are calling a "human capital crisis" within the government.

If the projections hold true, decades of institutional knowledge will be lost in the coming years, presenting the administration with the need to hire rather than outsource federal employees.

Younger members of Generation X have not been flocking to the federal government as a career the way the Baby Boomers did during the past 40 years. ◆

competition agenda," said Stan Soloway, president of the Professional Services Council, a business group that represents major government contractors such as Booz Allen Hamilton Inc. and Northrop Grumman Corp. "Clearly this administration has put an unprecedented emphasis on competition across the entire federal government. There's ample evidence that competition drives efficiency and keeps costs down."

War of Many Battles

Circular A-76, in fact, is just one part of the administration's effort to gain more management control and flexibility over federal personnel, an effort that has clashed with employee unions.

The most notable run-in was over the Homeland Security Act (PL 107-296) in 2002. Bush requested, and won, more authority to hire and fire employees and set aside union rights if it is necessary for national security purposes. Unions saw this as the wedge issue that put federal employees at odds with the administration. (*2002 Almanac, p. 7-3*)

The latest revisions to the A-76 process were a wake-up call for unions, the clearest sign that their power is being challenged.

"This has taken up a lot of our time," said Matthew Biggs, spokesman for the International Federation of Professional and Technical Engineers, which represents 40,000 federal engineers and other technical workers. "This has been an aggressive attack on the federal work-

Voting on the Run

Presidential candidates' low participation scores have affected key legislation

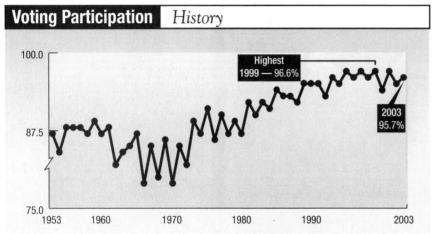

Voting Participation *History*

Highest
1999 — 96.6%

2003
95.7%

	RECORDED VOTES	PARTICIPATION RATE
2003 Data		
Senate	459	96.1%
House	675	95.6%
Total	1,134	95.7%

As John Kerry was preparing to fly to Des Moines to unveil his health care platform on May 15, his well-laid plans for furthering his presidential candidacy were suddenly complicated by his day job representing Massachusetts in the United States Senate. The Republican leadership had chosen that day for the climactic votes on President Bush's second major tax cut — sure to be among the defining issues of the 2004 campaign.

So, like the other five members of Congress then seeking the Democratic presidential nomination, Kerry scrambled his campaign schedule and was on hand to vote against the bill that ultimately became last year's $330 billion, 11-year tax cut (PL 108-27). (*2003 CQ Weekly, p. 3133*)

Such a decision was very nearly the exception rather than the rule during the year for those presidential aspirants. On average the six of them participated in just 51.6 percent of the year's roll call votes; taken as a group, they missed more than 1,500.

In contrast, members of the 108th Congress as a whole participated — meaning they cast "yea" or "nay" votes — a collective 95.7 percent of the time in the first session. That is a typical average for the past decade, which has seen the highest voting participation in the 50 years that Congressional Quarterly has been calculating the statistic. The

highest, 96.6 percent, was in 1999.

The would-be presidents say they set aside their fundraising and flesh-pressing in Iowa, New Hampshire and elsewhere for the year's most important and hotly contested votes — especially when their presence or absence would make a difference in the outcome, or when the vote was on an issue particularly dear to the lawmaker's political heart.

"He has been present for critical votes when his vote would have made a difference," spokesman Casey Aden-Wansbury said of Sen. Joseph I. Lieberman of Connecticut, for example.

Lieberman made a point of returning from the campaign trail Oct. 23, for example, to vote for a Democratic amendment that would have blocked Bush from transferring some federal government jobs to private contractors — an idea that organized labor is vigorously opposing, with the backing of all the Democratic presidential candidates. But two of Lieberman's rivals, Kerry and John Edwards of North Carolina, missed the roll call — and the amendment was rejected by a single vote, 47-48. (*2003 CQ Weekly, p. 2642*)

On the House side, the absence of a presidential candidate similarly appeared to determine defeat for the Democratic position in at least one instance. Richard A. Gephardt of Missouri and just one other lawmaker, fellow Democrat Ed Pastor of Arizona, were missing when the House voted, 217-216, on July 25 to pass an overhaul of the Head Start early-

childhood education program (HR 2210). Had either been present and joined all the other Democrats in opposition, the measure could have died on a tie ballot. (*2003 CQ Weekly, p. 3114*)

Candidates' Score Low

Gephardt's voting participation score — he voted "yea" or "nay" in just 9 percent of the roll calls — is the lowest recorded by CQ in at least the past 20 years for a healthy member of Congress who was in office throughout the year. A spokeswoman, Adella Jones, said Gephardt "has done his best to make substantive votes" in the past year. When he last ran for president 16 years ago, he voted in 18 percent of House roll calls. (*1987 Almanac, p. 48-C*)

Kerry had the lowest score among senators running for president: 36 percent. Lieberman's score was 46 percent and Edwards voted "yea" or "nay" 61 percent of the time. Bob Graham of Florida, who dropped out of the presidential race in October, voted in 68 percent of the year's 459 Senate roll calls.

By far the highest voting participation score among the presidential candidates belonged to Dennis J. Kucinich: 91 percent.

But Kucinich is unique among the contenders: His candidacy faces sufficiently long odds that he is preparing to seek a fifth term representing Cleveland in the House, making him the only presidential candidate also running for Congress this fall.

Gephardt and Edwards have staked their electoral futures on the presidency and are relinquishing their congressional seats this year, while Kerry and Lieberman are not up for re-election to the Senate in 2004, so none of them face any immediate parochial political heat for their absenteeism.

It has been an article of faith among political strategists in recent years that missing too many votes makes a lawmaker vulnerable to defeat. But it remains rare to find a concrete case when low participation, by itself, has been a central reason for the end of a congressional career. "It doesn't matter as much," said Thad Beyle, a political science professor at the University of North Carolina at Chapel Hill. "If you have somebody who's just not performing well, it could be used in a campaign . . . but it might not matter."

At the same time, there are several examples of lawmakers with comparatively poor scores who won with relative ease the year after. In three decades as Alaska's only House member, Republican Don Young has participated in fewer than 90 percent of the roll calls 19 times — including an 87.1 percent score in 2003, when the House average was 95.6 percent. The Alaska media have criticized him for his habitually low attendance, and so have his political opponents. But Young, who bristles when confronted on the subject, has won his last three elections with more than 60 percent of the vote.

"It's not something that comes to the forefront in an election," said Sarah Binder, a congressional expert and senior fellow at the Brookings Institution. "Unless a challenger makes a big deal out of it, it's not going to be an issue."

And almost without exception, the aggregate voting participation rate of Congress is lower in election years — and the roster of people with perfect scores is smaller. The past two years is an exception in the second instance: 27 lawmakers voted "yea" or "nay" on every roll call in 2002; in 2003, only 15 did so. (*Top scorers, this page*)

Among those who slipped off the list was Republican Fred Upton of Michigan. He was working on the longest active voting participation streak of anyone in the House, casting 3,587 roll call votes between the middle of 1997 and last Oct. 6 — when he left with a congressional delegation for Iraq and missed eight recorded votes.

While no one is close to reaching the

Leading Scorers: Voting Participation

The following six senators and nine House members were the only lawmakers who cast "yea" or "nay" votes on every roll call ballot conducted in 2003:

HOUSE REPUBLICANS
Tom Latham of Iowa
Frank A. LoBiondo of New Jersey
Jon Porter of Nevada
Denny Rehberg of Montana

HOUSE DEMOCRATS
Dale E. Kildee of Michigan
Jim Matheson of Utah
Nick J. Rahall II of West Virginia
Tim Ryan of Ohio
Tom Udall of New Mexico

SENATE REPUBLICANS
Susan Collins of Maine
Charles E. Grassley of Iowa
Olympia J. Snowe of Maine

SENATE DEMOCRATS
Daniel K. Akaka of Hawaii
Russell D. Feingold of Wisconsin
Carl Levin of Michigan

legendary streak of 18,401 consecutive yea-or-nay votes that Democrat William H. Natcher of Kentucky cast between 1953 and the month before he died in 1994, several members take pride in their perfect scores and have particular reasons for keeping their streaks alive.

Sens. Susan Collins and Olympia J. Snowe have had 100 percent participation scores in each of the past two years — a pattern that some Maine voters have come to expect because of Margaret Chase Smith (1949-73), the other Republican woman the state elected to the Senate. She "went for years without missing a vote," said Collins. "I continue to be inspired by her example."

However, some members with 100 percent scores in 2003 said they would not slavishly attend to that streak if some other matter — such as a particular problem back home — were to conflict with the balloting on second-tier legislation or a procedural question.

"It's no big deal if I miss a vote. There'd be a good reason, though," said Tom Latham, R-Iowa, who participated in every 2003 House vote. "Someone who's only striving for a streak may end up missing work that is more important."

Democrat Tim Ryan of Ohio posted a 100 percent score in his freshman year in the House, but he suggested that the streak would not last forever because "there are so many votes and so many aspects of the job and so many meetings taking place at the same time."

Academics and political strategists say there have been several reasons why the overall voting participating score has routinely been near or above 95 percent since the late 1980s, after climbing steadily above 90 percent only as that decade began. The potential for a law-

maker to hand an opponent an issue by missing too many votes is one. Another is the convenience and efficiency of modern transportation, with flights often arriving just in time for members to make an evening roll call.

And for several years now congressional leaders, of both parties and on both sides of the Capitol, have been arranging votes at times designed to maximize turnout — not only to inconvenience the fewest lawmakers but also to assist the majority whips in mustering the votes they need to advance legislation through closely divided chambers. Roll calls only on Tuesdays, Wednesdays and Thursdays have become the standard schedule.

Still, a spate of rank-and-file absences made the job sufficiently difficult for House GOP leaders on a series of bills this summer that they told their colleagues to improve their attendance records — or face potential reprisals. House Majority Whip Roy Blunt, R-Mo., told a closed-door caucus in September that when too many members were absent he often had to resort to leaning on GOP lawmakers to cast votes contrary to their positions or difficult to defend back home.

Ernie Fletcher, for example, was persuaded at one point to reverse course and vote to create a federally funded private-school voucher program in Washington, D.C. — a potential problem for his campaign for governor of Kentucky. He won despite that vote and a 69 percent voting participation score that was the lowest of any House Republican other than the Speaker, J. Dennis Hastert of Illinois, who by custom refrains from most votes. ◆

The GOP's Internal Divide

Conservatives dismayed with return to red ink are taking on their own party

When Congress last year took up the largest expansion of Medicare since its inception in 1965, fiscal conservatives in the Republican Party were seeing red.

"I came to Washington to reform Great Society programs, not to ratify and enlarge them," said freshman Rep. Tom Feeney of Florida. Despite a personal call from President Bush, Feeney voted no.

The truth is, the precise size of the new Medicare law — $400 billion over 10 years — had been decided months earlier, in the fiscal 2004 budget resolution (H Con Res 95). Feeney and other fiscal conservatives even voted for it.

But the Medicare bill became an emblem for budget hawks because it so exactly captured their biggest fear: that the Republican Party has slipped away from its long-held principle of small government and budgetary discipline, and has succumbed to the spending temptations that come with being the party in power.

"Republicans used to believe in fiscal responsibility, limited international entanglements and limited government. We have lost our way," Sen. Chuck Hagel of Nebraska wrote in the Omaha World-Herald in November.

CQ Weekly Jan. 17, 2004

"We have come loose from our moorings. The Medicare reform bill is a good example of our lack of direction, purpose and responsibility."

That the party can no longer claim the mantle of fiscal restraint is especially grating for the movement Republicans who took office in the House sweep of 1994 and who with Newt Gingrich, R-Ga. (1979-99), designed the "Contract With America," which included a constitutional amendment requiring a balanced budget. (*1994 Almanac, p. 22*)

It has also provided Democrats, long labeled by Republicans as "tax and spend liberals," with an opening, rhetorically at least, on fiscal matters. Former Gov. Howard Dean of Vermont, a Democratic frontrunner for president, has promised a balanced budget if he is elected.

"An economic policy built on reckless deficits and irresponsible tax cuts has brought two consecutive years of job loss for the first time in over half a century," Dean said Jan. 9 in response to the release of employment figures. On the campaign trail, he often points to his experience in balancing Vermont's budget.

Whether the deficit matters politically in this election year remains to be seen. There is usually a greater political price to be paid for attempts to balance the budget than for worsening the deficit. (*Political consequences, p. 61*)

But the two parties' role reversal on this issue is significant because it goes directly to the heart of how each side defines itself and what it stands for.

It has also provoked the most serious split in Republican ranks since Bush took office, with hard-core fiscal conservatives expressing strong dismay over the shift from surplus to deep deficit and congressional leaders and the president justifying the red ink as the result of the country's necessary responses to terrorism and the sluggish economy.

An Intraparty Battle

That split has already manifested itself politically. In the Pennsylvania Republican primary, where conservative Rep. Patrick J. Toomey is taking on Sen. Arlen Specter, who is more moderate, the two are sparring on this very issue.

The conservative Club for Growth, which ardently lobbied against the Medicare measure (PL 108-173), recently drafted a radio ad targeting Specter for supporting the legislation. The well-financed anti-tax, small-government group is backing Toomey, who was one of 25 Republicans who vot-

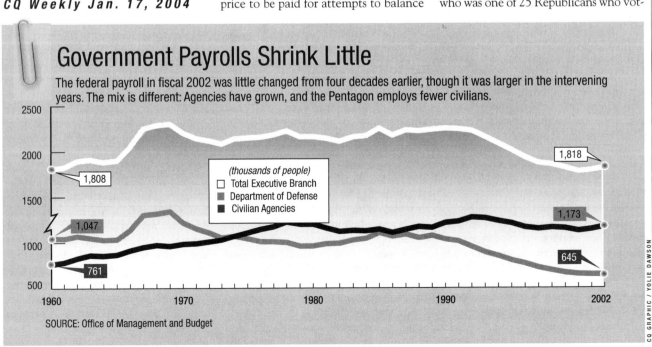

Government Payrolls Shrink Little

The federal payroll in fiscal 2002 was little changed from four decades earlier, though it was larger in the intervening years. The mix is different: Agencies have grown, and the Pentagon employs fewer civilians.

(thousands of people)
- ☐ Total Executive Branch
- ▨ Department of Defense
- ■ Civilian Agencies

1,808 — 1,818
1,047 — 1,173
761 — 645

1960   1970   1980   1990   2002

SOURCE: Office of Management and Budget

CQ GRAPHIC / YOLIE DAWSON

Fix the Deficit, Pay the Price

In fickle political and economic times, a sour economy can cost a leader his job. But what about a deepening sea of red ink? Recent history shows that trying to erase the deficit, rather than running one up, is more likely to hurt political careers.

Just ask former Vice President Walter F. Mondale, who was the 1984 Democratic presidential nominee. He got hammered for promising to reduce the Reagan-era budget deficit by two-thirds. "Let's tell the truth . . . Mr. Reagan will raise taxes, and so will I. He won't tell you. I just did." Mondale lost the election.

President George Bush broke his "no new taxes pledge" in an effort to start fixing the budget, only to lose re-election in 1992 to Bill Clinton. The election year was marked by a bad economy and the third-party candidacy of H. Ross Perot, who made "deficit" a household word.

Perot even drew millions of television viewers to his 30-minute campaign ads featuring pie charts and other graphics illustrating the danger of the deficit. When his lack of political experience was questioned during one debate, Perot confessed: "Well, they've got a point. I don't have any experience in running up a $4 trillion debt." The audience roared.

In 1994, House Democrats, after a 40-year reign, lost control of the chamber after passing, without a single Republican vote, Clinton's deficit reduction plan (PL 103-66) that included tax hikes. But Clinton defied the trend and was re-elected in 1996.

Too Abstract an Issue

This year, Republicans are counting on voters to pay little attention to the rising deficit, or at least on voters agreeing that the increased spending was needed to fight terrorism and pass tax cuts to boost the economy.

When voters are asked what is more important — creating jobs or reducing the deficit — the answer is overwhelmingly in favor of jobs, said GOP pollster David Winston. "The deficit is an abstract. The jobs are something that are real." The deficit matters only when it is seen as an impediment to growth, Winston added.

It is a view that troubled former Treasury Secretary Paul O'Neill, according to the recently published book, "The Price of Loyalty: George W. Bush, the White House and the Education of Paul O'Neill," by Ron Suskind.

According to Suskind, O'Neill recalled how the tax cut had caused a split in the Bush economic team. When he argued in November 2002 that the deficits hurt the economy, Vice President Dick Cheney cut him off and said, "Reagan proved deficits don't matter."

O'Neill was soon fired.

ed against the bill.

As Stephen Moore, the group's president, was reviewing the hard-hitting ad copy attacking Specter for his yes vote, he learned that another organization, the centrist Republican Main Street Partnership, had already launched its own radio spot criticizing Toomey for opposing the bill.

"It shows the condition our party is in, that you would actually have a Republican group trumpeting this bill," Moore said. "You have two parties in Washington now that are for bigger government."

Republicans who voted for the new law say it is a good start toward overhauling the program because it introduces private competition into the Medicare system. Conversely, Democrats who supported it also see it as a first step — toward an even greater expansion of the program. That means coming fights over Medicare will turn into the same crucible as the last one. And with Medicare as well as other social programs, smaller-government advocates can be expected to use the record budget deficit as a tool to fend off proposed program

expansions and even demand cuts.

"You will see a renewal of focus on waste, fraud and abuse," said Rep. Mike Pence, a second-term Indiana Republican who often stakes out positions to the right of his leadership. "It may be one of the positive consequences of the Medicare vote. A lot of conservatives who voted for the bill now have something to prove" about their commitment to smaller government, he said.

Unavoidable Costs

Bush and GOP congressional leaders argue that most of the increased spending on their watch has been an unavoidable response to the 2001 terrorist attacks and Iraq war. The tax cuts, they say, fired up a slow economy. Most conservative Republicans backed both the tax cuts and the defense and homeland security spending increases. Moore's group used television advertising last spring to attack two moderate Republican senators who insisted on a smaller tax cut than Bush proposed.

Democrats and fiscal conservatives, mindful of public sentiment on homeland defense and national security, have

focused on the tax cuts.

The nonpartisan Concord Coalition, which advocates a balanced budget, concluded in September that tax cuts had by then accounted for more than one-third of the deterioration of the federal balance sheet since 2001, while defense and homeland security-related spending increases were responsible for one-fifth of the shift from budget surpluses to budget deficits. The Medicare law and revenue losses resulting from the recession were other significant factors, the coalition reported.

At its core, the debate becomes an ideological one, with conservatives pursuing a "smaller government" focusing on the growth of domestic discretionary spending in recent years, rather than on the cost of tax cuts.

"Federal domestic spending has not exploded in the past few years. Neither is it true that government has contracted, and they want to see it beginning to shrink," said Robert Greenstein, executive director of the liberal-leaning Center on Budget and Policy Priorities.

Many liberals say the Republicans' real agenda is to cut taxes to the point where Congress has no choice but to shrink domestic spending and fulfill their long-held goal of a smaller government.

Reinforcing that view on the conservative side is Grover Norquist, president of Americans for Tax Reform and an adviser to the Bush re-election team, who has said he wants to reduce government "to the size where I can drag it into the bathroom and drown it in the bathtub."

The problem, conservatives say, is that Republicans now in a position to shrink the government find that control of the legislative and executive branches brings a more seductive power of the purse. Especially in an election year, Republican leaders are often not prepared to say "no" to colleagues who want funding for local projects or expensive provisions for favored interests. They cite thousands of funding "earmarks" that Republicans wrote into the fiscal 2004 spending bills.

"There's no shame here. Earmarks have increased fourfold under Republicans, and we have nobody to blame," said Rep. Jeff Flake of Arizona. "We are going to march ourselves right into the political minority if we continue to do that."

Such criticism infuriates House Budget Chairman Jim Nussle, R-Iowa. He noted that leaders have thus far found ways to honor the spending limits in the fiscal 2004 budget resolution, despite pressure from appropriators and other lawmakers to spend more.

Return of the Hawks

The fiscal conservatives can be expected to reassert themselves again this year when the fiscal 2005 budget and appropriations cycle begins, and some of their targets could be important to the president's re-election campaign platform.

"I don't foresee any additional spending for education. It has now been adequately funded," said Rep. Sam Johnson, R-Texas, a founding member of the conservative Republican Study Group.

Appearing at a Tennessee elementary school Jan. 8, Bush said that for fiscal 2005 he will ask for an additional $1 billion in annual spending on special education and another $1 billion boost in Title I aid to schools serving disadvantaged students.

"You want to support your president, but if it gets to the point where spending is starting to get beyond our means, well, we will have to ask our administration to change," Johnson said.

This conservative uprising, however, comes at a politically convenient time for Bush: Some of the most expensive initiatives — the tax cut, the Medicare overhaul, and reconstruction costs in Afghanistan and Iraq — are mostly paid for.

Bush said recently that his proposed 2005 budget will begin the process of cutting the deficit in half over the next five years. The president said he is using "reasonable [economic] growth assumptions" and counting on Congress to "continue to hold the line on spending." Nussle said Hill leaders have been working with the White House on deficit reduction ideas.

But many conservatives are skeptical of the president's commitment to lower spending. Only a strong mandate from voters will provide the impetus for lowering the deficit, they say.

"If Republicans are spending because they think it's the politically advantageous thing to do, they will not stop spending until they see it's politically advantageous to stop," said Brian M. Riedl, lead budget analyst at the Heritage Foundation. "I don't see the GOP turning the ship around in 2004, because in an election year there's more pressure to use government spending to win more votes."

Nussle argues that Congress' ability to control spending is frustrated by the 51-48-1 makeup of the Senate. "I don't feel like we are all that much in control," he said.

Conservatives such as Feeney, who was formerly Speaker of the Florida House, observed that increased spending sometimes is the inevitable result of mutually beneficial legislative dealmaking among the president and congressional leaders such as Senate Majority Leader Bill Frist, R-Tenn., and House Speaker J. Dennis Hastert, R-Ill.

"The president tries to help Frist; Frist tries to help Hastert; and Hastert tries to help the president," Feeney said. "Sometimes, nobody wants to say no to anybody."

"It's not a fertile environment for anti-spending conservatives to make the case, and it's even more difficult when you have a conservative president and conservative leaders in the House and Senate," he said.

And when a popular president gives his imprimatur to an initiative such as the greatest expansion of an already sizable government program — even if it is a Democratic one — it provides other members of his party with the cover they need to vote for it.

"George Bush is someone I support and want to see re-elected. But he is not an anti-big-government president, and in fact, he likes bigger government," said Moore of the Club for Growth. "Since he's the leader of the party, it gives a lot of leaders in the Congress the right to be for bigger government too." ◆

Joshua B. Bolten

As the Bush administration point man on the budget, Joshua B. Bolten will play a key role if the White House decides to do battle with lawmakers over spending this year.

Bolten showed a willingness last fall to delve into the details of congressional spending; he is now President Bush's chief advocate for domestic spending restraint. Bush has charged Bolten with writing a fiscal 2005 budget that seeks to halve the deficit by fiscal 2009 — a pledge that may be hard to fulfill in light of the politically difficult spending cuts it could require and the president's desires for robust defense spending and tax cuts.

As deputy White House chief of staff for policy, Bolten had a hand in most of Bush's early domestic legislative initiatives. He was tapped in the middle of 2003 to take over the Office of Management and Budget. Bolten's temperate personality has made him a more welcome figure on Capitol Hill than his predecessor, Mitchell E. Daniels Jr., who was not reluctant to publicly deride appropriators for what he viewed as their profligate ways. (Daniels is now running for governor of Indiana.)

But given the institutional tendency of Congress and the White House to clash over spending — no matter who is in the Oval Office — Bolten will have to face off with the guardians of the federal purse in any debate over deficit reduction.

Bolten kept a relatively low profile in his first year until the end of the appropriations process, when he engaged appropriators over a package of domestic spending add-ons. In the end, the White House agreed to a series of offsets and budgetary maneuvers that allowed Congress to extract more spending — but let Bush claim victory on his budgetary top line.

Rumsfeld, center, testifies to the Senate Armed Services Committee on May 7, flanked by other top Pentagon officials.

Stunned by Abuses, Congress 'Must Now Be Involved'

Furious lawmakers vow new depths of oversight, an end to no-questions Iraq policy

On any given day, Congress is full of outrage. Usually, it is the political kind; it makes for good rhetoric, but does not reflect anything more serious than that.

This time, the outrage was real. Even the hallway conversations on Capitol Hill were conducted with wide eyes, shaking heads, voices barely under control. Photographs of Iraqi prisoners stripped naked, piled on top of each other, covered with hoods and threatened with electrocution were brutal and undeniable evidence that the United States' goals of building a better Iraq had gone tragically wrong.

The images shocked the system of a Congress that, until now, had gone along with nearly everything President Bush had asked of it, authorizing the Iraq operation and keeping the money flowing with few or no strings attached. The anger was thus intensified as lawmakers considered the reaction of the public to a war that they had authorized, paid for, and supported with relatively little oversight.

"We risk losing public support for this conflict," Sen. John McCain, R-Ariz., told Defense Secretary Donald H. Rumsfeld during a May 7 hearing of the Senate Armed Services Committee. "As Americans turned away from the Vietnam War, they may turn away from this one unless this issue is quickly resolved with full disclosure immediately."

As the scandal's scope broadened the week of May 3, lawmakers found ways to indicate to the administration that Congress would no longer take a no-questions-asked approach on Iraq.

"Congress, having not been informed, must now be involved," said Rep. Ike Skelton of Missouri, the top Democrat on the House Armed Services Committee.

Rumsfeld was summoned to Capitol Hill for back-to-back hearings on the abuses at the Abu Ghraib prison near Baghdad. Other military and intelligence officials streamed in and out of the Capitol complex, giving closed-door briefings to lawmakers. The crisis had taken on a powerful momentum, and it was hard to tell where it would end — with high-profile resignations, perhaps, or even pressure within Congress for the United States to speed up its timetable for disengaging from Iraq.

The House adopted a resolution (H Res 627) condemning the abuses, scolding the Pentagon for not disclosing them earlier and demanding regular briefings from the Defense Department in the future, and the Senate planned a vote on its own resolution the week of May 10.

Indeed, it was the administration's failure to warn lawmakers of the enormity of the case and its devastating international implications that left senators and House members seething. They could understand how such an incident might happen with young soldiers and inept commanders. But they could not understand and would be slow to forgive the administration for keeping the case from them until it broke on the evening news.

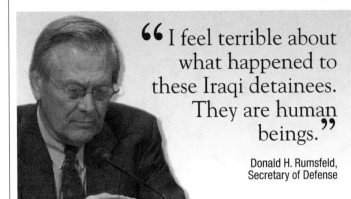

❝I feel terrible about what happened to these Iraqi detainees. They are human beings.❞

Donald H. Rumsfeld,
Secretary of Defense

❝Mr. Secretary, I must tell you that we do not like these types of surprises here in the Congress.❞

Sen. Mark Pryor, D-Ark.

"Mr. Secretary," said Sen. Mark Pryor, D-Ark., looking down at Rumsfeld from the Armed Services Committee rostrum, "I must tell you that we do not like these type of surprises here in the Congress."

That hearing, and a subsequent one in front of the House Armed Services Committee, amounted to a fight for his career for Rumsfeld, who had quickly become the main target of congressional criticism as the week progressed.

"I feel terrible about what happened to these Iraqi detainees," Rumsfeld said in his opening statement. "They are human beings. They were in U.S. custody. Our country had an obligation to treat them right. We didn't, and that was wrong.

"So to those Iraqis who were mistreated by members of the U.S. armed forces, I offer my deepest apology."

And though Chairman John W. Warner, R-Va., pronounced the secretary's statement "strong and in every sense heartfelt," the matter is far from closed. Warner promised more hearings from his committee, as did Sen. Pat Roberts, R-Kan., who chairs the Senate Intelligence Committee.

A Lethal Combination

The fact that Republicans were in such a rush to schedule hearings illustrated the depth of concern and anger in Congress, on multiple levels.

"This mistreatment of prisoners represents an appalling and totally unacceptable breach of military regulations and conduct," Warner said. "Most significant, the replaying of these images day after day throughout the Middle East, and indeed the world, has the potential to undermine the substantial gains — emphasize the substantial gains — toward the goal of peace and freedom in various operation areas of the world, most particularly Iraq, and the substantial sacrifice by our forces, those of our allies, in the war on terror."

McCain, who suffered years of torture and solitary confinement as an American prisoner of war in Vietnam, was one of the first to react to news reports and photos depicting the abuses. "The rules for the treatment of prisoners of war are very clear," he said. "There's no justification for this kind of treatment."

Much of the fury was rooted in the way lawmakers learned of the abuse. Many said the Pentagon should have told them in March, when an internal military report by Maj. Gen. Antonio M. Taguba documented the abuses. Even House Majority Leader Tom DeLay, R-Texas, one of the most committed supporters of the war, vented frustration. "If we are going to be part of this," he said, "we ought to be completely briefed."

And while Bush maintains he was not told about the mil-

itary report, or the pictures either, other lawmakers saw the omission as just the latest in a pattern of secrecy by the administration.

"There's a lot that they don't share with us, and they do so at their own risk, because we get angry," said Senate Armed Services member Joseph I. Lieberman, D-Conn., who made his support for the Iraq war a defining theme of his run for the presidency earlier this year. "There will be a lot of oversight now."

One of the first tests of that oversight will come when Congress decides how many strings to attach to the next funding request.

In a stroke of timing that either added to members' apprehensions about the course of the war or simply lumped all the bad news into one week, Bush on May 5 asked Congress for an additional $25 billion for military action in Iraq and Afghanistan. Appropriators say they want greater accountability this time than in past requests, and they are wary of the president's proposal that the money be structured as a "contingency reserve fund." (*2004 CQ Weekly, p. 1084*)

But their anger also spoke to a broader issue. Since it authorized the Iraq war in 2002, Congress has stuck with the entire war effort, despite the absence of weapons of mass destruction, the deadly violence by insurgents, the strained relations with allies and the increasingly expensive occupation. (*2003 CQ Weekly, p. 2783*)

Now, lawmakers are left struggling to convince the rest of the world that the Iraqis actually are better off now.

"These are political professionals who see how damaging this is in the eyes of the world, and how impossible it is to recover," said Alton Frye, director of the Congress and Foreign Policy program at the Council on Foreign Relations.

"This is lethal to the fundamental posture of intervening in Iraq, and it could go well beyond Iraq as well."

The Oversight Challenge

Lawmakers are vowing to become more engaged in their oversight duties. Among other things, Congress will have to deal with its failure to notice the widespread reliance on private contractors in Iraq and the ramifications of that policy, including the possibility that the use of civilian contractors to interrogate prisoners might have been a setup for the disaster that followed. (*2004 CQ Weekly, p. 1067*)

"It is a duty upon us to leave no stone unturned, to reveal all of the facts, to give the assurance that it will not happen again, and to place into the military such authorities as they need" to address the problems, Warner said.

Roberts said he and West Virginia Sen. John D. Rockefeller IV, the ranking Democrat on the Intelligence panel, had agreed that "we must take a much more activist role in looking at issues of detention throughout this conflict."

Congress has had a number of obstacles that have limited its oversight of the war until now. The Bush administration has not made life easy for its critics in Congress, and responsibility for security programs in Iraq has been so dispersed that the oversight jurisdiction has been spread out among different committees.

But the biggest obstacle has been self-imposed: Some lawmakers say they have deliberately held back from asking pointed questions while U.S. troops were in battle.

Now, Republicans find themselves grasping for ways to step up oversight of the administration without doing the one thing they have said they would never do: undermine their support for the U.S. troops who are not implicated in the scandal.

"When I look at what happened over there, it's deplorable. But there's so many people over there that it's going to be impossible not to have a few bad apples," said Senate Armed Services member John Ensign, R-Nev.

"I just hope this doesn't take anything away from the Pat Tillmans of the world and the other heroes," said Ensign, referring to the former National Football League player who was killed April 22 in Afghanistan.

The key to whether the new intensity of congressional oversight will be successful is "how hard they push to get to the organizational causes" of the abuse of the prisoners, which could include the use of private contractors, said Joel D. Aberbach, director of the Center for American Politics and Public Policy at UCLA, who has conducted studies of congressional oversight.

While the abuses may indeed have been committed by "a few bad apples," Aberbach said, "you don't have people taking pictures of themselves abusing the prisoners unless they have some reason to believe that activity is acceptable and sanctioned in some way."

Damage Control

Bush clearly sensed the scope of the political damage. His aides, who almost never leak internal disputes to the press, quickly spread word that he had scolded Rumsfeld on May 5 for not alerting him that the photos existed and that there was a military report documenting the abuses. Bush himself

confirmed the account the next day.

He appeared on Arabic television networks to try to convince viewers that the images did not represent what Americans truly stand for. And on May 6, during an appearance with Jordan's King Abdullah II, Bush offered a public apology.

"I told him I was sorry for the humiliation suffered by the Iraqi prisoners, and the humiliation suffered by their families," Bush said. "I told him I was equally sorry that people who have been seeing those pictures didn't understand the true nature and heart of America. I assured him Americans, like me, didn't appreciate what we saw, that it made us sick to our stomachs."

The apology did not keep Bush's Democratic rival for the presidency, Sen. John Kerry of Massachusetts, from blasting the president's handling of the scandal.

"Today, I have a message for the men and women of our armed forces: As commander in chief, I will honor your commitment, and I will take responsibility for the bad as well as the good," Kerry said May 6 during a campaign event at a California high school. "As president, I will not be the last to know what is going on in my command."

The Escalating Crisis

There were, of course, lawmakers who might have gone a bit beyond genuine anger.

Somehow, the House managed to turn bipartisan outrage into yet another partisan food fight, as Republicans and Democrats battled over whether a resolution condemning the abuses should also include a call for congressional investigations.

Democrats supported the language, Republicans did not, and the resolution was adopted, 365-50, amid complaints from Minority Whip Steny H. Hoyer, D-Md., that the Republican majority should have reached out to Democrats. The number of opposing votes, he said, "should have been zero." (*2004 CQ Weekly, p. 1104*)

A hooded and wired Iraqi prisoner reportedly was told he would be electrocuted if he fell off a box.

REUTERS PHOTO / THE NEW YORKER

Unfolding Story of Abu Ghraib

2003
OCTOBER-DECEMBER
According to reports, Iraqi prisoners at Abu Ghraib were abused by personnel charged with their care. Photographs of those abuses were taken by insiders at the prison.

2004
JANUARY 16
In a one-paragraph news release, the U.S. Central Command announces an investigation is under way into "reported incidents of detainee abuse at a Coalition Forces detention facility." No further information is released because to do so would "hinder the investigation," the release says.

JANUARY 19
Lt. Gen. Ricardo Sanchez, commander of the Combined Joint Task Force in Iraq, requests a high-level investigator be appointed to look into the abuse charges.

JANUARY 31
Maj. Gen. Antonio M. Taguba, deputy commanding general for support in Kuwait, is appointed to lead the investigation.

FEBRUARY 26
Asked about 17 military personnel under investigation for mistreatment of Abu Ghraib prisoners, Sanchez says, "They are suspended from their duties. . . . I can't give you any more information than that."

Minority Leader Nancy Pelosi of California and other Democrats called on Rumsfeld to resign. The Democratic Congressional Campaign Committee launched an online petition demanding his resignation. Rep. Charles B. Rangel, D-N.Y., said he should be impeached.

From the Republican side, DeLay blasted Rep. John P. Murtha, D-Pa., a Vietnam veteran and longtime defense hawk, for saying the Iraq war would be "unwinnable" without a major change in direction, such as sending more troops and resources.

"To say this morning, while our troops are under enemy fire — while American blood is flowing on the battlefield — that this war is unwinnable is an insult to every man and woman who has ever fought and sacrificed under the flag of this nation," DeLay said at a news conference.

"This is what the heirs of [Franklin D.] Roosevelt and [John F.] Kennedy have become: a collection of appeasing

who see our every casualty in Iraq as a potential campaign gimmick," he added.

Other Republicans accused Democrats of trying to play events for partisan advantage, particularly in calling for Rumsfeld's resignation. Some, including Sen. Jon Kyl, R-Ariz., said critics risked encouraging the enemy.

"People should hold their fire and just wait until the facts come in, and we can discuss this in a nonpartisan and a constructive way, rather than in a way that might be misread by our enemies," Kyl said. "Because the more this kind of criticism occurs, the more the enemy may take from it that we are divided, that we no longer have the commitment or the will to see this conflict to an end."

Tough Week for Rumsfeld

Democrats, particularly in the House, spared nothing in attacking Rumsfeld. They seemed emboldened by signs that his career might be in trouble.

His "leadership of the Pentagon has unnecessarily jeopardized the safety of American troops, and it has seriously undermined our ability to prosecute the war on terrorism," Pelosi said in a statement. "He has been dismissive of international law, of world opinion, and of the Congress."

A few Republicans defended Rumsfeld, and Bush rejected demands that the secretary resign. But comments from others were muted and qualified.

In the packed Senate Armed Services Committee hearing carried live on all the national television networks, Rumsfeld apologized not only to the Iraqi detainees, but also to the lawmakers who had to find out about the abuses through the media.

"I failed to recognize how important it was to elevate a matter of such gravity to the highest levels, including the president and the members of Congress," Rumsfeld said. This time, he was determined not to make the same mistake. Rumsfeld warned the committee that there are additional photographs, and even videos, of the prison abuse that could surface in the coming weeks.

The Defense secretary had a lot of

More photos of U.S. guards with Iraqi prisoners began appearing in early May. At the far right, Saddam Saleh, a former Abu Ghraib prisoner, holds a picture of himself alongside other Iraqis while in captivity.

REUTERS PHOTO / THE NEW YORKER

REUTERS PHOTO / OLEG POPOV

MARCH 3
Taguba report is completed. It charges a lengthy list of abuses of prisoners at Abu Ghraib. The report is classified as secret and is not released outside the Pentagon.

MARCH 20
Brig. Gen. Mark Kimmitt, chief military spokesman in Iraq, announces at a briefing that "six military personnel have been charged with criminal offenses" including cruelty, maltreatment, assault and indecent acts. He declines to elaborate.

APRIL 28
CBS News airs a story on the Abu Ghraib abuses, including photographs of prisoners in degrading positions with their guards standing close by. The network had delayed the story for two weeks at the request of Joint Chiefs of Staff Chairman Gen. Richard B. Myers.

MAY 5
Senate Armed Services Committee demands Defense Secretary Donald H. Rumsfeld appear at a hearing.

MAY 6
New photos of prisoner abuse are published. House Minority Leader Nancy Pelosi, D-Calif., holds a news conference in which she calls for Rumsfeld's resignation.

MAY 7
Rumsfeld and Pentagon leaders appear before both the Senate and House Armed Services committees. In the Senate hearing, Rumsfeld admits that there are more photos and some videos of prisoner abuse. Committee members complain they first heard about the abuse from media reports. Senate Armed Services Chairman John W. Warner, R-Va., says he receives hundreds of calls from the Pentagon but, "I did not receive such a call in this case."

Negroponte Appointed Ambassador to Iraq

This summer, John D. Negroponte will become the first ambassador that the United States has had in Baghdad in 14 years. The Senate confirmed him, 95-3, on May 6, after a debate in which his qualifications were minimally questioned but President Bush's policies in Iraq were ridiculed by several Democrats. (*2004 CQ Weekly, p. 1101*)

Foreign Relations Chairman Richard G. Lugar, R-Ind., who noted Negroponte's experience in "dangerous predicaments," pushed the nomination through the Senate in just 17 days. (*2004 CQ Weekly, p. 1039*)

Since shortly after the Sept. 11 attacks, Negroponte, 64, has been the U.S. ambassador to the United Nations. He plans to arrive for his new assignment July 1, a day after Iraqi sovereignty is to be transferred from the U.S.-led Coalition Provisional Authority, headed by L. Paul Bremer III, to an as-yet-undetermined interim Iraqi government. It is unclear how Iraqis will react to that government and how that government will treat U.S. officials,

REUTERS PHOTO / LARRY DOWNING

Negroponte

especially given the U.S. abuse of Iraqi prisoners.

Sen. Tom Harkin, D-Iowa, said Negroponte was wrong for the job because he "showed a callous disregard for human rights abuses" by the Honduran military when he was ambassador there in the 1980s. But Sen. Joseph R. Biden Jr. of Delaware, the top Democrat on Foreign Relations, praised him for accepting "the most difficult and, at this moment, most dangerous job in U.S. diplomacy."

With a staff of up to 3,000, the Baghdad post is on course to become the world's largest U.S. embassy. The last envoy was April C. Glaspie, who left Iraq in the summer of 1990 shortly before Saddam Hussein invaded Kuwait, the precursor to the Persian Gulf War. She formally remained ambassador into the next year. (*1991 Almanac, p. 455*)

---

amends to make. Warner, a former secretary of the Navy, spoke for nearly everyone in Congress when he scolded Rumsfeld for not telling him earlier about the report's existence.

"In my 25 years on this committee, I've received hundreds of calls day and night from top — all levels — top and all levels, uniformed and civilian, in the Department of Defense when they in their judgment felt it was necessary," Warner said. "I did not receive such a call in this case."

Other committee members grilled Rumsfeld relentlessly, particularly McCain, who was not satisfied when the secretary could not provide a direct answer about who might have ordered the abuses.

"In all due respect, you've got to answer this question," McCain said. "This is a pretty simple, straightforward question: Who was in charge of the interrogations?"

Democrats, meanwhile, pressed Rumsfeld about reports that the International Committee of the Red Cross had warned U.S. officials of abuse of prisoners in Iraq more than a year ago. "How do we know that there isn't a broader problem here?" asked committee member Robert C. Byrd, D-W.Va.

Rumsfeld got off considerably easier in the House hearing, at least on the Republican side.

"We are engaged in a complex and global war on terror and are operating against terrorists in two major the-

aters," said Chairman Duncan Hunter, R-Calif. "We need to judge the department on its performance in that war, not on its public relations skills or the frequency with which a few egos on Capitol Hill get bruised. In that area, the secretary and his colleagues have consistently demonstrated excellent management skills and superior military judgment."

Can It Be Fixed?

It was difficult to see what, short of some dramatic gesture from the administration, could defuse the ire and criticism on Capitol Hill, though many lawmakers offered advice.

Some, including Roberts, said an immediate, symbolic gesture to repudiate the abuses would be to shut down the Abu Ghraib prison.

Finding a substantive policy fix, however, could be harder.

In the Senate, as members rushed to confirm John D. Negroponte as the first U.S. ambassador to Iraq since the 1991 Persian Gulf War, leaders of the Foreign Relations Committee warned that unless the administration moves soon to implement a more detailed plan for turning over power in Iraq, the mission may face insurmountable problems.

Negroponte, currently U.S. ambassador to the United Nations, is uniquely qualified for what will be a "difficult assignment," said Committee Chairman Richard G. Lugar, R-Ind. But he added that Bush "must communicate"

a clearer strategy for moving toward democracy in Iraq.

"The announcement of a flexible but detailed plan would prove we have a strategy," he said.

Lugar, who has repeatedly prodded the administration to provide more details about its strategy for shifting power to the Iraqis, said he would hold more hearings in May "to monitor developments and to illuminate for the American people the challenges and responsibilities that we face in Iraq."

The panel's ranking Democrat, Joseph R. Biden Jr. of Delaware, called for "snap elections" soon in Iraq to choose a body that would oversee and lend legitimacy to the establishment of a permanent new government and the drafting of a constitution.

He also said Bush should bring a plan to NATO and lobby for the help of member countries to patrol borders in Iraq and otherwise bolster efforts to bring security there. And he urged that all U.S.-run prisons in Iraq be opened to international observers and aid organizations in order to begin to restore trust of Iraqis.

Other lawmakers will have their own ideas on how to get back on the right track. But as the events of the week proved, Bush and Congress face an even bigger challenge: finding a way to live down the horrifying images and make amends with the Arab world.

So far, no one has. ◆

Congress Gropes for Next Move In Response to Abuse Scandal

Quick Contents

Lawmakers are trying to learn the extent of the abuses at Iraq's Abu Ghraib prison. The chambers' divergent approaches, however, could hobble efforts.

Members of the House and Senate trickled out from behind closed doors on Capitol Hill May 12 after viewing unreleased photos that showed U.S. soldiers abusing Iraqi prisoners. Most of the lawmakers were grim, some outraged, a few shaken.

It was "like looking at the rings of hell," said Sen. Richard J. Durbin, an Illinois Democrat. "But this is a hell of our own creation."

The photos, which depicted prisoners tied up, cowering before snarling dogs or being forced to masturbate, certainly gave lawmakers a close-up view of the cruel behavior of U.S. personnel at the Abu Ghraib prison outside Baghdad. But the photos did little to answer the overriding question of how extensive the abuse was or how high up the chain of command lawmakers should place the responsibility.

Was the mistreatment and torture limited to a "handful of bad actors" stationed at Abu Ghraib who were poorly trained and barely supervised? Or was it symptomatic of far more widespread use of illegal interrogation techniques on suspects in the war on terror, overseen or condoned by senior military and intelligence officials?

By the end of the week of May 10, after 10 hearings, lawmakers were not much closer to

CQ Weekly May 15, 2004

finding out where, between those two extremes, the truth was to be found. And despite countless statements of outrage from Capitol Hill, it also remained unclear how hard congressional leaders would push to uncover the truth. If evidence of high-level complicity were uncovered, would senior GOP leaders really call for the resignation of Donald H. Rumsfeld, Bush's embattled Defense secretary? Were they prepared to use their powers, if needed, to subpoena or censure Pentagon officials?

The 108th Congress, after all, has not been known for its oversight of the Bush administration's stewardship of the war in Iraq. And House GOP leaders already were moving to provide some measure of cover to the White House.

California Rep. Jane Harman, the ranking Democrat on the House Select Intelligence Committee, warned that Congress' duty to provide meaningful oversight of the executive branch would be put to the test in the coming weeks. "The world is tuned in, and America is on trial," Harman said. "Congress will be on trial, too, if it doesn't act."

Different Paths

Just a week after the broadcast of graphic pictures of prisoner abuse at Abu Ghraib by the CBS news program "60 Minutes II" produced bipartisan outrage across Capitol Hill, the House and Senate already were diverging on how best to handle the blossoming scandal.

In the Senate, leaders pledged open investigations and bipartisan cooperation. Senators from both parties demanded a public accounting of what went wrong and signaled their willingness to swiftly and repeatedly call a wide range of defense policy makers before committees.

On May 10, the Senate adopted, on a 92-0 vote, a resolution (S Res 356) denouncing the abuses at Abu Ghraib and calling for thorough investigations by both the Senate and the executive branch. (*2004 CQ Weekly, p. 1170*)

"It's never comfortable when you're exercising oversight over decisions made by your own party," said Susan Collins, a moderate Maine Republican who sits on the Senate Armed Services Committee. "But it's part of our responsibility."

John W. Warner, the Virginia Republican who chairs the panel, won praise from Demo-

Rumsfeld, left, visits Abu Ghraib prison during a surprise May 13 visit to Iraq. He has told Congress that six investigations into the prison abuse scandal are under way.

crats for quickly calling open hearings with Pentagon investigators. Warner, a former secretary of the Navy and one of the Pentagon's leading allies on Capitol Hill, said he was acting in the military's best interests.

"I'm trying to get the facts out so the military can heal itself, hold those that are accountable and get on with its business," Warner said. "Here at home there's such a sense of despair and dismay as to how the proud uniform of the military has been so tarnished and desecrated by a handful of bad actors. So we've got to get the facts out."

After calling Rumsfeld to Capitol Hill's first open hearing on prisoner abuses May 7, Warner convened another pair of open hearings May 11 featuring Army investigators and intelligence officials. He says he plans further hearings.

His strategy of openness and bipartisan cooperation, backed by Majority Leader Bill Frist, R-Tenn., was aimed at demonstrating to the public that the Senate was serious about the prisoner abuse and capable of investigating it in a determined, nonpartisan manner.

"Chairman Warner is a very honorable, thoughtful leader who understands the constitutional and institutional ramifications of these issues and has conducted a very bipartisan investigation," said Democratic Sen. Hillary Rodham Clinton of New York, a member of the panel.

The scene was much different in the House, where the previous week's facade of unified bipartisan anger over the prisoner abuses quickly crumbled. (*Lawmakers*, p. 63)

GOP leaders dismissed a call by Minority Leader Nancy Pelosi, D-Calif., for a "full congressional investigation" and accused Democrats of politicizing the crisis. Majority Leader Tom DeLay, R-Texas, blasted Democratic presidential candidate Sen. John Kerry of Massachusetts for including a campaign fundraising appeal in an e-mailed petition calling for Rumsfeld's resignation.

"They're profiteering off a horrible event, and, frankly, it's disgusting," DeLay said.

DeLay also mounted a spirited defense of the White House's Iraq policy, dismissing criticism from Democrats, some of whom have called Bush's handling of the Iraq war inept.

"The policy's not wrong," he said.

"We tried their way, and we got 9/11. Appeasement doesn't work."

Some House Republicans argued that too many facts about the prison abuses had been made public. As evidence that a more cautious approach was needed, they pointed to the May 11 beheading of Nicholas Berg, a civilian from Pennsylvania who had vanished in Iraq. Berg's captors said they killed him to avenge the U.S. abuse of Iraqi prisoners.

Indeed, as Warner's May 11 hearing was being broadcast live on TV, other Pentagon officials, including Rumsfeld, were testifying in private before the House Appropriations Subcommittee on Defense.

House Armed Services Chairman Duncan Hunter, R-Calif., who held an open hearing on the prisoner abuses on May 7, said he also would close the doors at his panel's next hearing on the issue.

"I'm not going to have it in open air," Hunter said.

A Pentagon official, who agreed to discuss the Defense Department's views on the condition of anonymity, defended the practice of closing hearings. While public hearings allow widespread airing of an issue, military officials often are limited in the answers they can provide, he said.

For example, questions about what kind of information interrogators are seeking from prisoners, what strategies they are using and what they are learning are all classified matters.

"If you really want to get the facts and deal with the thorny issues that may include classified information, you go [for a] closed hearing," the official said.

Six Probes Under Way

One crucial question that Congress has yet to figure out is how far up the chain of command responsibility for the mistreatment rests.

Army Maj. Gen. Antonio M. Taguba, who conducted the initial investigation of the abuse at Abu Ghraib and completed a preliminary report in March, told the Armed Services panel on May 11 that he "did not find any evidence of a policy or a direct order to these soldiers to do what they did."

Taguba attributed the abuse to a small group of soldiers at the prison who were not properly trained, disciplined or led by their superiors.

But that hearing exposed differ-ences within the Pentagon that have left lawmakers confused. Stephen Cambone, the undersecretary of Defense for intelligence, asserted that responsibility for abuse of Iraqi prisoners rested with Brig. Gen. Janis L. Karpinski, the former commander of the military police personnel at Abu Ghraib prison.

Cambone told the Armed Services panel that policy makers in Washington and top commanders in Iraq had made clear that the Geneva Convention for humane treatment of prisoners should be observed.

But Taguba said that military intelligence officials had "tactical control of all units that were residing at Abu Ghraib," including military police. And he said it was clear from his probe that the military police did not receive training in the Geneva Convention and its requirements.

"You have two entirely different kinds of viewpoints on this issue," said a frustrated Sen. Edward M. Kennedy, D-Mass.

Rumsfeld told the Senate Appropriations Subcommittee on Defense on May 12 that six separate investigations into prisoner mistreatment were under way and that so far none had uncovered evidence of systemic abuse.

But many lawmakers remain skeptical that the abuses at Abu Ghraib were the isolated, spontaneous actions of a few enlisted personnel.

"The despicable actions described in Gen. Taguba's report not only reek of abuse, they reek of an organized effort and methodical preparation for interrogation," said Sen. Carl Levin of Michigan, the ranking Democrat on the Armed Services panel.

And one of the Senate's leading human rights advocates, Vermont Democrat Patrick J. Leahy, charged that the mistreatment of Iraqis at Abu Ghraib was part of a wider pattern of abuse by the U.S. military of people detained in the war on terror.

Leahy has complained for nearly a year to an array of senior officials in the Bush administration about alleged mistreatment of prisoners, mainly in Afghanistan. His questions have largely gone unanswered.

"It appears to be exactly the same techniques used in Afghanistan as were used in Iraq," he told Rumsfeld. "I don't think they're getting their techniques over the Internet. There's obviously some systemic training."

The investigation that lawmakers are most eagerly awaiting news on is being led by Maj. Gen. George R. Fay. Fay is examining whether military intelligence had a role in the abuses at the Iraqi prison and how high up in the chain of command knowledge of the abuses went.

"The key . . . is the Fay report," said Senate Select Intelligence Chairman Pat Roberts, R-Kan., adding that he hoped Fay would have an interim report completed by early June.

Widespread Frustrations

Part of the problem with Congress' struggle to learn of the extent of the prison abuse scandal is the difficulties that lawmakers say they have had in getting information out of the Bush administration.

From the lawmakers' standpoint, Congress has been purely accommodating in giving the White House the political and financial support to wage its global war on terrorism since the Sept. 11 attacks. It passed resolutions giving the president broad authority to use military force against terrorists (PL 107-40) and to remove Iraqi dictator Saddam Hussein from power (PL 107-243). *(2001 Almanac, p. 7-8; 2002 Almanac, p. 9-3)*

Since the spring of last year, lawmakers also have provided $166 billion for war efforts in Iraq and Afghanistan in two supplemental appropriations bills that had few strings attached (PL 108-11, PL 108-106). *(2003 CQ Weekly, p. 3105)*

But lawmakers, including some Republicans, say the administration has taken such support as its due and balked at answering tough questions about Iraq. Senate Foreign Relations Chairman Richard G. Lugar, R-Ind., has said the White House cut him out of the information loop on Iraq.

In April, the Defense Department refused to send a senior official to a hearing that Lugar held to discuss the administration's plan for turning over limited sovereignty to an interim Iraqi government on June 30. *(2004 CQ Weekly, p. 915)*

For their part, Democrats complain that any time they try to hold the administration accountable for its Iraq strategy — asking, for example, whether enough troops were deployed to keep the peace or why there is no concrete handover plan — their patriotism is questioned.

"They have been unaccountable for the policy," Pelosi said of the administration. "They will not account for the funds, and all they can do is lob charges of unpatriotism."

Across the Potomac River at the Pentagon, officials are equally frustrated by the outrage spewing from Capitol Hill. Defense Department officials say privately that until the photos of abuse at Abu Ghraib were aired by CBS, most members of Congress showed little interest in the treatment of prisoners in Iraq. They estimate that several dozen lawmakers visited Abu Ghraib, but only to view the torture room used by former Iraqi dictator Saddam Hussein.

On May 13, Republican Sen. Rick Santorum of Pennsylvania inadvertently provided a glimpse into the limited congressional focus on the prisoner abuse issue when he told reporters that his office had received two letters last June from the brother of an American soldier accused of mistreating Iraqi prisoners at Camp Bucca in southern Iraq. The letter said the soldier, Master Sgt. Lisa Girman of the 320th Military Police Battalion based in Ashley, Pa., was being punished unfairly for doing her job.

Santorum agreed to meet with Girman on Feb. 2 but had to cancel after Senate offices were closed following the discovery of the toxin ricin. He said his scheduler called Girman to reschedule, but Girman did not return the call.

Santorum, apparently, did not press the issue further. "We did everything we could," said his spokesman, Robert Traynham.

Before the Abu Ghraib abuses surfaced, nearly all of Congress' concerns about treatment of prisoners were focused on Afghanistan and a special facility at the Guantanamo Bay naval base in Cuba that holds terror suspects.

Some lawmakers also expressed concerns about the administration's decision to classify terror suspects as enemy combatants rather than prisoners of war, a practice that gives the military more latitude to detain suspects and limit their legal rights.

But Pentagon officials maintain that there was little response after the military announced March 20 that six military personnel in Iraq had been charged with criminal offenses involving mistreatment of prisoners, includ-

ing cruelty, maltreatment, assault and indecent acts.

"Overall, the Congress abdicated its responsibility to provide oversight for this detention system that was set up around the world after Sept. 11," said Tom Malinowski, Washington advocacy director for Human Rights Watch, a group that has pressed the Bush administration on the rights of detainees since 2002.

Early Warning Claims

Pentagon officials also challenge the charge by some lawmakers that they were trying to hide the prison abuse problem from Congress. Rather, they say, they were guilty of not realizing its implications.

Taguba's report was still being vetted and had not reached senior officials when CBS broke the story of the prisoner abuse on April 28. While senior officials, such as Rumsfeld and Gen. Richard B. Myers, the chairman of the Joint Chiefs of Staff, knew beforehand that CBS was planning to air its exposé, that information had not filtered down to lower levels at the Pentagon. "We just had no sense that it was an issue," said a Defense official who asked not to be named.

Many lawmakers also have complained that Rumsfeld failed to warn them about the CBS broadcast when he met with Senate and House members several hours before the broadcast of the pictures. Pentagon officials also challenge that claim.

According to a Defense Department list, warnings of the upcoming broadcast were provided to Congress on April 28, several hours before the "60 Minutes II" broadcast.

In the House, only the Armed Services Committee was warned, according to the list. But in the Senate, the list indicated, staff-level warnings were provided to Warner; Levin; Republican Ted Stevens of Alaska, the chairman of the Appropriations Defense Subcommittee; and Daniel K. Inouye of Hawaii, the subcommittee's ranking Democrat.

Some lawmakers who had constituents allegedly involved in the abuse also were informed. According to the list, they were Democrats Robert C. Byrd of West Virginia, Barbara A. Mikulski of Maryland, Paul S. Sarbanes of Maryland and Charles E. Schumer of New York, and Republican Arlen Specter of Pennsylvania.

"They didn't get to see the pictures until the program ran," acknowledged the Defense official. "I can certainly understand their unhappiness. But I also believe their claim they didn't know isn't true either."

Continuing Questions

Warner says it will take some time to get answers to lawmakers' questions about the abuse scandal. "We're just going to continue to pick up the facts as we can waiting for Gen. Fay's report."

But as long as those questions remain unanswered, there is a danger that other important defense and foreign policy business on Capitol Hill may get derailed by continuing questioning about the prisoner abuse.

Both the House and Senate are scheduled to take up their versions of the fiscal 2005 defense authorization bill the week of May 17. During the same week, Lugar plans to hold another two days of hearings on the June 30 handover, this time with Deputy Defense Secretary Paul D. Wolfowitz and Deputy Secretary of State Richard L. Armitage as the main witnesses. Congress will also be debating the Bush administration's May 12 request for a $25 million war reserve fund. (*Defense authorization, 2004 CQ Weekly, p. 1162; appropriations, p. 1126*)

The potential for those deliberations to be eclipsed by the prison abuse issue was evident at a May 13 hearing of the Senate Armed Services Committee that was supposed to be focused on Bush's $25 billion supplemental funding request.

Warner tried to stop Kennedy from grilling Wolfowitz about the prisoner abuse. A defiant Kennedy dared Warner to rule him out of order.

"I've been on this committee for 24 years, I've been in the Senate 42 years, and I have never been denied the opportunity to question any person that's come before a committee on what I wanted to ask for it," the Massachusetts Democrat said. "And I resent it and reject it on a matter of national importance."

Warner backed down. The questions about prison abuse went on. ◆

New Tensions Test the Limits Of Bush's Sway in Congress

White House finds more Republicans willing to buck its agenda as troubles mount

For most of this year, President Bush has enjoyed the strongest relationship with Congress of any president in decades. He has benefited from a widespread network of allies in both the House and Senate, and rank-and-file Republicans have not forgotten who campaigned so hard to help them win back the Senate.

But this fall, Bush's safety net of support in the Republican-run Congress is being tested like never before.

All over Capitol Hill, jaws are hanging open over Bush's $87 billion request for a year's worth of military operations and reconstruction in Iraq and Afghanistan. The Treasury is expecting a deficit approaching $500 billion for the fiscal year that started Oct. 1, and a recent New York Times-CBS News Poll showed that a majority of the public says Congress should say no to the whole thing. That will not happen, but it is increasingly likely Congress will try to limit the damage by turning at least some of the $20.3 billion for rebuilding Iraq into a loan rather than a grant.

There is also the growing unease in GOP ranks over joblessness, the reach of the 2001 anti-terrorism law (PL 107-56) into Americans' privacy, and the deepening deficits that many believe will get even worse if Congress enacts an expensive Medicare prescription drug benefit. Furthermore, Bush's job approval ratings, once a source of phenomenal political strength for not only him but also congressional Republicans, have fallen to a new low. In fact, they have dipped below the approval ratings he was getting before the Sept. 11 terrorist attacks. *(Polling, p. 73)*

The conditions are producing the greatest tensions in the Bush-Congress relationship since Republicans won majorities in both chambers in the midterm election 11 months ago. Their differences are still relatively small, and they fall far short of all-out internal warfare. But the White House is finding that Republicans are willing to vote against its proposals, if only on second-tier issues — such as overtime rules and media consolidation — and in ways that do not threaten the central themes of Bush's presidency.

The frequency of these Republican push-backs against the president has been increasing, and shows signs of picking up even more as the first session of the 108th Congress moves into its final weeks. If the trend continues next year, it could make it more difficult for Republicans to present a unified front as they campaign to keep one-party government in place beyond November 2004.

Still, there are limits to how far Republicans will go in de-

" They're going to get some pretty tough questions because the people at home are asking us tough questions. "

— Sen. Chuck Hagel, R-Neb., on the tension between Congress and the White House

fying Bush on the issues that define his presidency. On the economy, the war on terrorism and the war in Iraq, Republicans restrict themselves to tinkering at the margins.

In part, that is because Republicans say they agree with Bush on the broad themes — that tax cuts are the right way to stimulate the economy, that new criminal justice powers were needed to fight terrorism at home, and that giving up on rebuilding Iraq would allow that nation to slip into chaos and lead to greater problems down the road.

No Longer Invincible

"There are ways to push back. Members will find the right thing to do," said Jim Kolbe, R-Ariz., chairman of the House Appropriations Foreign Operations Subcommittee. In the end, Congress will approve Bush's spending request for Iraq, he predicted, "because people don't want to be seen as saying we didn't follow through. Regardless of whether you felt we should or should not be there, we have to follow through."

Hill Republicans also will probably limit their rebellions because an all-out defeat of Bush's basic principles on the economy or foreign policy could damage them as well in the process. Knowing that such an effort would not only undermine him but also might drag them down, they make sure any rebellion is more of a tap on the shoulder than a full-force shove. "If Bush does badly, they're likely to pay, too," said Barbara Sinclair, a professor of American politics at UCLA.

"They really don't have any alternatives right now," said Merle Black, a professor of political science at Emory University. Having invested themselves so deeply in Bush's agenda, he said, "they've just got to tough it out and hope the situation improves."

At the moment, public attitudes toward Iraq are not improving, for either the White House or congressional Republicans. Faced with incredulous questions from their constituents — why would the United States give money to a country that has the second-largest oil reserves in the world? — Republicans are warming to the idea of lending the reconstruction funds to Iraq and expecting the country to pay it back with its oil revenues.

When they return from a recess the week of Oct. 13, senators expect a showdown vote on an amendment to the fiscal 2004 supplemental spending package (S 1689) that would turn $10 billion of the reconstruction funds Bush has requested into long-term loans. The proposal is by two Republicans: Kay Bailey Hutchison of Texas, the vice chairwoman of the GOP Conference, and Susan Collins of Maine. (*2003 CQ Weekly, p. 2451*)

"In a rare instance, they're politically tone deaf to the way this is being perceived," freshman GOP Rep. Tom Feeney of Florida said of the White House. He co-wrote an article for National Review Online with Stephen Moore, president of the conservative Club for Growth, advocating the loan approach.

Making the reconstruction funds a loan would be a relatively mild rebellion compared with other proposals that will not succeed, such as separating the reconstruction money from the rest of the package and killing it entirely, as Senate Democrats tried to do. But it would be a rejection of the administration's insistence that Iraq has enough debt already and cannot take on any more.

Moreover, some of the specific details in the request have made Hill Republicans cringe. Democrats had a field day with such items as $3.6 million for 600 radios and satellite telephones — at a cost of $6,000 each — and $2.6 million for 80 pickup trucks, at a cost of $33,000 each. A statement released by Senate Minority Leader Tom Daschle, D-S.D., noted dryly that "prices in the United States for a new truck begin at $14,000."

Even Republican leaders who normally would line up quickly behind Bush are finding themselves short of material to work with.

"The level of detail presented by the White House is something that's going to cause us more trouble than help," said Ohio's Deborah Pryce, chairwoman of the House Republican Conference. She said the White House had more work to do to make "the complete and proper case" that the reconstruction money should be a grant, not a loan.

Second-Tier Setbacks

The loan-vs.-grant debate is the most visible congressional challenge to the White House at the moment, but it follows a series of recent rebukes on other issues, at the hands of Republicans as well as Democrats.

Last month, the Senate voted, with the support of six Republicans, to block the administration's proposed changes in overtime regulations, which Democrats contend could make as many as 8 million workers ineligible for the extra pay.

The provision of the Labor, Health and Human Services, and Education spending bill (HR 2660) could complicate negotiations on the final bill. On Oct. 2, the House approved a non-binding motion endorsing the Senate language, with 21 Republicans defying a veto threat from Bush. Such "motions to instruct" are only symbolic, but they often provide a low-risk way for lawmakers to express their true feelings on an issue. (*2003 CQ Weekly, p. 2440*)

There have been other setbacks to the administration. With the support of 12 Republicans, the Senate voted in September to overturn a Federal Communications Commis-

President Showing Vulnerability

Recent polls appear to show President Bush's standing with the American people slipping.

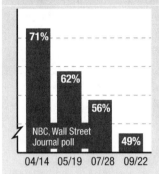
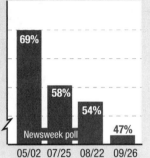
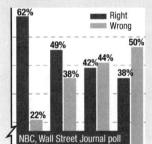
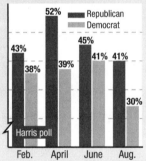
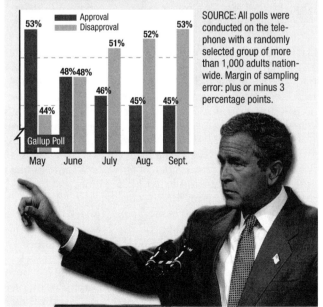

73

Recent Congressional Rejections of Bush Policy

Since July, President Bush has faced a series of setbacks from Congress, with Republicans joining Democrats to reject a half-dozen of the administration's policies. While most do not rise to the level of issues that will define the Bush presidency, taken together they have raised the level of tension between Bush and Congress. And they signal a shift in a relationship that since the 2002 election has been dominated by a powerful president at the height of his popularity.

PATRIOT ACT:	**OVERTIME:**	**MEDIA CONSOLIDATION:**	**PRIVATIZATION:**	**AVIATION:**	**CUBA TRAVEL:**
On July 22, in an amendment to the Commerce-Justice-State appropriations bill (HR 2799), the House voted 309-118 to kill funding for a provision of the 2001 anti-terrorism law (PL 107-56) that lets police conduct searches and seize evidence without advanced notice. *(2003 CQ Weekly, p. 1905)*	On Sept. 10, the Senate adopted 55-45 an amendment to the social services appropriations bill (HR 2660) to block changes in federal overtime rules. On Oct. 2, the House voted 221-203 to instruct conferees to accept the Senate position. *(2003 CQ Weekly, p. 2440)*	On Sept. 16, on a 55-40 vote, the Senate adopted a resolution (S J Res 17) to overturn a Federal Communications Commission rule that would let large media firms own more television stations and newspapers. *(2003 CQ Weekly, p. 2303)*	In an amendment to the Transportation-Treasury appropriations bill (HR 2989), the House voted 220-198 Sept. 9 to stop the administration from privatizing thousands of federal jobs. *(2003 CQ Weekly, p. 2224)*	Under pressure from Democrats and some Republicans, House GOP leaders are expected to send a bill to reauthorize the Federal Aviation Administration (HR 2115) back to conference committee to rewrite or drop its privatization language. *(2003 CQ Weekly, p. 2357)*	Also on the Transportation-Treasury bill Sept. 9, the House voted 227-188 to lift the ban on most travel to Cuba. *(2003 CQ Weekly, p. 2224)*

sion rule that would let large media conglomerates get larger. And the House, normally the chamber the White House can count on for support, has voted to stop the administration from privatizing thousands of federal jobs and to lift the ban on most travel to Cuba. (2003 CQ *Weekly*, pp. 2303, 2224)

Some Democratic strategists say those votes could create momentum for Congress to mount broader challenges on bigger issues. "One of the most important parts of the Bush image is effectiveness. He talks tax cuts, he gets tax cuts," said Democratic pollster Anna Greenberg. The recent defeats, she said, undermine that image.

"I really feel a different dynamic on Capitol Hill," said Democratic strategist Michael Lux. On issues such as Iraq, the economy and Medicare, Lux said, "they went home over the August recess, and I think they got the hell scared out of them."

But independent public opinion analysts say issues such as media regulation, overtime and privatization of federal jobs are not the kind that burn themselves into the public memory. "These were important issues, but they're not so large that they will resonate across the country," said Andrew Kohut, director of the Pew Research Center for the People and the Press.

Now, Republicans are taking heat on the big issues that do resonate. Con-

stituents are critical of the rising costs and mounting U.S. death toll in Iraq and are questioning whether the administration's economic and anti-terrorism policies are working. (2003 CQ *Weekly*, p. 2198)

"It's a very different situation than we've seen in the last two years," said Sen. Chuck Hagel, R-Neb., a member of the Foreign Relations Committee who has criticized Bush for not giving other nations a big enough role in rebuilding Iraq. The public sees "a drain on the Treasury. We're taking casualties. . . . We've never been in the Middle East as deeply as this. All of this adds up to a very unsteady public that wants some answers."

Damage Control

The White House has been concerned enough about Republican anxiety that Vice President Dick Cheney and other administration officials have been on Capitol Hill to press Bush's case for the funds.

They know any nervousness that spills into public view generates headlines and creates political problems for Bush. "I think everyone is concerned about the cost," said Sam Brownback, R-Kan., a member of the Senate Appropriations Committee. "People are starting to ask more questions now: Why $87 billion? Is it needed? Is it structured in the right way?"

To answer those questions, Cheney

has met with the Senate and House Republican conferences, and the administration has made top officials such as Defense Secretary Donald H. Rumsfeld, Ambassador L. Paul Bremer III, the top civilian official in Iraq, and General John P. Abizaid, commander of the United States Central Command, widely available to explain the request at length in committee hearings.

In addition, the White House has been circulating information to Hill Republicans who want to support the request but have no idea how to defend it to their constituents.

That strategy acknowledged the reality behind many of the criticisms during several recent hearings on Iraq. For Republicans such as Pete V. Domenici of New Mexico, a member of the Senate Appropriations Committee, the pointed questions were less about opposing the funding than about needing a good set of talking points to make the case to skeptics back home.

"I think there is a substantial majority of Americans who think we should have gone to war, who still think it was the right decision, but who are fragile because they don't understand the plan," Domenici told Bremer at an Appropriations hearing Sept. 22. He suggested Bremer hold news conferences on a regular basis to explain the plan for rebuilding Iraq and report on its progress.

"They're going to get some pretty tough questions, because the people at home are asking us tough questions," Hagel said.

Former lawmakers say the GOP is keenly aware that it can take dissent only so far, especially in the House.

"I think you'll see great reluctance among rank-and-file Republicans to pile on in this situation," said John Edward Porter, R-Ill. (1980-2001), a former House appropriator and now a partner at Hogan & Hartson LLP.

Instead, Porter suggested, Republicans may simply let Democrats pose the tough questions — including those they secretly would like to ask themselves — so the issues get aired without GOP fingerprints. "There will be enough questions raised . . . that it will give great pause to the administration if it decides to ask for another supplemental," Porter said.

Talking Points

To help congressional Republicans convince the public — and perhaps themselves — that the funding is justified, one set of White House talking points noted that $87 billion is less than 4 percent of next year's federal budget. While Iraq's total reconstruction needs are projected at $50 billion to $75 billion, the administration says it expects the United States to have to pay only $20 billion and that other nations and Iraq itself ultimately will cover the rest.

In addition, the White House says the Iraq costs have been higher than expected because it was difficult before the war to get an accurate picture of the deterioration of Iraq's electrical, water and sewage systems.

A second set of White House talking points offered explanations for some of the troublesome line items in the reconstruction funding request, such as $50,000 a bed for two new Iraqi prisons and $9 million to improve postal service. The administration said the cost for the prison beds is less than the U.S. average and Iraq is running out of prison space for criminals and terrorists, and that most of the postal money is actually to repair looted post offices.

Even that information may not be much help to the administration's cause. "I would have thought the one thing the Iraqis were good at was providing plenty of prison space," Rep. David R. Obey of Wisconsin, the ranking Democrat on Appropriations, remarked to Bremer during a Sept. 24 hearing of the Foreign Operations Appropriations Subcommittee.

Until now, the closest Bush came to a

serious push-back from the Republican Congress came in the spring, on his economic policy. Under pressure from Democrats and moderate Senate Republicans, Congress slashed the second major tax cut of his presidency from the $674 billion he requested to the $350 billion he signed (PL 108-27). Even there, however, Congress never seriously questioned whether there would be a tax cut at all. And conservative leaders have made it clear they hardly consider a $350 billion tax cut a defeat. (*CQ Weekly*, p. 1309)

Now, despite real unease among Republicans over the stagnant jobs picture, the core of Bush's economic program is not under attack from within his own party. And the deteriorating deficit picture is still justified by many as acceptable in a time of war.

Aware that polls show jobs are the voters' top concern, Senate Majority Leader Bill Frist of Tennessee and other GOP leaders unveiled a "jobs and growth" agenda Oct. 2. But rather than outlining new initiatives, it was mainly a repackaging of legislation already moving through Congress — such as the energy bill (HR 6), limits on class action lawsuits (S 274) and a reauthorization of the Small Business Administration (S 1375) — that emphasizes their economic impact.

In general, Republicans agree that tax cuts have been the right way to stimulate the economy, so any new initiatives will continue in that vein. The Senate Finance Committee approved a

tax package (S 1637) on Oct. 1 that would give targeted tax relief to manufacturers. (*Taxes, p. 2428*)

The next day, the Senate rejected the latest Democratic attempt to pare Bush's tax cuts. An amendment by Democrat Joseph R. Biden Jr. of Delaware that would have raised taxes on the wealthiest Americans as a way to pay for the $87 billion Iraq supplemental was killed on a tabling motion, 57-42.

In the debate, Republicans advocated staying the course on Bush's economic policy. "The thing we need to do is to keep the growth occurring in this country, and you do that by low interest rates and low taxes," Brownback said.

Cornerstone of Terrorism War

Congress also is displaying the limits of its challenges to Bush on one of the cornerstones of the president's war against terrorism: the 2001 law known as the Patriot Act.

While polls have not shown strong public opposition to the law, there are other signs of anxiety. More than 175 cities and counties, as well as the states of Vermont, Alaska and Hawaii, have adopted resolutions criticizing the law. And Attorney General John Ashcroft recently went on a nationwide speaking tour to defend the law after the House voted overwhelmingly, with the support of 113 Republicans, to bar the application of a provision that allows police to conduct searches and seize evidence without notifying the subjects in advance. (*CQ Weekly, p. 1905*)

The celebration at the signing of the homeland defense spending bill Oct. 1 belied tensions between Congress and Bush, shown shaking hands with Sen. Patrick J. Leahy, D-Vt.

"The whole Patriot Act is one big secret," said Rep. C. L. "Butch" Otter, the Idaho Republican who sponsored the amendment, noting that the Justice Department has refused to release records of how it has been used in most cases.

Any legislative backlash, however, will be piecemeal. Otter is preparing a second amendment that would strip the attorney general's power to investigate religious institutions. And Sen. Larry E. Craig of Idaho, a former member of the GOP leadership, is planning to introduce a bill with Democrat Richard J. Durbin of Illinois that would rein in the FBI's subpoena powers and the power of law enforcement agencies to use "roving wiretaps," which follow suspects to any telephone lines they use.

But Otter says he has no intention of challenging the entire law. He believes some of it was necessary.

The Medicare Challenge

Overhauling Medicare, a potentially defining issue for Bush, may prove to be the exception to the rule of the Bush-Congress relationship.

Thirteen conservative Republicans who voted for the House version of the bill (HR 1) signed a letter to Speaker J. Dennis Hastert, R-Ill., saying they will not do so again if the final agreement does not include private competition and cost controls. These Republicans say the letter is not an idle threat, because the idea of creating a new, open-ended entitlement truly contradicts their basic view of the proper size and cost of the federal government. (2003 CQ *Weekly*, p. 2446)

"The letter should be taken quite literally," said its lead author, Rep. Patrick J. Toomey of Pennsylvania. "It's much more important to get a good bill than to get just any bill, and we're very serious about that."

Rep. Marsha Blackburn of Tennessee, a co-author of the letter, said she could no longer keep silent. "One of the things I learned while I was in the statehouse is that it's very easy to just keep your mouth shut and vote no," she said. "But that's not fair to everyone who's involved. It's much more honest to get involved in how the legislation is shaped."

These Republicans insist their letter was meant more to help the House negotiators' bargaining position than to challenge the president, and they say their goal is to improve the bill rather than to kill it. Some conservative leaders outside Congress, however, are open about their desire to stop the Medicare bill entirely.

"I think the question is whether or not we can change the political dynamics enough so that the bill becomes stymied," said Moore of the Club for Growth. The administration, he said, may "see it as a political winner in 2004, and our job as conservatives is to convince them that the politics actually work the other way."

Although Bush insists he wants a bill, and held a highly publicized meeting with House and Senate negotiators Sept. 25 to urge them to keep working, he has not been personally involved in the negotiations and therefore has plenty of room to distance himself if the negotiations fail.

Furthermore, there is some question whether Bush is using all of the tools at his disposal to make sure the bill passes. Three of the Republicans who signed the letter said they have gotten no feedback from the White House at all since they released it Sept. 17.

The fact that Republicans are venting their concerns at all is remarkable for a party that historically has frowned upon airing its differences in public.

That level of party discipline has helped Bush, for the most part, win greater compliance from a Republican Congress than the most recent Democratic presidents, Bill Clinton and Jimmy Carter, did from Congresses that were even more solidly Democratic.

"The prevailing wisdom is, 'If we fight in public, that's what Democrats do,'" said Lewis L. Gould, a professor emeritus in American history at the University of Texas at Austin and author of the forthcoming "Grand Old Party: A History of the Republicans." "When it's a president they agree with, and they endorse the policies in their general concept, it wouldn't make sense to get into fratricidal conflicts like the Democrats do."

Republicans are also aware that despite his declining overall approval ratings, Bush is still tremendously popular with their core supporters. "Most Republican voters still love him, and certainly the activists do," Sinclair said.

In addition, they are conscious of the presidential election politics that are already well under way, and the mileage Democratic presidential candidates are getting from criticizing Bush's policies on Iraq and the economy and his efforts to safeguard, if not expand, the Patriot Act.

Not all Republicans buy the argument that they should keep their differences private, however. "Our role now, as stewards of the funds, is to make sure the money is being spent wisely, with benchmarks to make sure it's being spent wisely," Kolbe said of the Iraq supplemental.

"It's never easy to criticize a president who you love and respect, and who is, of course, of your own party," said Feeney, who has advocated loans rather than grants for Iraq and was also one of the 13 House Republicans who signed the Medicare letter. "You have an obligation, when you think your friends are making mistakes, to speak up."

And the fact that other Republicans have been relatively restrained in questioning the administration in public on Iraq does not mean the tough questions have not been raised in private, some are quick to point out.

"They have been. It's just that they haven't been public," said Sen. George V. Voinovich, R-Ohio, a member of the Foreign Relations Committee.

By using the hearings and the floor debate to vent their frustrations over the cost of the Iraq request — even while making it clear they will ultimately vote for it — congressional Republicans say they are still having an impact by putting pressure on the administration to be more careful with its cost estimates and funding requests in the future.

Loyalty vs. Self-Preservation

"The administration is going to be put on notice that it can't just waltz in here and say, 'We're in charge of the foreign policy, you just give us the money,'" said Hagel.

Analysts agree. "The message is, 'This ticket is good for this trip only, and don't come back and ask us for another one,'" said Gould. "The peril for the administration is . . . what if they have to come back in June or July and say, 'Uh, we need another supplemental'?"

If that happens, the Republican tradition of discipline and loyalty will be pitted against the oldest tradition in politics: self-preservation. "The first rule of politics is to protect yourself," said former Democratic Rep. Dan Glickman of Kansas (1977-95), who now directs the Institute of Politics at Harvard's John F. Kennedy School of Government. "Yeah, party loyalty is important, but a smart senator or representative isn't going to do anything willingly that jeopardizes his or her career." ◆

Score Belies Bush's Success

Multiple votes on controversial issues skew president's support numbers

It was the year George W. Bush was supposed to have his clearest shot at getting his priorities through Congress. For the first time he had an entire year with Republican majorities in both the House and Senate, and their enthusiastic support for most of his agenda, together with his political strength as a wartime president, gave Bush the kind of bargaining power of which most presidents can only dream.

So it might seem ironic that Bush's success rate on votes in Congress actually fell slightly in 2003, making it the lowest rating of the three years of his presidency.

During the year, lawmakers sided with Bush on 78.7 percent of all the recorded votes in the House and Senate on which he staked out a clear position beforehand. By historical standards, that is still the highest success rate of any president since Lyndon B. Johnson, whose extraordinary support from Congress during his push for the Great Society programs is shaping up as the closest parallel to the Bush presidency.

But it is still lower than the 87 percent success rate Bush chalked up in 2001 or his 87.8 percent success rate in 2002, both years in which he had to deal with a Democratic Senate for all or part of the year.

Bush is now at approximately the level Johnson was in 1966, the third full year of his presidency, when Congress voted the way he wanted 79 percent of the time. That was the year when Johnson's legislative success rate — which started at 88 percent in 1964 and peaked at 93 percent in 1965 — began to erode, signaling that he could no longer expect to get everything he wanted.

Congressional Quarterly's annual presidential support studies, which have tracked every president's success rate at

Bush, shown here in May with Vice President Dick Cheney, left, and GOP leaders, saw his voting support dip in 2003.

CQ PHOTO / SCOTT J. FERRELL

the Capitol since Dwight D. Eisenhower took office in 1953, do not take into account whether the president's proposals became law. CQ looks at each House and Senate floor vote, determines whether the president had articulated a clear position before the roll was called, then notes the outcome.

If voting scores told everything about a president's success with Congress, historians might look on 2003 as the year in which Bush's effectiveness started to slip. But there is always more going on than the recorded votes indicate.

Partisan Shots, Quick Recoveries

Instead, analysts say the slight drop in last year's success rate says more about the partisan polarization of the Senate — in which the Republican leadership was more willing to bring up contentious items and the Democrats were more willing to block them —

than it does about Bush's effectiveness. *(Party unity, p. 32)*

"The overall fact is that the score is pretty damned good," said Charles O. Jones, a professor emeritus of political science at the University of Wisconsin-Madison. "It's more impressive than I imagined it would be. You almost get the impression that the Senate isn't working, and it certainly isn't working for the president."

And while lawmakers from both parties showed more willingness than in the past to vote against Bush's priorities, particularly on a series of second-tier items in the middle of the year, the other side of the story was that the president managed to get nearly all of the defeats reversed in the final bills — generally through negotiations that are not reflected in the voting records.

"There were drawbacks, but the president certainly got what he wanted," said George C. Edwards III, professor of political science and former director of the Center for Presidential Studies at Texas A&M University.

These results suggest Bush could easily see his support scores drop again in 2004, since congressional leaders in both parties expect partisanship to get worse as he stands for a second term and the GOP tries to maintain if not expand its congressional majorities on Election Day. But if his recoveries in 2003 are any indication, Bush may be able to survive even more voting defeats this year — as lawmakers vent their concerns over controversial issues and score points against each other — without suffering any real diminishment of his practical effectiveness with Congress.

"You have more continuity here than you have change," said John C. Fortier, a research associate at the conservative American Enterprise Institute. "The president really doesn't lose that much in Congress. There are certainly votes where he was beaten, but he doesn't lose anything in a big way."

Some of the 2003 defeats arguably were driven by Bush's actions. He pushed the Senate to keep trying to confirm his most conservative judicial nominees in the face of almost unanimous Democratic opposition, leading to repeated losses for the president on cloture votes in which the margins barely changed. And Bush declined to cut deals on some divisive issues before they reached the House and Senate floors — such as whether postwar reconstruction aid to Iraq should have been a grant or a loan — leading to defeats on issues that in the past might have been negotiated in his favor in advance of a floor vote.

"In some cases, they do push things rather than negotiate," Burdett Loomis, a professor of government at the University of Kansas, said of members of the Bush administration.

Still, most political scientists say a 79 percent success rate is nothing to be ashamed of — particularly when much of the coverage of Congress in 2003 focused on near-gridlock in the Senate.

More Votes

One difference between 2003 and the previous years is that there were more votes on issues where Bush had expressed a clear position, and therefore more chances for opponents to score victories. Congress took 174 votes on such issues, compared with 120 in 2001 and only 98 in 2002.

It was the highest number of presidential position votes since 1995, when President Bill Clinton faced off for the first time against new and assertive Republican majorities that had a lengthy agenda of their own.

Bush, of course, did not face an aggressive opposition party that was setting the legislative agenda. Clinton's success rate in Congress plummeted from 86.4 percent in 1994, the last year he had Democratic majorities to work with, to 36.2 percent in 1995. By contrast, Bush was driving the agenda in Congress with a freedom presidents rarely enjoy.

Part of the reason the number of presidential position votes increased in 2003, Jones observed, is that some of his more contentious domestic priorities returned after having been put on hold after the 2001 terrorist attacks.

In general, though, Bush stuck to his well-established pattern of taking positions on a relatively small number of high-priority issues, giving himself and Congress plenty of maneuvering room on the rest.

"He's taken stands on a very few issues, so a few issues are looming large," Edwards said. "It's a very narrow agenda, which is classic George W. Bush."

That the number of presidential position votes grew anyway points to another 2003 phenomenon: repetitive votes. Several issues came up repeatedly in various forms, as did the standoff between Bush and the Democrats over his picks for the federal appeals courts.

The result is that the roster of presidential support votes was dominated by a handful of high-profile items: the $350 billion tax cut package (PL 108-27), the $87.5 billion spending package on postwar Iraq and Afghanistan (PL 108-106), the Medicare overhaul and prescription drug benefit creation (PL 108-173), the stalled energy policy rewrite (HR 6) and the ban on a procedure called "partial birth" abortion (PL 108-105) by its opponents. Several of these were controversial enough to draw amendments, which inflated the number of times an issue showed up in the presidential support record — and often padded Bush's success rate.

The abortion measure, for example, generated eight votes in favor of Bush's position. Each chamber voted on passage of an initial version of the bill and adoption of the eventual conference agreement; in addition, each chamber defeated a substitute to make an exception to the ban if the mother's health was in danger. The Senate also defeated a Democratic amendment addressing the health of the mother, and the House defeated a Democratic motion to send the bill back to committee.

The judicial nominations, by contrast, added to Bush's share of defeats. Of the 119 presidential position votes in the Senate, 72 (61 percent) were on nominations, compared with only 43 in 2001 and 38 in 2002. Most of Bush's court picks were readily confirmed; of the 18 votes that were presidential defeats, most were repeated votes on appeals court nominees — including seven unsuccessful votes to advance the nomination of Miguel A. Estrada, four such cloture votes on Priscilla Owen and two on William H. Pryor Jr.

"It's a hardening of positions on both sides — a willingness of the Republican leadership to bring these up repeatedly and the Democrats to say, 'We're not going to go along,'" said Fortier.

The nomination votes show how polarized the Senate has become, particularly when the GOP is convinced that the repeated public setbacks for the most conservative judges can be turned into political victories at the polls, analysts said.

"I think the president can be characterized as having resolve, and the Republicans think it works to their advantage," said Edwards.

Short-Lived Rebellions

On legislative issues, Bush faced some defeats as well. Some were probably avoidable, analysts say in hindsight. But as a general rule, the setbacks on the floor had little bearing on the final results — because White House officials stared down their congressional opponents and almost always got what they wanted in the end.

In rapid succession, Congress voted against a series of Bush's policies this summer and early fall. The Senate voted to block his administration's proposed changes to overtime rules and his proposal to privatize some air traffic controllers. It also voted to nullify new Federal Communications Commission (FCC) rules, embraced by Bush, that would have allowed media conglomerates to own more television stations and newspapers. And appropriations bills in both the House and Senate included a rider to block part of that deregulation for a year. (*Overtime, 2003 CQ Weekly p. 2440; aviation, p. 2357; media consolidation, p. 3137*)

The House voted to stop the administration from turning thousands of federal jobs over to private businesses. And — for the first time, and over the president's clear objections — the Senate joined the House in voting for a spending bill rider that would have effectively ended the ban on travel to Cuba. (*Outsourcing, 2003 CQ Weekly p. 2224; Cuba travel, pp. 2642, 2224*)

In the end, though, a compromise attached to the omnibus fiscal 2004 appropriations measure (HR 2673) expected to clear Congress later this month would let a single company own more broadcast stations than it can now, although fewer than the FCC wanted. (*2003 CQ Weekly, p. 2964*)

And the other challenges to the White House disappeared quickly. At the insistence of White House emissaries to the talks on the final spending package, appropriators jettisoned the overtime and Cuba travel riders —

Presidential Success | *History*

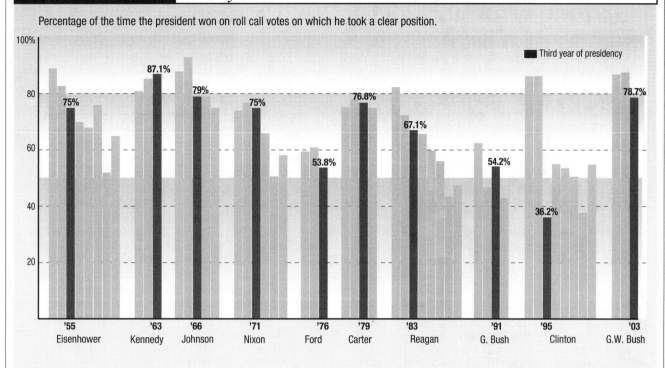

Percentage of the time the president won on roll call votes on which he took a clear position.

■ Third year of presidency

'55 Eisenhower · 75%
'63 Kennedy · 87.1%
'66 Johnson · 79%
'71 Nixon · 75%
'76 Ford · 53.8%
'79 Carter · 76.8%
'83 Reagan · 67.1%
'91 G. Bush · 54.2%
'95 Clinton · 36.2%
'03 G.W. Bush · 78.7%

both of which had drawn veto threats — and removed almost all of the teeth from the outsourcing language.

Also, a Senate filibuster of the Federal Aviation Administration reauthorization law (PL 108-176) fell away after the agency's administrator promised no air traffic control jobs would be privatized in 2004. (*2003 CQ Weekly, p. 3141*)

Not all of the defeats were on such relatively second-tier issues. After refusing to negotiate with lawmakers who thought Iraq should be required to pay back its reconstruction aid through future oil revenues, Bush suffered a defeat on the Iraq supplemental spending bill when the Senate adopted an amendment by Evan Bayh, D-Ind., that would have turned half the $20 billion in aid into a loan. That rebellion did not last long, however. After the Senate vote, White House negotiators pressured appropriators not to include any loan provisions in the final bill, and that is how the final version was written. (*2003 CQ Weekly, p. 2715*)

One defeat that did have a lasting impact happened in March, when the Senate — nervous about the cost of the Iraq war that had just started — chopped Bush's tax cut in half. It set what turned out to be a binding ceiling of $350 billion on the second major tax cut in three years, down from the $726 billion Bush originally asked for. Even there, however, most conservatives say a tax cut of that size was hardly a disappointment. (*2003 CQ Weekly, p. 740*)

Another Senate vote — which eliminated a provision from the budget resolution that assumed Congress would allow oil drilling in Alaska's Arctic National Wildlife Refuge — showed the president could not get his way on that issue and persuaded lawmakers to leave the provision out of the final energy agreement, which ended up stalling for other reasons. (*2003 CQ Weekly, p. 698*)

Still, analysts said, sometimes Bush's hard lines may have led to unnecessary defeats — particularly the loan vs. grant debate for the Iraq aid — which other presidents might have simply negotiated before the vote. "In some ways, that was crying for a negotiation," said Loomis.

Indeed, the number of Bush defeats in a Republican Senate was higher than it was in a Democratic Senate because the Democrats were less willing to bring bills to the floor before a deal had been reached, Fortier said.

Such recalcitrance in dealing with Congress may have helped Bush get what he wanted in the long run, however.

2003 Data	
Senate	89 victories
	30 defeats
House	48 victories
	7 defeats
Total Bush success rate:	78.7 percent

In his first two years, he used a dual-track legislative strategy, pursuing bipartisan agreements on some issues — notably the 2001 education overhaul (PL 107-110) — while trying to eke out bare victories on others by solidifying his GOP support and peeling away just enough Democrats to pass bills, said Fortier.

In 2003, the bipartisan strategy became nearly impossible and therefore disappeared, Fortier said. The Medicare overhaul, he noted, started as a bipartisan bill in the Senate and became a more partisan product in the end, as it became clear that Republicans and Democrats were so deeply dug into their ideological camps that the differences could not be bridged.

"I think Medicare is really the metaphor for it," agreed Loomis. "When push came to shove, they were willing to do it in a highly partisan way." ◆

Leading Scorers: Presidential Support

Support indicates those who in 2003 voted most often for President Bush's position. **Opposition** shows those who voted most often against his position. Scores are based on actual votes cast.

Members who missed half or more of the votes are not listed. Scores are rounded to one decimal; lawmakers with identical scores are listed alphabetically. *(2004 CQ Weekly, pp. 56, 58)*

Senate Support

Bunning

Nelson

Republicans		Democrats	
Bunning, Ky.	100.0%	Miller, Ga.	96.8%
McConnell, Ky.	100.0	Nelson, Neb.	79.8
Burns, Mont.	99.2	Breaux, La.	70.9
Grassley, Iowa	99.2	Lincoln, Ark.	60.5
Hatch, Utah	99.2	Pryor, Ark.	59.7
Kyl, Ariz.	99.2	Landrieu, La.	57.9
Santorum, Pa.	99.2	Conrad, N.D.	57.8
Sessions, Ala.	99.2	Nelson, Fla.	56.3
Coleman, Minn.	98.3	Bayh, Ind.	55.1
Dole, N.C.	98.3	Dorgan, N.D.	54.7
Frist, Tenn.	98.3	Byrd, W.Va.	53.9
Lugar, Ind.	98.3	Baucus, Mont.	53.8

Senate Opposition

Snowe

Edwards

Republicans		Democrats	
Chafee, R.I.	23.1%	Edwards, N.C.	58.7%
Snowe, Maine	18.5	Graham, Fla.	58.3
Collins, Maine	13.5	Corzine, N.J.	56.8
Specter, Pa.	10.6	Lautenberg, N.J.	56.3
McCain, Ariz.	9.2	Mikulski, Md.	56.0
Campbell, Colo.	7.0	Boxer, Calif.	55.6
Gregg, N.H.	7.0	Reed, R.I.	55.2
Murkowski, Alaska	6.7	Durbin, Ill.	54.5
Sununu, N.H.	5.2	Biden, Del.	54.1
Voinovich, Ohio	5.2	Harkin, Iowa	54.1
Graham, S.C.	5.1	Sarbanes, Md.	53.9
Shelby, Ala.	5.1		

House Support

Republicans

Republicans	
Blunt, Mo.	100.0%
Boehner, Ohio	100.0
Cantor, Va.	100.0
Chocola, Ind.	100.0
Cox, Calif.	100.0
Crane, Ill.	100.0
DeLay, Texas	100.0
Dreier, Calif.	100.0
Goss, Fla.	100.0
Harris, Fla.	100.0
Hart, Pa.	100.0
Knollenberg, Mich.	100.0
Linder, Ga.	100.0
McCrery, La.	100.0
Nunes, Calif.	100.0
Putnam, Fla.	100.0
Radanovich, Calif.	100.0
Reynolds, N.Y.	100.0
Smith, Texas	100.0
Sullivan, Okla.	100.0
Weller, Ill.	100.0

Lucas

Democrats	
Hall, Texas	85.2%
Lucas, Ky.	76.4
Cramer, Ala.	73.1
John, La.	69.1
Stenholm, Texas	67.3
Skelton, Mo.	61.8
Peterson, Minn.	58.5
Alexander, La.	56.4
Matheson, Utah	56.4
Davis, Tenn.	55.8
Dooley, Calif.	54.7
Marshall, Ga.	52.8
Taylor, Miss.	52.7

House Opposition

Paul

Jackson

Republicans		Democrats	
Paul, Texas	57.4%	Jackson, Ill.	90.9%
Leach, Iowa	42.6	Scott, Va.	90.7
Shays, Conn.	32.7	Delahunt, Mass.	90.4
Simmons, Conn.	32.7	Conyers, Mich.	89.8
Castle, Del.	30.9	Lee, Calif.	89.1
Boehlert, N.Y.	29.6	Stark, Calif.	89.1
Flake, Ariz.	29.6	Brown, Ohio	88.9
Johnson, Conn.	29.6	Filner, Calif.	88.9
Jones, N.C.	27.3	Miller, Calif.	88.7
Johnson, Ill.	25.9	Slaughter, N.Y.	88.7
		Waters, Calif.	88.5
		Owens, N.Y.	88.2

Bush's Domestic Vision: Help People Help Themselves

President's 'ownership society' plan must compete with other costly priorities

President Bush is devising a theme for the future by taking a page from the past. As he turns his attention from war and the economy to policy issues that are closer to home — and of interest to prospective voters — Bush has picked up a playbook that worked well for one of his predecessors, Bill Clinton, during the last year that had an incumbent president running for re-election.

The emerging domestic agenda for Bush's hoped-for second term draws inspiration from the landmark 1996 overhaul of welfare that ended more than 60 years of guaranteed federal cash assistance and required recipients to work as a condition of receiving aid. (*1996 Almanac, p. 6-3*)

Like Clinton, who used welfare overhaul to burnish his credentials with moderate swing voters, Bush wants to expand his "compassionate conservative" image by focusing on issues that matter to middle-income taxpayers, such as education, health care and retirement.

Unlike his Democratic predecessor, however, Bush also wants to mollify fiscal conservatives uncomfortable with the prospect of increased domestic spending and what they regard as a "big government" approach to domestic policy conundrums rooted in the Great Society and New Deal.

Bush believes the combination of less government and more personal responsibility that was the foundation for the new welfare law (PL 104-193) is the solution to a host of other public policy problems surrounding health insurance, retirement benefits and personal savings.

He touched on the theme lightly in his State of the Union address to Congress on Jan. 20. But he has been more explicit on the campaign trail, especially in appearances before prospective donors.

In the latter venues, he is actively promoting the notion of an "ownership society," in which the government has a diminished role in Americans' retirement savings, health insurance, and employment and education benefits. Individuals would be encouraged to act as investors in their own destiny by squirreling savings into tax-preferred personal accounts tied to stocks, bonds and other securities.

"The president . . . recognizes that government has a lot of answers, but at the end of the day, people have to be self-reliant," said Jay Lefkowitz, former domestic policy counsel for the Bush administration. "Government's job has become to help people become self-reliant."

This new agenda — consisting of the creation of at least five new types of savings accounts — represents a convergence of conservative tax doctrine and social policies. At the same time, he hopes the idea of creating dedicated accounts for such things as unexpected health expenses or a child's college tuition has political appeal and, at a minimum, creates the impression that voters have more control over their individual financial futures. (*Savings accounts, p. 82*)

Bush has already started to advance the concept in his campaign for re-election. "In a compassionate society, people respect one another, and they take responsibility for the decisions they make in life," he told a group of contributors in Orlando, Fla., last fall. "The culture of America is changing from one that has said, if it feels good, do it, and if you've got a problem, blame somebody else, to a culture in which each of us understands we're responsible for the decisions we make in life."

Assuming the argument resonates with voters, congressional supporters are ready to push legislation creating some of the accounts and perhaps even force some election-year test votes during the current session. Supporters also say an expanded discussion will at least legitimize the ideas, as was the case with plans to overhaul the federal Medicare program and fund programs to promote marriage.

"We call it setting the terms of the debate," said Robert Rector, senior research fellow for domestic policy studies at the Heritage Foundation.

But Bush still will have a difficult time selling Congress on the initiative. Democrats say Bush's true intention is to relieve government of its responsibilities and replace it with a free market that values profits more than a social safety net. What's more troublesome, though, to moderates from both parties is the possibility that creating tax breaks to spur savings will not help the poorest Americans — many of whom do not make enough to pay taxes.

They also fear a drain on revenue for the Treasury, which would help to dramatically increase the size of budget deficits. (*Deficit dilemma, p. 111*)

"I think there would be a lot of Democrats who would join in supporting bolstering assets for middle- and lower-income households, [but] most of the administration proposals don't really do that," said Peter R. Orszag, senior fellow in economic studies at the Brookings Institution and a former economic adviser to President Bill Clinton. "Their major effect is to provide tax breaks for saving that high-income households would have done anyway."

Accounts for Many Purposes

One aspect of the ownership society has already been written into law. Last year's Medicare overhaul law (PL 108-173) created "health savings accounts" that would allow anyone who pays high deductibles for health insurance to save and withdraw money tax-free to pay for medical expenses. The accounts — long sought by conservatives — would cost more than $6 billion over 10 years. (*2004 CQ Weekly, p. 238*)

Bush and his allies want to take the concept much further. In his State of the Union address, the president proposed expanding the accounts — currently limited to individuals with an annual deductible of at least $1,000 or families with deductibles of at least $2,000 — so that individuals could buy catastrophic health care coverage through the accounts and deduct 100 percent of the premiums from their taxes. (*Accounts, p. 85*)

Bush also wants to create "lifetime savings accounts" modeled on Roth IRAs but without any restrictions on when account holders could make withdrawals. Contributions would not be deductible, but earnings and withdrawals

Stenholm of Texas, standing, was one of the few Democrats to applaud Bush's proposal to overhaul the Social Security system.

would not be taxed. The money could be used for virtually any purpose — making a down payment on a house, unexpected medical expenses or even going on vacation.

His concept includes two retirement savings accounts: one that would be similar to an expanded Roth IRA but with fewer withdrawal restrictions, and one that would combine employer-based contribution retirement plans such as 401(k)s and increase contribution limits.

Congress already has a history of creating tax-preferred investment vehicles — such as Keoghs, IRAs and Roth IRAs — to spur savings. However, last year's creation of health savings accounts broke with precedent. While all of the older investment vehicles were taxed either when money was deposited or withdrawn, the medical accounts are not subject to taxation at any point in their existence. That tracks with conservative philosophy on taxation that opposes any tax associated with savings and investment.

The most ambitious component of the ownership society would be an overhaul of the Social Security system, whose costs will begin to exceed income from tax collections by 2018, according to program trustees' most recent projections.

Bush would like to fulfill a long-sought policy goal of conservatives and allow workers to divert some payroll taxes into savings accounts tied to stocks and bonds. Such "privatization" plans have been depicted as a way of solving the program's financing problems because private investments could deliver a significantly higher return than the securities the Social Security system holds and reduce the need for more long-term borrowing to pay retiree benefits.

"We should make the Social Security system a source of ownership for the American people," Bush said in his speech. "And we should limit the burden of government on this economy by acting as good stewards of taxpayers' dollars."

Changing Times

Conservatives say time is their ally in pushing the idea of an ownership society. Baby boomers who grew up during the prosperous 1950s tend to be more accepting of a reduced role for government than Americans who recall the Depression and New Deal.

The debate over Social Security provides some evidence for this belief. As recently as the mid-1990s, Social Security was regarded as an untouchable "third rail of American politics," and proposing to overhaul the system was so taboo that candidates who did could begin writing farewell speeches. But Bush used the issue during his 2000 presidential campaign to appeal to younger workers who were comfortable with the idea of private retirement accounts because many had them through their employers. Two years later, Senate Republican candidates Lindsay Graham of South Carolina, John E. Sununu of New Hampshire and Elizabeth Dole of North Carolina each touted privatizing Social Security during their campaigns, and won.

Will Privatization Work?

It is unclear whether such proposals actually would increase most Americans' nationwide private savings — or make enough of them financially secure. The nonpartisan Employee Benefit Research Institute estimates that retired Americans will have at least $45 billion less than they will need to cover basic expenses by 2030. While middle-income individuals could provide for their future by saving 5 percent of their annual salaries on top of the retirement benefits they expect to receive, many lower-income individuals lack the resources to save enough for retirement, the institute concluded.

Evidence additionally suggests that the creation of new tax-preferred investment options does not necessarily increase overall savings, but may simply lead people to shift their money among savings vehicles.

"The main criticism with the Bush proposals is that they don't necessarily create new savings incentives that are strong enough," said Reid Cramer, a research director at the New America Foundation. "They raise the contribution limits for these accounts, but the fear is that people will use them as tax shelters. They'll take money they already have and shift it over to tax-preferred accounts."

Cramer says the way 401(k) programs are used already illustrates that such accounts do not act as an incentive for lower-income workers to save extra money. For instance, a study by the Tax Policy Center and the Center on Budget and Policy Priorities shows that about 40 percent of employees earning more than $160,000 a year contribute the maximum allowable amount to their 401(k) retirement plans, but only 1 percent of people who make less than $40,000 annually put in the maximum amount.

Ownership Through Savings Accounts

President Bush favors a variety of tax-preferred savings accounts to help individuals cover retirement and certain other costs:

Health savings accounts (HSA)

Allows individuals under the age of 65 who have high-deductible health insurance policies to set aside, tax-free, money in these accounts to use later for health care needs. The money also would not be taxed when it is withdrawn. These accounts were established under the Medicare overhaul bill that became law in December (PL 108-173).

Lifetime savings accounts (LSA)

Would allow individuals to withdraw money at any time for such expenses as the down payment on a house, the purchase of a boat, medical care, or a vacation. After-tax contributions would be put into these accounts, but earnings on interest, dividends and capital gains would be tax-free.

Retirement savings accounts (RSA)

Would be similar to existing Roth IRA accounts, under which contributions are not tax-deductible, but withdrawals, including all earnings, would be tax-free. The accounts would have withdrawal restrictions.

Employer retirement savings accounts (ERSA)

Would try to combine everything that is now in the form of a 401(k) or 403(b) retirement account, with a possible increase in individual contribution limits.

Social Security

Would allow workers to divert a portion of the payroll taxes they now pay into the Social Security system to personal accounts that would be invested in stocks and bonds.

The tax policy center is a joint venture of the Brookings Institution and the Urban Institute.

Democrats also charge that Bush's policies would do little to help the most vulnerable populations, such as individuals near the poverty line who do not have health insurance.

"Rather than a society that restricts its rewards to a privileged few, we need an 'opportunity society' that allows all Americans to succeed," said Senate Minority Leader Tom Daschle, D-S.D., offering a twist on Bush's ownership society label.

But attempts to enact the ownership agenda will have to vie with other domestic priorities in a time of extremely tight budgets. Bush would have to pay for his bold proposals at a time when the government is running a nearly $500 billion deficit, largely because of his tax cuts and continued increases in domestic spending. Legislation authorizing any of the new savings accounts would also have to compete with costly domestic measures Congress already is considering, including bills reauthorizing the 1996 welfare law, the Head Start early-childhood program and the law governing special-education programs. Congress this year is expected to vote to spend an additional $3 billion on child care programs and another $2 billion on grants to states for special education.

Tight budgets last year scuttled an administration attempt to create personal re-employment accounts for jobless workers. The attempt came after the administration and Republican congressional leaders opted not to expand a supplemental unemployment insurance program amid signs that the economy was recovering and unemployment was on the decline.

The administration proposed creating personal accounts and awarding grants of up to $3,000 for out-of-work individuals to use for job training or counseling or for services such as child care that might help during an employment search. The House Education and the Workforce Committee approved a bill (HR 444) authorizing the program in March, but the measure died when budget writers could not fit its $3.6 billion, two-year price tag into the fiscal 2004 budget resolution (H Con Res 95). (2003 *CQ Weekly*, p. 1193)

Health Savings Accounts

Budget concerns notwithstanding, one aspect of the ownership society almost certain to be debated this year is Bush's proposed expansion of health savings accounts. Rising health costs continue to provide fodder for lively political debate, as they did during last year's Medicare debate.

Supporters of expanding the accounts say the proposal will encourage more people to open the tax-free accounts and have direct control over how and when they will spend on their future health care needs. Adherents of this view say individuals' ability to withdraw money from the accounts when they need it is preferable to having them rely on government-run programs that may overuse some services and not sufficiently address individuals' needs.

"The one thing we really haven't tried is letting consumers have a say," said Grace-Marie Turner, president of the Galen Institute, an Alexandria, Va., think tank that promotes free-market approaches to health policy. "This is giving people more control over their money and an incentive to spend those dollars wisely."

But skeptics see big problems with the proposal. Opponents say healthier individuals with money to spare will take advantage of the proposal and buy health plans with high deductibles in order to become eligible for the tax-free accounts. That would leave older, sicker individuals in more traditional insurance plans with lower deductibles — a situation that could drive up claims and costs for those plans until they become prohibitively expensive for employers to maintain.

Expanding the accounts the way Bush envisions would appeal to some businesses and workers. Employers would be able to contribute to a worker's medical savings account, and those contributions would not be included in the person's taxable income. The move could be attractive to small businesses that were struggling with health care costs. Those businesses could opt to buy cheaper health coverage with higher deductibles for their workers, and then set aside extra money in workers' medical savings accounts.

The Main Event: Social Security

The most heated debate, though, will be over Social Security and whether workers should be able to divert money now designated for the program into private savings accounts.

Three years ago, Bush appointed a commission to study ways to create private accounts. The panel suggested three options. The first two would allow workers to invest 2 percent or 4 percent of payroll taxes into private accounts. A third option would allow workers to contribute 1 percent of their annual income into a private account and receive a government match equaling 2.5 percent of their income up to a maximum of $1,000. The "transition" cost of sustaining the existing system and creating new accounts could be at least $2 trillion over the next 75 years.

Retirement Accounts No Sure Thing

Stock market declines have wreaked havoc with the nation's 401(k) accounts and may provide a preview of what could happen to individual Social Security accounts. Average per-person year-end 401(k) balances for select age groups:

	1999	2000	2001	2002
All accounts	$64,074	$63,470	$62,646	$57,668
Owners in their 50s with 30+ years in the program	160,917	145,555	136,657	120,987
Owners in their 60s with 30+ years in the program	209,900	188,880	175,542	156,180

SOURCE: EBRI/ICI Participant-Directed Retirement Plan Data Collection Project. Data come from a sample of 5.3 million participants.

CQ GRAPHICS / MARILYN GATES-DAVIS

Critics said the commission did not advocate a specific plan to send to Congress, effectively allowing Bush to talk about overhauling the system without having to dwell on how to pay for it.

"That has pretty much been the trend to his overall legislative program from Day One," said Rep. Robert T. Matsui of California, chairman of the Democratic Congressional Campaign Committee. "This is basically conceptualizing how the individual programs are put together, and that's it."

Democratic Resistance

Democrats are against making major changes to a social program they view as one of their party's proudest achievements, saying it is inappropriate to put retirement savings at risk in sometimes volatile securities markets. Since the Bush commission's report, Democrats have pointed to corporate scandals such as the collapse of energy giant Enron Corp. as evidence of the risk. Their resistance is expected to be particularly fierce in the wake of Bush's success reshaping Medicare.

However, some centrists say Democrats must propose alternatives or risk being branded obstructionists.

South Carolina Sen. Graham said the 2002 elections proved candidates can talk about private accounts without risking defeat.

Graham has proposed legislation (S 1878) that would allow younger workers to invest up to $1,300 of their Social Security taxes into private accounts each year. Low-income workers would receive a $500 matching deposit from the federal government. Those age 55 and older could remain in the existing system.

Graham would pay for the plan by cutting some tax breaks and other preferences for large corporations and investing the savings in the Social Security trust funds.

In the House, Reps. Charles W. Stenholm, D-Texas, and Jim Kolbe, R-Ariz., have led the fight for several years to create private accounts before the Social Security trust fund dries up.

However, stock market volatility and fear of antagonizing senior voters have prevented the measure from being brought up for votes.

The fund is projected to run out of money in 2042, according to the trustees' report. To continue benefits, Social Security will have to cash in Treasury IOUs from its trust fund. That will force the federal government to borrow more.

Lawmakers could seek to ensure the future health of the system by raising Social Security taxes or cutting retirees' benefits. But those options are not considered realistic in the current political climate.

Kolbe said Bush needs to show more leadership on the issue by proposing specific legislation. Otherwise, he said, the Social Security discussion will be confined to a few committee hearings.

But Lefkowitz, the former White House domestic policy counsel, says he believes Bush already has made strides by focusing debate on the issue.

"It is starting to get some traction, and any time you want to change the status quo, it is threatening to some people," he said. "You don't get better or stronger without making some changes. I think you'll continue to hear him talk about it." ◆

A Record to Run On

President previews re-election campaign message in his State of the Union address

During the weeks before George W. Bush delivered the final State of the Union address of this presidential term, White House officials insisted that he was not distracted by the onslaught of criticism directed at him by those who would oppose him in November.

The president was having no trouble remaining above the political fray, his aides said, while those vying for the 2000 Democratic presidential nomination described his policies day after day with various degrees of scorn. And Bush could be confident that his annual address to Congress, delivered with all the customary ceremony from the rostrum of the House chamber, would allow him to present a powerful image on national television of a president leading the nation. Conveniently, he would be doing so one night after the Democrats formally started their battle for the nomination at the Iowa caucuses.

But by the time Bush had finished speaking Jan. 20, he had made it clear that he was planning to be at least as much a political figure as a presidential one this year.

On the opening day of the sharply divided 108th Congress' second session, Bush delivered an address that revealed how closely he has been paying attention to the race for the Democratic nomination. He implicitly conceded that some of his would-be rivals' rhetorical punches had landed and that the time had come to make the case for his re-election.

In a point-by-point rebuttal to the seven Democrats still running for president, Bush laid out a combative defense of his handling of foreign policy, the Iraq war and the economy. He urged that the two major tax cuts enacted in the first three years of his administra-

Bush, escorted by Senate leaders, is greeted by lawmakers as he enters the House chamber Jan. 20.

tion (PL 107-16, PL 108-27) be extended indefinitely. And he leaned over the podium for emphasis as he warned the rest of the room not to change the recently signed Medicare prescription drug law (PL 108-173) or the overhaul of education programs (PL 107-110) that he signed two years ago.

One clear inference of the speech was that Bush is comfortable using the domestic and economic legislative accomplishments he has had so far, combined with his conduct of the war on terrorism, as the basis for his campaign. He actually made only a dozen specific requests for action by Congress, a smaller laundry list than either Bush or his predecessors have traditionally unfurled each January. Most of the initiatives on his list were designed to showcase a GOP commitment to job creation and to improving access to medical care.

For the benefit of Republican conservatives — the base of his political

support — Bush offered reassurances of their shared values, forcefully pledging to defend the institution of marriage as the union of a man and a woman, promoting sexual abstinence and anti-drug initiatives for teenagers, and calling on the sports world to stop the use of steroids. (*2004 CQ Weekly, p. 230*)

But by emphasizing themes that register as the highest priorities of voters in opinion polls — jobs and the economy, health care, the war in Iraq, education — portions of the address sounded like a first draft of a campaign stump speech. "We can go forward with confidence and resolve," he said in a line that sounded much like a campaign slogan, "or we can turn back to the old policies and old divisions."

Stephen Hess, a senior fellow at the Brookings Institution, a liberal-leaning think tank, said, "This was more of a campaign speech than [any other] I have seen a president give in a State of the Union message."

Battling Democrats

Bush was hoping to focus the nation on his roster of accomplishment at a time of intense squabbling among the Democratic candidates for president, whose own contest appeared much more complex and close-knit the week of Jan. 19. The weeks before the Iowa caucuses were heavy on intraparty attacks, most of them focused on Howard Dean, the former Vermont governor then seen as the front-runner. But he finished a weak third in Iowa, with 18 percent, behind two surging senators: John Kerry of Massachusetts, who had 38 percent, and John Edwards of North Carolina, who took 32 percent. After finishing fourth, with 11 percent, Rep. Richard A. Gephardt of Missouri abandoned his candidacy and announced his retirement from public life. (*2004 CQ Weekly, p. 213*)

85

The infighting had driven up the Democrats' negative poll ratings, said Republican strategist and pollster David Winston. "All of the Democrats, every single one of them, their image got worse" from November to January, he said, even among Democratic voters.

But if the White House assumed that it could take advantage of the Democrats' brawl and steal the spotlight by staging the speech a day after the caucuses, the calculation was off. Within 24 hours of the address, television networks were again leading their newscasts with the Democratic race, which was reshaped by Kerry's victory. National newspapers made similar decisions, devoting relatively scant coverage to the trips Bush made to Ohio, Arizona and New Mexico to expand on themes from his speech. (*2004 CQ Weekly, p. 193*)

United in Opposition

None of the Democratic aspirants attended the speech; instead, they descended on New Hampshire, where the primary is Jan. 27. They continued to delineate their differences while all pledging, if elected, to repel a common enemy: the policies of George W. Bush.

They disagree on how much of the recent tax cuts should be delayed or repealed to pay for domestic priorities, but they agree that the cuts were unfairly tilted to the wealthy and have done little to improve the economy. They stress that under Bush, there has been a net loss of jobs and a budget surplus turned into a projected deficit of $475 billion this year. (*Deficit, p. 111*)

The Democratic aspirants disagree on the wisdom of the congressional resolution that authorized the Iraq war (PL 107-243), but they are united in their contention that the administration based its case for the invasion on faulty intelligence, alienated major U.S. allies by going to war without United Nations support, and now is struggling to stabilize Iraq.

The presidential hopefuls also share the belief that Bush has underfunded his education program and that he has not adequately addressed the growing number of Americans without health insurance, while signing a Medicare prescription drug law that will prove inadequate in the long run.

Recent polling shows that Bush's personal popularity rating has climbed back to the high 50s after dipping last fall, when skepticism about his handling of the war and the economy was

Sen. Edward M. Kennedy, D-Mass., right, stays seated as Bush defends the Iraq war, which Kennedy opposed. Sens. Bob Graham, D-Fla., left, and Joseph R. Biden, Jr., D-Del., applaud.

at its peak. But voters also are saying they trust Democrats more than Bush to manage domestic priorities, including the economy, prescription drugs and other health care issues.

The constant pounding by the presidential candidates on these issues has not been lost on the administration. "This is a highly political White House that knows just what it's doing," said Norman J. Ornstein, resident scholar at the American Enterprise Institute, a conservative think tank. "They have been following the polls and the issues the Democrats are hammering away at."

Winston, the GOP pollster, said the timing of Bush's speech in between the Iowa and New Hampshire contests was intentional because "he has been getting hit for three months and he wanted to simply make the case" for his decisions. Bush set out to differ with his opponents, not attack them, he added. (*2004 CQ Weekly, p. 192*)

Making the Case

Bush stayed true to State of the Union tradition this year and never uttered the word "Democrats" in his 54-minute speech. But they were clearly whom he meant when he described "some in this chamber" and "critics" who voted against the war — and to the "skeptics" of his domestic policies, including "defenders" of the "status quo" on education.

"Some critics have said our duties in Iraq must be internationalized," Bush said with a hint of derision. "This particular criticism is hard to explain to our partners in Britain, Australia, Japan,

South Korea, the Philippines, Thailand, Italy, Spain, Poland, Denmark, Hungary, Bulgaria, Ukraine, Romania, the Netherlands . . ." At this point he was interrupted by cheers from the Republican side of the aisle. As those died down, he pressed on: ". . . Norway, El Salvador and the 17 other countries that have committed troops to Iraq."

He added, "There is a difference, however, between leading a coalition of many nations and submitting to the objections of a few. America will never seek a permission slip to defend the security of our people."

And in a direct response to Dean's comment in December that the capture of Iraqi leader Saddam Hussein had not made America safer, Bush declared that, "For all who love freedom and peace, the world without Saddam Hussein's regime is a better and safer place."

Another obvious difference of opinion between Bush and Democrats came when he noted that many of the central provisions of the anti-terrorism law known as the Patriot Act (PL 107-56) will expire next year. As he paused on that point, applause rang out from Democrats who believe the measure has overextended the reach of law enforcement. But Bush pressed ahead and urged Congress to renew the statute. (*2001 Almanac, p. 14-3*)

Domestic Initiatives

On the domestic front, Bush offered proposals — most of them modest, few of them new — meant to both answer his critics and motivate his party's conservative base.

In calling for making his tax cuts "permanent," he argued that stronger economic growth and job creation would result. "Unless you act, Americans face a tax increase. What the Congress has given, the Congress should not take away," he said.

He proposed a "Jobs for the 21st Century" plan, which includes $500 million in new funding to create job training partnerships between community colleges and employers, provide more college grants for low-income students and improve math skills of middle and high school students.

With the prescription drug law in hand, Bush resurrected past health care proposals, such as tax credits to help individuals purchase medical insurance. He added to his wish list legislation that would make catastrophic health insurance premiums 100 percent tax deductible for individuals who buy coverage as part of their new health savings accounts. (*2004 CQ Weekly, p. 202*)

From the start of his presidency, Bush has been particularly sensitive about economic issues. He is keenly aware that his father, George Bush, lost his bid for re-election in 1992 to Bill Clinton, who made the weak economy a central campaign theme.

"In 1992, there was this sense of, 'We're fine, we can coast to the election,' " Winston said. "What I think you are seeing with this group of Republicans is, 'Okay. We've done all of these things. What can we do next?' "

Wooing Conservatives

Four years ago, Bush campaigned as a "compassionate conservative" as he reached out to swing voters with promises to make improvements in some domestic areas, including education.

But in this State of the Union address, he emphasized social values as he set out to reinforce his ties to conservatives whose turnout is critical to Republicans in close elections.

"There's some folks that you need to let them know the light's still on," said former Rep. J.C. Watts of Oklahoma, (1995-2003) who now chairs GOPAC, a conservative Republican political action committee.

The president issued his strongest statement yet against gay marriage, which has become as fervently opposed as abortion by many social conservatives. He stopped short of calling for a constitutional amendment to ban the practice, as some conservatives demand, but declared that "our nation must defend the sanctity of marriage." (*Gay marriage, p. 105*)

Gary Bauer, a conservative activist who ran against Bush in the 2000 GOP presidential primaries and now heads American Values, said he was disappointed that Bush did not call on Congress to act immediately. But he said he was pleased that the White House appears to understand that one of the reasons the 2000 election between Bush and Al Gore was so close was that an estimated 4 million Christian conservatives stayed home. Polls have shown that people who regularly attend church are far more likely to vote Republican than Democratic.

"People say, 'What is a Christian conservative going to do? Vote for Howard Dean?' But if people lose enthusiasm, they just end up staying home," Bauer said.

All seven Democratic candidates oppose the proposed constitutional amendment, though there are some differences among them when discussing the legal differences between marriage and civil union. As governor, Dean signed a law granting limited legal rights through civil unions between homosexuals in Vermont.

A Light Session Ahead

Democratic leaders cited Bush's emphasis on social issues to underscore their criticism that his presidency's focus is all wrong and that he has paid insufficient attention to the economy. (*2004 CQ Weekly, p. 235*)

"The president spent almost as much time discussing steroid use among professional athletes as he did about the jobs crisis," said House Minority Whip Steny H. Hoyer of Maryland.

Some lawmakers said the speech was notable for what it did not contain, including a demand that Congress produce an overdue reauthorization of the highway and mass transit authorization law this year. Nor did he mention any new initiatives for homeland security, which Democrats argue has been underfunded. (*2004 CQ Weekly, p. 219*)

But Republicans said the growing deficit was what drove the decision not to trot out major new programs in the speech. For example, the president made no mention of his proposal, announced just the week before, to send astronauts back to the moon and on to Mars by 2030 — an idea criticized by both Democrats and GOP fiscal conservatives as unaffordable at this time. (*2004 CQ Weekly, p. 220*)

So while Democrats may have found Bush's plan for the next year to be lacking in substance, deficit hawks questioned whether the new initiatives contained in the speech were too much.

"It doesn't look like there's any real intention to cut back on the fastest spending pace since the Lyndon Johnson administration," said David Boaz, executive vice president of the Cato Institute, a libertarian think tank.

Sen. John McCain, R-Ariz., also doubted the president's promise to work with Congress to cut the deficit in half in the next five years. "Half of what and when?" he asked. "This deficit is out of control. . . . We have to stop the spending."

Debate over the budget will probably dominate the Congress this year, since little else is expected to get done as the presidential campaign intensifies. Republicans agree with the White House that they already have a strong set of accomplishments on which they can run for re-election: tax cuts, the education overhaul, the prescription drug benefit, the war on terrorism and the removal of Saddam Hussein from Iraq.

Republican leaders plan to keep Congress focused on a short list of priorities, such as extending the tax cuts, capping medical malpractice awards and pushing bills that can be cast as essential to growing jobs. In doing so, they also limit the time available for congressional Democrats to offer alternatives.

After reconvening for the new year to hear Bush's speech, the House considered minor measures the next day and then recessed for the week. Only two days of legislating are in store the week of Jan. 26. That is not unusual for this early in a new session, but House Minority Leader Nancy Pelosi of California says she is rankled by the paucity of work put forth by the Republicans.

"We have all of these challenges facing the American people, and we are barely here," she said.

A light congressional schedule, however, would probably suit Bush just fine. Not much usually happens in the fourth year of a presidential term, when the incumbent is seeking re-election. "There are certain things that, maybe if he's lucky, will be pushed through because he has a unified Congress," Hess said. "But basically they all want to go home and campaign." ◆

GOP's Support for Bush Showing Signs of Strain

Party line remains upbeat, but president's recent setbacks have kept doubt alive

Bush, shown here at a speech on Feb. 11, has had a rough ride on the Hill in recent weeks. Lawmakers in his own party say he should focus more on the economy. Those from the Midwest, a political battleground, are especially concerned about the loss of jobs in their states.

When White House political adviser Karl Rove got up to address House Republicans the first day of the GOP retreat in Philadelphia, on Jan. 29, he reminded them of recent reports that showed the economy was bouncing back. But Vernon J. Ehlers was having none of it.

The Michigan Republican, whose 3rd District includes the manufacturing-rich city of Grand Rapids, held up a copy of The Grand Rapids Press with a front-page headline: "10 Days, 4,600 Jobs Lost." The story detailed two major regional layoffs in the space of a week and a half and warned that a third was on the way.

What, Ehlers asked Rove, are we supposed to tell our constituents about that? The political mastermind had no good answer.

"Nobody does," Ehlers said in an interview. "But the point is that they need to pay more attention to job creation. The economy is recovering in much of the country, but the fact is that some states have suffered much greater job losses than others."

The exchange points to a new reality of this election year. For the first time since their triumph two years ago, some Republicans are showing signs of doubt that President Bush still has the political skills to help them — and himself — in November as much as he helped them when they recaptured the Senate and expanded their House majority in 2002.

Just two months ago, Bush seemed to have everything going for him in the upcoming elections. The economy was starting to grow again, Saddam Hussein had been captured, and Congress had delivered on the bulk of his agenda for the year, including the second major tax cut in three years and a new Medicare prescription drug benefit. Meanwhile, the Democrats running for his job were spending most of their time attacking each other. (*Republicans, p. 24*)

Lately, Bush's fortunes have taken some turns for the worse.

A report by David Kay, Bush's former chief arms inspector, suggested that the United States may never find weapons of mass destruction in Iraq. The federal budget deficit swelled to a projected $521 billion this year. New estimates by the White House indicated the Medicare prescription drug benefit would cost $139 billion more than Congress thought. As spending seemed to escalate out of control, Bush proposed sending people to Mars — an idea so embarrassing to fiscal conservatives that it quickly sank out of sight.

Bush's State of the Union address Jan. 20 got generally mediocre reviews. His performance on NBC's "Meet the Press" on Feb. 8, in which he defended his decision to go to war with Iraq, underwhelmed some Hill Republicans who thought it was defensive and inarticulate. His insistence that the economy is recovering, a position supported by most economic indicators, struck some Republicans as tone-deaf, particularly because unemployment has worsened in manufacturing states such as Michigan and Ohio.

A statement by one of his top economists — N. Gregory Mankiw, chairman of the White House Council of Economic

Advisers — that praised outsourcing as a "new way to do international trade" was slapped down in a rare rebellion by the House's top Republican, Speaker J. Dennis Hastert of Illinois. Hastert said the statement "fails a basic test of real economics. An economy suffers when jobs disappear."

Finally, several recent surveys have shown Bush either tied with or trailing the Democratic presidential front-runner, Sen. John Kerry of Massachusetts, a brainy but charisma-free candidate who had lagged behind his own party's rivals for months. According to a Gallup analysis, it is rare for an incumbent president to be behind in the polls at this point in the campaign season.

An ABC News-Washington Post poll of 1,003 adults Feb. 10-11 showed that the public's trust in Bush had fallen to the lowest point of his presidency, with 52 percent saying he was trustworthy and 45 percent saying he was not. A majority — 54 percent — said the administration exaggerated evidence that Iraq had weapons of mass destruction.

Moreover, the poll found that, for the first time, less than half of Americans said they believed the war was worth fighting. In the poll, Kerry led Bush among registered voters 52 percent to 43 percent.

Loyalty Remains Solid

In the long run, Bush's current troubles could turn out to be nothing more than a rough patch.

The economic recovery could start to produce jobs, as Federal Reserve Chairman Alan Greenspan predicted Feb. 11, taking care of the one big area that has lagged behind the rest of the economy. Six in 10 Americans still see Bush as a strong leader and approve of his handling of the war on terrorism, according to the poll.

Bush still has solid loyalty among Hill Republicans. "You can nitpick anybody, but the American people know that George Bush speaks from the heart, and he has the courage to act on it," said Sen. Jeff Sessions, R-Ala.

With nearly nine months left until the election, there is plenty of time for Bush's fortunes to reverse again. That is especially true considering the ups and downs he has experienced in public approval over the last nine months, in which the spectacularly quick victory in Iraq turned to chaos, then improved with the capture of Saddam, and in which the lackluster economy began to recover at a rapid pace.

President Slips in Voters' Eyes

Recent events have led voters to question President Bush's actions and his character. The slide in public opinion appears to be hurting him in terms of his re-election chances in November.

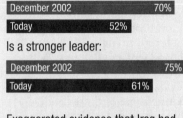

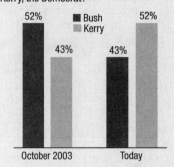

SOURCE: ABC News/Washington Post telephone polls of more than 1,000 adults nationwide. Margin of sampling error: plus or minus 3 percentage points.

In addition, few Republicans in Congress publicly question Bush's effectiveness. They say he has been battered by a period in which the Democratic presidential candidates have had the campaign stage to themselves, and that he will do fine when his campaign kicks into high gear.

The vast majority say there were plenty of reasons to remove Saddam from power in Iraq, and much to gain from the war, even if the weapons of mass destruction did not exist. The public may be open to that argument. In the ABC News-Washington Post poll, 57 percent said the war could be justified even if no such weapons are ever found.

"I think everyone understands that this is campaign season, and that some of the candidates who are attending these Democratic rallies have to explain their votes," said Senate Foreign Relations Chairman Richard G. Lugar, R-Ind., who has not been shy about challenging Bush on other issues.

But often more is revealed by Republican lawmakers' actions than by their words.

Watching What They Do

House Republicans are discussing budget ideas that would go further than Bush in cutting spending, raising the possibility that this year's budget will look very different from his proposal —

or possibly get stuck in deadlock between the House and the Senate. Some have called for Mankiw's resignation after his "outsourcing" remarks. Several Michigan GOP lawmakers gave Republican National Committee chairman Ed Gillespie an earful about the jobs situation in a private meeting.

And sometimes, the key is in their words. Moderates such as Sens. Olympia J. Snowe and Susan Collins, both of Maine, say they are concerned about the failure to find weapons of mass destruction in Iraq. Sen. Judd Gregg of New Hampshire, a fiscal conservative who opposed the Medicare law (PL 108-173), said Bush has "let the horses out of the barn" on spending and that "there's not much he can do" now that the prescription drug benefit has been enacted.

"There's no question that the recent polling on Republicans' credibility on the deficit, together with the recent polling on Bush vs. Kerry, is creating enormous anxiety in the Republican conference in general, and among the conservatives who have been lonely wolves crying in the wilderness" about the growing deficits, said Rep. Tom Feeney of Florida, a fiscal conservative.

Bush insists he will not play second fiddle to Congress in the effort to reduce the deficit. On Feb. 12, he renewed his veto threat against a $318 billion Senate highway bill (S 1072) shortly after it passed that chamber, saying it is too expensive. "The Senate today missed an important opportunity to rein in spending," White House press secretary Scott McClellan said in a statement. (*2004 CQ Weekly, p. 416*)

So far, no lawmakers have said they are worried that Bush's recent troubles will cost them their own seats. But some express concern that he could have trouble carrying key battleground states such as Michigan, particularly if job losses continue and voters do not think he takes the situation seriously.

"Certainly, there are some political implications, and you have to be mindful of that. Because the opposition will do everything they can to turn the heat up," said Rep. Joe Knollenberg, R-Mich.

As Ehlers said of the Michigan Republicans' meeting with Gillespie: "We think we're in good shape. We just want to make sure the president carries the state. It's not for us — it's for him."

Reading the Code

Most of the time, Republicans still avoid any direct verbal challenge to Bush. The preferred method is to speak in code, through the diplomatic, gently worded phrases that an employee at a large company might use to steer the corporate CEO away from trouble.

On the budget, for example, no one says Bush submitted a bad plan that does not do enough to cut the deficit. Instead, the conservative and moderate House Republicans who are discussing ideas for a spending freeze make their point in a more upbeat way. Almost to the word, they say the same thing: Bush's budget is a good start, and we can do even better.

"I think the consensus is that he's done a good job, but he needs to do more," Rep. Sue Myrick of North Carolina, who chairs the conservative Republican Study Committee, said Feb. 11 after a two-hour House Republican Conference meeting on the budget.

"I think it's a good start," said Rep. Jeb Hensarling of Texas. "I would just like to build on the president's budget to see if we can do more to protect the family budget from the federal budget."

Translation: Republicans do not want their base voters to get disgusted with federal spending growth and stay home on Election Day.

"I think the political concern is that the public will have a concern about the [deficit] numbers and that it will depress the voting among the base," said former Rep. Robert S. Walker, R-Pa. (1977-97),

chairman of Wexler & Walker Public Policy Associates.

Likewise, no one says the Mars mission was a poorly timed idea in the face of ballooning deficits. GOP leaders simply are not putting the mission in members' talking points. Instead, Republicans note, as did Sen. Craig Thomas of Wyoming, that "the Mars thing is pretty much gone" since Bush did not include it in his State of the Union address.

Another tactic is to pin the blame not on Bush, but on a faceless agency that reports to him, such as the Office of Management and Budget (OMB).

"I have some problems not with the president, but with the way OMB is treating some of these agencies," said Ohio Rep. David L. Hobson, who chairs the House Appropriations Subcommittee on Energy and Water Development. "They'll do the Mars thing, but the funding for waterways is shortchanged."

And to take the edge off any criticism clearly aimed at Bush, there is always the old standby: Congress is just as much to blame as the president.

"There's some concern about the Mars thing; there's concern about the deficit. But that's as much our responsibility as his," said Rep. Michael N. Castle of Delaware, co-chairman of the moderate Republican Tuesday Group.

It is becoming harder, however, for Republicans to ignore the stinging blows Bush is taking in the press — some at the hands of conservative columnists and editorial boards.

Harsh Reviews

Time magazine ran a cover story that asked, "Does Bush Have a Credibility Gap?" It was hardly the first media outlet to raise the question. A week earlier, conservative columnist Robert Novak, noting the failure to find weapons of mass destruction and the Medicare cost estimates that were $139 billion off, wrote that a lack of credibility was "the biggest problem he faces today."

While some congressional Republicans privately say they were not impressed by Bush's performance on "Meet the Press" — filled with long, awkward pauses as he formulated answers to questions about Iraq — conservative columnists have said so publicly.

Wall Street Journal columnist Peggy Noonan, a former speechwriter to President Ronald Reagan, wrote that Bush's performance was "not impressive" and that he "seemed tired, unsure and often bumbling."

National Review editor-at-large John

O'Sullivan wrote that Bush "should have been commanding and authoritative on every issue raised. Instead he seemed like a fundamentally nice guy slightly out of his depth. That's barely acceptable in a challenger; it's death and taxes in a man who has been president for three years."

Novak concluded: "It seems difficult for an incumbent president to lose amid economic recovery, but George W. Bush is showing it might be possible."

On Capitol Hill, Bush has plenty of defenders. But Republicans are in a position no politician likes: fielding questions about whether a president from their party has a credibility problem.

Some defend him enthusiastically. Sessions says it was Bush's predecessor, President Bill Clinton, who "had a big problem with the truth" and that Bush is "a straight shooter."

Others are not as enthusiastic. "I don't think this president has a credibility problem," said Snowe, a member of the Select Committee on Intelligence. "But we do have to answer these questions: Where are the weapons of mass destruction, what happened to the intelligence? And I think we have an obligation [to investigate], and the president understands that."

Rep. Mike Pence of Indiana, one of the fiscal conservatives pushing for more aggressive measures to cut the deficit, said Americans "understand the impact of the national recession and 9/11 and the war on terror. They're very forgiving of spending in an emergency. But now they're far enough away from that that they want us to return to our roots."

The Economy and Deficit

The biggest concerns by far for Republicans are the deficit and the failure of Bush's policies to create jobs more quickly, particularly in the states that have been losing manufacturing jobs.

Republicans in those states were clamoring for Bush to pay more attention to job creation even before Mankiw's comments about outsourcing. But his words quickly became a fundraising pitch for Democrats and an embarrassment to the GOP. Mankiw tried to recant in a letter to Hastert, saying, "My lack of clarity left the wrong impression that I praised the loss of U.S. jobs."

More important, some Republicans want Bush to do more to reassure constituents that he is aware of their job woes and is working to fix them, rather than just playing up good news about economic growth elsewhere.

"For them, it's a depression," Sen. George V. Voinovich said of his Ohio constituents. "He's got to talk to those people who are saying, 'Are you out there, Mr. President? Do you hear us?'"

Bush "did a great job" of reassuring them in a Jan. 21 speech on job training at a community college in Perrysburg Township, Voinovich said. "More of that has to be out there," he said.

OMB did announce a new initiative Feb. 13 to ease the regulatory burden on manufacturers to help them become more competitive. But Republicans such as Fred Upton of Michigan would like to see other measures as well, such as targeted tax relief. "A lot of my constituents just haven't seen" economic growth, he said. "We're hurting."

The deficit's growth, meanwhile, is making some Republicans nervous that constituents will be less willing to forgive Bush than they might have been at the height of his popularity.

"This administration was dealt a bad hand. They had a recession. They had the war on terror. They had 9/11," said Feeney. But after all of that, he said, "we did the biggest entitlement [expansion] since Lyndon Johnson" by creating the prescription drug benefit.

Though Democrats usually try to increase spending more than the GOP, Feeney said, "in this business, perception is reality, and Republicans are about to lose the war of perceptions."

It did not help matters when Bush proposed a budget that included an $18 million increase for the National Endowment for the Arts, Feeney added. "That's not a big budget issue. It's not going to bust the budget. But again, perception is reality." (2004 CQ Weekly, p. 371)

Those anxieties could have an important practical consequence this year. If Republicans forge ahead with plans to draft a significantly different budget than Bush proposed, they could get caught up in fights between the Senate and House, and among different factions of each chamber, over what they are willing to cut that would make a bigger dent in the deficit.

"Everybody's got their wish list of programs to cut, but can you get 218 votes for it?" Walker asked.

The Case for War

The concerns over the absence of weapons of mass destruction in Iraq are less widespread. It is a source of anxiety to some moderate Republicans who

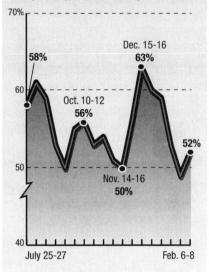

Approval Rises, Falls

The public has vacillated in its judgment about President Bush over the past several months. Percentage of poll respondents who said they approved of the job the president is doing:

58%

Dec. 15-16
63%

Oct. 10-12
56%

52%

Nov. 14-16
50%

July 25-27   Feb. 6-8

SOURCE: USA Today/CNN/Gallup telephone poll of at least 1,000 adults nationwide. Margin of sampling error, plus or minus 3 percentage points.

voted to authorize the war.

"I'm concerned about it," Collins said. "Although the war was justified for other reasons, if the David Kay report is accurate, it was a colossal failure of our intelligence."

But most Republicans say they are confident that the weapons fiasco is outweighed by the benefits of getting rid of a brutal dictator who supported Palestinian terrorists — making him a legitimate target in the war on terrorism — and who probably would have gotten more dangerous over time.

"It's a concern," Sen. Orrin G. Hatch of Utah, a member of the Intelligence panel, said of the absence of weapons of mass destruction. But there was no doubt Saddam had chemical weapons before and would have used weapons of mass destruction if he had gotten them, Hatch said.

There have been benefits since the war, Hatch said, including Libya's decision to renounce its weapons program. "That never would have happened if we hadn't gone in," he said.

If anything, some Republicans say, Bush should defend the war more aggressively rather than spend so much time responding to Democratic attacks on the weapons issue.

"What I'm hearing is that this is insanity, that the president needs to get more aggressive," said Jack A. Abramoff, a lobbyist at Greenberg Traurig and a top Republican fundraiser. "No one thinks that if Europe had had the foresight to take out Hitler in 1939, that they shouldn't have done it."

Even those who dismiss the weapons issue, however, express other concerns about Iraq — particularly the quality of the planning for the aftermath, in which the terrorist attacks by insurgents have continued long after the capture of Saddam.

At a Senate Foreign Relations Committee hearing Feb. 12, Lugar pressed Secretary of State Colin L. Powell to support an initiative he has launched to rethink how the federal government prepares for postwar reconstruction. Powell hedged, saying the president "has to have the flexibility to decide what he wants to do in these situations."

But Lugar said the turmoil in postwar Iraq and Afghanistan proves there needs to be, at the State Department or elsewhere, "a group of people who are, in fact, prepared to build nations."

"We're concerned about it, you're concerned about it, the country is concerned about it, because it just did not work very well," Lugar said.

Conservative groups, meanwhile, insist that Bush could still receive strong support from the base in November — particularly if he emphasizes issues that motivate them, such as ramping up the fight with Democrats to confirm his judicial nominees.

"I will tell you that for movement conservatives, the issue of judicial nominees trumps everything else," said Morton C. Blackwell, founder and president of the Leadership Institute, which recruits and trains conservatives for careers in politics and public policy.

And not all Republicans in the manufacturing states say they are worried about the jobs situation yet.

"We don't get as excitable in the Republican Party as others do. I mean, it's only February," said Rep. Steven C. LaTourette of Ohio. "If we're still talking about jobs in June, that'd be a different story."

Most Republicans say they expect many more plot twists in the coming months, and they expect Bush's support in the polls to bounce up and down a few more times. Right now, though, they are saying they would feel better if the president hit his stride a little sooner. ◆

Swing Voters Again the Key In Starkly Divided Nation

Loyalty or opposition to President Bush identifies most lawmakers and voters alike

The 2000 elections defined the United States as a 50-50 nation. George W. Bush was elected president by the slimmest of electoral vote margins and even lost the popular vote to Democrat Al Gore. The Senate was literally split 50-50, and Republicans clung to a narrow majority in the House.

Since then, the world has been turned upside down. Americans have lived through a tumultuous period marked by terrorism on American soil and U.S. soldiers sent to war overseas. On the domestic side, the economy has sputtered and health care costs have spiraled uncontrollably upward.

Yet it is unclear whether any of that will mean a sea change in this presidential election year. Indeed, almost nine months from Election Day 2004, it would appear that in strictly political terms, the country has picked up largely where it left off in 2000.

Bush seems headed toward another close battle as he seeks a second term; Republicans hold a narrow 51-seat majority in the Senate and fewer than 53 percent of the seats in the House. Virtually all the major national polls show that the public is still split down the middle on which party should control the White House and Congress.

One thing that has changed is the intensity of true believers in both the Republican and Democratic parties. Bush, who promised to be a uniter when he ran in 2000, has turned out to be a uniquely polarizing figure as president.

Most Republicans, voters and elected officials alike, have shown an unshakable faith in him. The furious anti-Bush sentiment among Democratic activists has been underscored by strong turnouts for many of the party's presidential nominating events and by the fervent response that candidates get when they criticize the president on the campaign trail.

What has not changed, though, is the fact that there are not enough hard-core partisans in the electorate to guarantee victory to either the Democrats or Republicans in the presidential race — and in the fight for control of Congress.

So once again the two parties are fighting intensely over the ever-elusive "swing voters" on whom so many recent elections have turned. The truth is, the 50-50 nation is a bit of a misnomer: It is more of a three-way split — much as it was four years ago — in which each party is grappling to add millions of independents and others who have no strong party affiliation to its hard-core base in order to win a majority.

The fact that a substantial portion of the electorate remains

Bush, who hopes to capitalize on military success in Iraq, visited Fort Carson, Colorado, in November 2003. Fort Carson has sent approximately 12,000 troops to Iraq.

up for grabs is demonstrated by the pronounced swings in the polls on the presidential race. In a CNN-USA Today-Gallup poll taken Feb. 16-17, Bush — who just weeks ago held solid leads over all of his potential Democratic challengers despite a decline in his public approval ratings — trailed by double-digit percentages both of the leading Democratic contenders: Massachusetts Sen. John Kerry and North Carolina Sen. John Edwards.

In congressional races, though, the GOP would appear to have some structural advantages.

Of the 34 contests for the Senate, 19 are for seats currently held by Democrats; 15 are for Republican-held seats. Of those 34, seven are for open seats, meaning there is no incumbent advantage. Five of those are currently held by Democrats and two by Republicans. And all five of the open Democratic seats are in the conservative-leaning South, where the party has been in decline for years.

On the House side, Democrats need a net gain of 12 seats to retake control of the chamber, a goal made difficult by the sharp reduction in the number of competitive districts as a result of redistricting and by other advantages that the incumbent party has. Specifically, Republicans handed themselves an almost-certain multiple-seat gain in Texas this year by pushing a highly partisan congressional district remapping through the GOP-controlled state legislature.

Despite the turmoil of the past three years, this year's races for the House, Senate and even the White House will be driven by the same fundamental principles that influence most modern-day elections during a presidential year: the degree that the presidential candidates have a "coattails effect" on the party tickets; the parties' success in raising money and recruiting candidates; and their ability to win the alliance of the swing voter in the battleground states.

Bush: Coattails or Drag?

As both parties battle for the White House and control of Congress, the benchmark for voters of all affiliations will be how they view Bush and his performance as president since 2001.

Already both sides are painting the picture that they think will work to the benefit of their candidates, Republicans to elevate appreciation of the president and his party, and Democrats to motivate their voters to oust the incumbent — and his congressional supporters.

Republicans contend that their support for Bush's leadership on economic policy — particularly his advocacy of tax cuts — has reversed a downturn that started at the end of Bill Clinton's presidency and is already well on the way to the next boom.

They point to the president's assertive projection of the nation's military might in making the case that the Bush White House has dealt a serious blow to the terrorist network responsible for the Sept. 11 attacks and removed the threat to world peace posed by Iraqi dictator Saddam Hussein.

Democrats argue that the tax cuts were aimed at the wealthiest Americans, provided only a short-term stimulus and added to huge budget deficits. They point to what they call a "jobless" economic recovery that they believe is the result of the Republicans' indifference to a growing trade imbalance and the outsourcing of American jobs to lower-paid workers in other countries.

Many Democrats also are attempting to tap into anger over the war, arguing that Bush misinformed the American public — severest critics say he lied — to justify the U.S.-led invasion of Iraq, and that he has bungled the aftermath at a dear cost of American lives, money and international reputation.

Whether either party's national sales pitch will have a major impact on the battles for Congress is open to question: The connection between presidential and congressional election outcomes has been weak in recent years. Even as Bush took the White House in 2000, Republicans endured a

A Portrait of Americans

In recent years, roughly equal numbers of U.S. voters have described themselves as Republicans or Democrats, with independents providing a sizable third group. When asked about their ideological leanings, most described themselves as moderates.

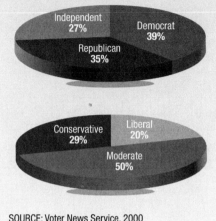

SOURCE: Voter News Service, 2000

net loss of four Senate seats and two House seats. And Clinton's easy re-election win in 1996 failed to restore control of Congress to the Democrats, who lost it two years earlier.

Raising Money, and Candidates

As has been the case for many years, the national Republican Party's congressional campaign committees have big leads over their Democratic counterparts — somewhat ironic given the fact that Democrats took the lead in pushing the campaign finance law overhaul that was enacted in 2002 (PL 107-155) and is first being implemented in this election cycle.

But on the individual candidate level, Democratic and Republican incumbents alike have piled up sizable campaign treasuries to avoid or fend off serious opposition. For example, the leading fundraiser among Senate incumbents seeking re-election is a Democrat, New York Charles E. Schumer, who had $23 million in total receipts and $20 million cash on hand as of Dec. 31. Although the state's candidate filing deadline is not until July 15, Schumer thus far has drawn no top-tier challenger.

Another element in the parties' congressional battles is candidate recruitment, which, like so much else in this cycle, is a mixed picture.

For example, each side has a Senate candidate trying again after a competi-

tive 2002 Senate bid: Former Rep. John Thune (1997-2003), who lost narrowly to Democratic Sen. Tim Johnson last time, will test Minority Leader Tom Daschle in South Dakota. Financier Erskine Bowles — a former Clinton administration chief of staff who ran creditably while losing to Republican celebrity candidate Elizabeth Dole in North Carolina — is seeking the seat that Democrat Edwards left open to run for president.

But each party has had flops. The Democrats have failed to find a top-tier candidate in Georgia and appear to be simply handing the GOP the seat that retiring Democratic Sen. Zell Miller has left open. Republicans, though, failed to produce the "A-list" challengers who they tried to talk into running against Democratic incumbents Blanche Lincoln of Arkansas, Harry Reid of Nevada and Byron L. Dorgan of North Dakota.

Perhaps the biggest unknown in the presidential race is whether the nation really is fixed in a "red state-blue state" dichotomy (named for the color-coding that TV networks use to signify the states won by Bush and Democrat Al Gore in the 2000 contest).

One question is whether dissatisfaction with Bush is deep enough for Democrats to pick off swing voters in states on the fringes of the conservative South: West Virginia, Kentucky, Tennessee, Arkansas, Louisiana and Florida.

Another is whether they can do that with New Englander Kerry at the top of the ticket. Would their chances improve with Southerner Edwards as a presidential or vice presidential nominee? And what impact would a Kerry-led ticket have on Democratic congressional races in the South, where the fight for Senate control in particular is likely to be decided?

Conversely, Bush's personal likability and image as a "war president" could help him penetrate the Democrats' "blue-state" base in the Northeast, industrial Midwest and West Coast.

So it can be said that, at least so far, there is no political tidal wave on the horizon that could either sweep the Democrats to a new era of dominance in Washington or give the Republicans an inarguable claim as the nation's majority party. As long as that remains the case, the possibility of voters rendering another split decision remains very real. ◆

Politics and Public Policy

Public *policymaking* refers to action that the government takes to address issues on the public agenda; implicit in the term is the process of reaching a decision about what action to take. It is the responsibility of the president, Congress, the judiciary and the bureaucracy to make, rule on and implement policy decisions. The articles in this section cover the most important policy issues that came before the federal government in late 2003 and early 2004.

The first article discusses the sweeping overhaul of Medicare passed in 2003 and the difficult questions that remain. The new plan marks the most significant structural change in the program's thirty-eight-year history, but many experts question whether it will work. For example, will Medicare recipients sign up for private drug plans? Will the overhaul reduce drug prices? How the plan will evolve in practice is a great unknown.

For lawmakers, the ten years since the passage of NAFTA—the North American Free Trade Agreement—have been an awakening to the complexities of trade policy. As the second article highlights, the loss of thousands of manufacturing jobs has led lawmakers to view more skeptically trade agreements that advocates say will create jobs simply by removing trade barriers. These misgivings may come into play as lawmakers vote on the Central American Free Trade Agreement, a broad trade bill that calls for removing tariffs and quotas on goods and services.

The third article looks at the congressional debate about gay marriage. The issue of a constitutional amendment to define marriage as a union between a man and a woman is political dynamite for both major parties, especially the Republicans, who control Congress and are more closely allied with social conservatives, who view gay marriage, like abortion and school prayer, as another threshold issue. It could, however, prove to be an irresistible wedge issue for the GOP to take advantage of in an election year.

The fourth article examines the ballooning deficit. The federal government's bottom line has swung $700 billion in just four years, from comfortable surpluses to a projected $475 billion deficit in 2004. So far, there has been no political price to pay by the White House or the Republican-controlled Congress.

New Plan Faces Rough Ride Through the Reality Mill

Next for Medicare rewrite: Hard questions and undetermined consequences

After 11 months of intense bargaining, Congress has produced a Medicare overhaul plan that is designed to reshape the way more than 40 million senior citizens and disabled Americans receive health care.

But will it work? The truth is, even the experts are not sure. How the plan will evolve in practice is the great unknown of the debate, and the answer has as much to do with human behavior and market forces as it does with actuarial and budgetary projections.

The Senate's 54-44 vote Nov. 25 to clear the conference report on the Medicare drug bill (HR 1 — H Rept 108-391) begins a new era for the popular federal entitlement program. It is to be transformed over the next two years into a mixed public-private system in which all beneficiaries will be eligible for prescription drug coverage and can enroll in new private health plans to provide integrated health care, including drug coverage. Insurers will compete against each other to offer both comprehensive managed care and drug-only policies.

The overhaul is to be accomplished with $400 billion that Congress set aside for the next 10 years in the fiscal 2004 budget resolution (H Con Res 95). Because Medicare beneficiaries are expected to incur $1.8 trillion in drug costs over the same period, according to Congressional Budget Office (CBO) estimates, the bill covers only a fraction of real costs.

Congress is betting that the new system will meet the health needs of seniors while sufficiently containing costs,

CQ Weekly Nov. 29, 2003

through competition, to accommodate current beneficiaries and the impending eligibility of the baby boom generation. Whether the system works will boil down to how beneficiaries respond to the changes and how insurers and health care providers calculate risk and profitability.

"It's asking a lot to put together a program with an inadequate level of resources relative to the magnitude of the problem and expect the beneficiaries, insurers and government agencies to piece it together seamlessly," said Thomas R. Oliver, a political scientist specializing in health policy at Johns Hopkins University.

The overhaul would create the first-ever outpatient Medicare drug benefit in 2006. Medicare recipients would buy coverage from private insurers, unless none offered such coverage in a given area. In that case, the government Medicare program would provide a fallback plan. The plan also calls for billions of dollars in payments to Medicare providers and to employers as part of an effort to discourage the companies from dropping retirees' drug coverage. (*2003 CQ Weekly, p. 1358*)

Experts say future Congresses will have to address unintended consequences arising from all the changes. Republicans and Democrats will almost certainly continue to blame each other for shortcomings in the system and will use Medicare as a cudgel in election campaigns, beginning next year. (*2003 CQ Weekly, p. 2885*)

Though details of the new system are still being developed, experts are already identifying potential trouble spots. What follows is look at five of the most pressing questions.

---

1. Will insurers participate in a revamped system?

One of the biggest assumptions built into the plan is that private insurance companies will compete against each other on price to provide drug coverage and integrated health care to Medicare beneficiaries. Accordingly, their participation is the linchpin of the overhaul effort.

Such a system would mimic the program that currently provides health benefits to federal government employees. If the plans do not choose to compete, the government will have to provide "fallback" drug-only plans and bear the burden of future increases in drug prices.

History has left some observers skeptical about whether insurers will play. Congress expanded Medicare's managed care program and renamed it Medicare+Choice in the 1997 Balanced Budget Act (PL 105-33), optimistic that encouraging more beneficiaries to join benefit-rich private health

plans would save money by managing seniors' care while offering them richer benefits, typically including drug coverage. The model was the array of health plans available to workers through employers. (*1997 Almanac, p. 6-3*)

But many of the private insurance plans that initially signed up for Medicare+Choice have dropped out, charging that the government's reimbursement rates were too low. The withdrawals have forced millions of senior citizens to find another private plan or return to

Frist touts a revamped Medicare system that relies more on private insurers.

the traditional Medicare program. Industry lobbyists have warned that unless the reimbursement levels and design of the new Medicare program promise insurers financial stability, the same outcome could occur.

Congress sought to accommodate the insurers by including provisions establishing risk adjustments that limit the amount of money an insurer can lose while providing a drug benefit. Lawmakers also added about $1.6 billion in payments for existing Medicare+Choice plans as an incentive to keep them in the program.

"They took steps to include attractive and favorable provisions for insurers, because if the plans don't want to play, they [Congress] have a real problem," said Paul Heldman, a health care analyst for Charles Schwab Capital Markets Washington Research Group.

Many experts say plans will want to participate in the early years, when federal subsidies are locked in. But the outlook is cloudier in later years, when risk adjustments and other sweeteners that Congress wrote into the overhaul plan lapse or prove inadequate. Some insurers may decide their Medicare business is not profitable enough. That is likeliest to happen in rural areas, where it is typically more expensive to assemble networks of hospitals, doctors and other providers.

Congress could step in and offer more subsidies. But that would put lawmakers in the uneasy position of paying more money to coerce private plans to stay in Medicare while expecting competition to control program costs.

"The fact is we really don't know how the market, in general, will respond," said Mark A. Peterson, a political scientist at the UCLA School of Public Policy and Social Research.

2. Will Medicare recipients sign up for private drug plans?

Despite the promise of drug coverage, some, such as the Alliance for Retired Americans, are critical of overhaul plans.

The introduction of Medicare drug coverage in 2006 will force beneficiaries to make a set of important calculations about their health care spending. Whether enough of them sign up to make the new benefit a success remains an open question.

The overhaul plan envisions creating a new version of Medicare+Choice called Medicare Advantage that features at least one, and possibly two, managed care health plans known as preferred provider organizations to serve beneficiaries who wish to leave traditional Medicare in a geographic region. Beneficiaries who want to remain in traditional Medicare could buy a privately administered drug-only plan.

Medicare recipients would have to decide which course to take based on such considerations as their annual drug costs and the premiums and co-payments each plan charges. The monthly premium for drug coverage is estimated to be around $35 per month, though the figure will vary by region and plan.

All plans would subsidize 75 percent of drug costs between $250 and $2,250. They also would offer "stop loss" coverage that would kick in after a beneficiary spent $3,600 out of pocket in a year. Beneficiaries then would have to pay 5 percent of the cost of each prescription or a co-payment of $2 to $5 for each prescription.

But because the overhaul plan does not have enough money to pay for drug coverage for every level of medical need, beneficiaries could land in the coverage gap — known in health parlance as a "doughnut hole" — that would leave them paying monthly premiums but getting no benefit. Beneficiaries with incomes less than 150 percent of the poverty level would be spared coverage gaps, though they would be subject to premiums based on a sliding scale and co-payments.

Experts think recipients who currently lack any drug coverage will probably enroll in large numbers. Even before the permanent benefit is created, beneficiaries in 2004 and 2005 will receive discount drug cards that would provide savings estimated at 15 percent to 25 percent per prescription.

But the bill will not meet the expectations of many seniors. People who take three or four medications daily for ailments such as high cholesterol or hypertension may fall into the doughnut hole because their drug spending, while high, may not break the $3,600 stop-loss barrier.

"There are going to be a lot of disappointed people who along about October or November are standing in line at the drugstore and find out, for example, that they are paying the full price and the government is not paying anything, or their plan is not paying anything," said Marilyn Moon, vice president and program director of health at the American Institutes for Research, at a forum sponsored by the Kaiser Family Foundation last month.

The consensus is that the drug benefit would most directly help the roughly 12 percent of Medicare beneficiaries who do not already have supplemental coverage, either through an employer-sponsored health plan or a self-purchased insurance policy such as Medigap. However, insurers will market the benefit to a much broader population, hoping to assemble the biggest cross-section of sick and healthy beneficiaries to make it easier to underwrite risks.

That broad marketing approach could result in other problems. Beneficiaries who purchase a drug policy but do not drop their existing supplemental coverage for other gaps in Medicare would have to deal with a new layer of government bureaucracy. "Who do they go to when there are problems?" asked Johns Hopkins' Oliver.

There also is the potential that some seniors who get confused by the choices will simply delay signing up for the drug benefit until they get sicker. They would probably have to pay financial penalties for delayed enrollment that plans are likely to levy. Delayed enrollment also could load the plans with sicker beneficiaries, driving up the cost of services and, by extension, plan members' premiums.

"The plans really need to encourage the younger, healthy seniors to sign up early," said Henry J. Aaron, senior fellow at the Brookings Institution, a Washington think tank.

Experts say it will be up to Congress or the federal Centers for Medicare and Medicaid Services to inform beneficiaries of coverage changes well in advance, and to establish telephone hotlines and other ways to cut through the program's red tape.

"I think beneficiaries will want an independent, user-friendly place they can go to for answers on how their benefit works, what drugs are covered and what drugs should be covered," said Tricia Neuman, director of the Medicare Policy Project at the Kaiser Family Foundation.

3. Will the overhaul reduce drug prices, through either negotiations or drug importation?

The Medicare system has a significant number of price controls that govern payments to doctors, hospitals, testing labs and other health providers. But it has no such requirements for drugs. That will remain so in the revamped system.

Insurance companies and entities known as pharmacy benefit managers will negotiate with drugmakers to determine the prices that beneficiaries end up paying. Plan architects also have included provisions designed to speed the approval of cheaper, generic versions of drugs — a move the CBO predicts will save the program about $600 million over 10 years.

Minnesota Republican Gov. Tim Pawlenty discusses drug importation in testimony before Senate Commerce Committee.

Lawmakers have been loath to impose price controls on prescription drugs, heeding drugmakers' warnings that such steps would inhibit future research and development because of the high costs of bringing drugs to market. But experts such as Moon, from the American Institutes for Research, say the government could use the Medicare system's purchasing power to negotiate significant volume discounts, as the Veterans Administration now does.

The Bush administration and its congressional allies argue that placing Medicare beneficiaries in large insurance pools is preferable to federal price regulation because such an arrangement would avoid price fixing and would rely on negotiations that will bring bigger discounts.

Each side has released estimates of how much the legislation would cut drug spending. Republicans say a hypothetical senior citizen who now spends $3,600 annually for prescription drugs would spend $1,380 under the plan. The GOP assumes prescription drug prices would fall 20 percent because of administrative savings from private plans.

Democrats say Republicans' estimates are overly optimistic and do not include the approximately $35 monthly premium. The Democrats estimate that average seniors' costs will drop from $3,600 to $2,520.

It may take years to prove or disprove those assertions. In the meantime, policy makers eager to show they are helping seniors with drug costs included language in the plan to allow the importation of drugs from Canada, where they often sell for less than in the United States, but only if the Health and Human Services secretary certifies the practice is safe.

In June, House lawmakers had pressed to include broader importation language in a Medicare bill that would allow the importation of drugs from Food and Drug Administration-approved plants in 25 countries. However, conferees scaled back the provision, heeding concerns from the administration and some in Congress that the practice would open the U.S. market to a flood of counterfeit medications. (2003 CQ *Weekly*, p. 2701)

The final bill language would at least theoretically reverse the 1987 Prescription Drug Marketing Act (PL 100-293), which allows the reimportation of prescription drugs only to the manufacturer of the drug or in specified instances, such as when the drugs are needed for emergency care. (1987 *Almanac*, p. 534)

Still, the Department of Health and Human Services has not certified importation as safe or cost-effective and is unlikely to do so. The department says it is impossible to track every drug that enters the country and verify its potency and efficacy.

"You can throw a lot of money at the agency for enforcement, but in the Internet age, when people can buy drugs online, it is very hard to control the flow of drugs," said Heldman of the Schwab Washington group.

The language will remove one ambiguity of current law by explicitly protecting individuals who carry drugs across the border from Canada for personal use. The Customs Service has informally allowed exceptions to the 1987 law when individuals declare drugs at the border and stipulate that they are for personal use, not for resale. Drug industry critics have organized busloads of seniors in border states to visit Canada and Mexico to buy cheaper medicine, saying such trips were the result of price-gouging in the U.S. market.

4. How will the government measure what beneficiaries earn for income-relating purposes?

One way architects of the Medicare overhaul hope to control program spending is through a provision that for the first time would tie premiums for Part B coverage of doctor bills and other outpatient care to beneficiaries' incomes. This is commonly but inaccurately referred to as "means testing." After a five-year phase-in beginning in 2007, singles with incomes of $80,000 and up or couples with $160,00 or more would have to pay higher premiums than other seniors. No such requirement applies to Medicare Part A, which covers hospital care and is

financed through payroll taxes. Similarly, low-income beneficiaries with incomes of less than 150 percent of the federal poverty line would pay premiums for drug coverage based on a sliding scale without any gaps.

Such "income relating" requirements mark the first departure from Medicare's historic principle of equality. Since its inception, the program has provided the same benefits for the same cost to all beneficiaries.

But the provision has practical implications as well. The government will have to find a way to instantaneously communicate information among insurers and program administrators to verify that a beneficiary is eligible for a certain level of assistance or must pay a higher premium, said Joseph Antos, an American Enterprise Institute scholar in health care and retirement policy, at the October Kaiser Family Foundation forum. That could pose challenges because lower-income beneficiaries easily could move up or down a sliding scale for premiums simply by making several hundred dollars more or less in a month.

There also is the sensitive question of how to determine income of beneficiaries, which is not specified in the bill. The easiest method, at least for wealthier beneficiaries, would be through tax returns. However, the additional scrutiny of the IRS could raise privacy concerns and alienate wealthier senior voters. On the other hand, voluntary reporting of income may be insufficient if cutoff levels for certain subsidies are the rule of law.

UCLA's Peterson says the effects of the income-relating provisions — estimated by CBO to save some $13.3 billion over 10 years — are more symbolic than monetary.

"The money they save is pretty insignificant in the bigger scheme of things," he said. "But symbolically, they're moving away from broad-based social insurance and adding a lot of administrative complexities in the process."

5. Will congressional politics reverse some overhaul efforts?

The fractious nature of the Medicare debate makes it likely that future Congresses will try to undo the provisions they most dislike. Already, opponents of the overhaul are talking about deleting some $12 billion in direct subsidies for insurers and language in the plan that prohibits the government from negotiating with pharmaceutical manufacturers to get the lowest drug prices for Medicare. (*2003 CQ Weekly, p. 2956*)

Arguably the biggest target is a provision to force the traditional Medicare system to compete directly with private plans on price in up to six metropolitan areas for up to six years, beginning in 2010.

The concept, known as "premium support," originated with House conservatives and was modified several times during negotiations to mollify Democrats and some moderate Republicans, who say it will undermine traditional Medicare. This time, the concerns are less about philosophy than about local politics.

Many lawmakers do not want the pilot program to take place in their districts and states. They fear that direct competition will create an insurance "death spiral" as healthier people leave Medicare for the private sector, leaving older and sicker recipients in the traditional program.

The higher costs of care for these individuals would probably drive up premiums for traditional Medicare in those markets and potentially lead to widely different Medicare premiums for senior citizens based solely on where they live.

"There is a real 'not in my back yard' mentality about this," said Heldman of the Schwab Washington group.

Seven Republican senators went on the record opposing the premium support demonstration this month, joining 36 of the chamber's Democrats and independent James M. Jeffords of Vermont in a letter to Senate Majority Leader Bill Frist, R-Tenn.

"Though some may consider this a demonstration project, we disagree. This appears to be a veiled attempt to institute this policy into law," the letter said. It was signed by Olympia J. Snowe and Susan Collins, both of Maine; John McCain of Arizona; Arlen Specter of Pennsylvania; Lincoln Chafee of Rhode Island; and Wayne Allard and Ben Nighthorse Campbell, both of Colorado. (*2003 CQ Weekly, p. 2827*)

Past pilot programs that aimed to spur competition by requiring private plans to bid for Medicare's business were killed by local opposition in Baltimore in 1996 and Denver in 1997. The demonstration project envisioned in the overhaul plan would target those metropolitan areas that have a higher number of Medicare beneficiaries in managed care.

Another part of the overhaul plan arousing parochial concerns is language that would require suppliers of durable medical equipment, such as canes and walkers, to compete for Medicare's business. The provision would do away with the practice of having Medicare pay a fixed rate for such supplies.

Members of Ohio's congressional delegation, including Republican Sens. George V. Voinovich and Mike DeWine, oppose the language. Ohio is the home state of Invacare, the

DeWine and other Ohioans object to durable medical equipment language.

world's largest manufacturer and distributor of home health care products. The level of opposition indicates this will remain an issue.

"When you try to make significant changes in the way a large-scale program operates, there are all kinds of consequences," said UCLA's Peterson. "This may be the contemporary high-water mark for conservative government. Who knows what Congress will look like in 10 years?" ◆

Ghost of NAFTA Haunts Future of Free Trade

Lawmakers burned by job losses in their districts unlikely to back similar legislation

Ten years ago, when the House was considering the North American Free Trade Agreement, Democratic Rep. John M. Spratt Jr., chairman of the Congressional Textile Caucus, swallowed hard and voted yes.

At the time, the textile industry that so dominates his South Carolina district had recognized for years that globalization and competition from low-wage countries would mean job losses, regardless of NAFTA. Spratt supported the legislation on the theory that even with its flaws, it represented the best chance for a deal that would send more U.S. textiles to Mexico even if it meant more competition from south of the border.

Now Spratt has some real regrets. After the loss of thousands of textile jobs in his home state over the past decade, he has a more skeptical view of agreements that advocates say will create jobs simply by breaking down trade barriers.

"It was based on blind faith that the market would operate to create new jobs," he said. "That flies in the face of everything we have seen in the last 25 or 30 years."

Spratt's misgivings about NAFTA will help guide his thinking when the Central American Free Trade Agreement — a broad trade bill that would remove tariffs and quotas on goods and services in that region — comes up for a vote. "What makes the United States Trade Representative and the Bush administration think CAFTA will work out any better or any differently?" he asked in a recent interview.

Indeed, NAFTA (PL 103-182) was a turning point in how members view trade policy, and lawmakers' positions are heavily colored by their experiences. Proponents see vast new choices for U.S. consumers, investment in Mexico that has helped political reforms take hold and a foundation for the largest free-trade bloc in the world. Foes still hear Ross Perot's "giant sucking sound," illustrated by Mexican and Chinese workers doing jobs once held by U.S. workers but at much lower wages and often in abysmal conditions.

But for lawmakers such as Spratt, the years since NAFTA have represented an awakening to the complexities of trade policy. He is one of a class of lawmakers that is now more knowledgeable about trade agreements that may come before Congress, more questioning of their potential benefits

Trade talks often provoke protests. Marchers protesting at the Free Trade Area of the Americas conference last month.

and more wary of their consequences.

The result is Congress may be more reluctant to pass broad free-trade legislation in the future. Spratt, if he decides to vote against CAFTA, could be joined by dozens of House members, including Minority Leader Nancy Pelosi of California and other leading Democrats. Some Republicans also are more hesitant on such legislation.

"Congressional support for future trade liberalization is in serious doubt," says Howard Rosen, a consultant to the Center for National Policy, a nonpartisan think tank, after analyzing major trade votes in Congress over the past 30 years.

Already, trade jitters have had a political impact. The White House is under pressure from Democrats who keep reminding voters about the 2.7 million manufacturing jobs that have vanished during the Bush administration.

In Congress, partisanship and polarization on trade have replaced the consensus of the late 1980s. The 2001 House vote, 215-214, on restoring fast-track trade negotiating authority showed how shaky support has become. The political heat surrounding Bush's decision the week of Dec. 1 to remove steel tariffs further illustrates the passion surrounding trade matters. Where there are moments of bipartisanship, they are often situational, such as efforts to get tough with China or the World Trade Organization. *(Fast track, 2002 Almanac, p. 18-3; steel, 2003 CQ Weekly p. 2998)*

"NAFTA has borne the brunt of all the wishes on both sides," said Rep. Ellen O. Tauscher of California, a Democrat who favors free trade. "It is still a lightning rod for those issues."

Life After NAFTA

This heated debate at home will affect Bush's ability to position the United States as the leading voice on free trade. Some recent White House actions — accepting the farm bill (PL 107-171) in 2002, slapping tariffs on steel, and taking on China over textiles — have betrayed its free-trade principles. The more Bush bends to protectionist sentiments, the more difficulty he will likely have convincing trade partners that they should do anything differently. *(2002 Almanac, p. 4-3)*

While the accord created a free-trade zone among Canada, Mexico and the United States, NAFTA was enacted primarily to eliminate tariffs and quotas on trade between the

Even the strongest proponents of free trade concede that global free trade agreements result in an inevitable flow of U.S. jobs to other countries. The Bush administration has agreed to extend trade adjustment assistance benefits to workers who lose their jobs and cannot find new jobs at comparable pay. Here, U.S. Trade Representative Robert B. Zoellick, left, Panamanian President Mireya Moscoso and Trade Minister Joaquin Jacome speak at a session of the Free Trade Area of the Americas (FTAA) meetings held in Miami in November 2003. Fundamental questions remain about the FTAA, and parties on both sides of the debate insist that the lessons of NAFTA must not be ignored.

United States and Mexico; U.S.-Canadian commerce was already relatively free of barriers. Some tariffs, specifically in the agricultural sector, are being phased out only now.

The legislation marked the first major trade deal with a developing country, which spurred worries that U.S. companies would rush to Mexico to exploit low-wage workers and take advantage of lax enforcement of environmental laws. To win passage, President Bill Clinton had to include side agreements designed to get Mexico to improve labor and environmental standards.

Despite the imprimatur of Clinton, his party's control of both the House and Senate and a vigorous push from the nation's business community, NAFTA was a tough fight. The House approved it Nov. 17, 1993, with bipartisan support, and it sailed to victory in the Senate three days later. The months of raucous debate preceding the votes were filled with highly optimistic and pessimistic predictions of the number of U.S. jobs that would be created or eliminated. (*1993 Almanac, p. 171*)

There have turned out to be elements of truth in the arguments of both sides.

A study produced by the Congressional Budget Office last spring found that U.S. exports to Mexico rose from $1.1 billion in 1994 to $10.3 billion in 2001. The CBO concluded that these are modest numbers in the context of the entire U.S. economy, but they represent an increase in commercial activity in spite of a severe recession and a currency crisis in Mexico in the mid-1990s.

The CBO, however, estimated NAFTA's effect on the gross domestic products of both countries was no more than a few billion dollars. That is a fraction of the U.S. economy but represents substantially more for Mexico, with an economy roughly 1/20th the size — the United States has a gross domestic product of $11.1 trillion annually compared with $900 billion for Mexico.

Yet critics still blame NAFTA for dislocating workers. Rep.

Sherrod Brown, D-Ohio, is fond of saying that in his district, west of Cleveland, "Trade is a four-letter word: J-O-B-S."

Public Citizen's Global Trade Watch, which has spearheaded opposition to unfettered trade liberalization, asserts that 525,094 workers lost their jobs because of NAFTA between 1994 and 2002. That figure is based on government data counting workers who filed for benefits under a special trade adjustment assistance program created by the agreement.

Gary Clyde Hufbauer, a senior fellow at the Institute for International Economics, had initially predicted U.S. job gains because of NAFTA. He now maintains that it is hard to determine what has happened. "I do not think anyone has ever successfully linked trade policy to total U.S. employment," he said.

Even members of Congress who concede that trade plays a role in job creation or destruction dismiss those who would lay all economic woes on the doorstep of the agreement.

"NAFTA, NAFTA, NAFTA," chants Rep. Cass Ballenger, R-N.C., summing up the campaign mantra of his opponents. While he has taken heat politically for his vote endorsing it, he said NAFTA tells only part of the story of job losses in his state.

Recalling Ross Perot's 1992 campaign warning that NAFTA would send jobs south of the border, Ballenger commented, "Where the hell had he been for the last 25 years?"

Annual U.S. trade with its six free-trade partners:
(in billions of dollars)

$251.3 — Exports
$375.1 — Imports

Annual U.S. trade with all 38 nations under consideration for free-trade agreements:
(in billions of dollars)

$59.3 — Exports
$75.2 — Imports

SOURCE: Congressional Budget Office

Free Trade Foes Cite Job Losses ...

Tracking the number of jobs lost to NAFTA and other free-trade initiatives is imprecise at best. An Economic Policy Institute study calculated job losses based on the effects of trade flows on 192 industries measured against the backdrop of growing trade deficits from 1994-2000. While trade proponents say the numbers are inflated and fail to account adequately for a range of other global economic conditions, the data offer a nationwide snapshot of the basis for opposition to free-trade policies.

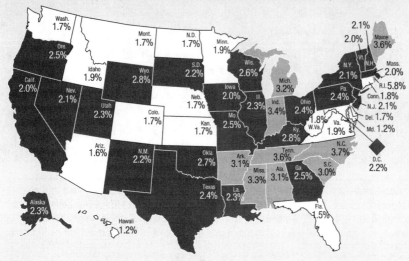

Job losses as a percentage of the labor force

| 3.0%-5.8% | 2.0%-2.8% | 1.2%-1.9% |

Trade-Related Job Losses 1994-2000

State	Losses	State	Losses	State	Losses
Alabama	-63,239	Kentucky	-50,948	North Dakota	-5,788
Alaska	-6,972	Louisiana	-44,940	Ohio	-135,139
Arizona	-32,461	Maine	-22,357	Oklahoma	-42,266
Arkansas	-37,469	Maryland	-31,057	Oregon	-41,124
California	-309,762	Massachusetts	-64,434	Pennsylvania	-142,221
Colorado	-34,982	Michigan	-152,061	Rhode Island	-29,164
Connecticut	-31,431	Minnesota	-49,925	South Carolina	-54,233
Delaware	-6,467	Mississippi	-41,338	South Dakota	-8,458
D.C.	-6,558	Missouri	-68,392	Tennessee	-96,355
Florida	-100,047	Montana	-7,521	Texas	-227,559
Georgia	-89,736	Nebraska	-15,312	Utah	-22,523
Hawaii	-7,116	Nevada	-16,493	Vermont	-6,283
Idaho	-11,021	New Hampshire	-12,936	Virginia	-66,083
Illinois	-139,537	New Jersey	-84,749	Washington	-45,739
Indiana	-102,873	New Mexico	-16,733	West Virginia	-14,458
Iowa	-31,770	New York	-179,288	Wisconsin	-73,476
Kansas	-23,248	North Carolina	-133,219	Wyoming	-6,977

SOURCE: Economic Policy Institute analysis of Census Bureau, Bureau of Labor Statistics data

In the decades leading up to NAFTA, Ballenger, who made millions manufacturing packaging for textiles, said some of his best customers were moving their operations overseas. For him, this movement of jobs is simply part of the historic cycle of textilemakers shifting to lower-wage markets to stay competitive.

Treasury Secretary John W. Snow got to the heart of the struggle in saying, "Clearly, the NAFTA accord has been a success. But as everybody knows it is a double-entry hook on trade. Trade necessitates some displacement."

The public relations problem for NAFTA proponents is that the benefits — shelves full of inexpensive toys, appliances and clothes in U.S. stores produced more cheaply overseas — are "dif-

fuse," he said.

But, Snow acknowledged, "The direct hurts are more concrete, palpable and discernable," in a given region or community, and influences broad public perceptions. "It is easy to get 25 people together," said Snow. "It is hard to get 25 million together."

The Battles Intensify

For many members of Congress, NAFTA was the high-water mark for bipartisan consensus, and even then the water was not very high. Since then, with few exceptions, trade battles have become more bitter and the vote margins have narrowed.

When trade ministers from the 34 nations that may someday compose the Free Trade Area of the Americas (FTAA) met in Miami in November, they were greeted by union members, human rights advocates and environmentalists vowing to stop what they call "NAFTA on steroids." There were clashes with police. In fact, the Miami-Dade police force offered to embed reporters attending the meeting the way the Pentagon did during major conflict operations in Iraq this year.

Other gatherings of high-level trade officials have also turned bloody. Rep. Marcy Kaptur, D-Ohio, compares the bloodshed in Miami this year, in Seattle in 1999 during WTO meetings and in Genoa in 2001 during the Group of Eight trade talks to that of the struggle to end slavery and enshrine civil rights.

"It is as great as the battle to throw off slavery," she said. "We lose soldiers but we are winning the war."

Free-traders, meanwhile, say protests and passions aside, they are making strides when Congress actually votes on trade legislation. The Africa Growth and Opportunity Act (PL 106-200) opened commerce with sub-Saharan African countries and expanded trade with Caribbean countries. (*2000 Almanac, p. 20-24*)

The Jordan Free Trade Agreement (PL 107-43) was viewed as a victory for tougher environmental standards in trade pacts as well as a move to strengthen ties with an ally in the war against terrorism. These passed with bipartisan support, as did agreements with Chile (PL 108-77) and Singapore (PL 108-78) this year, though immigration provisions robbed supporters of the huge victories they had expected. (*2003 CQ Weekly, pp. 1985, 1923, 1767; 2001 Almanac, p. 19-6*)

Also, though the 2002 vote was close, restoration of the president's fast-track negotiating power (PL 107-212) meant Bush could move ahead quickly on trade agreements without hearing objections from trade partners who until then were hesitant to agree to pacts that Congress could rewrite.

What is more, after recovering from the setback in Seattle, the United States led the successful launch of the first WTO round in eight years in 2001, and in 2000 Congress cleared the way for China's entry into the WTO (PL 106-286). These developments are a sign that Congress, with a modest level of bipartisanship, is willing to stay the course on trade even amid uncertainty and job losses. (*2000 Almanac, p. 20-3*)

Rep. David Dreier, R-Calif., among the most ardent free-trade supporters in Congress, acknowledged that trade votes will continue to be tough. "Protectionism thrives on anxiety," he said. "We just need a higher level of growth so we can create more jobs."

Recent trade data shows a stubborn trend of the United States consuming much more of what other countries make than world markets buying U.S. output. The last time the United States had a trade surplus was 1975. The trade deficit has now grown to what many economists view as an unsustainable level. It was $41.3 billion in September; on an annual basis, it exceeds $100 billion with China alone.

But as Federal Reserve Board Chairman Alan Greenspan noted the week of Nov. 17, even though these numbers represent a record trade imbalance, the ongoing trade deficit poses less of a threat to economic vitality than "creeping protectionism."

Yet where there is a Spratt, there is a Ballenger or a Rep. Howard Coble, R-N.C., another textile state member, who, though concerned by job losses, views the 97.3 percent increase in his state's exports over the past decade as "staggeringly good numbers."

Rep. Jennifer Dunn, R-Wash., whose district has also been hurt by job losses, said constituents are still able to view trade rationally. Layoffs at Boeing Co. in her state have not resulted from the trend of shifting even well-paying, high-skill jobs overseas, she says.

And while another big employer in her state, Microsoft Corp., employs engineers in India, payrolls at home are growing as well, she pointed out.

... Supporters Tout Major Benefits

What supporters point to as the benefits of trade agreements are not nearly as visible as lost jobs and may take years to materialize. Below are some examples:

$1,600 TAX CUT FOR U.S. FAMILIES

In testimony earlier this year, U.S. Trade Representative Robert B. Zoellick told the House Ways and Means Committee:

" The U.S. proposal for a zero-tariff world is a major tax cut that would directly save America's working families more than $18 billion per year on the import taxes they currently pay in the form of higher prices. The dynamic, pro-business, pro-consumer and pro-competitive effects of slashing tariffs would mean that America's national income would increase by $95 billion under the U.S. goods proposal. Together with the tax cut from lower tariffs, that would mean an economic gain of about $1,600 per year for the average family of four."

U.S. exports to trading partners rise

Since NAFTA was signed, U.S. exports to both Canada and Mexico have grown substantially:

(in billions of dollars)

Mexico
1994 $50.8
2002 $97.5

Canada
1994 $114.4
2002 $160.9

Tariffs almost totally removed from incoming goods

Average tariff rate on goods — which translate directly to lower consumer costs — coming into the United States from Mexico:

1993 12%
2001 1.3%

The United States gains a more stable neighbor

Mexico — a hotbed of political and economic unrest for decades — has shown marked strides in both areas during the past decade. The progress includes:

- Jobs at export-manufacturing companies pay about 37 percent more than jobs in manufacturing companies that produce for domestic Mexican consumption.
- Foreign investment in Mexico has grown three-fold since 1993 to $11.7 billion per year. Less than 20 percent of that investment is from the United States.
- Farm production is up by more than 50 percent since 1993 and exports to the United States have increased.
- After 71 years of rule by the Institutional Revolutionary Party, opposition party candidate Vicente Fox was elected president in July 2000. Some political observers credit NAFTA and economic gains, at least in part, for that change.

Source: U.S. Trade Representative

Bush's Trade Agenda

So far, the Bush administration has had some major trade victories, such as securing fast-track authority and passage of the Chile and Singapore accords. Also, U.S. Trade Representative Robert B. Zoellick has launched trade liberalization talks with countries on every continent.

The ambitious agenda that includes the Australia and Central American agreements, the WTO round, the FTAA and bilateral agreements with Bahrain and Morocco means labor and environmental issues will be big factors as most of these would-be partners are developing countries.

"We do think that NAFTA is very

relevant to a lot of the discussions on CAFTA and FTAA," said Thea Lee, assistant director for international economics for the AFL-CIO. "We will be working this issue pretty hard."

The same is true of environmental groups. While the National Wildlife Federation and the League of Conservation Voters supported NAFTA, the groups have been disappointed by what they view as ineffectual side agreements. These provided funds to monitor and assist with compliance with Mexico's environmental and labor laws.

They now stand with the Sierra Club and other environmental groups in opposing new trade liberalization if in the NAFTA model. The groups contend that the NAFTA side agreements did not work and instead set the stage for powerful companies to undermine environmental regulations.

With China's emergence as an economic force, trade concerns resonate beyond a small circle of liberal activists. With its low wages, China is now taking jobs from other developing countries, notably Mexico. And its refusal to let its currency float has distorted trade enough to lead even pro-trade business groups and the Bush administration to scold Chinese officials. (2003 *CQ Weekly*, p. 2198)

"There is a seething in this country among people who had well-paying manufacturing jobs and have been put out of work because of investment in Red China," said Rep. Dana Rohrabacher, R-Calif.

Of the administration's trade agenda items, the most immediate is CAFTA — the accord with El Salvador, Guatemala, Honduras, Costa Rica and Nicaragua.

Many House Democrats who voted for the Chile and Singapore agreements warned that, to win passage, CAFTA must include enforceable labor provisions based on the core labor standards of the International Labor Organization, included in the Jordan Free Trade Agreement.

Also, U.S. textile, sugar and citrus producers are looking for exemptions in the agreement, which the White House does not want to provide. But members from the Carolinas, Florida and Louisiana are standing firm.

"We have made it clear that we must learn from the mistakes of NAFTA," said Rep. Ileana Ros-Lehtinen, R-Fla. "Florida is an important state for

the president politically."

"CAFTA is a real problem," said Rep. Robert T. Matsui, D-Calif., who continues to support NAFTA and led efforts to restore fast-track authority during the Clinton administration.

The free-trade agreement with Australia probably will not raise labor and environmental concerns because Australia's standards are equal to or better than those of the United States.

Tugs of War Outside Congress

The FTAA, meanwhile, is in less immediate peril in Congress because negotiations are still at an early stage. Negotiators from the various countries have not yet settled fundamental questions about the scope of what will be included in the agreement.

The same is true elsewhere on the global stage. WTO talks on the current trade round collapsed in Cancun, Mexico, in September. Agricultural subsidies in all countries, including the United States, played a major role in the breakdown. Future efforts to bridge the divide between rich and poor nations, a stated focus of the current round, could be jeopardized without more progress on agriculture. 2003 (*CQ Weekly*, p. 1340)

If there is bipartisan cooperation in Congress on trade, it is on efforts for free trade to become fair trade. That means better enforcement of the terms of commerce, bolder defense of U.S. trade remedies and programs that train workers for jobs that have yet to be created rather than fighting to retrieve ones already lost.

"Many who have been free-traders have to reconsider anti-dumping actions, safeguards and other tools they had been skeptical of," said Rep. Phil English, R-Pa. "Some of this may be necessary to achieve a soft landing."

Perhaps no trade issue has brought Republicans and Democrats together like China's alleged manipulation of its currency to gain a trade advantage by making its goods artificially cheap. A half-dozen bipartisan resolutions and a bill have been introduced deploring China's actions.

Additionally, there was bipartisan support for extra money for the fiscal 2004 Commerce, Justice and State spending bill (HR 2799) for monitoring and enforcing trade terms with China, which is part of an omnibus spending bill (HR 2673) to be taken up by the House the week of Dec. 8. Zoel-

lick's office would be given additional funds to review compliance with trade agreements.

The administration, though, has demonstrated that it understands the importance of domestic trade politics and interests, even if it has meant angering U.S. trading partners.

In 2002, Bush provoked the ire of trading partners around the world by slapping tariffs on a range of imported steel products. The 2002 farm bill was popular with U.S. farmers hurt by imports, but it outraged other countries and helped end WTO talks in Cancun.

Finally, after long resistance to using safeguards included in the legislation to normalize trade relations with China, the administration announced the week of Nov. 17 that it would stem the flow of certain textile imports.

But Rep. Cal Dooley of California, a leading pro-trade Democrat, cautioned that a more confrontational approach could backfire if WTO decisions do not go in the United States' favor.

Zoellick has shown more interest in providing assistance to developing countries so they will be better able to attain acceptable labor and environmental standards, a parallel effort to negotiating trade agreements known as capacity building.

But these steps cannot reverse the inevitable flow of U.S. jobs to other countries under global free trade agreements. Even the most ardent free-traders concede that. To address this, the administration has agreed to extend trade adjustment assistance benefits to farmers and a wage insurance to workers who are unlikely to find new jobs at comparable pay when their import-sensitive jobs disappear.

Even a free-trade proponent such as Ballenger, who is retiring from Congress after this term, agrees that the administration can do more to assure workers that they will not be abandoned in the throes of a changing trade picture and its economic consequences. He noted that North Carolina gave President Bush one of his largest victories in 2000, but acknowledges that winning big there in 2004 will require sensitivity to the jobs lost in his home state.

"I've told people in the administration, 'If you don't start paying more attention to trade adjustment assistance and fair trade, you are going to have a heck of a time,' " he said. ◆

Parties Wary of Political Risk In Stands on Gay Marriage

Social conservatives move issue of same-sex unions to top of priority list

For the past decade, the political debate over gay rights has revolved around such basic legal questions as privacy and equity. And bit by bit, Congress, some states and several courts have gradually made way for homosexual men and women to participate openly in American society without fear of legalized discrimination or public censure.

From television sitcoms such as "Will & Grace" to campaigns by openly gay candidates for state, local and federal offices, gay life has entered the mainstream of popular culture and politics. Indeed, both Democrats and Republicans have increasingly steered clear of making gay rights a defining issue for or against either party. Gays, it turned out, voted on both sides.

But all of a sudden, the Supreme Judicial Court of Massachusetts has thrown the delicate balance out of kilter. In a 4-3 decision, the justices said same-sex couples have a right to marry under the state Constitution. The Nov. 18 decision, which has broad implications for both state and federal laws, has

Gay rights supporters in San Francisco celebrate the Massachusetts Supreme Judicial Court's decision that the state's Constitution guarantees gay couples the right to marry.

effectively taken gay rights out of bedrooms, workplaces and other venues of everyday life and forced the question on a bedrock social institution — marriage.

Social conservatives, who have long focused their political energies on "family values" issues such as abortion and school prayer, now view gay marriage as another threshold issue. They say the Massachusetts court ruling, along with a related opinion from the U.S. Supreme Court, show that the institution of marriage is under threat from an activist judiciary.

In the wake of the court opinions, they want to force Congress and state legislatures to impose the ultimate legal sanction — an amendment to the U.S. Constitution that would define marriage exclusively as a union between a man and a woman.

"If we are going to be redefining marriage, who should decide: unelected judges, or the people and their elected representatives?" said Republican Rep. Marilyn Musgrave of Colorado, sponsor of a proposed constitutional amendment in the House (H J Res 56).

Such a dramatic step poses significant risks for both Democrats and Republicans, however.

Democrats will have to decide how much they want to resist the initiative, fearing their own backlash from swing voters who may feel tolerant about gay rights but are telling pollsters that they are much more uncomfortable with the prospect of giving same-sex couples a moral and religious imprimatur of marriage.

But a rush to constitutional judgment on gay marriage also poses problems for President Bush and congressional Republicans. Embracing such permanent and wide-scale language could brand them as unnecessarily intolerant, not just with generic swing voters, but also with gays and lesbians who have been much more willing to join the Republican ranks than, for example, blacks or other ethnic minorities. Bush won 25 percent of the gay vote in 2000, triple his share of the black vote, for example.

"A federal marriage amendment has the potential to ignite a culture war," said Mark Mead, the political director of the Log Cabin Republicans, an increasingly influential organization of gay members of the GOP. "As conservative Republicans, we know what can happen when you ignite a cultural war."

Meanwhile, many homosexuals and some gay rights groups appear content to leave well enough alone and not push for changes to federal statutes regarding gay marriage.

"There are political perils for both parties on this issue that I think both sides need to worry about," said Dan Hofrenning, a political scientist at St. Olaf College in Northfield, Minn.

An Irresistible Topic?

Still, if Congress moves to affirm the socially accepted definition of marriage could prove politically irresistible in an election year, helping the GOP firm up its base among religious conservatives and brand Democrats as out of step with mainstream public sentiment. The prospect is especially alluring because the Democrats' current presidential front-runner, Howard Dean, signed the nation's first civil unions law while he was governor of Vermont. Civil unions convey some, though not all, of the same legal rights that marriage does.

Some social conservative groups have made sending a constitutional amendment to the states for ratification their top priority for Congress this year and are stoking grass-roots sentiment in favor of the measure in daily e-mail messages to supporters.

"When you look at the Republican Party base, this has now, at least temporarily, superseded abortion as a hot-button issue," said Larry J. Sabato, a University of Virginia political scientist.

Musgrave's constitutional amendment — Colorado Republican Wayne Allard has introduced a companion measure in the Senate (S J Res 26) — would define marriage as "the union of a man and a woman."

A two-thirds supermajority in both chambers is needed for adoption. After that, three-fourths, or 38, of the 50 state legislatures would have to ratify the amendment for it to become the law of the land. At that point, it would supplant a 1996 law (PL 104-199) aimed at preventing homosexual couples from getting married and would essentially protect that ban from all legal challenges. (*1996 Almanac, p. 5-26*)

This is not the first time that Musgrave, who is still in her freshman term, has taken a leading role on the issue. As a state legislator, she led the successful effort in Colorado to enact a law blocking same-sex marriages.

Musgrave, who represents a staunchly Republican northeast Colorado district, depicts the issue as a philosophical battle between Congress and the courts.

"We've got a judiciary that's just out of control," she said.

But Musgrave represents only one faction within a considerably fragmented Republican caucus.

GOP lawmakers who favor states' rights worry that the amendment would set a dangerous precedent and undercut states' traditional roles as the entities that set legal aspects of marriage. Others are skeptical, as a matter of principle, about rushing to amend the Constitution.

"I firmly believe marriage should be between a man and a

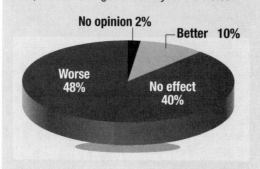

Many See Negative Effect If Same-Sex Couples Are Allowed to Marry

"Just your best guess, do you think that allowing two people of the same sex to legally marry will change our society for the better, will it have no effect, or will it change our society for the worse?"

No opinion 2%
Better 10%
Worse 48%
No effect 40%

SOURCE: Sept. 19-21, 2003, CNN/USA Today/Gallup telephone poll of 1,003 randomly selected adults nationwide. Margin of sampling error: plus or minus 3 percentage points.

woman," said Elton Gallegly of California, a senior Republican on the House Judiciary Committee. "I'm just not certain how far we should be going legislatively on this, particularly when it involves the Constitution."

Republican leaders in the House and Senate have said they support the amendment. But they prefer to move it only in the event that the 1996 law, known as the Defense of Marriage Act, is declared unconstitutional. Experts on both sides of the gay marriage debate have questioned whether the law would pass such a test. The discussion has been moot, however, because no state yet has passed a law legalizing same-sex marriages.

"If the courts begin to tear [the 1996 law] down, we have a responsibility to address it, and all options are indeed on the table," Senate Majority Leader Bill Frist, R-Tenn., said late last year.

Though the president has no formal role in this process, Bush's public support for an amendment would influence deliberations.

So far, Bush's enthusiasm has been measured.

Asked during a December interview on ABC television whether he supported a constitutional amendment banning same-sex marriage, he gave a carefully worded answer that balanced a certain sensitivity to states' rights with a defense of the traditional view of marriage.

"If necessary, I will support a constitutional amendment which would honor marriage between a man and a woman, codify that," Bush said. At the same time, he added, "the position of this administration is that, you know, whatever legal arrangements people want to make, they're allowed to make, so long as it's embraced by the state."

Sensitive Timing

Deciding what strategy to take has become more of a delicate political gambit as American acceptance of gays and lesbians has grown in the past eight years since Congress last acted to significantly limit their rights.

Last year, for example, the Episcopal Church promoted an openly gay priest, the Rev. V. Gene Robinson, to be bishop of the diocese of New Hampshire. There also are positive depictions of gay characters on popular television shows, such as "Queer Eye for the Straight Guy."

In many ways, gay rights advocates say, it is difficult to believe it has been just a decade since the storm of controversy over President Bill Clinton's "don't ask, don't tell" policy on homosexuals in the military, which was generally credited as working against Clinton and the Democratic Party just as the new administration was taking power. (*Gays in the military, 2004 CQ Weekly, p. 88*)

And when it comes to redefining the institution of marriage to accommodate gays and lesbians, Americans are decidedly mixed in their messages.

For instance, when asked in a recent National Public Radio poll whether they were for or against allowing homosexuals to marry, 56 percent of respondents said they were opposed to the idea. But when asked where they stood on laws that would allow same-sex couples to form civil unions that would give them some of the legal rights of married couples, a smaller percentage — 49 percent — were opposed. (*2004 CQ Weekly, p. 88*)

An ABC News poll in September found that 55 percent of the respondents thought that gay marriages should be illegal, but 60 percent of those opposed to the concept of gay marriage said it was not worth amending the Constitution to bar them.

"The dynamic we're dealing with is not clear," said David Winston, a Republican pollster who advises the GOP congressional leadership. "We've had one legal case in Massachusetts, and we don't know what that means."

The debate over gay marriage, with its cultural and religious overtones, recalls the bitter fight over school prayer, experts say.

In 1962, the Supreme Court ruled in *Engel v. Vitale* that it was unconstitutional for New York school officials to mandate a particular daily prayer. Then, as now, social conservatives implored Congress to pass a constitutional amendment to override the court.

For years, supporters tried without success to muster the necessary two-thirds in the House and Senate for a constitutional amendment to permit organized, recited school prayer.

Like Bush, President Ronald Reagan assiduously courted social conservatives. And, like Bush so far, Reagan spoke in favor of the amendment but did not push hard for it.

"The religious right was disappointed that Ronald Reagan didn't give the all-out effort to get the two-thirds necessary to get the amendment process started," Hofrenning said. "It'll be interesting how much of a priority George Bush makes same-sex marriage."

Conservative Pressure

Supporters of the proposed amendment to ban gay marriage worry that allowing same-sex couples to wed would confer added legitimacy on homosexuality, which social conservatives generally abhor. Allowing gays to wed, according to this line of reasoning, would cheapen and undermine an institution that is already battered by high divorce rates and out-of-wedlock births among heterosexuals.

The Family Research Council, one of the most prominent backers of the amendment, has sent out blanket e-mail messages to build support for the measure. The group is also asking political candidates to pledge that they will oppose allowing gays to marry.

But many lawmakers who are opposed to gay marriage are still reluctant to commit to supporting a constitutional amendment while the 1996 law is on the books.

"Until you know the lay of the legal analysis, it's hard to know what is the appropriate legislative response," said George Allen of Virginia, chairman of the National Republican Senatorial Committee.

The question of whether governments should confer gay marriage rights first surfaced more than a decade ago. In 1993, Hawaii's Supreme Court ruled that the state Legislature would have to show a "compelling state interest" in order to stop three homosexual couples who were trying to get married.

It was the first court ruling in the nation to open the possibility of legalized same-sex marriage.

Congress responded in 1996 — a presidential election year — by passing the Defense of Marriage Act, which gave states permission not to recognize same-sex marriages performed in other states. It also defined marriage as "a legal union between one man and one woman."

The House debated the measure for two days as lawmakers angrily disagreed over whether the bill was necessary or constitutional. Opponents charged that Republican congressional leaders advanced the bill in part to goad Democrats into defending gay marriage. In the end, the majority of lawmakers concluded that endorsing gay marriage was too risky, and the House voted 342-67 to pass the bill.

The Senate voted on the legislation under a bipartisan agreement to hold back-to-back votes on the bill and on a measure aimed at barring most job-related bias against homosexuals. The same sex marriage ban passed 85-14, but the discrimination measure lost on a 49-50 vote.

Clinton, the first presidential candidate to openly woo gay voters, endorsed the bill. Even so, he signed the legislation in the early morning hours

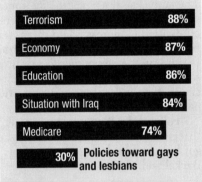

Gay/Lesbian Policy Ranks Low Among Voter Concerns

"From a list of some of the issues that will probably be discussed in next year's presidential election campaigns, please indicate how important the candidates' positions on that issue will be in influencing your vote for president — extremely important, very important, somewhat important, or not important."

Figures show percentage of respondents who said selected issues were extremely or very important:

Issue	Percentage
Terrorism	88%
Economy	87%
Education	86%
Situation with Iraq	84%
Medicare	74%
Policies toward gays and lesbians	30%

SOURCE: Dec. 5-7, 2003, CNN/USA Today/Gallup telephone poll of 1,083 randomly selected adults nationwide. Margin of sampling error: plus or minus 3 percentage points.

of Sept. 21 without public witnesses or comment.

Social conservatives soon after began lobbying state legislatures to codify that homosexuals should be prohibited from marrying. Thirty-four states have passed laws to that effect. Three states — Alaska, Nebraska and Nevada — have ratified constitutional amendments banning gay marriage. Hawaii's law followed a voter-ratified constitutional amendment empowering its Legislature to define marriage. (*State laws, p. 110*)

Gay rights activists also have been pressing the issue state-by-state since 1971, when a gay couple unsuccessfully sued to get a Minnesota marriage license.

They argue that no two people should be denied the rights and responsibilities of marriage simply because they are both of the same sex. Furthermore, they say, it is not enough to allow same-sex couples to enter into civil unions and domestic partnerships because those relationships do not have the universal recognition — and all of the legal rights — that marriage conveys. (*Marriage benefits, p. 109*)

"We're talking to the voters and we're talking to the judges," said David S. Buckel, senior staff attorney at Lambda Legal, a gay rights group. "What this is really about is what each state is going to decide to do."

Activists such as Buckel want to avoid an emotional national debate and fight for same-sex benefits at the local level, where employers and public entities have been increasingly receptive to the idea of offering same-sex couples access to health insurance, pension coverage and other benefits. The activists say advocating for same-sex benefits before the Republican-controlled Congress could prompt a backlash and prompt lawmakers into expanding the amendment's wording so that it bars not only same-sex marriages, but civil unions and domestic partner benefits as well.

"Folks understand if you try to take three giant leaps forward, you might get knocked back three giant leaps," Buckel said.

Cases Affirm Gay Rights

The issue moved back to the national stage last year after two high-profile court decisions.

On June 26, the Supreme Court ruled 6-3 in *Lawrence v. Texas* that a Texas law barring sexual acts between people of the same sex was an unconstitutional violation of individual "liberty" under the 5th and 14th Amendments.

Five months later, the Massachusetts Supreme Judicial Court ruled that under the Massachusetts Constitution, same-sex couples cannot be denied the right to marry. The state's legislature was given until the summer to write a new law.

Although the justices in the Texas case did not address the question of gay marriage, social conservatives decried the decision — which established a constitutional right to sexual intercourse for homosexuals — as a precursor to an eventual court ruling to overturn the 1996 Defense of Marriage Act.

"The Texas case showed clearly that the courts are going to do what they want," said Connie Mackey, vice president for government affairs at the Fam-

ily Research Council.

Her concern is echoed by GOP lawmakers.

"The Massachusetts Supreme Court has confirmed the suspicion of many that, absent some action from Congress in the form of a constitutional amendment, Massachusetts is just the beginning," said John Cornyn, R-Texas, chairman of the Senate Judiciary Subcommittee on the Constitution, Civil Rights and Property Rights. Even so, Cornyn has not decided whether to support Allard's proposed amendment.

The Massachusetts case is significant because it could trigger a sequence of events culminating in the first legal test of the 1996 law.

The Massachusetts court gave the state legislature 180 days to work out the details. Since then, the state Senate has asked the court whether it would be sufficient for the legislature to pass a law allowing same-sex civil unions that would confer some of the legal rights married couples enjoy but would avoid redefining the term "marriage."

The legislature also has scheduled a Feb. 11 joint session to vote on a state constitutional amendment that would bar same-sex marriages. But under Massachusetts law, the amendment would have to pass not only this year, but also once again in the next legislative session, before being put to state voters for ratification. That means the amendment could not take effect until November 2006 at the earliest.

Conservatives in Massachusetts say they hope to satisfy the state's high court by passing legislation allowing same-sex couples to enter into civil unions. They would like to then amend the Massachusetts constitution at some point to bar same-sex marriage, then repeal the civil union law.

But legal scholars say that unless the court allows the legislature to satisfy its ruling with a civil unions law, Massachusetts will become the first state to legalize same-sex marriage.

Social conservatives are convinced that if that happens, a homosexual couple armed with a Massachusetts marriage license will file a lawsuit to force another state, or the federal government, to honor it. That could spark a direct legal challenge to the 1996 law, which social conservatives and their congressional allies fear would succeed in the courts.

While Massachusetts may be ahead of other states in allowing same-sex marriage, it is not the first to extend legal rights to homosexual partners. Last year, California enacted domestic-partnership benefits for same-sex couples. In 2000, the Vermont legislature passed and Dean signed its law to allow gays to enter into civil unions. And on Jan. 8, New Jersey lawmakers cleared a bill that would allow the state to extend some benefits to same-sex partners. Democratic Democratic Gov. James E. McGreevey is expected to sign it.

Existing Law on Shaky Ground?

A court challenge might indeed prove destructive to the 1996 federal law, legal scholars say. Prospective plaintiffs could challenge the law as an unconstitutional violation of the "liberty" inherent in the 14th Amendment clause that guarantees equal protection for all people under the law or in the Fifth Amendment clause guaranteeing due process of law.

By distinguishing between same-sex and opposite-sex marriages, the 1996 law "violates the core principles of equality and equal dignity for gays and straights that the Supreme Court finds in *Lawrence v. Texas*," said Laurence Tribe, a constitutional law scholar at Harvard University who has urged the Massachusetts legislature to heed the state court decision.

Congress claimed constitutional authority to pass the 1996 law under a provision that gives Congress the power to define how states shall extend "full faith and credit" to the "public Acts, Records and judicial Proceedings of every other State."

But the "full faith and credit" clause traditionally has been applied to reciprocal recognition of judgments and decrees — such as divorces — but not legislation or licensing laws.

Arguments for a constitutional amendment banning gay marriage are expected to intensify if there are more court rulings endorsing expanded rights for same-sex couples.

Gay rights advocates are currently waging courtroom battles in several other states. In New Jersey, seven gay and lesbian couples are appealing a state court ruling that denied them marriage rights. In Indiana, three same-sex couples are challenging that state's marriage laws.

Rulings for the plaintiffs in those

cases could spur congressional leaders to move an amendment before the courts decide on the constitutionality of the 1996 law.

Bush still might score political points even if he does not endorse the proposed amendment. For example, he could underscore his support for heterosexual marriage and imply that his Democratic opponent would undermine it.

Dean is particularly vulnerable because of his role in enacting the nation's first civil union law.

"It may not find its way into Bush's speeches, but it will be there in the presidential campaign on the Republican side, especially if Howard Dean is the Democratic nominee," Sabato said.

It is still unclear how such tactics would play with moderate voters, especially in the suburbs. "Elected officials who are gambling their careers are walking on tiptoes" by considering passing the amendment, said Grover Norquist, president of Americans for Tax Reform, a GOP insider with close ties to the White House who does not favor action on an amendment this year.

Some Republicans are still haunted by the fallout from a speech given at their national convention in 1992 by presidential candidate Patrick J. Buchanan, who had mounted a challenge to the renomination of President George Bush.

Buchanan railed against Americans whose views differed from those of social conservatives, saying there was a "cultural war" to be waged "for the soul of America." The speech tarred Republicans as the party of intolerance and was a factor in Clinton's victory that year.

Norquist is not the only Republican loyalist wary of the amendment. Gay Republicans and other homosexuals who would consider supporting Bush are urging party leaders to avoid the gay marriage issue.

Mead said the Log Cabin Republicans, who favor giving gay couples the right to marry, will not support any Republican candidate who backs an amendment against same-sex marriage. Were the amendment to gain traction in Congress, Mead said, his organization would redirect its resources to "a ground game of defeating the amendment" in the states.

Some conservatives in both chambers — including House Judiciary Chairman F. James Sensenbrenner Jr.,

Marriage Legal Rights and Duties

Federal law confers more than 1,000 rights and responsibilities to married couples. Some examples follow:

Finances

• **Taxes:** Married couples generally can be treated as one economic unit under federal tax law. They can choose to file separate tax returns or to file jointly and pool deductions. Spouses also can make gifts to each other and can transfer property to each other without being subject to a gift or transfer tax. Individuals can inherit property from a deceased spouse without paying certain estate taxes.

• **Social Security:** Marital status helps determine whether someone is eligible for Social Security payments, and, if so, how much that person can receive. A husband or wife can receive Social Security benefits when their spouse dies or becomes disabled.

Employment

• **Medical leave:** Employees can get unpaid leave to care for a seriously ill spouse.

• **Health insurance:** Under the 1985 COBRA law (PL 99-272), a person can receive health insurance coverage under a deceased spouse's plan for up to 36 months.

Veterans' Benefits

• **Survivor:** If a member of the military is killed in action or dies as a result of a disability incurred during a war, his or her spouse can collect some benefits. When a veteran's death was not connected to service, his or her spouse can receive a monthly pension.

Crimes

• **Spousal privilege:** People generally can refuse to testify in civil and criminal cases against their husbands or wives.

Responsibilities

• **Child support:** Generally, when children are born to married couples, spouses are automatically responsible for child support, should they divorce.

• **Debts:** Under state laws, spouses are generally both liable, to some degree, for debts incurred for necessary items such as food and shelter.

R-Wis., and House Speaker J. Dennis Hastert, R-Ill. — have said that while they oppose gay marriage, congressional action on a constitutional amendment should wait until the 1996 law is reviewed in federal court.

"Federal law under the 1996 Defense of Marriage Act already provides that other states need not recognize marriage licenses granted to same-sex couples under Massachusetts law or any other state law," Sensenbrenner said after the Massachusetts ruling.

Internal Disagreements

The GOP is further fragmented by disagreements among social conservatives who want Congress to pass the

amendment over how broadly to word it.

Groups including the conservative Merrifield, Va.-based Alliance for Marriage, which drafted the language used in the House and Senate resolutions, chiefly want to bar same-sex marriage. The proposed constitutional amendment by Musgrave and Allard would add language declaring that nothing in the Constitution or the constitution of any state, nor state of federal law, "shall be construed to require that marital status or the legal incidents thereof be conferred upon unmarried couples or groups."

Supporters say that language is intended to bar only gay marriages and would not invalidate other types of

Same-Sex Marriage Landscape

None of the 50 states currently allows same-sex marriages, although some have no law against them. The map below shows differing laws across the country:

KEY:

- **35 states** have laws banning same-sex marriages and the recognition of such marriages that occur in other states. These states do not give spousal rights to same-sex couples.
- **California and Hawaii** both have laws banning same-sex marriages, but provide some spousal rights to unmarried couples, including those of the same sex.
- **Massachusetts** has no law on same-sex marriage, but the state's supreme court ruled in November that same-sex couples cannot be denied the legal rights of marriage, and handed the issue to the legislature to work out details by summer.
- **Vermont** allows "civil unions" that provide spousal rights to same-sex couples.
- **New Jersey's** Legislature has passed a bill the governor is expected to sign that would recognize some domestic partnerships, including same-sex couples, but falls short of establishing civil unions as in Vermont.
- **10 states** have no laws precluding same-sex marriages, nor do they have any laws providing spousal rights.

SOURCE: Human Rights Campaign

CQ GRAPHICS / YOLIE DAWSON

same-sex unions, such as those allowed in Vermont. But critics say the "legal incidents thereof" language would also effectively bar civil unions and domestic partnerships.

Matt Daniels, president of the Alliance for Marriage, said the group is working on new language that would block gay marriages but allow state legislatures to recognize civil unions and other same-sex partnerships.

That approach does not sit well with some other groups on the political right, including the Family Research Council and Focus on the Family, who want the Constitution to block same-sex unions and domestic partnerships as well as marriages.

Socially conservative activists privately concede that they are willing to support the Alliance for Marriage language if necessary, but there are still plenty of social conservatives who would not be entirely satisfied with an amendment that focuses solely on same-sex marriages.

Disagreements aside, virtually everyone familiar with the debate says it would be far easier to push a constitutional amendment banning gay marriage through the House than the Senate.

When some other constitutional amendments, such as one to allow Congress to ban flag burning, have come before the House since Republicans took control in 1995, they have garnered the necessary two-thirds majority needed for passage with ease. That is partly because the chamber's rules allow the Republican majority to set parameters for debate and block substitute measures that could peel off GOP votes.

Even so, an amendment banning gay marriage is far more politically treacherous than one on flag desecration.

Gay rights advocates have already been courting members in the House, trying to build resistance to a constitutional amendment.

Winnie Stachelberg, political direc-

tor for the Human Rights Campaign, a leading gay rights group, said Republicans and Democrats are concerned about the pitfalls surrounding the issue and are wary of focusing on gay marriage while other issues — Social Security, the economy, the rebuilding of Iraq — dominate the agenda for typical voters.

"We're working aggressively in both bodies to ensure we have those numbers," Stachelberg said. "A lot of Republicans and Democrats see this as something that could backfire."

In the Senate, lobbyists for and against a constitutional amendment are wooing moderate Republicans and Democrats to secure the necessary two-thirds majority. But with the chamber closely divided and a majority of Democrats likely to vote against the measure, amendment supporters will probably not gain much ground.

Frist has not outlined a plan for bringing any proposal to the floor. The constitutional amendment is under the jurisdiction of the Senate Judiciary Committee, and Chairman Orrin G. Hatch, R-Utah, has not taken a stance on the proposal.

Democrats Under Less Pressure

Gay rights groups have not pressed Democrats because the groups know the minority party has no control over the congressional agenda. Moreover, many Democrats have insulated themselves by favoring civil unions but opposing same-sex marriage. That stance has not cost the lawmakers significant support from gay rights activists.

"Without a doubt, the gay rights groups are going to give [Democrats] a pass," said David Garrow, a law professor at Emory University. "No one is going to demand or expect that Howard Dean is going to endorse gay marriage."

Democratic candidates could win over moderate voters by portraying their Republican opponents as intolerant of homosexuals, analysts say.

They also could argue that, between the war on terrorism, the U.S. occupation of Iraq, and the still-struggling economy, it is inappropriate for Congress to concentrate on amending the Constitution to reinforce the existing federal law.

"Most people are not coming to their dinner tables each night saying, 'What can we do to prevent the scourge of gay marriage?' " said Democratic pollster Mark Mellman. ◆

Federal Deficit Heads Deeper Into the Red

After posting four consecutive surpluses at the turn of the century — the first since 1969 and the longest string since the end of the 1920s — the federal books now show steadily worsening record deficits for fiscal 2003 and 2004.

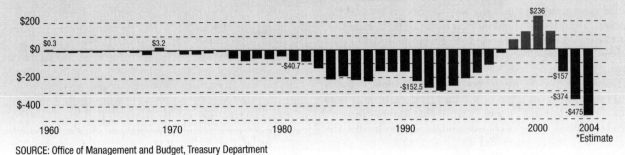

SOURCE: Office of Management and Budget, Treasury Department

With Half-Trillion in Red Ink, U.S. Inc. Looks Bad on Paper

Swing from record surplus to record deficit took just three years

The national enterprise called the U.S. government is hemorrhaging money. The past fiscal year went into the books as a budgetary disaster of record proportion, and the current year's outlook is even worse — much worse.

The nation's bottom line has swung $700 billion in just four years, careering from a surplus of $236 billion in fiscal 2000 to a projected shortfall of about $500 billion for the current year.

If the federal government were a publicly traded corporation called U.S. Inc., analysts might wonder how its managers have survived this long. There would almost certainly be scrutiny of its books. Potential investors in the enterprise would be wary of a prospectus showing operating losses in 30 of the past 35 years, huge projected deficits for years to come, accumulated debt of $7 trillion, about $165 billion in interest payments this year on borrowed money, worldwide security challenges and a domestic clientele demanding more services.

The current picture is particularly remarkable because three years ago the forecast was entirely sunny. In fiscal years 1998 through 2001, the federal balance sheets were in the black, more than $400 billion was trimmed from the national debt, and the outlook for the next decade was bright with opportunity.

But in 2001, it all unraveled. In just one year, the U.S. budget plunged from a $127 billion surplus, in fiscal 2001, to a $158 billion deficit, in fiscal 2002 — a $285 billion swing. A recession of eight months' duration undermined revenue. The chief executive and board of directors — President Bush and Congress — further reduced the income stream with history-making tax cuts, then poured more money into defense and homeland security after the Sept. 11 terrorist attacks. More tax cuts and a deficit of $158 billion followed in

fiscal 2002. In fiscal 2003, which ended Sept. 30, the deficit hit a record $374 billion.

So far, U.S. Inc. shareholders — taxpayers and voters — do not appear concerned about the trend. If voters are anxious about the deficit, their concern is offset by their view of how the rest of government is run. In the 2002 midterm elections, they gave the president's Republican Party control of the Senate and a larger House majority. And this year Bush continues to easily out-poll his Democratic rivals.

But any leeway this management team is getting from voters may be negated by the deficit itself. The estimated half-trillion dollar shortfall for fiscal 2004, which began last October, is taking away the government's room to maneuver. Looming in the not-too-distant future are substantial increases in the costs of two of the largest and most protected federal spending programs, Social Security and Medicare, the inevitable result of the impending retirement of the baby boom generation. The security and rebuilding costs in Iraq and Afghanistan are also expected to continue into the future.

In other words, what appeared a couple of years ago to be a rosy future of back-to-back budget surpluses and declining debt now seems to be just the opposite. The phrase "deficits as far as the eye can see" has returned to the budgetary lexicon.

"We are risking a decade of unusually large deficits at a particularly bad time. They will not go away on their own. Hard choices are going to have to be made on tax and spending policies," said Robert L. Bixby, executive director of the Concord Coalition, a nonpartisan fiscal watchdog group.

"That is the 10-year outlook. The future looks even worse," he said.

At risk as Bush and lawmakers come to grips with the budget dilemma are the health of the recovering economy and funding for federal programs Americans have come to take for granted — and even the possibility that tax increases or curbs on the defense spending will eventually be required to control the deficit.

The International Monetary Fund, which monitors Third World governments much the way the Securities and Exchange Commission stands watch over public companies, has warned that the mounting U.S. government debt could undermine the world economy by putting pressure on global interest rates.

Democrats in Congress and on the presidential campaign trail are making an issue of the budget deficit, and now deficit reduction has become part of the administration's agenda — along with tax cut extensions, new tax breaks, the ongoing war on terrorism and the latest starter, a moon-to-Mars space exploration initiative.

Bush and congressional leaders justify deficit spending in the past three years as the necessary response to the recession and the war on terrorism. The president also suggests that the budget would be healthier if Congress were not so hungry for spending.

"The deficit, we've got a plan to cut it in half over the next five years. It means Congress is going to have to toe the line when it comes to spending," Bush said during a Dec. 16 television interview. "They can't, particularly in campaign years, try to be all things to all people and overspend. But I think we're making good progress. I'm satisfied with the progress we've made."

No Longer a Dirty Word

For corporate executives or politicians, the first step toward solving a problem is to define what it is. Not only do the White House and the warring factions in Congress disagree on what to do about the deficit, there is no consensus on whether the flood of red ink is a serious problem.

"This is clearly a bipartisan problem. The denial is . . . universal," said Pete Peterson, Concord Coalition president and chairman of the Blackstone Group, a private investment firm. "Because the political will has been so lacking, it will probably take a crisis of some magnitude to get action."

In such an atmosphere, reducing the deficit will be difficult. Neither tax increases nor spending cuts are attractive to politicians, particularly in an election year. A booming economy and an accompanying surge in revenue in the late 1990s made balancing the budget look deceptively easy. But many economists say economic growth alone will not produce sufficient revenue to balance the budget this time around.

In a previous political era, large budget deficits would have prompted outraged Republican deficit hawks to warn of dire economic consequences, ac-

What Is the Deficit?

Most years, the government spends more on everything from fighter jets to Medicare reimbursements to federal worker salaries than it collects in taxes and other revenues. The difference, in every year but five since 1960, has been a deficit that the government has had to borrow to cover. The annual red ink has accumulated to almost $7 trillion in total federal government debt, about 25 times more than in 1960.

cuse the White House and Congress of selling out future generations and demand legislation or even a constitutional amendment to impose fiscal responsibility. (*2004 CQ Weekly*, p. 169)

Deficit critics still warn that without action to balance the budget or at least keep deficits small, a rise in interest rates and other factors will drag down the economy. They see government borrowing in competition with the private sector for available capital, especially in a humming economy.

But many Republican leaders, whose party stormed to control of Congress in the 1994 elections while demanding a balanced budget, now mostly shrug off the deficit.

"The Soviet Union had a balanced budget," House Majority Leader Tom DeLay, R-Texas, said in December. "Well, you can raise taxes until you balance it, but the economy will go into the toilet."

The White House calls the deficit "manageable" and promises to cut it in half over five years. The current budget deficits, the administration argues, represent relatively small percentages of the nation's gross domestic product (GDP), compared with the deficits of the 1980s. The 2003 deficit represented 3.4 percent of GDP; by contrast, the deficits of the mid-1980s routinely hovered around 5 percent of GDP.

Cutting the deficit in half in actual dollar terms, says Treasury Secretary John W. Snow, would "get the deficit down around 2 percent of GDP, which, by historic standards, is low."

Democrats lambaste Republicans as fiscally reckless in their pursuit of more tax cuts as the deficit increases. But at the same time, the minority party accuses the GOP of short-changing domestic programs and homeland security.

Despite projections suggesting that the deficit will not go away without major changes in policy, the most significant legislative actions last year moved in the opposite direction. Lawmakers cleared and Bush signed into law a $330 billion tax cut package (PL 108-27), a prescription drug benefit that will add $400 billion or more to the cost of Medicare through 2013 (PL 108-173), and two supplemental spending bills providing $166 billion for military action and rebuilding in Iraq and Afghanistan (PL 108-11, PL 108-106). (*2003 CQ Weekly*, pp. 3105, 3106, 3121, 3133)

The deficit will probably get more respect this year. Democrats are expected to invoke the deficit to fight GOP-backed tax cuts. Conservative Republicans are counting on the deficit to bolster their efforts to challenge spending increases. (*Deficit politics*, p. 60)

Even so, one of the first bills to be tackled this year will be a reauthorization of federal highway and mass transit programs. Bills pending in the House and Senate (HR 3550, S 1072, S 1978) would spend significantly more than the $247 billion proposed by the administration over six years. The House bill is expected to cost $375 billion, the Senate measure $311 billion.

"What the White House is afraid of, and what I'm afraid of, and what budget hawks should be afraid of, is the transportation bill," said a GOP senator who spoke on the condition he not be named. "What's their line in the sand?"

Is It Structural?

In the eyes of many budget experts, the four-year run of surpluses that started in 1998 was a phenomenon unlikely to be repeated in light of the nation's spending demands and changes in the revenue base. Their view is that the budget has returned to what is called a "structural" deficit, meaning

How Big Is the Deficit?

The deficit is estimated to widen to $475 billion or more for the current fiscal year, which ends Sept. 30, from $374.2 billion in fiscal 2003. Both are records in absolute terms, but not when measured against the size of the U.S. economy. This year's projected deficit would amount to about 4.2 percent of gross domestic product, an increase over last year's 3.4 percent of GDP, but still below the 6 percent recorded in 1983.

it will persist unless revenue increases or spending cuts are enacted.

"We have seen a return to the types of structural deficits we had in the '70s and '80s," said Stephen Moore, a prominent conservative economist and president of the Club for Growth. "You've got no forces for fiscal discipline right now either on Capitol Hill or in the White House."

Former Treasury Secretary Robert E. Rubin, a deficit hawk, warns that a structural deficit would have a corrosive effect on the economy. In a recent paper, Rubin said chronic deficits will lead to an increase of 1 to 2 percentage points in long-term interest rates and impose a significant strain on the economy.

He went on to say large deficits could bring on a cavalcade of other economic problems, including lower stock prices and a sharp decline in the value of the dollar. Rubin warned that financial markets and foreign investors will lose confidence in the ability of the U.S. political system to control the deficit and will demand higher interest rates to protect against the risk of inflation.

But other economists dispute the conclusion that deficits increase interest rates. Rates sometimes move in the opposite direction from what analysts expect, and often move in cycles that do not appear linked to the federal budget. Interest rates dropped as deficits skyrocketed in the 1980s. Recently, rates have remained near record lows despite the return of large deficits.

During a Jan. 13 conference call with reporters, Rubin did not advocate immediate tax increases to cut the deficit. Economists generally agree that deficits are tolerable in the short term because they are a natural result of a soft economy, and because some ac-

tions to balance the budget — such as tax increases or limits on payments to individuals — could slow the economic recovery. (*2004 CQ Weekly, p. 141*)

Economists also have shifting opinions on when a deficit is harmful. Several economists contend that the $374.2 billion fiscal 2003 deficit, which amounted to 3.4 percent of GDP, was not excessive given the need for an economic stimulus.

"You could argue that the [2003] budget deficit is not in itself troublesome, and on balance is helpful, because it's stimulative," said Robert Hormatz, vice chairman of Goldman Sachs.

But many economists fear that deficits of that magnitude would have negative effects if carried over the long term.

"You can't run deficits of 3, 4, 5 percent of GDP year after year after year and not have economic consequences," said Barry Anderson, a former top official at both the Congressional Budget Office (CBO) and the Office of Management and Budget (OMB).

"I think we're screwed," said Brookings Institution economist William Gale. "The administration does not have a policy to deal with this. They say their policy is cutting spending and making the economy grow. But what their policy really is increasing spending, and the only way they can think of to make the economy grow is by cutting taxes. And cutting taxes to raise growth is not going to raise revenue."

Looking at the Assumptions

Even some White House allies view halving the deficit in five years as politically infeasible.

"Cutting [the] deficit in half will be very, very difficult," G. William Hoagland, top budget adviser to Senate Majority Leader Bill Frist, R-Tenn., warned in a recent memo to senators. "Will it require mandatory spending reductions next year to achieve the goal?"

The difficulty Hoagland perceived is illustrated by current budget forecasts. The most recent White House outlook, issued in July, predicted that the deficit will spike at $475 billion this year, then back off to $226 billion by fiscal 2008.

Those figures were based on some debatable assumptions about federal spending: ignoring the multi-year costs of occupying and rebuilding Iraq and pegging overall increases in non-

defense discretionary accounts at slightly more than 1 percent a year. OMB did not include in its calculations the cost of a politically popular but expensive long-term adjustment of the alternative minimum tax (AMT).

OMB Director Joshua B. Bolten has acknowledged that the AMT "does still need to be addressed" to avoid a taxpayer revolt. A remedy could add about $600 billion to the deficit over 10 years.

Similarly and possibly more unrealistic is the latest CBO "baseline," or projection of the deficit as it would be without any changes in current law. CBO's latest figures, produced in August, ignore the Medicare prescription drug law and the possibility that the 2001 or 2003 tax cuts will be extended past their current expiration dates.

Assuming that the tax cuts will expire, CBO offers a more optimistic forecast in which the budget nears balance in 2011 and produces a $211 billion surplus in 2013.

Instead of relying on White House estimates or the CBO's baseline, most budget analysts devise their own, plugging in educated guesses about future legislation.

Virtually all of those calculations envision deficits much larger than those projected by the White House, reflecting continuing demands for spending and tax cuts. Some analyses conclude that without major steps to balance spending and revenue, deficits will average about 3.5 percent of GDP for the near future.

After modifying CBO's baseline to assume permanent tax cuts, changes in the AMT, and appropriated spending increases at the rate of inflation and population growth, Brookings scholars Alice M. Rivlin and Isabel Sawhill forecast deficits greater than $400 billion in each of the next five fiscal years, including a $499 billion deficit in 2009, the year when the White House says the red ink can be in the neighborhood of $250 billion. The Brookings baseline predicts deficits in excess of 3 percent of GDP throughout the next decade.

Another, more optimistic, forecast was produced by CBO using assumptions specified by the congressional "Blue Dog" coalition, a group of fiscally conservative House Democrats. It shows deficits in the mid-$300 billion range for most of the next decade, including a deficit of $340 billion, or 2.3 percent of GDP, in 2009. The Blue

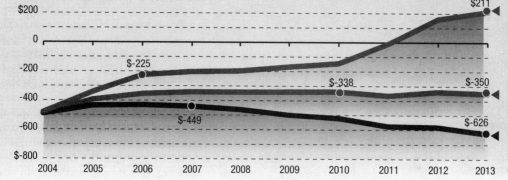

Budget Projections Differ Over Next 10 Years

Depending on expectations about how Congress might change government policies, different analysts project a range of possible deficit or surplus scenarios. How various estimates compare:

Congressional Budget Office baseline presumes current policies are unchanged and tax cuts are allowed to expire as scheduled

Blue Dog Coalition forecast presumes extension of tax cuts, changes in alternative minimum tax and passage of administration spending proposals

Brookings Institution forecast presumes extension of tax cuts and changes in alternative minimum tax

SOURCE: Congressional Budget Office, Brookings Institution

Dogs generally followed the Brookings approach, but assumed that spending appropriated by Congress would increase at Bush's lower estimates.

To be sure, economic forecasts have fluctuated wildly over the past few years, and the same kind of handwringing over the deficit occurring now was a central feature of the last era of supposedly uncontrollable deficits in 1982-96.

Forecasting is an Art

Developments beyond the control of policymakers — including swings in the economy, world events or revolutionary changes such as the development of the Internet — constantly affect the bottom line, usually to a greater extent than changes in fiscal policy.

Consequently, some conservatives do not buy the idea that it is impossible for economic growth to erase the current deficit, much as the boom in the late 1990s produced sudden budget surpluses.

"If you look at the Congressional Budget Office, it has never been right in any of its predictions. They're

always off," DeLay said. "They try to predict 10 years, 20 years out, and frankly, it's hard to predict what's going to happen next year."

The budget surpluses in fiscal 1998-2001 came out of the blue, appearing after Congress and President Bill Clinton spent months hammering out a plan (PL 105-33) that called for a surplus beginning in 2002. A surging economy and stock market produced a wave of unexpected tax revenue that dwarfed the impact of the delicately negotiated deficit reduction package. (*1997 Almanac, p. 2-3*)

When Bush took office in 2001, both CBO and OMB assumed that the revenue flow of the late 1990s would continue. Both agencies predicted budget surpluses totaling $5.6 trillion from 2002 to 2011.

Those projections helped bolster Republican tax-cutting efforts. They also prompted Federal Reserve Chairman Alan Greenspan to warn that large surpluses could be dangerous, because the government might retire its accumulated debt and begin investing in the private sector. (*2004 CQ Weekly, p. 138*)

Analysts explain the budget surpluses of 1998-2001 as a product of an economic "bubble" that provided a windfall to the Treasury as a result of circumstances unlikely to be repeated.

While the economy grew at a healthy clip in the 1990s, the amount of federal revenue as a percentage of the economy also increased, peaking at 20.8 percent of GDP in 2000, compared with a historical average of about 18 percent. (*2004 CQ Weekly, p. 144*)

A big factor in that revenue growth, according to economists and budget analysts, was the stock market's climb, which produced a wave of tax revenue from capital gains on stock sales. The booming high-technology sector also helped, as workers redeeming their lucrative stock options were often taxed at the then-top income tax rate of 39.6 percent, set by the 1993 deficit-reduction package (PL 103-66). The record bonuses awarded to Wall Street executives also proved lucrative for U.S. coffers. (*1993 Almanac, p. 107*)

Some tax experts conclude that even if the current economy rebounds, it is unlikely to produce a similar boost in tax revenue because the heyday of stock options is over.

Last year's reduction of the top income tax rate to 35 percent and the creation of a 15 percent tax rate for capital gains income also lead some analysts to conclude that the revenue bubble of the late 1990s and 2000 is unlikely to reappear. The 2001 tax cut package (PL 107-16) cut the top income tax rate to 35 percent from 39.6 percent. (*2004 CQ Weekly, p. 169*)

"We had very strong economic growth and a booming stock market during the '90s that produced very large income gains among those in the top quintile of the income distribution, who are precisely the folks that we had raised taxes on in 1990 and 1993," said former CBO Director Robert D. Reischauer. "While we could experience another surge of income among the top income earners in America, we've changed the tax code in ways that will ensure that the same dividend will not flow into the Treasury's pocket."

CBO Director Douglas J. Holtz-

Why Is It So Big?

As recently as 2001, the government was forecasting that a period of budget surpluses would continue for many years. Since then, three tax cuts, a recession, the stock market slump, the war against terrorism and the invasion of Iraq have caused the deficit to widen as the combination of factors has pushed spending higher and revenues lower.

Eakin is somewhat more hopeful that the budget-balancing revenue increase of the 1990s might be repeated. "I don't know if it's a one-time thing," he said. "I don't see the next one coming right away, but that doesn't rule it out."

Bolten said in December that "Treasury receipts [are] only beginning to reflect a recovering economy." That signals that there will probably not be a big change in the administration's long-term deficit forecast, despite a GDP growth rate of 8.2 percent in the third quarter of 2003.

Federal revenue peaked at about $2 trillion in 2000, but has dropped in each of the past three years. The administration's latest estimate of fiscal 2003 revenue is $269 billion less than the 2000 figure. Federal revenue was 16.4 percent of GDP last year, 4.4 points short of the high-water mark in 2000, when revenue equaled 20.8 percent of the economy.

OMB predicts that the revenue figure will bottom out at 16 percent next year, before rising.

Disappearing Surplus

Bush, unlike either his predecessor Clinton or his father, did not need to slay the deficit dragon when he took office. Instead, he inherited huge surpluses, at least according to the OMB and CBO forecasts.

It was, according to Bush's first budget proposal, "an unprecedented moment in history." With that kind of money, it seemed, everything was possible: tax cuts, debt reduction and increased spending for both the military

Does It Matter?

Many economists agree with the Bush administration that a deficit amounting to less than 5 percent of GDP is not a serious threat to the economy. But the retirement of the baby boom generation will increase Social Security and Medicare costs dramatically beginning in 2008. A large budget deficit might stifle economic growth by pushing interest rates higher, and it might squeeze government resources, creating pressure for tax increases or cuts in big-ticket programs, including retirement and health care.

and non-defense programs. (*2001 Almanac, p. 5-3*)

By August of 2001, six months after Bush sent his first budget proposal to Congress, it was apparent that the projections were far off the mark. A recession had begun in March, and a slump in the stock market had washed away billions of dollars in forecasted tax revenue from capital gains.

Then came Sept. 11. The White House and Congress virtually ignored the deteriorating budget outlook as billions of dollars were provided to fight terrorism. (*2001 Almanac, p. 2-59*)

The slumping economy quashed any talk of slowing implementation of the 2001 tax cut package in an effort to head off a budget deficit. The White House's top priority after the 2002 elections was to further stimulate the economy with more tax cuts. The 2003 tax package accelerated income tax rate cuts enacted in 2001 and included new tax breaks intended to spur business investment.

"That's how we balance the budget," DeLay said. "You cut taxes, it leaves more money in people's pockets. They save, they invest, the economy grows. And from the economy, the revenue to the government grows. As we restrain spending and revenue grow in the government, we'll get back to balance."

Although both OMB and CBO predict that the economy will grow at about 3 percent annually over the long term, they nevertheless forecast continuing budget deficits.

Economic growth rate averaged about 4 percent in the late 1990s, when deficits evaporated, but economists generally agree that such an expansion rate is not possible over a decade.

And should the economy post 4 percent growth from 2004 to 2013, the budget would still be in the red over that period by an average of $260 billion per year, according to an analysis by Rubin and two economists that uses higher spending levels than those assumed by the White House.

Beyond near-term worries over the much-debated impact of budget deficits on the economy, there is a impending problem everyone acknowledges. The retirement of the baby boom generation will put stress on the federal budget as the boomers begin to draw Social Security checks and Medicare payments near the end of this decade.

When that happens, there will

be fewer individuals under the age of 65 to finance the benefits of retirees. According to the Social Security Administration, there are now 3.4 workers for each Social Security beneficiary. In 2030, the number will be 2.1.

"In 2008, the first members of the baby boom generation will turn 62, and from that moment on the federal budget will be driven by new demographic realities," said Charles Kolb, president of the Committee for Economic Development, a business-sponsored research group.

Unless taxes are substantially increased or payments are slashed, providing benefits for the coming wave of retirees will require a great deal of government borrowing. The problem will be even worse if large deficits increase the accumulated debt the government is carrying when the baby boomers retire. (*2004 CQ Weekly, p. 157*)

Wild cards in the budget outlook include the uncertainties created by the war on terrorism, the long-term cost of the 2001 and 2003 tax cuts, and the cost of the Medicare drug plan in the next decade.

The administration's commitment to fighting terrorism is open-ended. The tax cuts may or may not be extended.

The drug plan was estimated to cost $400 billion through 2013 — a rather uncertain bet in itself. The cost over the subsequent decade is expected to more than double.

"It's easy to expect this [prescription drug] bill to cost over $1 trillion in the second 10 years and perhaps approach $2 trillion," said CBO's Holtz-Eakin.

The cost of extending the tax cuts — all of which are scheduled to expire by the end of 2010 — would probably ensure large deficits. In 2013 alone, CBO estimates, extension of the tax cuts would add $325 billion to the deficit.

No one is looking to the military for help in reducing the budget deficit. The "peace dividend" that followed the end of the Cold War and helped create the most recent surpluses is a fading memory, and defense analysts warn of a budget crunch at the Pentagon in the coming years despite steady funding increases. Several big-ticket weapons systems are scheduled to come off assembly lines at almost the same time. (*2004 CQ Weekly, p. 154*)

A Disaster in the Making

The debate over the causes, significance and future course of the budget deficit will not be resolved during the

Deficits and Economic Performance

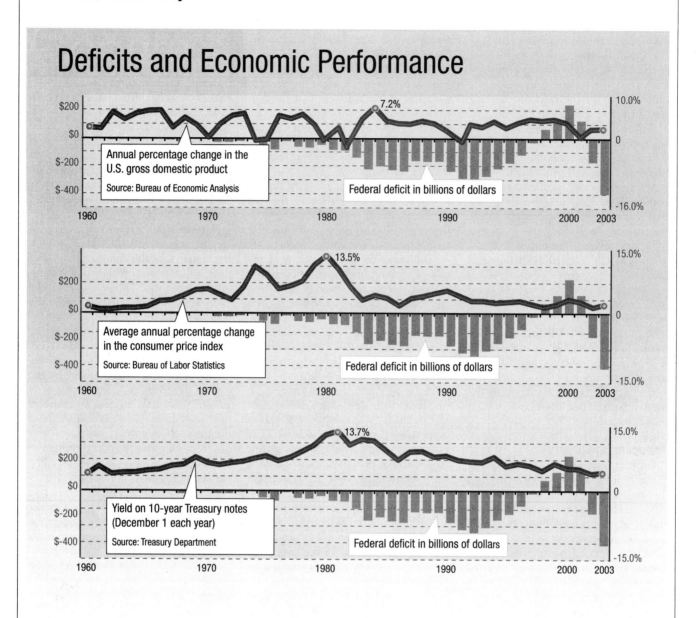

Annual percentage change in the U.S. gross domestic product

Source: Bureau of Economic Analysis

7.2%

Federal deficit in billions of dollars

Average annual percentage change in the consumer price index

Source: Bureau of Labor Statistics

13.5%

Federal deficit in billions of dollars

Yield on 10-year Treasury notes (December 1 each year)

Source: Treasury Department

13.7%

Federal deficit in billions of dollars

upcoming election-year budget process.

The administration budget proposal to be sent to Congress on Feb. 2 will embody a wait-and-see approach, letting the resurgent economy and a hard line on spending determine the fiscal fortunes of the government.

The White House projection for cutting the deficit in half within five years will be based chiefly on a slow increase in appropriated spending. The administration has long argued that the big increases in appropriations during the final years of the Clinton administration cannot and should not be sustained.

Bush's previous efforts to impose restraint on domestic appropriations have begun to bear fruit. Bolten said overall domestic spending unrelated to homeland security will increase by 3 percent

from fiscal 2003 to fiscal 2004, assuming that the Senate clears the omnibus spending package (HR 2673 — H Rept 108-401) after lawmakers reconvene on Jan. 20. In the last budget year of the Clinton administration, such spending increased by 15 percent. (*2004 CQ Weekly, p. 148*)

But Bush's Republican allies on Capitol Hill, particularly the old-school lawmakers who populate the top tiers of the Appropriations committees, have proven difficult to control. It will be especially difficult to scale back expectations for spending on popular programs or lawmakers' pet projects.

Senior appropriations aides in both parties predict that the appropriations process may break down this year as Congress works from Bush budget allocations that will prove too

frugal to permit passage of the 13 fiscal 2005 spending bills.

The upcoming appropriations cycle will be a "disaster," predicts House Appropriations Committee Chief of Staff James W. Dyer.

Congressional action on the highway bill will provide an early signal of whether Congress can or intends to follow Bush's lead.

The year ahead, then, could represent a federal budget on autopilot, one in which the performance of the economy — and the revenue that it produces — will largely determine whether the fiscal health of the federal enterprise will improve, as Bush is betting, or deteriorate to the point that the next administration and the next Congress will have to take steps they are now unwilling to contemplate. ◆

Appendix

The Legislative Process in Brief

Note: Parliamentary terms used below are defined in the glossary.

Introduction of Bills

A House member (including the resident commissioner of Puerto Rico and nonvoting delegates of the District of Columbia, Guam, the Virgin Islands and American Samoa) may introduce any one of several types of bills and resolutions by handing it to the clerk of the House or placing it in a box called the hopper. A senator first gains recognition of the presiding officer to announce the introduction of a bill.

As the usual next step in either the House or Senate, the bill is numbered, referred to the appropriate committee, labeled with the sponsor's name and sent to the Government Printing Office so that copies can be made for subsequent study and action. House and Senate bills may be jointly sponsored and carry several senators' names. A bill written in the executive branch and proposed as an administration measure usually is introduced by the chairman of the congressional committee that has jurisdiction, as a courtesy to the White House.

Bills—Prefixed with HR in the House, S in the Senate, followed by a number. Used as the form for most legislation, whether general or special, public or private.

Joint Resolutions—Designated H J Res or S J Res. Subject to the same procedure as bills, with the exception of a joint resolution proposing an amendment to the Constitution. The latter must be approved by two-thirds of both houses and is then sent directly to the administrator of general services for submission to the states for ratification instead of being presented to the president for his approval.

Concurrent Resolutions—Designated H Con Res or S Con Res. Used for matters affecting the operations of both houses. These resolutions do not become law.

Resolutions—Designated H Res or S Res. Used for a matter concerning the operation of either house alone and adopted only by the chamber in which it originates.

Committee Action

With few exceptions, bills are referred to the appropriate standing committees. The job of referral formally is the responsibility of the Speaker of the House and the presiding officer of the Senate, but this task usually is carried out on their behalf by the parliamentarians of the House and Senate. Precedent, statute and the jurisdictional mandates of the committees as set forth in the rules of the House and Senate determine which committees receive what kinds of bills. Bills are technically considered "read for the first time" when referred to House committees.

When a bill reaches a committee it is placed on the committee's calendar. Failure of a committee to act on a bill is equivalent to killing it and most fall by the legislative roadside. The measure can be withdrawn from the committee's purview only by a discharge petition signed by a majority of the House membership on House bills, or by adoption of a special resolution in the Senate. Discharge attempts rarely succeed and the Senate procedure has not been used for decades.

The first committee action taken on a bill usually is a request for comment on it by interested agencies of the government. The committee chairman may assign the bill to a subcommittee for study and hearings, or it may be considered by the full committee. Hearings may be public, closed (executive session) or both. A subcommittee, after considering a bill, reports to the full committee its recommendations for action and any proposed amendments.

The full committee then votes on its recommendation to the House or Senate. This procedure is called "ordering a bill reported." Occasionally a committee may order a bill reported unfavorably; most of the time a report, submitted by the chairman of the committee to the House or Senate, calls for favorable action on the measure since the committee can effectively "kill" a bill by simply failing to take any action.

After the bill is reported, the committee chairman instructs the staff to prepare a written report. The report describes the purposes and scope of the bill, explains the committee revisions, notes proposed changes in existing law and, usually, includes the views of the executive branch agencies consulted. Often committee members opposing a measure issue dissenting minority statements that are included in the report.

Usually, the committee "marks up" or proposes amendments to the bill. If the amendments are substantial and the measure is complicated, the committee may order a "clean bill" introduced, which will embody the proposed amendments. The original bill then is put aside and the clean bill, with a new number, is reported to the floor.

The chamber must approve, alter or reject the committee amendments before the bill itself can be put to a vote.

Floor Action

After a bill is reported back to the house where it originated, it is placed on the calendar.

There are five legislative calendars in the House, issued in one cumulative calendar titled *Calendars of the United States House of Representatives and History of Legislation.* The House calendars are:

The Union Calendar to which are referred bills raising revenues, general appropriations bills and any measures directly or indirectly appropriating money or property. It is the Calendar of the Committee of the Whole House on the State of the Union.

This graphic shows the most typical way in which proposed legislation is enacted into law. There are more complicated, as well as simpler, routes, and most bills never become law. The process is illustrated with two hypothetical bills, House bill No. 1 (HR 1) and

Senate bill No. 2 (S 2). Bills must be passed by both houses in identical form before they can be sent to the president. The path of HR 1 is traced by a gray line, that of S 2 by a black line. In practice, most bills begin as similar proposals in both houses.

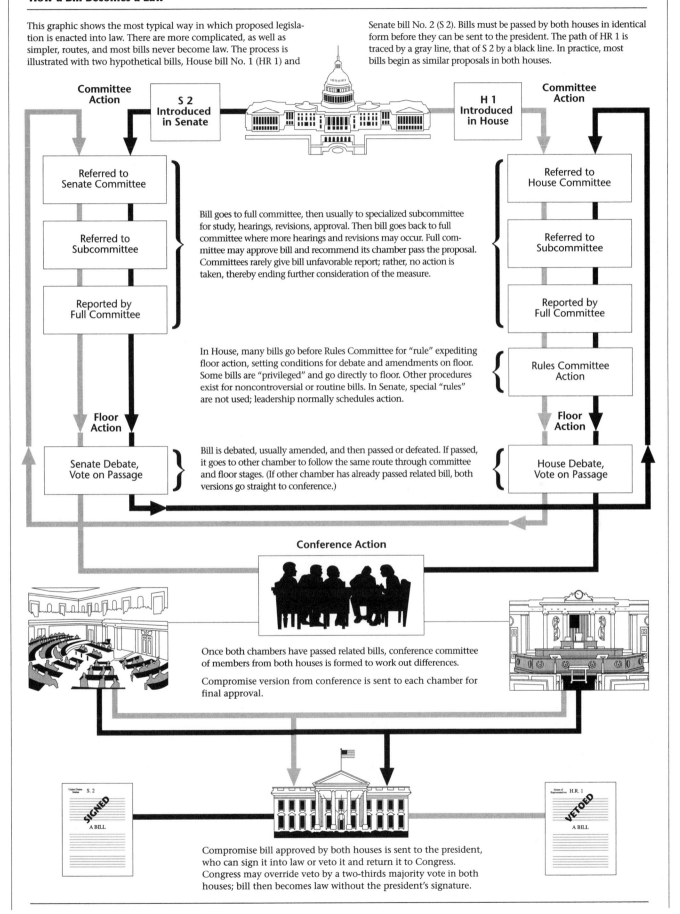

Committee Action

S 2 Introduced in Senate

Referred to Senate Committee

Referred to Subcommittee

Reported by Full Committee

Floor Action

Senate Debate, Vote on Passage

H 1 Introduced in House

Committee Action

Referred to House Committee

Referred to Subcommittee

Reported by Full Committee

Rules Committee Action

Floor Action

House Debate, Vote on Passage

Bill goes to full committee, then usually to specialized subcommittee for study, hearings, revisions, approval. Then bill goes back to full committee where more hearings and revisions may occur. Full committee may approve bill and recommend its chamber pass the proposal. Committees rarely give bill unfavorable report; rather, no action is taken, thereby ending further consideration of the measure.

In House, many bills go before Rules Committee for "rule" expediting floor action, setting conditions for debate and amendments on floor. Some bills are "privileged" and go directly to floor. Other procedures exist for noncontroversial or routine bills. In Senate, special "rules" are not used; leadership normally schedules action.

Bill is debated, usually amended, and then passed or defeated. If passed, it goes to other chamber to follow the same route through committee and floor stages. (If other chamber has already passed related bill, both versions go straight to conference.)

Conference Action

Once both chambers have passed related bills, conference committee of members from both houses is formed to work out differences.

Compromise version from conference is sent to each chamber for final approval.

S 2 SIGNED A BILL

H.R. 1 VETOED A BILL

Compromise bill approved by both houses is sent to the president, who can sign it into law or veto it and return it to Congress. Congress may override veto by a two-thirds majority vote in both houses; bill then becomes law without the president's signature.

The House Calendar to which are referred bills of public character not raising revenue or appropriating money.

The Corrections Calendar to which are referred bills to repeal rules and regulations deemed excessive or unnecessary when the Corrections Calendar is called the second and fourth Tuesday of each month. (Instituted in the 104th Congress to replace the seldom-used Consent Calendar.) A three-fifths majority is required for passage.

The Private Calendar to which are referred bills for relief in the nature of claims against the United States or private immigration bills that are passed without debate when the Private Calendar is called the first and third Tuesdays of each month.

The Discharge Calendar to which are referred motions to discharge committees when the necessary signatures are signed to a discharge petition.

There is only one legislative calendar in the Senate and one "executive calendar" for treaties and nominations submitted to the Senate.

Debate. A bill is brought to debate by varying procedures. In the Senate the majority leader, in consultation with the minority leader and others, schedules the bills that will be taken up for debate. If it is urgent or important it can be taken up in the Senate either by unanimous consent or by a majority vote.

In the House, precedence is granted if a special rule is obtained from the Rules Committee. A request for a special rule usually is made by the chairman of the committee that favorably reported the bill. The request is considered by the Rules Committee in the same fashion that other committees consider legislative measures. The committee proposes a resolution providing for immediate consideration of the bill. The Rules Committee reports the resolution to the House where it is debated and voted on in the same fashion as regular bills.

The resolutions providing special rules are important because they specify how long the bill may be debated and whether it may be amended from the floor. If floor amendments are banned, the bill is considered under a "closed rule."

When a bill is debated under an "open rule," amendments may be offered from the floor. Committee amendments always are taken up first but may be changed, as may all amendments up to the second degree; that is, an amendment to an amendment to an amendment is not in order.

Duration of debate in the House depends on whether the bill is under discussion by the House proper or before the House when it is sitting as the Committee of the Whole House on the State of the Union. In the former, the amount of time for debate is allocated with an hour for each member if the measure is under consideration without a rule. In the Committee of the Whole the amount of time agreed on for general debate is equally divided between proponents and opponents. At the end of general discussion, the bill is often read section by section for amendment. Debate on an amendment is limited to five minutes for each side; this is called the "five-minute rule." In practice, amendments regularly are debated more than ten minutes, with members gaining the floor by offering pro forma amendments or obtaining unanimous consent to speak longer than five minutes.

Senate debate usually is unlimited. It can be halted only by unanimous consent or by "cloture," which requires a three-fifths majority of the entire Senate except for proposed changes in the Senate rules. The latter requires a two-thirds vote.

The House considers almost all important bills within a parliamentary framework known as the Committee of the Whole. It is not a committee as the word usually is understood; it is the full House meeting under another name for the purpose of speeding action on legislation. Technically, the House sits as the Committee of the Whole when it considers any tax measure or bill dealing with public appropriations. Upon adoption of a special rule, the Speaker declares the House resolved into the Committee of the Whole and appoints a member of the majority party to serve as the chairman. The rules of the House permit the Committee of the Whole to meet when a quorum of 100 members is present on the floor and to amend and act on bills. When the Committee of the Whole has acted, it "rises," the Speaker returns as the presiding officer of the House and the member appointed chairman of the Committee of the Whole reports the action of the committee and its recommendations. The Committee of the Whole cannot pass a bill; instead it reports the measure to the full House with whatever changes it has approved. The full House then may pass or reject the bill — or, on occasion, recommit the bill to committee. Amendments adopted in the Committee of the Whole may be put to a second vote in the full House.

Votes. Voting on bills may occur repeatedly before they are finally approved or rejected. The House votes on the rule for the bill and on various amendments to the bill. Voting on amendments often is a more illuminating test of a bill's support than is the final tally. Sometimes members approve final passage of bills after vigorously supporting amendments that, if adopted, would have scuttled the legislation.

The Senate has three different methods of voting: an untabulated voice vote, a standing vote (called a division) and a recorded roll call to which members answer "yea" or "nay" when their names are called. The House also employs voice and standing votes, but since January 1973 yeas and nays have been recorded by an electronic voting device, eliminating the need for time-consuming roll calls.

After amendments to a bill have been voted upon, a vote may be taken on a motion to recommit the bill to committee. If carried, this vote is usually a death blow to the bill. If the motion is unsuccessful, the bill then is "read for the third time." After the third reading a vote on passage is taken. The final vote may be followed by a motion to reconsider, and this motion may be followed by a move to lay the motion on the table. Usually, those voting for the bill's passage vote for the tabling motion, thus safeguarding the final passage action. With that, the bill has been formally passed by the chamber.

Action in Second Chamber

After a bill is passed it is sent to the other chamber. This body may then take one of several steps. It may pass the bill as is — accepting the other chamber's language. It may send the bill to committee for scrutiny or alteration, or reject the entire bill, advising the other chamber of its actions. Or it simply may ignore the bill submitted while it continues work on its own version of the proposed legislation. Frequently, one chamber may approve a version of a bill that is greatly at variance with the version already passed by the other chamber, and then substitute its contents for the language of the other, retaining only the latter's bill number.

Often the second chamber makes only minor changes. If these are readily agreed to by the other chamber, the bill then is routed to the president. However, if the opposite chamber significantly alters the bill submitted to it, the measure usually is "sent to conference." The chamber that has possession of the "papers" (engrossed bill, engrossed amendments, messages of transmittal) requests a conference and the other chamber may agree to it. If the second chamber does not agree, the bill dies.

Conference Action

A conference works out conflicting House and Senate versions of a legislative bill. The conferees usually are senior members from the committees that managed the legislation who are appointed by the presiding officers of the two houses. Under this arrangement the conferees of one house have the duty of trying to maintain their chamber's position in the face of amending actions by the conferees (also referred to as "managers") of the other house.

The number of conferees from each chamber may vary, the range usually being from seven to nine members in each group, depending on the length or complexity of the bill involved. But a majority vote controls the action of each group so that a large representation does not give one chamber a voting advantage over the other chamber's conferees.

Theoretically, conferees are not allowed to write new legislation in reconciling the two versions before them, but this curb sometimes is bypassed. Many bills have been put into acceptable compromise form only after new language was provided by the conferees. Frequently the ironing out of difficulties takes days or even weeks. Conferences on involved, complex and controversial bills sometimes are particularly drawn out.

As a conference proceeds, conferees reconcile differences between the versions, but generally they grant concessions only insofar as they remain sure that the chamber they represent will accept the compromises. Occasionally, uncertainty over how either house will react, or the positive refusal of a chamber to back down on a disputed amendment, results in an impasse, and the bills die in conference even though each was approved by its sponsoring chamber.

When the conferees have reached agreement, they prepare a conference report embodying their recommendations (compromises) and a joint explanatory statement. The report, in document form, must be submitted to each house. The conference report must be approved by each house. Consequently, approval of the report is approval of the compromise bill. In the order of voting on conference reports, the chamber that asked for a conference yields to the other chamber the opportunity to vote first.

Final Action

After a bill has been passed by both the House and Senate in identical form, all of the original papers are sent to the enrolling clerk of the chamber in which the bill originated. The clerk then prepares an enrolled bill, which is printed on parchment paper.

When this bill has been certified as correct by the secretary of the Senate or the clerk of the House, depending on which chamber originated the bill, it is signed first (no matter whether it originated in the Senate or House) by the Speaker of the House and then by the president of the Senate. It is next sent to the White House to await action.

If the president approves the bill, he signs it, dates it and usually writes the word "approved" on the document. If the president does not sign it within 10 days (Sundays excepted) and Congress is in session, the bill becomes law without his signature.

If Congress adjourns *sine die* at the end of the second session the president can pocket veto a bill and it dies without Congress having the opportunity to override.

A president vetoes a bill by refusing to sign it and, before the ten-day period expires, returning it to Congress with a message stating his reasons. The message is sent to the chamber that originated the bill. If no action is taken on the message, the bill dies. Congress, however, can attempt to override the president's veto and enact the bill, "the objections of the president to the contrary notwithstanding." Overriding a veto requires a two-thirds vote of those present in each chamber, who must number a quorum and vote by roll call.

If the president's veto is overridden by a two-thirds vote in both houses, the bill becomes law. Otherwise it is dead.

When bills are passed finally and signed, or passed over a veto, they are given law numbers in numerical order as they become law. There are two series of numbers, one for public and one for private laws, starting at the number "1" for each two-year term of Congress. They are then identified by law number and by Congress — for example, Private Law 10, 105th Congress; Public Law 33, 106th Congress (or PL 106-33).

The Budget Process in Brief

Through the budget process, the president and Congress decide how much to spend and tax during the upcoming fiscal year. More specifically, they decide how much to spend on each activity, ensure that the government spends no more than that and spends it only for that activity and report on that spending at the end of each budget cycle.

The President's Budget

The law requires that, by the first Monday in February, the president submit to Congress his proposed federal budget for the next fiscal year, which begins on October 1. To accomplish this the president establishes general budget and fiscal policy guidelines. Based on these guidelines, executive branch agencies make requests for funds and submit them to the White House's Office of Management and Budget (OMB) nearly a year before the start of a new fiscal year. The OMB, receiving direction from the president and administration officials, reviews the agencies' requests and develops a detailed budget by December. From December to January the OMB prepares the budget documents, so that the president can deliver it to Congress in February.

The president's budget is the executive branch's plan for the next year — but it is just a proposal. After receiving it, Congress has its own budget process to follow from February to October. Only after Congress passes the required spending bills — and the president signs them — has the government created its actual budget.

Action in Congress

Congress first must pass a "budget resolution" — a framework within which the members of Congress will make their decisions about spending and taxes. It includes targets for total spending, total revenues and the deficit, and allocations within the spending target for the two types of spending — discretionary and mandatory.

Discretionary spending, which currently accounts for about 33 percent of all federal spending, is what the president and Congress must decide to spend for the next year through the thirteen annual appropriations bills. It includes money for such activities as the FBI and the Coast Guard, for housing and education, for NASA and highway and bridge construction and for defense and foreign aid.

Mandatory spending, which currently accounts for 67 percent of all spending, is authorized by laws that have already been passed. It includes entitlement spending — such as for Social Security, Medicare, veterans' benefits and food stamps — through which individuals receive benefits because they are eligible based on their age, income or other criteria. It also includes interest on the national debt, which the government pays to individuals and institutions that hold Treasury bonds and other government securities. The only way the president and Congress can change the spending on entitlement and other mandatory programs is if they change the laws that authorized the programs.

Currently, the law requires that legislation that would raise mandatory spending or lower revenues — compared to existing law — be offset by spending cuts or revenue increases. This requirement, called "pay-as-you-go" is designed to prevent new legislation from increasing the deficit.

Once Congress passes the budget resolution, legislators turn their attention to passing the 13 annual appropriations bills and, if they choose, "authorizing" bills to change the laws governing mandatory spending and revenues.

Congress begins by examining the president's budget in detail. Scores of committees and subcommittees hold hearings on proposals under their jurisdiction. The House and Senate Armed Services Authorizing Committees, and the Defense and Military Construction Subcommittees of the Appropriations Committees, for instance, hold hearings on the president's defense budget. The White House budget director, cabinet officers and other administration officials work with Congress as it accepts some of the president's proposals, rejects others and changes still others. Congress can change funding levels, eliminate programs or add programs not requested by the president. It can add or eliminate taxes and other sources of revenue, or make other changes that affect the amount of revenue collected. Congressional rules require that these committees and subcommittees take actions that reflect the congressional budget resolution.

The president's budget, the budget resolution and the appropriations or authorizing bills measure spending in two ways — "budget authority" and "outlays." Budget authority is what the law authorizes the federal government to spend for certain programs, projects or activities. What the government actually spends in a particular year, however, is an outlay. For example, when the government decides to build a space exploration system, the president and Congress may agree to appropriate $1 billion in budget authority. But the space system may take ten years to build. Thus, the government may spend $100 million in outlays in the first year to begin construction and the remaining $900 million during the next nine years as the construction continues.

Congress must provide budget authority before the federal agencies can obligate the government to make outlays. When Congress fails to complete action on one or more of the regular annual appropriations bills before the fiscal year begins on October 1, budget authority may be made on a temporary basis through continuing resolutions. Continuing resolutions make budget authority available for limited periods of time, generally at rates related through some formula to the rate provided in the previous year's appropriation.

Monitoring the Budget

Once Congress passes and the president signs the federal appropriations bills or authorizing laws for the fiscal year, the government monitors the budget through (1) agency program managers and budget officials, including the Inspectors General, who report only to the agency head; (2) the Office of Management and Budget; (3) congressional committees; and (4) the General Accounting Office, an auditing arm of Congress.

This oversight is designed to (1) ensure that agencies comply with legal limits on spending and that agencies use budget authority only for the purposes intended; (2) see that programs are operating consistently with legal requirements and existing policy; and (3) ensure that programs are well managed and achieving the intended results.

The president may withhold appropriated amounts from obligation only under certain limited circumstances — to provide for contingencies, to achieve savings made possible through changes in requirements or greater efficiency of operations or as otherwise provided by law. The Impoundment Control Act of 1974 specifies the procedures that must be followed if funds are withheld. Congress can also cancel previous authorized budget authority by passing a rescissions bill — but it also must be signed by the president.

Glossary of Congressional Terms

AA—(See Administrative Assistant.)

Absence of a Quorum—Absence of the required number of members to conduct business in a house or a committee. When a quorum call or roll-call vote in a house establishes that a quorum is not present, no debate or other business is permitted except a motion to adjourn or motions to request or compel the attendance of absent members, if necessary by arresting them.

Absolute Majority—A vote requiring approval by a majority of all members of a house rather than a majority of members present and voting. Also referred to as constitutional majority.

Account—Organizational units used in the federal budget primarily for recording spending and revenue transactions.

Act—(1) A bill passed in identical form by both houses of Congress and signed into law by the president or enacted over the president's veto. A bill also becomes an act without the president's signature if he does not return it to Congress within ten days (Sundays excepted) and if Congress has not adjourned within that period. (2) Also, the technical term for a bill passed by at least one house and engrossed.

Ad Hoc Select Committee—A temporary committee formed for a special purpose or to deal with a specific subject. Conference committees are ad hoc joint committees. A House rule adopted in 1975 authorizes the Speaker to refer measures to special ad hoc committees, appointed by the Speaker with the approval of the House.

Adjourn—A motion to adjourn is a formal motion to end a day's session or meeting of a house or a committee. A motion to adjourn usually has no conditions attached to it, but it sometimes may specify the day or time for reconvening or make reconvening subject to the call of the chamber's presiding officer or the committee's chairman. In both houses, a motion to adjourn is of the highest privilege, takes precedence over all other motions, is not debatable and must be put to an immediate vote. Adjournment of a house ends its legislative day. For this reason, the House or Senate sometimes adjourns for only one minute, or some other very brief period of time, during the course of a day's session. The House does not permit a motion to adjourn after it has resolved into Committee of the Whole or when the previous question has been ordered on a measure to final passage without an intervening motion.

Adjourn for More Than Three Days—Under Article I, Section 5 of the Constitution, neither house may adjourn for more than three days without the approval of the other. The necessary approval is given in a concurrent resolution to which both houses have agreed.

Adjournment *Sine Die*—Final adjournment of an annual or two-year session of Congress; literally, adjournment without a day. The two houses must agree to a privileged concurrent resolution for such an adjournment. A sine die adjournment precludes Congress from meeting again until the next constitutionally fixed date of a session (Jan. 3 of the following year) unless Congress determines otherwise by law or the president calls it into special session. Article II, Section 3 of the Constitution authorizes the president to adjourn both houses until such time as the president thinks proper when the two houses cannot agree to a time of adjournment. No president, however, has ever exercised this authority.

Adjournment to a Day (and Time) Certain—An adjournment that fixes the next date and time of meeting for one or both houses. It does not end an annual session of Congress.

Administration Bill—A bill drafted in the executive office of the president or in an executive department or agency to implement part of the president's program. An administration bill is introduced in Congress by a member who supports it or as a courtesy to the administration.

Administrative Assistant (AA)—The title usually given to a member's chief aide, political advisor and head of office staff. The administrative assistant often represents the member at meetings with visitors or officials when the member is unable (or unwilling) to attend.

Adoption—The usual parliamentary term for approval of a conference report. It is also commonly applied to amendments.

Advance Appropriation—In an appropriation act for a particular fiscal year, an appropriation that does not become available for spending or obligation until a subsequent fiscal year. The amount of the advance appropriation is counted as part of the budget for the fiscal year in which it becomes available for obligation.

Advance Funding—A mechanism whereby statutory language may allow budget authority for a fiscal year to be increased, and obligations to be incurred, with an offsetting decrease in the budget authority available in the succeeding fiscal year. If not used, the budget authority remains available for obligation in the succeeding fiscal year. Advance funding is sometimes used to provide contingency funding of a few benefit programs.

Adverse Report—A committee report recommending against approval of a measure or some other matter. Committees usually pigeonhole measures they oppose instead of reporting them adversely, but they may be required to report them by a statutory rule or an instruction from their parent body.

Advice and Consent—The Senate's constitutional role in consenting to or rejecting the president's nominations to executive branch and judicial offices and treaties with other nations. Confirmation of nominees requires a simple majority vote of senators present and voting. Treaties must be approved by a two-thirds majority of those present and voting.

Aisle—The center aisle of each chamber. When facing the presiding officer, Republicans usually sit to the right of the aisle, Democrats to the left. When members speak of "my side of the aisle" or "this side," they are referring to their party.

Amendment—A formal proposal to alter the text of a bill, resolution, amendment, motion, treaty or some other text. Technically, it is a motion. An amendment may strike out (eliminate) part of a text, insert new text or strike out and insert — that is, replace all or part of the text with new text. The texts of amendments considered on the floor are printed in full in the Congressional Record.

Amendment in the Nature of a Substitute—Usually, an amendment to replace the entire text of a measure. It strikes out everything after the enacting clause and inserts a version that may be somewhat, substantially or entirely different. When a committee adopts extensive amendments to a measure, it often incorporates them into such an amendment. Occasionally, the term is applied to an amendment that replaces a major portion of a measure's text.

Amendment Tree—A diagram showing the number and types of amendments that the rules and practices of a house permit to be offered to a measure before any of the amendments is voted on. It shows the relationship of one amendment to the others, and it may also indicate the degree of each amendment, whether it is a perfecting or substitute amendment, the order in which amendments may be offered and the order in which they are put to a vote. The same type of diagram can be used to display an actual amendment situation.

Annual Authorization—Legislation that authorizes appropriations for a single fiscal year and usually for a specific amount. Under the rules of the authorization-appropriation process, an annually authorized agency or program must be reauthorized each year if it is to receive appropriations for that year. Sometimes Congress fails to enact the reauthorization but nevertheless provides appropriations to continue the program, circumventing the rules by one means or another.

Appeal—A member's formal challenge of a ruling or decision by the presiding officer. On appeal, a house or a committee may overturn the ruling by majority vote. The right of appeal ensures the body against arbitrary control by the chair. Appeals are rarely made in the House and are even more rarely successful. Rulings are more frequently appealed in the Senate and occasionally overturned, in part because its presiding officer is not the majority party's leader, as in the House.

Apportionment—The action, after each decennial census, of allocating the number of members in the House of Representatives to each state. By law, the total number of House members (not counting delegates and a resident commissioner) is fixed at 435. The number allotted to each state is based approximately on its proportion of the nation's total population. Because the Constitution guarantees each state one representative no matter how small its population, exact proportional distribution is virtually impossible. The mathematical formula currently used to determine the apportionment is called the Method of Equal Proportions. (See Method of Equal Proportions.)

Appropriated Entitlement—An entitlement program, such as veterans' pensions, that is funded through annual appropriations rather than by a permanent appropriation. Because such an entitlement law requires the government to provide eligible recipients the benefits to which they are entitled, whatever the cost, Congress must appropriate the necessary funds.

Appropriation—(1) Legislative language that permits a federal agency to incur obligations and make payments from the Treasury for specified purposes, usually during a specified period of time. (2) The specific amount of money made available by such language. The Constitution prohibits payments from the Treasury except "in Consequence of Appropriations made by Law." With some exceptions, the rules of both houses forbid consideration of appropriations for purposes that are unauthorized in law or of appropriation amounts larger than those authorized in law. The House of Representatives claims the exclusive right to originate appropriation bills — a claim the Senate denies in theory but accepts in practice.

At-Large—Elected by and representing an entire state instead of a district within a state. The term usually refers to a representative rather than to a senator. (See Apportionment; Congressional District; Redistricting.)

August Adjournment—A congressional adjournment during the month of August in odd-numbered years, required by the Legislative Reorganization Act of 1970. The law instructs the two houses to adjourn for a period of at least thirty days before the second day after Labor Day, unless Congress provides otherwise or if, on July 31, a state of war exists by congressional declaration.

Authorization—(1) A statutory provision that establishes or continues a federal agency, activity or program for a fixed or indefinite period of time. It may also establish policies and restrictions and deal with organizational and administrative matters. (2) A statutory provision, as described in (1), may also, explicitly or implicitly, authorize congressional action to provide appropriations for an agency, activity or program. The appropriations may be authorized for one year, several years or an indefinite period of time, and the authorization may be for a specific amount of money or an indefinite amount ("such sums as may be necessary"). Authorizations of specific amounts are construed as ceilings on the amounts that subsequently may be appropriated in an appropriation bill, but not as minimums; either house may appropriate lesser amounts or nothing at all.

Authorization-Appropriation Process—The two-stage procedural system that the rules of each house require for establishing and funding federal agencies and programs: first, enactment of authorizing legislation that creates or continues an agency or program; second, enactment of appropriations legislation that provides funds for the authorized agency or program.

Automatic Roll Call—Under a House rule, the automatic ordering of the yeas and nays when a quorum is not present on a voice or division vote and a member objects to the vote on that ground. It is not permitted in the Committee of the Whole.

Backdoor Spending Authority—Authority to incur obligations that evades the normal congressional appropriations process because it is provided in legislation other than appropriation acts. The most common forms are borrowing authority, contract authority and entitlement authority.

Baseline—A projection of the levels of federal spending, revenues and the resulting budgetary surpluses or deficits for the upcoming and subsequent fiscal years, taking into account laws enacted to date and assuming no new policy decisions. It provides a benchmark for measuring the budgetary effects of proposed changes in federal revenues or spending, assuming certain economic conditions.

Bells—A system of electric signals and lights that informs members of activities in each chamber. The type of activity taking place is indicated by the number of signals and the interval between them. When the signals are sounded, a corresponding number of lights are lit around the perimeter of many clocks in House or Senate offices.

Bicameral—Consisting of two houses or chambers. Congress is a bicameral legislature whose two houses have an equal role in enacting legislation. In most other national bicameral legislatures, one house is significantly more powerful than the other.

Bigger Bite Amendment—An amendment that substantively changes a portion of a text including language that had previously been amended. Normally, language that has been amended may not be amended again. However, a part of a sentence that has been changed by amendment, for example, may be changed again by an amendment that amends a "bigger bite" of the text — that is, by an amendment that also substantively changes the unamended parts of the sentence or the entire section or title in which the previously amended language appears. The biggest possible bite is an amendment in the nature of a substitute that amends the entire text of a measure. Once adopted, therefore, such an amendment ends the amending process.

Bill—The term for the chief vehicle Congress uses for enacting laws. Bills that originate in the House of Representatives are designated as HR, those in the Senate as S, followed by a number assigned in the order in which they are introduced during a two-year Congress. A bill becomes a law if passed in identical language by both houses and signed by the president, or passed over the president's veto, or if the president fails to sign it within ten days after receiving it while Congress is in session.

Bill of Attainder—An act of a legislature finding a person guilty of treason or a felony. The Constitution prohibits the passage of such a bill by the U.S. Congress or any state legislature.

Bills and Resolutions Introduced—Members formally present measures to their respective houses by delivering them to a clerk in the chamber when their house is in session. Both houses permit any number of members to join in introducing a bill or resolution. The first member listed on the measure is the sponsor; the other members listed are its cosponsors.

Bills and Resolutions Referred—After a bill or resolution is introduced, it is normally sent to one or more committees that have jurisdiction over its subject, as defined by House and Senate rules and precedents. A Senate measure is usually referred to the committee with jurisdiction over the predominant subject of its text, but it may be sent to two or more committees by unanimous consent or on a motion offered jointly by the majority and minority leaders. In the House, a rule requires the Speaker to refer a measure to the committee that has primary jurisdiction. The Speaker is also authorized to refer measures sequentially to additional committees and to impose time limits on such referrals.

Bipartisan Committee—A committee with an equal number of members from each political party. The House Committee on Standards of Official Conduct and the Senate Select Committee on Ethics are the only bipartisan, permanent full committees.

Borrowing Authority—Statutory authority permitting a federal agency, such as the Export-Import Bank, to borrow money from the public or the Treasury to finance its operations. It is a form of backdoor spending. To bring such spending under the control of the congressional appropriation process, the Congressional Budget Act requires that new borrowing authority shall be effective only to the extent and in such amounts as are provided in appropriations acts.

Budget—A detailed statement of actual or anticipated revenues and expenditures during an accounting period. For the national government, the period is the federal fiscal year (Oct. 1 to Sept. 30). The budget usually refers to the president's budget submission to Congress early each calendar year. The president's budget estimates federal government income and spending for the upcoming fiscal year and contains detailed recommendations for appropriation, revenue and other legislation. Congress is not required to accept or even vote directly on the president's proposals, and it often revises the president's budget extensively. (See Fiscal Year.)

Budget Act—Common name for the Congressional Budget and Impoundment Control Act of 1974, which established the basic procedures of the current congressional budget process; created the House and Senate Budget Committees; and enacted procedures for reconciliation, deferrals and rescissions. (See Budget Process; Deferral; Impoundment; Reconciliation; Rescission. See also Gramm-Rudman-Hollings Act of 1985.)

Budget and Accounting Act of 1921—The law that, for the first time, authorized the president to submit to Congress an annual budget for the entire federal government. Before passage of the act, most federal agencies sent their budget requests to the appropriate congressional committees without review by the president.

Budget Authority—Generally, the amount of money that may be spent or obligated by a government agency or for a government program or activity. Technically, it is statutory authority to enter into obligations that normally result in outlays. The main forms of budget authority are appropriations, borrowing authority and contract authority. It also includes authority to obligate and expend the proceeds of offsetting receipts and collections. Congress may

make budget authority available for only one year, several years or an indefinite period, and it may specify definite or indefinite amounts.

Budget Enforcement Act of 1990—An act that revised the sequestration process established by the Gramm-Rudman-Hollings Act of 1985, replaced the earlier act's fixed deficit targets with adjustable ones, established discretionary spending limits for fiscal years 1991 through 1995, instituted pay-as-you-go rules to enforce deficit neutrality on revenue and mandatory spending legislation and reformed the budget and accounting rules for federal credit activities. Unlike the Gramm-Rudman-Hollings Act, the 1990 act emphasized restraints on legislated changes in taxes and spending instead of fixed deficit limits.

Budget Enforcement Act of 1997—An act that revised and updated the provisions of the Budget Enforcement Act of 1990, including by extending the discretionary spending caps and pay-as-you-go rules through 2002.

Budget Process—(1) In Congress, the procedural system it uses (a) to approve an annual concurrent resolution on the budget that sets goals for aggregate and functional categories of federal expenditures, revenues and the surplus or deficit for an upcoming fiscal year; and (b) to implement those goals in spending, revenue and, if necessary, reconciliation and debt-limit legislation. (2) In the executive branch, the process of formulating the president's annual budget, submitting it to Congress, defending it before congressional committees, implementing subsequent budget-related legislation, impounding or sequestering expenditures as permitted by law, auditing and evaluating programs and compiling final budget data. The Budget and Accounting Act of 1921 and the Congressional Budget and Impoundment Control Act of 1974 established the basic elements of the current budget process. Major revisions were enacted in the Gramm-Rudman-Hollings Act of 1985 and the Budget Enforcement Act of 1990.

Budget Resolution—A concurrent resolution in which Congress establishes or revises its version of the federal budget's broad financial features for the upcoming fiscal year and several additional fiscal years. Like other concurrent resolutions, it does not have the force of law, but it provides the framework within which Congress subsequently considers revenue, spending and other budget-implementing legislation. The framework consists of two basic elements: (1) aggregate budget amounts (total revenues, new budget authority, outlays, loan obligations and loan guarantee commitments, deficit or surplus and debt limit); and (2) subdivisions of the relevant aggregate amounts among the functional categories of the budget. Although it does not allocate funds to specific programs or accounts, the budget committees' reports accompanying the resolution often discuss the major program assumptions underlying its functional amounts. Unlike those amounts, however, the assumptions are not binding on Congress.

By Request—A designation indicating that a member has introduced a measure on behalf of the president, an executive agency or a private individual or organization. Members often introduce such measures as a courtesy because neither the president nor any person other than a member of Congress can do so. The term, which appears next to the sponsor's name, implies that the member who introduced the measure does not necessarily endorse it. A House rule dealing with by-request introductions dates from 1888, but the practice goes back to the earliest history of Congress.

Byrd Rule—The popular name of an amendment to the Congressional Budget Act that bars the inclusion of extraneous matter in any reconciliation legislation considered in the Senate. The ban is enforced by points of order that the presiding officer sustains. The provision defines different categories of extraneous matter, but it also permits certain exceptions. Its chief sponsor was Sen. Robert C. Byrd, D-W.Va.

Calendar—A list of measures or other matters (most of them favorably reported by committees) that are eligible for floor consideration. The House has five calendars; the Senate has two. A place on a calendar does not guarantee consideration. Each house decides which measures and matters it will take up, when and in what order, in accordance with its rules and practices.

Calendar Wednesday—A House procedure that on Wednesdays permits its committees to bring up for floor consideration nonprivileged measures they have reported. The procedure is so cumbersome and susceptible to dilatory tactics, however, that it is rarely used.

Call Up—To bring a measure or report to the floor for immediate consideration.

Casework—Assistance to constituents who seek assistance in dealing with federal and local government agencies. Constituent service is a high priority in most members' offices.

Caucus—(1) A common term for the official organization of each party in each house. (2) The official title of the organization of House Democrats. House and Senate Republicans and Senate Democrats call their organizations "conferences." (3) A term for an informal group of members who share legislative interests, such as the Black Caucus, Hispanic Caucus and Children's Caucus.

Censure—The strongest formal condemnation of a member for misconduct short of expulsion. A house usually adopts a resolution of censure to express its condemnation, after which the presiding officer reads its rebuke aloud to the member in the presence of his or her colleagues.

Chairman—The presiding officer of a committee, a subcommittee or a task force. At meetings, the chairman preserves order, enforces the rules, recognizes members to speak or offer motions and puts questions to a vote. The chairman of a committee or subcommittee usually appoints its staff and sets its agenda, subject to the panel's veto.

Chamber—The Capitol room in which a house of Congress normally holds its sessions. The chamber of the House of Representatives, officially called the Hall of the House, is considerably larger than that of the Senate because it must accommodate 435 representatives, four delegates and one resident commissioner. Unlike the Senate chamber, members have no desks or assigned seats. In both chambers, the floor slopes downward to the well in front of the presiding officer's raised desk. A chamber is often referred to as "the floor," as when members are said to be on or going to the floor. Those expressions usually imply that the member's house is in session.

Christmas Tree Bill—Jargon for a bill adorned with amendments, many of them unrelated to the bill's subject, that provide benefits for interest groups, specific states, congressional districts, companies and individuals.

Classes of Senators—A class consists of the thirty-three or thirty-four senators elected to a six-year term in the same general election. Because the terms of approximately one-third of the senators expire every two years, there are three classes.

Clean Bill—After a House committee extensively amends a bill, it often assembles its amendments and what is left of the bill into a new measure that one or more of its members introduces as a "clean bill." The revised measure is assigned a new number.

Clerk of the House—An officer of the House of Representatives responsible principally for administrative support of the legislative process in the House. The clerk is invariably the candidate of the majority party.

Cloakrooms—Two rooms with access to the rear of each chamber's floor, one for each party's members, where members may confer privately, sit quietly or have a snack. The presiding officer sometimes urges members who are conversing too loudly on the floor to retire to their cloakrooms.

Closed Hearing—A hearing closed to the public and the media. A House committee may close a hearing only if it determines that disclosure of the testimony to be taken would endanger national security, violate any law or tend to defame, degrade or incriminate any person. The Senate has a similar rule. Both houses require roll-call votes in open session to close a hearing.

Closed Rule—A special rule reported from the House Rules Committee that prohibits amendments to a measure or that only permits amendments offered by the reporting committee.

Cloture—A Senate procedure that limits further consideration of a pending proposal to thirty hours in order to end a filibuster. Sixteen senators must first sign and submit a cloture motion to the presiding officer. One hour after the Senate meets on the second calendar day thereafter, the chair puts the motion to a yea-and-nay vote following a live quorum call. If three-fifths of all senators (sixty if there are no vacancies) vote for the motion, the Senate must take final action on the cloture proposal by the end of the thirty hours of consideration and may consider no other business until it takes that action. Cloture on a proposal to amend the Senate's standing rules requires approval by two-thirds of the senators present and voting.

Code of Official Conduct—A House rule that bans certain actions by House members, officers and employees; requires them to conduct themselves in ways that "reflect creditably" on the House; and orders them to adhere to the spirit and the letter of House rules and those of its committees. The code's provisions govern the receipt of outside compensation, gifts and honoraria and the use of campaign funds; prohibit members from using their clerk-hire allowance to pay anyone who does not perform duties commensurate with that pay; forbids discrimination in members' hiring or treatment of employees on the grounds of race, color, religion, sex, handicap, age or national origin; orders members convicted of a crime who might be punished by imprisonment of two or more years not to participate in committee business or vote on the floor until exonerated or reelected; and restricts employees' contact with federal agencies on matters in which they have a significant financial interest. The Senate's rules contain some similar prohibitions.

College of Cardinals—A popular term for the subcommittee chairmen of the appropriations committees, reflecting their influence over appropriation measures. The chairmen of the full appropriations committees are sometimes referred to as popes.

Comity—The practice of maintaining mutual courtesy and civility between the two houses in their dealings with each other and in members' speeches on the floor. Although the practice is largely governed by long-established customs, a House rule explicitly cautions its members not to characterize any Senate action or inaction, refer to individual senators except under certain circumstances, or quote from Senate proceedings except to make legislative history on a measure. The Senate has no rule on the subject but references to the House have been held out of order on several occasions. Generally the houses do not interfere with each other's appropriations although minor conflicts sometimes occur. A refusal to receive a message from the other house has also been held to violate the practice of comity.

Committee—A panel of members elected or appointed to perform some service or function for its parent body. Congress has four types of committees: standing, special or select, joint, and, in the House, a Committee of the Whole. Committees conduct investigations, make studies, issue reports and recommendations and, in the case of standing committees, review and prepare measures on their assigned subjects for action by their respective houses. Most committees divide their work among several subcommittees. With rare exceptions, the majority party in a house holds a majority of the seats on its committees, and their chairmen are also from that party.

Committee Jurisdiction—The legislative subjects and other functions assigned to a committee by rule, precedent, resolution or statute. A committee's title usually indicates the general scope of its jurisdiction but often fails to mention other significant subjects assigned to it.

Committee of the Whole—Common name of the Committee of the Whole House on the State of the Union, a committee consisting of all members of the House of Representatives. Measures from the union calendar must be considered in the Committee of the Whole before the House officially completes action on them; the committee often considers other major bills as well. A quorum of the committee is 100, and it meets in the House chamber under a chairman appointed by the Speaker. Procedures in the Committee of the Whole expedite consideration of legislation because of its smaller quorum requirement, its ban on certain motions and its five-minute rule for debate on amendments. Those procedures usually permit more members to offer amendments and participate in the debate on a measure than is normally possible. The Senate no longer uses a Committee of the Whole.

Committee Ratios—The ratios of majority to minority party members on committees. By custom, the ratios of most committees reflect party strength in their respective houses as closely as possible.

Committee Report on a Measure—A document submitted by a committee to report a measure to its parent chamber. Customarily, the report explains the measure's purpose, describes provisions and any amendments recommended by the committee and presents arguments for its approval.

Committee Veto—A procedure that requires an executive department or agency to submit certain proposed policies, programs or action to designated committees for review before implementing them. Before 1983, when the Supreme Court declared that a legislative veto was unconstitutional, these provisions permitted committees to veto the proposals. Committees no longer conduct this type of policy review, and the term is now something of a misnomer. Nevertheless, agencies usually take the pragmatic approach of trying to reach a consensus with the committees before carrying out their proposals, especially when an appropriations committee is involved.

Concur—To agree to an amendment of the other house, either by adopting a motion to concur in that amendment or a motion to concur with an amendment to that amendment. After both houses have agreed to the same version of an amendment, neither house may amend it further, nor may any subsequent conference change it or delete it from the measure. Concurrence by one house in all amendments of the other house completes action on the measure; no vote is then necessary on the measure as a whole because both houses previously passed it.

Concurrent Resolution—A resolution that requires approval by both houses but does not need the president's signature and therefore cannot have the force of law. Concurrent resolutions deal with the prerogatives or internal affairs of Congress as a whole. Designated H. Con. Res. in the House and S. Con. Res. in the Senate, they are numbered consecutively in each house in their order of introduction during a two-year Congress.

Conferees—A common title for managers, the members from each house appointed to a conference committee. The Senate usually authorizes its presiding officer to appoint its conferees. The Speaker appoints House conferees, and under a rule adopted in 1993, can remove conferees "at any time after an original appointment" and also appoint additional conferees at any time. Conferees are expected to support the positions of their houses despite their personal views, but in practice this is not always the case. The party ratios of conferees generally reflect the ratios in their houses. Each house may appoint as many conferees as it pleases. House conferees often outnumber their Senate colleagues; however, each house has only one vote in a conference, so the size of its delegation is immaterial.

Conference—(1) A formal meeting or series of meetings between members representing each house to reconcile House and Senate differences on a measure (occasionally several measures). Because one house cannot require the other to agree to its proposals, the conference usually reaches agreement by compromise. When a conference completes action on a measure, or as much action as appears possible, it sends its recommendations to both houses in the form of a conference report, accompanied by an explanatory statement. (2) The official title of the organization of all Democrats or Republicans in the Senate and of all Republicans in the House of Representatives. (See Party Caucus.)

Conference Committee—A temporary joint committee formed for the purpose of resolving differences between the houses on a measure. Major and controversial legislation usually requires conference committee action. Voting in a conference committee is not by individuals but within the House and Senate delegations. Consequently, a conference committee report requires the support of a majority of the conferees from each house. Both houses require that conference committees open their meetings to the public. The Senate's rule permits the committee to close its meetings if a majority of conferees in each delegation agree by a roll-call vote. The House rule permits closed meetings only if the House authorizes them to do so on a roll-call vote. Otherwise, there are no congressional rules governing the organization of, or procedure in, a conference committee. The committee chooses its chairman, but on measures that go to conference annually, such as general appropriation bills, the chairmanship traditionally rotates between the houses.

Conference Report—A document submitted to both houses that contains a conference committee's agreements for resolving their differences on a measure. It must be signed by a majority of the conferees from each house separately and must be accompanied by an explanatory statement. Both houses prohibit amendments to a conference report and require it to be accepted or rejected in its entirety.

Congress—(1) The national legislature of the United States, consisting of the House of Representatives and the Senate. (2) The national legislature in office during a two-year period. Congresses are numbered sequentially; thus, the 1st Congress of 1789–1791 and the 106th Congress of 1999–2001. Before 1935, the two-year period began on the first Monday in December of odd-numbered years. Since then it has extended from January of an odd-numbered year through noon on Jan. 3 of the next odd-numbered year. A Congress usually holds two annual sessions, but some have had three sessions and the 67th Congress had four. When a Congress expires, measures die if they have not yet been enacted.

Congressional Accountability Act of 1995 (CAA)—An act applying eleven labor, workplace and civil rights laws to the legislative branch and establishing procedures and remedies for legislative branch employees with grievances in violation of these laws. The following laws are covered by the CAA: the Fair Labor

Standards Act of 1938; Title VII of the Civil Rights Act of 1964; Americans with Disabilities Act of 1990; Age Discrimination in Employment Act of 1967; Family and Medical Leave Act of 1993; Occupational Safety and Health Act of 1970; Chapter 71 of Title 5, U.S. Code (relating to federal service labor-management relations); Employee Polygraph Protection Act of 1988; Worker Adjustment and Retraining Notification Act; Rehabilitation Act of 1973; and Chapter 43 of Title 38, U.S. Code (relating to veterans' employment and reemployment).

Congressional Budget and Impoundment Control Act of 1974—The law that established the basic elements of the congressional budget process, the House and Senate Budget Committees, the Congressional Budget Office and the procedures for congressional review of impoundments in the form of rescissions and deferrals proposed by the president. The budget process consists of procedures for coordinating congressional revenue and spending decisions made in separate tax, appropriations and legislative measures. The impoundment provisions were intended to give Congress greater control over executive branch actions that delay or prevent the spending of funds provided by Congress.

Congressional Budget Office (CBO)—A congressional support agency created by the Congressional Budget and Impoundment Control Act of 1974 to provide nonpartisan budgetary information and analysis to Congress and its committees. CBO acts as a scorekeeper when Congress is voting on the federal budget, tracking bills to ensure they comply with overall budget goals. The agency also estimates what proposed legislation would cost over a five-year period. CBO works most closely with the House and Senate Budget Committees.

Congressional Directory—The official who's who of Congress, usually published during the first session of a two-year Congress.

Congressional District—The geographical area represented by a single member of the House of Representatives. For states with only one representative, the entire state is a congressional district. As of 2001 seven states had only one representative each: Alaska, Delaware, Montana, North Dakota, South Dakota, Vermont and Wyoming.

Congressional Record—The daily, printed and substantially verbatim account of proceedings in both the House and Senate chambers. Extraneous materials submitted by members appear in a section titled "Extensions of Remarks." A "Daily Digest" appendix contains highlights of the day's floor and committee action plus a list of committee meetings and floor agendas for the next day's session.

Although the official reporters of each house take down every word spoken during the proceedings, members are permitted to edit and "revise and extend" their remarks before they are printed. In the Senate section, all speeches, articles and other material submitted by senators but not actually spoken or read on the floor are set off by large black dots, called bullets. However, bullets do not appear when a senator reads part of a speech and inserts the rest. In the House section, undelivered speeches and materials are printed in a distinctive typeface. The term "permanent Record" refers to the bound volumes of the daily Records of an entire session of Congress.

Congressional Research Service (CRS)—Established in 1917, a department of the Library of Congress whose staff provide nonpartisan, objective analysis and information on virtually any subject to committees, members and staff of Congress. Originally the Legislative Reference Service, it is the oldest congressional support agency.

Congressional Support Agencies—A term often applied to three agencies in the legislative branch that provide nonpartisan information and analysis to committees and members of Congress: the Congressional Budget Office, the Congressional Research Service of the Library of Congress and the General Accounting Office. A fourth support agency, the Office of Technology Assessment, formerly provided such support but was abolished in the 104th Congress.

Congressional Terms of Office—A term normally begins on Jan. 3 of the year following a general election and runs two years for representatives and six years for senators. A representative chosen in a special election to fill a vacancy is sworn in for the remainder of the predecessor's term. An individual appointed to fill a Senate vacancy usually serves until the next general election or until the end of the predecessor's term, whichever comes first. Some states, however, require their governors to call a special election to fill a Senate vacancy shortly after an appointment has been made.

Constitutional Rules—Constitutional provisions that prescribe procedures for Congress. In addition to certain types of votes required in particular situations, these provisions include the following: (1) the House chooses its Speaker, the Senate its president pro tempore and both houses their officers; (2) each house requires a majority quorum to conduct business; (3) less than a majority may adjourn from day to day and compel the attendance of absent members; (4) neither house may adjourn for more than three days without the consent of the other; (5) each house must keep a journal; (6) the yeas and nays are ordered when supported by one-fifth of the members present; (7) all revenue-raising bills must originate in the House, but the Senate may propose amendments to them. The Constitution also sets out the procedure in the House for electing a president, the procedure in the Senate for electing a vice president, the procedure for filling a vacancy in the office of vice president and the procedure for overriding a presidential veto.

Constitutional Votes—Constitutional provisions that require certain votes or voting methods in specific situations. They include (1) the yeas and nays at the desire of one-fifth of the members present; (2) a two-thirds vote by the yeas and nays to override a veto; (3) a two-thirds vote by one house to expel one of its members and by both houses to propose a constitutional amendment; (4) a two-thirds vote of senators present to convict someone whom the House has impeached and to consent to ratification of treaties; (5) a two-thirds vote in each house to remove political disabilities from persons who have engaged in insurrection or rebellion or given aid or comfort to the enemies of the United States; (6) a majority vote in each house to fill a vacancy in the office of vice president; (7) a majority vote of all states to elect a president in the House of Representatives when no candidate receives a majority of the electoral votes; (8) a majority vote of all senators when the Senate elects a vice president under the same circumstances; and (9) the casting vote of the vice president in case of tie votes in the Senate.

Contempt of Congress—Willful obstruction of the proper functions of Congress. Most frequently, it is a refusal to obey a subpoena to appear and testify before a committee or to produce documents demanded by it. Such obstruction is a misdemeanor and persons cited for contempt are subject to prosecution in federal courts. A house cites an individual for contempt by agreeing to a privileged resolution to that effect reported by a committee. The presiding officer then refers the matter to a U.S. attorney for prosecution.

Continuing Body—A characterization of the Senate on the theory that it continues from Congress to Congress and has existed continuously since it first convened in 1789. The rationale for the theory is that under the system of staggered six-year terms for senators, the terms of only about one-third of them expire after each Congress and, therefore, a quorum of the Senate is always in office. Consequently, under this theory, the Senate, unlike the House, does not have to adopt its rules at the beginning of each Congress because those rules continue from one Congress to the next. This makes it extremely difficult for the Senate to change its rules against the opposition of a determined minority because those rules require a two-thirds vote of the senators present and voting to invoke cloture on a proposed rules change.

Continuing Resolution (CR)—A joint resolution that provides funds to continue the operation of federal agencies and programs at the beginning of a new fiscal year if their annual appropriation bills have not yet been enacted; also called continuing appropriations. Continuing resolutions are enacted shortly before or after the new fiscal year begins and usually make funds available for a specified period. Additional resolutions are often needed after the first expires. Some continuing resolutions have provided appropriations for an entire fiscal year. Continuing resolutions for specific periods customarily fix a rate at which agencies may incur obligations based either on the previous year's appropriations, the president's budget request, or the amount as specified in the agency's regular annual appropriation bill if that bill has already been passed by one or both houses. In the House, continuing resolutions are privileged after Sept. 15.

Contract Authority—Statutory authority permitting an agency to enter into contracts or incur other obligations even though it has not received an appropriation to pay for them. Congress must eventually fund them because the government is legally liable for such payments. The Congressional Budget Act of 1974 requires that new contract authority may not be used unless provided for in advance by an appropriation act, but it permits a few exceptions.

Correcting Recorded Votes—The rules of both houses prohibit members from changing their votes after a vote result has been announced. Nevertheless, the Senate permits its members to withdraw or change their votes, by unanimous consent, immediately after the announcement. In rare instances, senators have been granted unanimous consent to change their votes several days or weeks after the announcement. Votes tallied by the electronic voting system in the House may not be changed. But when a vote actually given is not recorded during an oral call of the roll, a member may demand a correction as a matter of right. On all other alleged errors in a recorded vote, the Speaker determines whether the circumstances justify a change. Occasionally, members merely announce that they were incorrectly recorded; announcements can occur hours, days or even months after the vote and appear in the Congressional Record.

Cosponsor—A member who has joined one or more other members to sponsor a measure.

Credit Authority—Authority granted to an agency to incur direct loan obligations or to make loan guarantee commitments. The Congressional Budget Act of 1974 bans congressional consideration of credit authority legislation unless the extent of that authority is made subject to provisions in appropriation acts.

C-SPAN—Cable-Satellite Public Affairs Network, which provides live, gavel-to-gavel coverage of Senate floor proceedings on one cable television channel and coverage of House floor proceedings on another channel. C-SPAN also televises important committee hearings in both houses. Each house also transmits its televised proceedings directly to congressional offices.

Current Services Estimates—Executive branch estimates of the anticipated costs of federal programs and operations for the next and future fiscal years at existing levels of service and assuming no new initiatives or changes in existing law. The president

submits these estimates to Congress with the annual budget and includes an explanation of the underlying economic and policy assumptions on which they are based, such as anticipated rates of inflation, real economic growth and unemployment, plus program caseloads and pay increases.

Custody of the Papers—Possession of an engrossed measure and certain related basic documents that the two houses produce as they try to resolve their differences over the measure.

Dance of the Swans and the Ducks—A whimsical description of the gestures some members use in connection with a request for a recorded vote, especially in the House. When members want their colleagues to stand in support of the request, they move their hands and arms in a gentle upward motion resembling the beginning flight of a graceful swan. When they want their colleagues to remain seated to avoid such a vote, they move their hands and arms in a vigorous downward motion resembling a diving duck.

Dean—Within a state's delegation in the House of Representatives, the member with the longest continuous service.

Debate—In congressional parlance, speeches delivered during consideration of a measure, motion or other matter, as distinguished from speeches in other parliamentary situations, such as one-minute and special order speeches when no business is pending. Virtually all debate in the House of Representatives is under some kind of time limitation. Most debate in the Senate is unlimited; that is, a senator, once recognized, may speak for as long as he or she chooses, unless the Senate invokes cloture.

Debt Limit—The maximum amount of outstanding federal public debt permitted by law. The limit (or ceiling) covers virtually all debt incurred by the government except agency debt. Each congressional budget resolution sets forth the new debt limit that may be required under its provisions.

Deferral—An impoundment of funds for a specific period of time that may not extend beyond the fiscal year in which it is proposed. Under the Impoundment Control Act of 1974, the president must notify Congress that he is deferring the spending or obligation of funds provided by law for a project or activity. Congress can disapprove the deferral by legislation.

Deficit—The amount by which the government's outlays exceed its budget receipts for a given fiscal year. Both the president's budget and the annual congressional budget resolution provide estimates of the deficit or surplus for the upcoming and several future fiscal years.

Degrees of Amendment—Designations that indicate the relationships of amendments to the text of a measure and to each other. In general, an amendment offered directly to the text of a measure is an amendment in the first degree, and an amendment to that amendment is an amendment in the second degree. Both houses normally prohibit amendments in the third degree — that is, an amendment to an amendment to an amendment.

Delegate—A nonvoting member of the House of Representatives elected to a two-year term from the District of Columbia, the territory of Guam, the territory of the Virgin Islands or the territory of American Samoa. By law, delegates may not vote in the full House but they may participate in debate, offer motions (except to reconsider) and serve and vote on standing and select committees. On their committees, delegates possess the same powers and privileges as other members and the Speaker may appoint them to appropriate conference committees and select committees.

Denounce—A formal action that condemns a member for misbehavior; considered by some experts to be equivalent to censure. (See Censure.)

Dilatory Tactics—Procedural actions intended to delay or prevent action by a house or a committee. They include, among others, offering numerous motions, demanding quorum calls and recorded votes at every opportunity, making numerous points of order and parliamentary inquiries and speaking as long as the applicable rules permit. The Senate rules permit a battery of dilatory tactics, especially lengthy speeches, except under cloture. In the House, possible dilatory tactics are more limited. Speeches are always subject to time limits and debate-ending motions. Moreover, a House rule instructs the Speaker not to entertain dilatory motions and lets the Speaker decide whether a motion is dilatory. However, the Speaker may not override the constitutional right of a member to demand the yeas and nays, and in practice usually waits for a point of order before exercising that authority. (See Cloture.)

Discharge a Committee—Remove a measure from a committee to which it has been referred in order to make it available for floor consideration. Noncontroversial measures are often discharged by unanimous consent. However, because congressional committees have no obligation to report measures referred to them, each house has procedures to extract controversial measures from recalcitrant committees. Six discharge procedures are available in the House of Representatives. The Senate uses a motion to discharge, which is usually converted into a discharge resolution.

District Office—Representatives maintain one or more offices in their districts for the purpose of assisting and communicating with constituents. The costs of maintaining these offices are paid from members' official allowances. Senators can use the official expense allowance to rent offices in their home state, subject to a funding formula based on their state's population and other factors.

District Work Period—The House term for a scheduled congressional recess during which members may visit their districts and conduct constituency business.

Division Vote—A vote in which the chair first counts those in favor of a proposition and then those opposed to it, with no record made of how each member votes. In the Senate, the chair may count raised hands or ask senators to stand, whereas the House requires members to stand; hence, often called a standing vote. Committees in both houses ordinarily use a show of hands. A division usually occurs after a voice vote and may be demanded by any member or ordered by the chair if there is any doubt about the outcome of the voice vote. The demand for a division can also come before a voice vote. In the Senate, the demand must come before the result of a voice vote is announced. It may be made after a voice vote announcement in the House, but only if no intervening business has transpired and only if the member was standing and seeking recognition at the time of the announcement. A demand for the yeas and nays or, in the House, for a recorded vote, takes precedence over a division vote.

Doorkeeper of the House—A former officer of the House of Representatives who was responsible for enforcing the rules prohibiting unauthorized persons from entering the chamber when the House is in session. The doorkeeper was usually the candidate of the majority party. In 1995 the office was abolished and its functions transferred to the sergeant at arms.

Effective Dates—Provisions of an act that specify when the entire act or individual provisions in it become effective as law. Most acts become effective on the date of enactment, but it is sometimes necessary or prudent to delay the effective dates of some provisions.

Electronic Voting—Since 1973 the House has used an electronic voting system to record the yeas and nays and to conduct recorded votes. Members vote by inserting their voting cards in one of the boxes at several locations in the chamber. They are given at least fifteen minutes to vote. When several votes occur immediately after each other, the Speaker may reduce the voting time to five minutes on the second and subsequent votes. The Speaker may allow additional time on each vote but may also close a vote at any time after the minimum time has expired. Members can change their votes at any time before the Speaker announces the result. The House also uses the electronic system for quorum calls. While a vote is in progress, a large panel above the Speaker's desk displays how each member has voted. Smaller panels on either side of the chamber display running totals of the votes and the time remaining. The Senate does not have electronic voting.

Enacting Clause—The opening language of each bill, beginning "Be it enacted by the Senate and House of Representatives of the United States of America in Congress assembled..." This language gives legal force to measures approved by Congress and signed by the president or enacted over the president's veto. A successful motion to strike it from a bill kills the entire measure.

Engrossed Bill—The official copy of a bill or joint resolution as passed by one chamber, including the text as amended by floor action and certified by the clerk of the House or the secretary of the Senate (as appropriate). Amendments by one house to a measure or amendments of the other also are engrossed. House engrossed documents are printed on blue paper; the Senate's are printed on white paper.

Enrolled Bill—The final official copy of a bill or joint resolution passed in identical form by both houses. An enrolled bill is printed on parchment. After it is certified by the chief officer of the house in which it originated and signed by the House Speaker and the Senate president pro tempore, the measure is sent to the White House for the president's signature.

Entitlement Program—A federal program under which individuals, businesses or units of government that meet the requirements or qualifications established by law are entitled to receive certain payments if they seek such payments. Major examples include Social Security, Medicare, Medicaid, unemployment insurance and military and federal civilian pensions. Congress cannot control their expenditures by refusing to appropriate the sums necessary to fund them because the government is legally obligated to pay eligible recipients the amounts to which the law entitles them.

Equality of the Houses—A component of the Constitution's emphasis on checks and balances under which each house is given essentially equal status in the enactment of legislation and in the relations and negotiations between the two houses. Although the House of Representatives initiates revenue and appropriation measures, the Senate has the right to amend them. Either house may initiate any other type of legislation, and neither can force the other to agree to, or even act on, its measures. Moreover, each house has a potential veto over the other because legislation requires agreement by both. Similarly, in a conference to resolve their differences on a measure, each house casts one vote, as determined by a majority of its conferees. In most other national bicameral legislatures, the powers of one house are markedly greater than those of the other.

Ethics Rules—Several rules or standing orders in each house that mandate certain standards of conduct for members and congressional employees in finance, employment, franking and other areas. The Senate Permanent Select Committee on Ethics and the House Committee on Standards of Official Conduct investigate alleged violations of conduct and recommend appropriate actions to their respective houses.

Exclusive Committee—(1) Under the rules of the Republican Conference and House Democratic Caucus, a standing committee whose members usually cannot serve on any other standing committee. As of 2000 the Appropriations, Energy and Commerce (beginning in the 105th Congress), Ways and Means and Rules Committees were designated as exclusive committees. (2) Under the rules of the two party conferences in the Senate, a standing committee whose members may not simultaneously serve on any other exclusive committee.

Executive Calendar—The Senate's calendar for committee reports on its executive business, namely treaties and nominations. The calendar numbers indicate the order in which items were referred to the calendar but have no bearing on when or if the Senate will consider them. The Senate, by motion or unanimous consent, resolves itself into executive session to consider them.

Executive Document—A document, usually a treaty, sent by the president to the Senate for approval. It is referred to a committee in the same manner as other measures. Resolutions to ratify treaties have their own "treaty document" numbers. For example, the first treaty submitted in the 106th Congress would be "Treaty Doc 106-1."

Executive Order—A unilateral proclamation by the president that has a policy-making or legislative impact. Members of Congress have challenged some executive orders on the grounds that they usurped the authority of the legislative branch. Although the Supreme Court has ruled that a particular order exceeded the president's authority, it has upheld others as falling within the president's general constitutional powers.

Executive Privilege—The assertion that presidents have the right to withhold certain information from Congress. Presidents have based their claim on (1) the constitutional separation of powers; (2) the need for secrecy in military and diplomatic affairs; (3) the need to protect individuals from unfavorable publicity; (4) the need to safeguard the confidential exchange of ideas in the executive branch; and (5) the need to protect individuals who provide confidential advice to the president.

Executive Session—(1) A Senate meeting devoted to the consideration of treaties or nominations. Normally, the Senate meets in legislative session; it resolves itself into executive session, by motion or by unanimous consent, to deal with its executive business. It also keeps a separate Journal for executive sessions. Executive sessions are usually open to the public, but the Senate may choose to close them.

Expulsion—A member's removal from office by a two-thirds vote of his or her house; the supermajority is required by the Constitution. It is the most severe and most rarely used sanction a house can invoke against a member. Although the Constitution provides no explicit grounds for expulsion, the courts have ruled that it may be applied only for misconduct during a member's term of office, not for conduct before the member's election. Generally, neither house will consider expulsion of a member convicted of a crime until the judicial processes have been exhausted. At that stage, members sometimes resign rather than face expulsion. In 1977 the House adopted a rule urging members convicted of certain crimes to voluntarily abstain from voting or participating in other legislative business.

Extensions of Remarks—An appendix to the daily Congressional Record that consists primarily of miscellaneous extraneous material submitted by members. It often includes members' statements not delivered on the floor, newspaper articles and editorials, praise for a member's constituents and noteworthy letters received by a member, among other material. Representatives supply the bulk of this material; senators submit very little. "Extensions of Remarks" pages are separately numbered, and each number is preceded by the letter "E." Materials may be placed in the Extensions of Remarks section only by unanimous consent. Usually, one member of each party makes the request each day on behalf of his or her party colleagues after the House has completed its legislative business of the day.

Federal Debt—The total amount of monies borrowed and not yet repaid by the federal government. Federal debt consists of public debt and agency debt. Public debt is the portion of the federal debt borrowed by the Treasury or the Federal Financing Bank directly from the public or from another federal fund or account. For example, the Treasury regularly borrows money from the Social Security trust fund. Public debt accounts for about 99 percent of the federal debt. Agency debt refers to the debt incurred by federal agencies such as the Export-Import Bank but excluding the Treasury and the Federal Financing Bank, which are authorized by law to borrow funds from the public or from another government fund or account.

Filibuster—The use of obstructive and time-consuming parliamentary tactics by one member or a minority of members to delay, modify or defeat proposed legislation or rules changes. Filibusters are also sometimes used to delay urgently needed measures to force the body to accept other legislation. The Senate's rules permitting unlimited debate and the extraordinary majority it requires to impose cloture make filibustering particularly effective in that chamber. Under the stricter rules of the House, filibusters in that body are short-lived and therefore ineffective and rarely attempted.

Fiscal Year—The federal government's annual accounting period. It begins Oct. 1 and ends on the following Sept. 30. A fiscal year is designated by the calendar year in which it ends and is often referred to as FY. Thus, fiscal year 1998 began Oct. 1, 1997, ended Sept. 30, 1998, and is called FY98. In theory, Congress is supposed to complete action on all budgetary measures applying to a fiscal year before that year begins. It rarely does so.

Five-Minute Rule—A House rule that limits debate on an amendment offered in Committee of the Whole to five minutes for its sponsor and five minutes for an opponent. In practice, the committee routinely permits longer debate by two devices: the offering of pro forma amendments, each debatable for five minutes, and unanimous consent for a member to speak longer than five minutes. Consequently, debate on an amendment sometimes continues for hours. At any time after the first ten minutes, however, the committee may shut off debate immediately or by a specified time, either by unanimous consent or by majority vote on a nondebatable motion. The motion, which dates from 1847, is also used in the House as in Committee of the Whole, where debate also may be shut off by a motion for the previous question.

Floor—The ground level of the House or Senate chamber where members sit and the houses conduct their business. When members are attending a meeting of their house they are said to be on the floor. Floor action refers to the procedural actions taken during floor consideration such as deciding on motions, taking up measures, amending them and voting.

Floor Manager—A majority party member responsible for guiding a measure through its floor consideration in a house and for devising the political and procedural strategies that might be required to get it passed. The presiding officer gives the floor manager priority recognition to debate, offer amendments, oppose amendments and make crucial procedural motions.

Frank—Informally, members' legal right to send official mail postage free under their signatures; often called the franking privilege. Technically, it is the autographic or facsimile signature used on envelopes instead of stamps that permits members and certain congressional officers to send their official mail free of charge. The franking privilege has been authorized by law since the first Congress, except for a few months in 1873. Congress reimburses the U.S. Postal Service for the franked mail it handles.

Function or Functional Category—A broad category of national need and spending of budgetary significance. A category provides an accounting method for allocating and keeping track of budgetary resources and expenditures for that function because it includes all budget accounts related to the function's subject or purpose such as agriculture, administration of justice, commerce and housing and energy. Functions do not necessarily correspond with appropriations acts or with the budgets of individual agencies. As of 2000 there were twenty functional categories, each divided into a number of subfunctions.

Gag Rule—A pejorative term for any type of special rule reported by the House Rules Committee that proposes to prohibit amendments to a measure or only permits amendments offered by the reporting committee.

Galleries—The balconies overlooking each chamber from which the public, news media, staff and others may observe floor proceedings.

General Accounting Office (GAO)—A congressional support agency, often referred to as the investigative arm of Congress. It evaluates and audits federal agencies and programs in the United States and abroad on its initiative or at the request of congressional committees or members.

General Appropriation Bill—A term applied to each of the thirteen annual bills that provide funds for most federal agencies and programs and also to the supplemental appropriation bills that contain appropriations for more than one agency or program.

Germaneness—The requirement that an amendment be closely related — in terms of subject or purpose, for example — to the text it proposes to amend. A House rule requires that all amendments be germane. In the Senate, only amendments offered to general appropriation bills and budget measures or proposed under cloture must be germane. Germaneness rules can be waived by suspension of the rules in both houses, by unanimous consent agreements in the Senate and by special rules from the Rules Committee in the House. Moreover, presiding officers usually do not enforce germaneness rules on their own initiative; therefore, a nongermane amendment can be adopted if no member raises a point of order against it. Under cloture in the Senate, however, the chair may take the initiative to rule amendments out of order as not being germane, without a point of order being made. All House debate must be germane except during general debate in the Committee of the Whole, but special rules invariably require that such debate be "confined to the bill." The Senate requires germane debate only during the first three hours of each daily session. Under the precedents of both houses, an amendment can be relevant but not necessarily germane. A crucial factor in determining germaneness in the House is how the subject of a measure or matter is defined. For example, the subject of a measure authorizing construction of a naval vessel is defined as being the construction of a single vessel; therefore, an amendment to authorize an additional vessel is not germane.

Gerrymandering—The manipulation of legislative district boundaries to benefit a particular party, politician or minority group. The term originated in 1812 when the Massachusetts legislature redrew the lines of state legislative districts to favor the party of Gov. Elbridge Gerry, and some critics said one district looked like a salamander. (See also Congressional District; Redistricting.)

Gramm-Rudman-Hollings Act of 1985—Common name for the Balanced Budget and Emergency Deficit Control Act of 1985, which established new budget procedures intended to balance the federal budget by fiscal year 1991. (The timetable subsequently was extended and then deleted.) The act's chief sponsors were senators Phil Gramm (R-Texas), Warren Rudman (R-N.H.) and Ernest Hollings (D-S.C.).

Grandfather Clause—A provision in a measure, law or rule that exempts an individual, entity or a defined category of individuals or entities from complying with a new policy or restriction. For example, a bill that would raise taxes on persons who reach the age of sixty-five after a certain date inherently grandfathers out those who are sixty-five before that date. Similarly, a Senate rule limiting senators to two major committee assignments also grandfathers some senators who were sitting on a third major committee before a specified date.

Grants-in-Aid—Payments by the federal government to state and local governments to help provide for assistance programs or public services.

Hearing—Committee or subcommittee meetings to receive testimony on proposed legislation during investigations or for oversight purposes. Relatively few bills are important enough to justify formal hearings. Witnesses often include experts, government officials, spokespersons for interested groups, officials of the General Accounting Office and members of Congress.

Hold—A senator's request that his or her party leaders delay floor consideration of certain legislation or presidential nominations. The majority leader usually honors a hold for a reasonable period of time, especially if its purpose is to assure the senator that the matter will not be called up during his or her absence or to give the senator time to gather necessary information.

Hold (or Have) the Floor—A member's right to speak without interruption, unless he or she violates a rule, after recognition by the presiding officer. At the member's discretion, he or she may yield to another member for a question in the Senate or for a question or statement in the House, but may reclaim the floor at any time.

Hold-Harmless Clause—In legislation providing a new formula for allocating federal funds, a clause to ensure that recipients of those funds do not receive less in a future year than they did in the current year if the new formula would result in a reduction for them. Similar to a grandfather clause, it has been used most frequently to soften the impact of sudden reductions in federal grants. (See Grandfather Clause.)

Hopper—A box on the clerk's desk in the House chamber into which members deposit bills and resolutions to introduce them. In House jargon, to drop a bill in the hopper is to introduce it.

Hour Rule—A House rule that permits members, when recognized, to hold the floor in debate for no more than one hour each. The majority party member customarily yields one-half the time to a minority member. Although the hour rule applies to general debate in Committee of the Whole as well as in the House, special rules routinely vary the length of time for such debate and its control to fit the circumstances of particular measures.

House As In Committee of the Whole—A hybrid combination of procedures from the general rules of the House and from the rules of the Committee of the Whole, sometimes used to expedite consideration of a measure on the floor.

House Calendar—The calendar reserved for all public bills and resolutions that do not raise revenue or directly or indirectly appropriate money or property when they are favorably reported by House committees.

House Manual—A commonly used title for the handbook of the rules of the House of Representatives, published in each Congress. Its official title is Constitution, Jefferson's Manual and Rules of the House of Representatives.

House of Representatives—The house of Congress in which states are represented roughly in proportion to their populations, but every state is guaranteed at least one representative. By law, the number of voting representatives is fixed at 435. Four delegates and one resident commissioner also serve in the House; they may vote in their committees but not on the House floor. Although the House and Senate have equal legislative power, the Constitution gives the House sole authority to originate revenue measures. The House also claims the right to originate appropriation measures, a claim the Senate disputes in theory but concedes in practice. The House has the sole power to impeach, and it elects the president when no candidate has received a majority of the electoral votes. It is sometimes referred to as the lower body.

Immunity—(1) Members' constitutional protection from lawsuits and arrest in connection with their legislative duties. They may not be tried for libel or slander for anything they say on the floor of a house or in committee. Nor may they be arrested while attending sessions of their houses or when traveling to or from sessions of Congress, except when charged with treason, a felony or a breach of the peace. (2) In the case of a witness before a committee, a grant of protection from prosecution based on that person's testimony to the committee. It is used to compel witnesses to testify who would otherwise refuse to do so on the constitutional ground of possible selfincrimination. Under such a grant, none of a witness's testimony may be used against him or her in a court proceeding except in a prosecution for perjury or for giving a false statement to Congress. (See also Contempt of Congress.)

Impeachment—The first step to remove the president, vice president or other federal civil officers from office and to disqualify them from any future federal office "of honor, Trust or Profit." An impeachment is a formal charge of treason, bribery or "other high Crimes and Misdemeanors." The House has the sole power of impeachment and the Senate the sole power of trying the charges and convicting. The House impeaches by a simple majority vote; conviction requires a two-thirds vote of all senators present.

Impeachment Trial, Removal and Disqualification—The Senate conducts an impeachment trial under a separate set of twenty-six rules that appears in the Senate Manual. Under the Constitution, the chief justice of the United States presides over trials of the president, but the vice president, the president pro tempore or any other senator may preside over the impeachment trial of another official.

The Constitution requires senators to take an oath for an impeachment trial. During the trial, senators may not engage in colloquies or participate in arguments, but they may submit questions in writing to House managers or defense counsel. After the trial concludes, the Senate votes separately on each article of impeachment without debate unless the Senate orders the doors closed for private discussions. During deliberations senators may speak no more than once on a question, not for more than ten minutes on an interlocutory question and not more than fifteen minutes on the final question. These rules may be set aside by unanimous consent or suspended on motion by a two-thirds vote.

The Senate's impeachment trial of President Clinton in 1999 was only the second such trial involving a president. It continued for five weeks, with the Senate voting not to convict on the two impeachment articles.

Senate impeachment rules allow the Senate, at its own discretion, to name a committee to hear evidence and conduct the trial, with all senators thereafter voting on the charges. The impeachment trials of three federal judges were conducted this way, and the Supreme Court upheld the validity of these rules in Nixon v. United States, 506 U.S. 224, 1993.

An official convicted on impeachment charges is removed from office immediately. However, the convicted official is not barred from holding a federal office in the future unless the Senate, after its conviction vote, also approves a resolution disqualifying the convicted official from future office. For example, federal judge Alcee L. Hastings was impeached and convicted in 1989, but the Senate did not vote to bar him from office in the future. In 1992 Hastings was elected to the House of Representatives, and no challenge was raised against seating him when he took the oath of office in 1993.

Impoundment—An executive branch action or inaction that delays or withholds the expenditure or obligation of budget authority provided by law. The Impoundment Control Act of 1974 classifies impoundments as either deferrals or rescissions, requires the president to notify Congress about all such actions and gives Congress authority to approve or reject them.

Inspector General (IG) In the House of Representatives—A position established with the passage of the House Administrative Reform Resolution of 1992. The duties of the office have been revised several times and are now contained in House Rule II. The inspector general (IG), who is subject to the policy direction and oversight of the Committee on House Administration, is appointed for a Congress jointly by the Speaker and the majority and minority leaders of the House. The IG communicates the results of audits to the House officers or officials who were the subjects of the audits and suggests appropriate corrective measures. The IG submits a report of each audit to the Speaker, the majority and minority leaders and the chairman and ranking minority member of the House Administration Committee; notifies these five members in the case of any financial irregularity discovered; and reports to the Committee on Standards of Official Conduct on possible violations of House rules or any applicable law by any House member, officer or employee. The IG's office also has certain duties to audit various financial operations of the House that had previously been performed by the General Accounting Office.

Instruct Conferees—A formal action by a house urging its conferees to uphold a particular position on a measure in conference. The instruction may be to insist on certain provisions in the measure as passed by that house or to accept a provision in the version passed by the other house. Instructions to conferees are not binding because the primary responsibility of conferees is to reach agreement on a measure and neither House can compel the other to accept particular provisions or positions.

Investigative Power—The authority of Congress and its committees to pursue investigations, upheld by the Supreme Court but limited to matters related to, and in furtherance of, a legitimate task of the Congress. Standing committees in both houses are permanently authorized to investigate matters within their jurisdictions. Major investigations are sometimes conducted by temporary select, special or joint committees established by resolutions for that purpose.

Some rules of the House provide certain safeguards for witnesses and others during investigative hearings. These permit counsel to accompany witnesses, require that each witness receive a copy of the committee's rules and order the committee to go into closed session if it believes the testimony to be heard might defame, degrade or incriminate any person. The committee may subsequently decide to hear such testimony in open session. The Senate has no rules of this kind.

Item Veto—Item veto authority, which is available to most state governors, allows governors to eliminate or reduce items in legislative measures presented for their signature without vetoing the entire measure and sign the rest into law. A similar authority was briefly granted to the U.S. president under the Line Item Veto Act of 1996. According to the majority opinion of the Supreme Court in its 1998 decision overturning that law, a constitutional amendment would be necessary to give the president such item veto authority.

Jefferson's Manual—Short title of Jefferson's Manual of Parliamentary Practice, prepared by Thomas Jefferson for his guidance when he was president of the Senate from 1797 to 1801. Although it reflects English parliamentary practice in his day, many procedures in both houses of Congress are still rooted in its basic precepts. Under a House rule adopted in 1837, the manual's provisions govern House procedures when applicable and when they are not inconsistent with its standing rules and orders. The Senate, however, has never officially acknowledged it as a direct authority for its legislative procedure.

Johnson Rule—A policy instituted in 1953 under which all Democratic senators are assigned to one major committee before any Democrat is assigned to two. The Johnson Rule is named after its author, Sen. Lyndon B. Johnson, D-Texas, then the Senate's Democratic leader. Senate Republicans adopted a similar policy soon thereafter.

Joint Committee—A committee composed of members selected from each house. The functions of most joint committees involve investigation, research or oversight of agencies closely related to Congress. Permanent joint committees, created by statute, are sometimes called standing joint committees. Once quite numerous, only four joint committees remained as of 2002: Joint Economic, Joint Taxation, Joint Library and Joint Printing. None has authority to report legislation.

Joint Resolution—A legislative measure that Congress uses for purposes other than general legislation. Similar to a bill, it has the force of law when passed by both houses and either approved by the president or passed over the president's veto. Unlike a bill, a joint resolution enacted into law is not called an act; it retains its original title. Most often, joint resolutions deal with such relatively limited matters as the correction of errors in existing law, continuing appropriations, a single appropriation or the establishment of permanent joint committees. Unlike bills, however, joint resolutions also are used to propose constitutional amendments; these do not require the president's signature and become effective only when ratified by three-fourths of the states. The House designates joint resolutions as H.J. Res., the Senate as S.J. Res. Each house numbers its joint resolutions consecutively in the order of introduction during a two-year Congress.

Joint Session—Informally, any combined meeting of the Senate and the House. Technically, a joint session is a combined meeting to count the electoral votes for president and vice president or to hear a presidential address, such as the State of the Union message; any other formal combined gathering of both houses is a joint meeting. Joint sessions are authorized by concurrent resolutions and are held in the House chamber, because of its larger seating capacity. Although the president of the Senate and the Speaker sit side by side at the Speaker's desk during combined meetings, the former presides over the electoral count and the latter presides on all other occasions and introduces the president or other guest speaker. The president and other guests may address a joint session or meeting only by invitation.

Joint Sponsorship—Two or more members sponsoring the same measure.

Journal—The official record of House or Senate actions, including every motion offered, every vote cast, amendments agreed to, quorum calls and so forth. Unlike the Congressional Record, it does not provide reports of speeches, debates, statements and the like. The Constitution requires each house to maintain a Journal and to publish it periodically.

Junket—A member's trip at government expense, especially abroad, ostensibly on official business but, it is often alleged, for pleasure.

Killer Amendment—An amendment that, if agreed to, might lead to the defeat of the measure it amends, either in the house in which the amendment is offered or at some later stage of the legislative process. Members sometimes deliberately offer or vote for such an amendment in the expectation that it will undermine support for the measure in Congress or increase the likelihood that the president will veto it.

King of the Mountain (or Hill) Rule—(See Queen of the Hill Rule.)

LA—(See Legislative Assistant.)

Lame Duck—Jargon for a member who has not been reelected, or did not seek reelection, and is serving the balance of his or her term.

Lame Duck Session—A session of a Congress held after the election for the succeeding Congress, so-called after the lame duck members still serving.

Last Train Out—Colloquial name for last must-pass bill of a session of Congress.

Law—An act of Congress that has been signed by the president, passed over the president's veto or allowed to become law without the president's signature.

Lay on the Table—A motion to dispose of a pending proposition immediately, finally and adversely; that is, to kill it without a direct vote on its substance. Often simply called a motion to table, it is not debatable and is adopted by majority vote or without objection. It is a highly privileged motion, taking precedence over all others except the motion to adjourn in the House and all but three additional motions in the Senate. It can kill a bill or resolution, an amendment, another motion, an appeal or virtually any other matter.

Tabling an amendment also tables the measure to which the amendment is pending in the House, but not in the Senate. The House does not allow the motion against the motion to recommit, in Committee of the Whole, and in some other situations. In the Senate it is the only permissible motion that immediately ends debate on a proposition, but only to kill it.

(The) Leadership—Usually, a reference to the majority and minority leaders of the Senate or to the Speaker and minority leader of the House. The term sometimes includes the majority leader in the House and the majority and minority whips in each house and, at other times, other party officials as well.

Legislation—(1) A synonym for legislative measures: bills and joint resolutions. (2) Provisions in such measures or in substantive amendments offered to them. (3) In some contexts, provisions that change existing substantive or authorizing law, rather than provisions that make appropriations.

Legislation on an Appropriation Bill—A common reference to provisions changing existing law that appear in, or are offered as amendments to, a general appropriation bill. A House rule prohibits the inclusion of such provisions in general appropriation bills unless they retrench expenditures. An analogous Senate rule permits points of order against amendments to a general appropriation bill that propose general legislation.

Legislative Assistant (LA)—A member's staff person responsible for monitoring and preparing legislation on particular subjects and for advising the member on them; commonly referred to as an LA.

Legislative Day—The day that begins when a house meets after an adjournment and ends when it next adjourns. Because the House of Representatives normally adjourns at the end of a daily session, its legislative and calendar days usually coincide. The Senate, however, frequently recesses at the end of a daily session, and its legislative day may extend over several calendar days, weeks or months. Among other uses, this technicality permits the Senate to save time by circumventing its morning hour, a procedure required at the beginning of every legislative day.

Legislative History—(1) A chronological list of actions taken on a measure during its progress through the legislative process. (2) The official documents relating to a measure, the entries in the Journals of the two houses on that measure and the Congressional Record text of its consideration in both houses. The documents include all committee reports and the conference report and joint explanatory statement, if any. Courts and affected federal agencies study a measure's legislative history for congressional intent about its purpose and interpretation.

Legislative Process—(1) Narrowly, the stages in the enactment of a law from introduction to final disposition. An introduced measure that becomes law typically travels through reference to committee; committee and subcommittee consideration; report to the chamber; floor consideration; amendment; passage; engrossment; messaging to the other house; similar steps in that house, including floor amendment of the measure; return of the measure to the first house; consideration of amendments between the houses or a conference to resolve their differences; approval of the conference report by both houses; enrollment; approval by the president or override of the president's veto; and deposit with the Archivist of the United States. (2) Broadly, the political, lobbying and other factors that affect or influence the process of enacting laws.

Legislative Veto—A procedure, declared unconstitutional in 1983, that allowed Congress or one of its houses to nullify certain actions of the president, executive branch agencies or independent agencies. Sometimes called congressional vetoes or congressional disapprovals. Following the Supreme Court's 1983 decision, Congress amended several legislative veto statutes to require enactment of joint resolutions, which are subject to presidential veto, for nullifying executive branch actions.

Limitation on a General Appropriation Bill—Language that prohibits expenditures for part of an authorized purpose from funds provided in a general appropriation bill. Precedents require that the language be phrased in the negative: that none of the funds provided in a pending appropriation bill shall be used for a specified authorized activity. Limitations in general appropriation bills are permitted on the grounds that Congress can refuse to fund authorized programs and, therefore, can refuse to fund any part of them as long as the prohibition does not change existing law. House precedents have established that a limitation does not change existing law if it does not impose additional duties or burdens on executive branch officials, interfere with their discretionary authority or require them to make judgments or determinations not required by existing law. The proliferation of limitation amendments in the 1970s and early 1980s prompted the House to adopt a rule in 1983 making it more difficult for members to offer them. The rule bans such amendments during the reading of an appropriation bill for amendments, unless they are specifically authorized in existing law. Other limitations may be offered after the reading, but the Committee of the Whole can foreclose them by adopting a motion to rise and report the bill back to the House. In 1995 the rule was amended to allow the motion to rise and report to be made only by the majority leader or his or her designee. The House Appropriations Committee, however, can include limitation provisions in the bills it reports.

Line Item—An amount in an appropriation measure. It can refer to a single appropriation account or to separate amounts within the account. In the congressional budget process, the term usually refers to assumptions about the funding of particular programs or accounts that underlie the broad functional amounts in a budget resolution. These assumptions are discussed in the reports accompanying each resolution and are not binding.

Line-Item Veto—(See Item Veto.)

Line Item Veto Act of 1996—A law, in effect only from January 1997 until June 1998, that granted the president authority intended to be functionally equivalent to an item veto, by amending the Impoundment Control Act of 1974 to incorporate an approach known as enhanced rescission. Key provisions established a new procedure that permitted the president to cancel amounts of new discretionary appropriations (budget authority), new items of direct spending (entitlements) or certain limited tax benefits. It also required the president to notify Congress of the cancellation in a special message within five calendar days after signing the measure. The cancellation would become permanent unless legislation disapproving it was enacted within thirty days. On June 25, 1998, in Clinton v. City of New York the Supreme Court held the Line Item Veto Act unconstitutional, on the grounds that its cancellation provisions violated the presentment clause in Article I, clause 7, of the Constitution.

Live Pair—A voluntary and informal agreement between two members on opposite sides of an issue, one of whom is absent for a recorded vote, under which the member who is present withholds or withdraws his or her vote to offset the failure to vote by the member who is absent. Usually the member in attendance announces that he or she has a live pair, states how each would have voted and votes "present." In the House, under a rules change enacted in the 106th Congress, a live pair is only permitted on the rare occasions when electronic voting is not used.

Live Quorum—In the Senate, a quorum call to which senators are expected to respond. Senators usually suggest the absence of a quorum, not to force a quorum to appear, but to provide a pause in the proceedings during which senators can engage in private discussions or wait for a senator to come to the floor. A senator desiring a live quorum usually announces his or her intention, giving fair warning that there will be an objection to any unanimous consent request that the quorum call be dispensed with before it is completed.

Loan Guarantee—A statutory commitment by the federal government to pay part or all of a loan's principal and interest to a lender or the holder of a security in case the borrower defaults.

Lobby—To try to persuade members of Congress to propose, pass, modify or defeat proposed legislation or to change or repeal existing laws. Lobbyists attempt to promote their preferences or those of a group, organization or industry. Originally the term referred to persons frequenting the lobbies or corridors of legislative chambers in order to speak to lawmakers. In a general sense, lobbying includes not only direct contact with members but also indirect attempts to influence them, such as writing to them or persuading others to write or visit them, attempting to mold public opinion toward a desired legislative goal by various means and contributing or arranging for contributions to members' election campaigns. The right to lobby stems from the First Amendment to the Constitution, which bans laws that abridge the right of the people to petition the government for a redress of grievances.

Lobbying Disclosure Act of 1995—The principal statute requiring disclosure of — and also, to a degree, circumscribing — the activities of lobbyists. In general, it requires lobbyists who spend more than 20 percent of their time on lobbying activities to register and make semiannual reports of their activities to the clerk of the House and the secretary of the Senate, although the law provides for a number of exemptions. Among the statute's prohibitions, lobbyists are not allowed to make contributions to the legal defense fund of a member or high government official or to reimburse for official travel. Civil penalties for failure to comply may include fines of up to $50,000. The act does not include grassroots lobbying in its definition of lobbying activities.

The act amends several other lobby laws, notably the Foreign Agents Registration Act (FARA), so that lobbyists can submit a single filing. Since the measure was enacted, the number of lobby registrations has risen from about 12,000 to more than 20,000. In 1998 expenditures on federal lobbying, as disclosed under the Lobbying Disclosure Act, totaled $1.42 billion. The 1995 act supersedes the 1946 Federal Regulation of Lobbying Act, which was repealed in Section 11 of the 1995 Act.

Logrolling—Jargon for a legislative tactic or bargaining strategy in which members try to build support for their legislation by promising to support legislation desired by other members or by accepting amendments they hope will induce their colleagues to vote for their bill.

Lower Body—A way to refer to the House of Representatives, which is considered pejorative by House members.

Mace—The symbol of the office of the House sergeant at arms. Under the direction of the Speaker, the sergeant at arms is responsible for preserving order on the House floor by holding up the mace in front of an unruly member, or by carrying the mace up and down the aisles to quell boisterous behavior. When the House is in session, the mace sits on a pedestal at the Speaker's right; when the House is in Committee of the Whole, it is moved to a lower pedestal. The mace is forty-six inches high and consists of thirteen ebony rods bound in silver and topped by a silver globe with a silver eagle, wings outstretched, perched on it.

Majority Leader—The majority party's chief floor spokesperson, elected by that party's caucus — sometimes called floor leader. In the Senate, the majority leader also develops the party's political and procedural strategy, usually in collaboration with other party officials and committee chairmen. The majority leader negotiates the Senate's agenda and committee ratios with the minority leader and usually calls up measures for floor action. The chamber traditionally concedes to the majority leader the right to determine the days on which it will meet and the hours at which it will convene and adjourn. In the House, the majority leader is the Speaker's deputy and heir apparent and helps plan the floor agenda and the party's legislative strategy and often speaks for the party leadership in debate.

Managers—(1) The official title of members appointed to a conference committee, commonly called conferees. The ranking majority and minority managers for each house also manage floor consideration of the committee's conference report. (2) The members who manage the initial floor consideration of a measure. (3) The official title of House members appointed to present impeachment articles to the Senate and to act as prosecutors on behalf of the House during the Senate trial of the impeached person.

Mandatory Appropriations—Amounts that Congress must appropriate annually because it has no discretion over them unless it first amends existing substantive law. Certain entitlement programs, for example, require annual appropriations.

Markup—A meeting or series of meetings by a committee or subcommittee during which members mark up a measure by offering, debating and voting on amendments to it.

Means-Tested Programs—Programs that provide benefits or services to low-income individuals who meet a test of need. Most are entitlement programs, such as Medicaid, food stamps and Supplementary Security Income. A few—for example, subsidized housing and various social services—are funded through discretionary appropriations.

Members' Allowances—Official expenses that are paid for or for which members are reimbursed by their houses. Among these are the costs of office space in congressional buildings and in their home states or districts; office equipment and supplies; postage-free mailings (the franking privilege); a set number of trips to and from home states or districts, as well as travel elsewhere on official business; telephone and other telecommunications services; and staff salaries.

Member's Staff—The personal staff to which a member is entitled. The House sets a maximum number of staff and a monetary allowance for each member. The Senate does not set a maximum staff level, but it does set a monetary allowance for each member. In each house, the staff allowance is included with office expenses allowances and official mail allowances in a consolidated allowance. Representatives and senators can spend as much money in their consolidated allowances for staff, office expenses or official mail, as long as they do not exceed the monetary value of the three allowances combined. This provides members with flexibility in operating their offices.

Method of Equal Proportions—The mathematical formula used since 1950 to determine how the 435 seats in the House of Representatives should be distributed among the fifty states in the apportionment following each decennial census. It minimizes as much as possible the proportional difference between the average district population in any two states. Because the Constitution guarantees each state at least one representative, fifty seats are automatically apportioned. The formula calculates priority numbers for each state, assigns the first of the 385 remaining seats to the state with the highest priority number, the second to the state with the next highest number and so on until all seats are distributed. (See Apportionment.)

Midterm Election—The general election for members of Congress that occurs in November of the second year in a presidential term.

Minority Leader—The minority party's leader and chief floor spokesman, elected by the party caucus; sometimes called minority floor leader. With the assistance of other party officials and the ranking minority members of committees, the minority leader devises the party's political and procedural strategy.

Minority Staff—Employees who assist the minority party members of a committee. Most committees hire separate majority and minority party staffs but they also may hire nonpartisan staff. Senate rules state that a committee's staff must reflect the relative number of its majority and minority party committee members, and the rules guarantee the minority at least one-third of the funds available for hiring partisan staff. In the House, each committee is authorized thirty professional staff, and the minority members of most committees may select up to ten of these staff (subject to full committee approval). Under House rules, the minority party is to be "treated fairly" in the apportionment of additional staff resources. Each House committee determines the portion of its additional staff it allocates to the minority; some committees allocate one-third; and others allot less.

Modified Rule—A special rule from the House Rules Committee that permits only certain amendments to be offered to a measure during its floor consideration or that bans certain specified amendments or amendments on certain subjects.

Morning Business—In the Senate, routine business that is to be transacted at the beginning of the morning hour. The business consists, first, of laying before the Senate, and referring to committees, matters such as messages from the president and the House, federal agency reports and unreferred petitions, memorials, bills and joint resolutions. Next, senators may present additional petitions and memorials. Then committees may present their reports, after which senators may introduce bills and resolutions. Finally, resolutions coming over from a previous day are taken up for consideration. In practice, the Senate adopts standing orders that permit senators to introduce measures and file reports at any time, but only if there has been a morning business period on that day. Because the Senate often remains in the same legislative day for several days, weeks or months at a time, it orders a morning business period almost every calendar day for the convenience of senators who wish to introduce measures or make reports.

Morning Hour—A two-hour period at the beginning of a new legislative day during which the Senate is supposed to conduct routine business, call the calendar on Mondays and deal with other matters described in a Senate rule. In practice, the morning hour very rarely, if ever, occurs, in part because the Senate frequently recesses, rather than adjourns, at the end of a daily session. Therefore the rule does not apply when the senate next meets. The Senate's rules reserve the first hour of the morning for morning business. After the completion of morning business, or at the end of the first hour, the rules permit a motion to proceed to the consideration of a measure on the calendar out of its regular order (except on Mondays). Because that normally debatable motion is not debatable if offered during the morning hour, the majority leader may, but rarely does, use this procedure in anticipating a filibuster on the motion to proceed. If the Senate agrees to the motion, it can consider the measure until the end of the morning hour, and if there is no unfinished business from the previous day it can continue considering it after the morning hour. But if there is unfinished business, a motion to continue consideration is necessary, and that motion is debatable.

Motion—A formal proposal for a procedural action, such as to consider, to amend, to lay on the table, to reconsider, to recess or to adjourn. It has been estimated that at least eighty-five motions are possible under various circumstances in the House of Representatives, somewhat fewer in the Senate. Not all motions are created equal; some are privileged or preferential and enjoy priority over others. Some motions are debatable, amendable or divisible, while others are not.

Multiple and Sequential Referrals—The practice of referring a measure to two or more committees for concurrent consideration (multiple referral) or successively to several committees in sequence (sequential referral). A measure may also be divided into several parts, with each referred to a different committee or to several committees sequentially (split referral). In theory this gives all committees that have jurisdiction over parts of a measure the opportunity to consider and report on them.

Before 1975, House precedents banned such referrals. A 1975 rule required the Speaker to make concurrent and sequential referrals "to the maximum extent feasible." On sequential referrals, the Speaker could set deadlines for reporting the measure. The Speaker ruled that this provision authorized him to discharge a committee from further consideration of a measure and place it on the appropriate calendar of the House if the committee fails to meet the Speaker's deadline. The Speaker also used combinations of concurrent and sequential referrals. In 1995 joint referrals were prohibited. Now each measure is referred to a primary committee and also may be referred, either concurrently or sequentially, to one or more other committees, but usually only for consideration of portions of the measure that fall within the jurisdiction of each of those other committees.

In the Senate, before 1977 concurrent and sequential referrals were permitted only by unanimous consent. In that year, a rule authorized a privileged motion for such a referral if offered jointly by the majority and minority leaders. Debate on the motion and all amendments to it is limited to two hours. The motion may set deadlines for reporting and provide for discharging the committees involved if they fail to meet the deadlines. To date, this procedure

has never been invoked; multiple referrals in the Senate continue to be made by unanimous consent.

Multiyear Appropriation—An appropriation that remains available for spending or obligation for more than one fiscal year; the exact period of time is specified in the act making the appropriation.

Multiyear Authorization—(1) Legislation that authorizes the existence or continuation of an agency, program or activity for more than one fiscal year. (2) Legislation that authorizes appropriations for an agency, program or activity for more than one fiscal year.

Nomination—A proposed presidential appointment to a federal office submitted to the Senate for confirmation. Approval is by majority vote. The Constitution explicitly requires confirmation for ambassadors, consuls, "public Ministers" (department heads) and Supreme Court justices. By law, other federal judges, all military promotions of officers and many high-level civilian officials must be confirmed.

Oath of Office—Upon taking office, members of Congress must swear or affirm that they will "support and defend the Constitution...against all enemies, foreign and domestic," that they will "bear true faith and allegiance" to the Constitution, that they take the obligation "freely, without any mental reservation or purpose of evasion," and that they will "well and faithfully discharge the duties" of their office. The oath is required by the Constitution, and the wording is prescribed by a statute. All House members must take the oath at the beginning of each new Congress. Usually, the member with the longest continuous service in the House swears in the Speaker, who then swears in the other members. The president of the Senate or a surrogate administers the oath to newly elected or reelected senators.

Obligation—A binding agreement by a government agency to pay for goods, products, services, studies and the like, either immediately or in the future. When an agency enters into such an agreement, it incurs an obligation. As the agency makes the required payments, it liquidates the obligation. Appropriation laws usually make funds available for obligation for one or more fiscal years but do not require agencies to spend their funds during those specific years. The actual outlays can occur years after the appropriation is obligated, as with a contract for construction of a submarine that may provide for payment to be made when it is delivered in the future. Such obligated funds are often said to be "in the pipeline." Under these circumstances, an agency's outlays in a particular year can come from appropriations obligated in previous years as well as from its current-year appropriation. Consequently, the money Congress appropriates for a fiscal year does not equal the total amount of appropriated money the government will actually spend in that year.

Off-Budget Entities—Specific federal entities whose budget authority, outlays and receipts are excluded by law from the calculation of budget totals, although they are part of government spending and income. As of early 2001, these included the Social Security trust funds (Federal Old-Age and Survivors Insurance Fund and the Federal Disability Insurance Trust Fund) and the Postal Service. Government-sponsored enterprises are also excluded from the budget because they are considered private rather than public organizations.

Office of Management and Budget (OMB)—A unit in the Executive Office of the President, reconstituted in 1970 from the former Bureau of the Budget. The Office of Management and Budget (OMB) assists the president in preparing the budget and in formulating the government's fiscal program. The OMB also plays a central role in supervising and controlling implementation of the budget, pursuant to provisions in appropriations laws, the Budget

Enforcement Act and other statutes. In addition to these budgetary functions, the OMB has various management duties, including those performed through its three statutory offices: Federal Financial Management, Federal Procurement Policy and Information and Regulatory Affairs.

Officers of Congress—The Constitution refers to the Speaker of the House and the president of the Senate as officers and declares that each house "shall chuse" its "other Officers," but it does not name them or indicate how they should be selected. A House rule refers to its clerk, sergeant at arms and chaplain as officers. Officers are not named in the Senate's rules, but Riddick's Senate Procedure lists the president pro tempore, secretary of the Senate, sergeant at arms, chaplain and the secretaries for the majority and minority parties as officers. A few appointed officials are sometimes referred to as officers, including the parliamentarians and the legislative counsels. The House elects its officers by resolution at the beginning of each Congress. The Senate also elects its officers, but once elected Senate officers serve from Congress to Congress until their successors are chosen.

Omnibus Bill—A measure that combines the provisions of several disparate subjects into a single and often lengthy bill.

One-Minute Speeches—Addresses by House members that can be on any subject but are limited to one minute. They are usually permitted at the beginning of a daily session after the chaplain's prayer, the pledge of allegiance and approval of the Journal. They are a customary practice, not a right granted by rule. Consequently, recognition for one-minute speeches requires unanimous consent and is entirely within the Speaker's discretion. The Speaker sometimes refuses to permit them when the House has a heavy legislative schedule or limits or postpones them until a later time of the day.

Open Rule—A special rule from the House Rules Committee that permits members to offer as many floor amendments as they wish as long as the amendments are germane and do not violate other House rules.

Order of Business (House)—The sequence of events prescribed by a House rule during the meeting of the House on a new legislative day that is supposed to take place, also called the general order of business. The sequence consists of (1) the chaplain's prayer; (2) reading and approval of the Journal; (3) the pledge of allegiance; (4) correction of the reference of public bills to committee; (5) disposal of business on the Speaker's table; (6) unfinished business; (7) the morning hour call of committees and consideration of their bills; (8) motions to go into Committee of the Whole; and (9) orders of the day. In practice, the House never fully complies with this rule. Instead, the items of business that follow the pledge of allegiance are supplanted by any special orders of business that are in order on that day (for example, conference reports; the corrections, discharge or private calendars; or motions to suspend the rules) and by other privileged business (for example, general appropriation bills and special rules) or measures made in order by special rules or unanimous consent. The regular order of business is also modified by unanimous consent practices and orders that govern recognition for one-minute speeches (which date from 1937) and for morning-hour debates, begun in 1994. By this combination of an order of business with privileged interruptions, the House gives precedence to certain categories of important legislation, brings to the floor other major legislation from its calendars in any order it chooses and provides expeditious processing for minor and noncontroversial measures.

Order of Business (Senate)—The sequence of events at the beginning of a new legislative day, as prescribed by Senate rules and standing orders. The sequence consists of (1) the chaplain's prayer; (2) the pledge of allegiance; (3) the designation of a temporary presiding officer if any; (4) Journal reading and approval; (5) recognition of the majority and minority leaders or their designees under the standing order; (6) morning business in the morning hour; (7) call of the calendar during the morning hour (largely obsolete); and (8) unfinished business from the previous session day.

Organization of Congress—The actions each house takes at the beginning of a Congress that are necessary to its operations. These include swearing in newly elected members, notifying the president that a quorum of each house is present, making committee assignments and fixing the hour for daily meetings. Because the House of Representatives is not a continuing body, it must also elect its Speaker and other officers and adopt its rules.

Original Bill—(1) A measure drafted by a committee and introduced by its chairman or another designated member when the committee reports the measure to its house. Unlike a clean bill, it is not referred back to the committee after introduction. The Senate permits all its legislative committees to report original bills. In the House, this authority is referred to in the rules as the "right to report at any time," and five committees (Appropriations, Budget, House Administration, Rules and Standards of Official Conduct) have such authority under circumstances specified in House Rule XIII, clause 5.

(2) In the House, special rules reported by the Rules Committee often propose that an amendment in the nature of a substitute be considered as an original bill for purposes of amendment, meaning that the substitute, as with a bill, may be amended in two degrees. Without that requirement, the substitute may only be amended in one further degree. In the Senate, an amendment in the nature of a substitute automatically is open to two degrees of amendment, as is the original text of the bill, if the substitute is offered when no other amendment is pending.

Original Jurisdiction—The authority of certain committees to originate a measure and report it to the chamber. For example, general appropriation bills reported by the House Appropriations Committee are original bills, and special rules reported by the House Rules Committee are original resolutions.

Other Body—A commonly used reference to a house by a member of the other house. Congressional comity discourages members from directly naming the other house during debate.

Outlays—Amounts of government spending. They consist of payments, usually by check or in cash, to liquidate obligations incurred in prior fiscal years as well as in the current year, including the net lending of funds under budget authority. In federal budget accounting, net outlays are calculated by subtracting the amounts of refunds and various kinds of reimbursements to the government from actual spending.

Override a Veto—Congressional enactment of a measure over the president's veto. A veto override requires a recorded two-thirds vote of those voting in each house, a quorum being present. Because the president must return the vetoed measure to its house of origin, that house votes first, but neither house is required to attempt an override, whether immediately or at all. If an override attempt fails in the house of origin, the veto stands and the measure dies.

Oversight—Congressional review of the way in which federal agencies implement laws to ensure that they are carrying out the intent of Congress and to inquire into the efficiency of the implementation and the effectiveness of the law. The Legislative Reorganization Act of 1946 defined oversight as the function of exercising continuous watchfulness over the execution of the laws by the executive branch.

Oxford-Style Debate—The House held three Oxford-style debates in 1994, modeled after the famous debating format favored by the Oxford Union in Great Britain. Neither chamber has held Oxford-style debates since then. The Oxford-style debates aired nationally over C-SPAN television and National Public Radio. The organized event featured eight participants divided evenly into two teams, one team representing the Democrats (then holding the majority in the chamber) and the other the Republicans. Both teams argued a single question chosen well ahead of the event. A moderator regulated the debate, and began it by stating the resolution at issue. The order of the speakers alternated by team, with a debater for the affirmative speaking first and a debater for the opposing team offering a rebuttal. The rest of the speakers alternated in kind until all gained the chance to speak.

Parliamentarian—The official advisor to the presiding officer in each house on questions of procedure. The parliamentarian and his or her assistants also answer procedural questions from members and congressional staff, refer measures to committees on behalf of the presiding officer and maintain compilations of the precedents. The House parliamentarian revises the House Manual at the beginning of every Congress and usually reviews special rules before the Rules Committee reports them to the House. Either a parliamentarian or an assistant is always present and near the podium during sessions of each house.

Party Caucus—Generic term for each party's official organization in each house. Only House Democrats officially call their organization a caucus. House and Senate Republicans and Senate Democrats call their organizations conferences. The party caucuses elect their leaders, approve committee assignments and chairmanships (or ranking minority members, if the party is in the minority), establish party committees and study groups and discuss party and legislative policies. On rare occasions, they have stripped members of committee seniority or expelled them from the caucus for party disloyalty.

Pay-as-You-Go (PAYGO)—A provision first instituted under the Budget Enforcement Act of 1990 that applies to legislation enacted before Oct. 1, 2002. It requires that the cumulative effect of legislation concerning either revenues or direct spending should not result in a net negative impact on the budget. If legislation does provide for an increase in spending or decrease in revenues, that effect is supposed to be offset by legislated spending reductions or revenue increases. If Congress fails to enact the appropriate offsets, the act requires presidential sequestration of sufficient offsetting amounts in specific direct spending accounts. Congress and the president can circumvent this requirement if both agree that an emergency requires a particular action or if a law is enacted declaring that deteriorated economic circumstances make it necessary to suspend the requirement.

Permanent Appropriation—An appropriation that remains continuously available, without current action or renewal by Congress, under the terms of a previously enacted authorization or appropriation law. One such appropriation provides for payment of interest on the public debt and another the salaries of members of Congress.

Permanent Authorization—An authorization without a time limit. It usually does not specify any limit on the funds that may be appropriated for the agency, program or activity that it authorizes, leaving such amounts to the discretion of the appropriations committees and the two houses.

Permanent Staff—Term used formerly for committee staff authorized by law, who were funded through a permanent authorization and also called statutory staff. Most committees were authorized thirty permanent staff members. Most committees also were permitted additional staff, often called investigative staff, who were authorized by annual or biennial funding resolutions. The Senate eliminated the primary distinction between statutory and investigative staff in 1981. The House eliminated the distinction in 1995 by requiring that funding resolutions authorize money to hire both types of staff.

Personally Obnoxious (or Objectionable)—A characterization a senator sometimes applies to a president's nominee for a federal office in that senator's state to justify his or her opposition to the nomination.

Pocket Veto—The indirect veto of a bill as a result of the president withholding approval of it until after Congress has adjourned sine die. A bill the president does not sign but does not formally veto while Congress is in session automatically becomes a law ten days (excluding Sundays) after it is received. But if Congress adjourns its annual session during that ten-day period the measure dies even if the president does not formally veto it.

Point of Order—A parliamentary term used in committee and on the floor to object to an alleged violation of a rule and to demand that the chair enforce the rule. The point of order immediately halts the proceedings until the chair decides whether the contention is valid.

Pork or Pork Barrel Legislation—Pejorative terms for federal appropriations, bills or policies that provide funds to benefit a legislator's district or state, with the implication that the legislator presses for enactment of such benefits to ingratiate himself or herself with constituents rather than on the basis of an impartial, objective assessment of need or merit. The terms are often applied to such benefits as new parks, post offices, dams, canals, bridges, roads, water projects, sewage treatment plants and public works of any kind, as well as demonstration projects, research grants and relocation of government facilities. Funds released by the president for various kinds of benefits or government contracts approved by him allegedly for political purposes are also sometimes referred to as pork.

Postcloture Filibuster—A filibuster conducted after the Senate invokes cloture. It employs an array of procedural tactics rather than lengthy speeches to delay final action. The Senate curtailed the postcloture filibuster's effectiveness by closing a variety of loopholes in the cloture rule in 1979 and 1986.

Power of the Purse—A reference to the constitutional power Congress has over legislation to raise revenue and appropriate monies from the Treasury. Article I, Section 8 states that Congress "shall have Power To lay and collect Taxes, Duties, Imposts and Excises, [and] to pay the Debts." Section 9 declares: "No Money shall be drawn from the Treasury, but in Consequence of Appropriations made by Law."

Preamble—Introductory language describing the reasons for and intent of a measure, sometimes called a whereas clause. It occasionally appears in joint, concurrent and simple resolutions but rarely in bills.

Precedent—A previous ruling on a parliamentary matter or a long-standing practice or custom of a house. Precedents serve to control arbitrary rulings and serve as the common law of a house.

President of the Senate—One constitutional role of the vice president is serving as the presiding officer of the Senate, or president of the Senate. The Constitution permits the vice president to cast a vote in the Senate only to break a tie, but the vice president is not required to do so.

President Pro Tempore—Under the Constitution, an officer elected by the Senate to preside over it during the absence of the vice president of the United States. Often referred to as the "pro tem," this senator is usually a member of the majority party with the longest continuous service in the chamber and also, by virtue of seniority, a committee chairman. When attending to committee and other duties the president pro tempore appoints other senators to preside.

Presiding Officer—In a formal meeting, the individual authorized to maintain order and decorum, recognize members to speak or offer motions and apply and interpret the chamber's rules, precedents and practices. The Speaker of the House and the president of the Senate are the chief presiding officers in their respective houses.

Previous Question—A nondebatable motion which, when agreed to by majority vote, usually cuts off further debate, prevents the offering of additional amendments and brings the pending matter to an immediate vote. It is a major debate-limiting device in the House; it is not permitted in Committee of the Whole in the House or in the Senate.

Private Bill—A bill that applies to one or more specified persons, corporations, institutions or other entities, usually to grant relief when no other legal remedy is available to them. Many private bills deal with claims against the federal government, immigration and naturalization cases and land titles.

Private Calendar—Commonly used title for a calendar in the House reserved for private bills and resolutions favorably reported by committees. The private calendar is officially called the Calendar of the Committee of the Whole House.

Private Law—A private bill enacted into law. Private laws are numbered in the same fashion as public laws.

Privilege—An attribute of a motion, measure, report, question or proposition that gives it priority status for consideration. Privileged motions and motions to bring up privileged questions are not debatable.

Privilege of the Floor—In addition to the members of a house, certain individuals are admitted to its floor while it is in session. The rules of the two houses differ somewhat but both extend the privilege to the president and vice president, Supreme Court justices, cabinet members, state governors, former members of that house, members of the other house, certain officers and officials of Congress, certain staff of that house in the discharge of official duties and the chamber's former parliamentarians. They also allow access to a limited number of committee and members' staff when their presence is necessary.

Pro Forma Amendment—In the House, an amendment that ostensibly proposes to change a measure or another amendment by moving "to strike the last word" or "to strike the requisite number of words." A member offers it not to make any actual change in the measure or amendment but only to obtain time for debate.

Pro Tem—A common reference to the president pro tempore of the Senate or, occasionally, to a Speaker pro tempore. (See President Pro Tempore; Speaker Pro Tempore.)

Procedures—The methods of conducting business in a deliberative body. The procedures of each house are governed first by applicable provisions of the Constitution, and then by its standing rules and orders, precedents, traditional practices and any statutory rules that apply to it. The authority of the houses to adopt rules in addition to those specified in the Constitution is derived from Article I, Section 5, clause 2, of the Constitution, which states: "Each House may determine the Rules of its Proceedings...." By rule, the House of Representatives also follows the procedures in Jefferson's Manual that are not inconsistent with its standing rules and orders. Many Senate procedures also conform with Jefferson's provisions, but by practice rather than by rule. At the beginning of each Congress, the House uses procedures in general parliamentary law until it adopts its standing rules.

Proxy Voting—The practice of permitting a member to cast the vote of an absent colleague in addition to his or her own vote. Proxy voting is prohibited on the floors of the House and Senate, but the Senate permits its committees to authorize proxy voting, and most do. In 1995, House rules were changed to prohibit proxy voting in committee.

Public Bill—A bill dealing with general legislative matters having national applicability or applying to the federal government or to a class of persons, groups or organizations.

Public Debt—Federal government debt incurred by the Treasury or the Federal Financing Bank by the sale of securities to the public or borrowings from a federal fund or account.

Public Law—A public bill or joint resolution enacted into law. It is cited by the letters "PL" followed by a hyphenated number. The digits before the hyphen indicate the number of the Congress in which it was enacted; the digits after the hyphen indicate its position in the numerical sequence of public measures that became law during that Congress. For example, the Budget Enforcement Act of 1990 became PL 101-508 because it was the 508th measure in that sequence for the 101st Congress. (See also Private Law.)

Qualification (of Members)—The Constitution requires members of the House of Representatives to be twenty-five years of age at the time their terms begin. They must have been citizens of the United States for seven years before that date and, when elected, must be "Inhabitant[s]" of the state from which they were elected. There is no constitutional requirement that they reside in the districts they represent. Senators are required to be thirty years of age at the time their terms begin. They must have been citizens of the United States for nine years before that date and, when elected, must be "Inhabitant[s]" of the states in which they were elected. The "Inhabitant" qualification is broadly interpreted, and in modern times a candidate's declaration of state residence has generally been accepted as meeting the constitutional requirement.

Queen of the Hill Rule—A special rule from the House Rules Committee that permits votes on a series of amendments, especially complete substitutes for a measure, in a specified order, but directs that the amendment receiving the greatest number of votes shall be the winning one. This kind of rule permits the House to vote directly on a variety of alternatives to a measure. In doing so, it sets aside the precedent that once an amendment has been adopted, no further amendments may be offered to the text it has amended. Under an earlier practice, the Rules Committee reported "king of the hill" rules under which there also could be votes on a series of amendments, again in a specified order. If more than one of the amendments was adopted under this kind of rule, it was the last amendment to receive a majority vote that was considered as having been finally adopted, whether or not it had received the greatest number of votes.

Quorum—The minimum number of members required to be present for the transaction of business. Under the Constitution, a quorum in each house is a majority of its members: 218 in the House and 51 in the Senate when there are no vacancies. By House rule, a quorum in Committee of the Whole is 100. In practice, both houses usually assume a quorum is present even if it is not, unless a member makes a point of no quorum in the House or suggests the absence of a quorum in the Senate. Consequently, each house transacts much of its business, and even passes bills, when only a few members are present. For House and Senate committees, chamber rules allow a minimum quorum of one-third of a committee's members to conduct most types of business.

Quorum Call—A procedure for determining whether a quorum is present in a chamber. In the Senate, a clerk calls the roll (roster) of senators. The House usually employs its electronic voting system.

Ramseyer Rule—A House rule that requires a committee's report on a bill or joint resolution to show the changes the measure, and any committee amendments to it, would make in existing law. The rule requires the report to present the text of any statutory provision that would be repealed and a comparative print showing, through typographical devices such as stricken-through type or italics, other changes that would be made in existing law. The rule, adopted in 1929, is named after its sponsor, Rep. Christian W. Ramseyer, R-Iowa. The Senate's analogous rule is called the Cordon Rule.

Rank or Ranking—A member's position on the list of his or her party's members on a committee or subcommittee. When first assigned to a committee, a member is usually placed at the bottom of the list, then moves up as those above leave the committee. On subcommittees, however, a member's rank may not have anything to do with the length of his or her service on it.

Ranking Member—(1) Most often a reference to the minority member with the highest ranking on a committee or subcommittee. (2) A reference to the majority member next in rank to the chairman or to the highest ranking majority member present at a committee or subcommittee meeting.

Ratification—(1) The president's formal act of promulgating a treaty after the Senate has approved it. The resolution of ratification agreed to by the Senate is the procedural vehicle by which the Senate gives its consent to ratification. (2) A state legislature's act in approving a proposed constitutional amendment. Such an amendment becomes effective when ratified by three-fourths of the states.

Reapportionment—(See Apportionment.)

Recess—(1) A temporary interruption or suspension of a meeting of a chamber or committee. Unlike an adjournment, a recess does not end a legislative day. Because the Senate often recesses from one calendar day to another, its legislative day may extend over several calendar days, weeks or even months. (2) A period of adjournment for more than three days to a day certain, especially over a holiday or in August during odd-numbered years.

Recess Appointment—A presidential appointment to a vacant federal position made after the Senate has adjourned sine die or has adjourned or recessed for more than thirty days. If the president submits the recess appointee's nomination during the next session of the Senate, that individual can continue to serve until the end of the session even though the Senate might have rejected the nomination. When appointed to a vacancy that existed thirty days before the end of the last Senate session, a recess appointee is not paid until confirmed.

Recommit—To send a measure back to the committee that reported it; sometimes called a straight motion to recommit to distinguish it from a motion to recommit with instructions. A successful motion to recommit kills the measure unless it is accompanied by instructions.

Recommit a Conference Report—To return a conference report to the conference committee for renegotiation of some or all of its agreements. A motion to recommit may be offered with or without instructions.

Recommit with Instructions—To send a measure back to a committee with instructions to take some action on it. Invariably in the House and often in the Senate, when the motion recommits to a standing committee, the instructions require the committee to report the measure "forthwith" with specified amendments.

Reconciliation—A procedure for changing existing revenue and spending laws to bring total federal revenues and spending within the limits established in a budget resolution. Congress has applied reconciliation chiefly to revenues and mandatory spending programs, especially entitlements. Discretionary spending is controlled through annual appropriation bills.

Recorded Vote—(1) Generally, any vote in which members are recorded by name for or against a measure; also called a record vote or roll-call vote. The only recorded vote in the Senate is a vote by the yeas and nays and is commonly called a roll-call vote. (2) Technically, a recorded vote is one demanded in the House of Representatives and supported by at least one-fifth of a quorum (forty-four members) in the House sitting as the House or at least twenty-five members in Committee of the Whole.

Recorded Vote by Clerks—A voting procedure in the House where members pass through the appropriate "aye" or "no" aisle in the chamber and cast their votes by depositing a signed green (yea) or red (no) card in a ballot box. These votes are tabulated by clerks and reported to the chair. The electronic voting system is much more convenient and has largely supplanted this procedure. (See Committee of the Whole; Recorded Vote; Teller Vote.)

Redistricting—The redrawing of congressional district boundaries within a state after a decennial census. Redistricting may be required to equalize district populations or to accommodate an increase or decrease in the number of a state's House seats that might have resulted from the decennial apportionment. The state governments determine the district lines. (See Apportionment; Congressional District; Gerrymandering.)

Referral—The assignment of a measure to committee for consideration. Under a House rule, the Speaker can refuse to refer a measure if the Speaker believes it is "of an obscene or insulting character."

Report—(1) As a verb, a committee is said to report when it submits a measure or other document to its parent chamber. (2) A clerk is said to report when he or she reads a measure's title, text or the text of an amendment to the body at the direction of the chair. (3) As a noun, a committee document that accompanies a reported measure. It describes the measure, the committee's views on it, its costs and the changes it proposes to make in existing law; it also includes certain impact statements. (4) A committee document submitted to its parent chamber that describes the results of an investigation or other study or provides information it is required to provide by rule or law.

Representative—An elected and duly sworn member of the House of Representatives who is entitled to vote in the chamber. The Constitution requires that a representative be at least twenty-five years old, a citizen of the United States for at least seven years and an inhabitant of the state from which he or she is elected. Customarily, the member resides in the district he or she represents. Representatives are elected in even-numbered years to two-year terms that begin the following January.

Reprimand—A formal condemnation of a member for misbehavior, considered a milder reproof than censure. The House of Representatives first used it in 1976. The Senate first used it in 1991. (See also Censure; Code of Official Conduct; Denounce; Ethics Rules; Expulsion; Seniority Loss.)

Rescission—A provision of law that repeals previously enacted budget authority in whole or in part. Under the Impoundment Control Act of 1974, the president can impound such funds by sending a message to Congress requesting one or more rescissions and the reasons for doing so. If Congress does not pass a rescission bill for the programs requested by the president within forty-five days of continuous session after receiving the message, the president must make the funds available for obligation and expenditure. If the president does not, the comptroller general of the

United States is authorized to bring suit to compel the release of those funds. A rescission bill may rescind all, part or none of an amount proposed by the president, and may rescind funds the president has not impounded.

Reserving the Right To Object—Members' declaration that at some indefinite future time they may object to a unanimous consent request. It is an attempt to circumvent the requirement that members may prevent such an action only by objecting immediately after it is proposed.

Resident Commissioner from Puerto Rico—A nonvoting member of the House of Representatives, elected to a four-year term. The resident commissioner has the same status and privileges as delegates. Like the delegates, the resident commissioner may not vote in the House or Committee of the Whole.

Resolution—(1) A simple resolution; that is, a nonlegislative measure effective only in the house in which it is proposed and not requiring concurrence by the other chamber or approval by the president. Simple resolutions are designated H. Res. in the House and S. Res. in the Senate. Simple resolutions express non-binding opinions on policies or issues or deal with the internal affairs or prerogatives of a house. (2) Any type of resolution: simple, concurrent or joint. (See Concurrent Resolution; Joint Resolution.)

Resolution of Inquiry—A resolution usually simple rather than concurrent calling on the president or the head of an executive agency to provide specific information or papers to one or both houses.

Resolution of Ratification—The Senate vehicle for agreeing to a treaty. The constitutionally mandated vote of two-thirds of the senators present and voting applies to the adoption of this resolution. However, it may also contain amendments, reservations, declarations or understandings that the Senate had previously added to it by majority vote.

Revenue Legislation—Measures that levy new taxes or tariffs or change existing ones. Under Article I, Section 7, clause 1 of the Constitution, the House of Representatives originates federal revenue measures, but the Senate can propose amendments to them. The House Ways and Means Committee and the Senate Finance Committee have jurisdiction over such measures, with a few minor exceptions.

Revise and Extend One's Remarks—A unanimous consent request to publish in the Congressional Record a statement a member did not deliver on the floor, a longer statement than the one made on the floor or miscellaneous extraneous material.

Revolving Fund—A trust fund or account whose income remains available to finance its continuing operations without any fiscal year limitation.

Rider—Congressional slang for an amendment unrelated or extraneous to the subject matter of the measure to which it is attached. Riders often contain proposals that are less likely to become law on their own merits as separate bills, either because of opposition in the committee of jurisdiction, resistance in the other house or the probability of a presidential veto. Riders are more common in the Senate.

Roll Call—A call of the roll to determine whether a quorum is present, to establish a quorum or to vote on a question. Usually, the House uses its electronic voting system for a roll call. The Senate does not have an electronic voting system; its roll is always called by a clerk.

Rule—(1) A permanent regulation that a house adopts to govern its conduct of business, its procedures, its internal organization, behavior of its members, regulation of its facilities, duties of

an officer or some other subject it chooses to govern in that form. (2) In the House, a privileged simple resolution reported by the Rules Committee that provides methods and conditions for floor consideration of a measure or, rarely, several measures.

Rule Twenty-Two—A common reference to the Senate's cloture rule. (See Cloture)

Second-Degree Amendment—An amendment to an amendment in the first degree. It is usually a perfecting amendment.

Secretary of the Senate—The chief financial, administrative and legislative officer of the Senate. Elected by resolution or order of the Senate, the secretary is invariably the candidate of the majority party and usually chosen by the majority leader. In the absence of the vice president and pending the election of a president pro tempore, the secretary presides over the Senate. The secretary is subject to policy direction and oversight by the Senate Committee on Rules and Administration. The secretary manages a wide range of functions that support the administrative operations of the Senate as an organization as well as those functions necessary to its legislative process, including record keeping, document management, certifications, housekeeping services, administration of oaths and lobbyist registrations. The secretary is responsible for accounting for all funds appropriated to the Senate and conducts audits of Senate financial activities. On a semiannual basis the secretary issues the Report of the Secretary of the Senate, a compilation of Senate expenditures.

Section—A subdivision of a bill or statute. By law, a section must be numbered and, as nearly as possible, contain "a single proposition of enactment."

Select or Special Committee—A committee established by a resolution in either house for a special purpose and, usually, for a limited time. Most select and special committees are assigned specific investigations or studies but are not authorized to report measures to their chambers. However, both houses have created several permanent select and special committees and have given legislative reporting authority to a few of them: the Ethics Committee in the Senate and the Intelligence Committees in both houses. There is no substantive difference between a select and a special committee; they are so called depending simply on whether the resolution creating the committee calls it one or the other.

Senate—The house of Congress in which each state is represented by two senators; each senator has one vote. Article V of the Constitution declares that "No State, without its Consent, shall be deprived of its equal Suffrage in the Senate." The Constitution also gives the Senate equal legislative power with the House of Representatives. Although the Senate is prohibited from originating revenue measures, and as a matter of practice it does not originate appropriation measures, it can amend both. Only the Senate can give or withhold consent to treaties and nominations from the president. It also acts as a court to try impeachments by the House and elects the vice president when no candidate receives a majority of the electoral votes. It is often referred to as "the upper body," but not by members of the House.

Senate Manual—The handbook of the Senate's standing rules and orders and the laws and other regulations that apply to the Senate, usually published once each Congress.

Senator—A duly sworn elected or appointed member of the Senate. The Constitution requires that a senator be at least thirty years old, a citizen of the United States for at least nine years and an inhabitant of the state from which he or she is elected. Senators are usually elected in even-numbered years to six-year terms that begin the following January. When a vacancy occurs before the end of a term, the state governor can appoint a replacement to fill the position until a successor is chosen at the state's next general election or, if specified under state law, the next feasible date for such an election, to serve the remainder of the term. Until the Seventeenth Amendment was ratified in 1913, senators were chosen by their state legislatures.

Senatorial Courtesy—The Senate's practice of declining to confirm a presidential nominee for an office in the state of a senator of the president's party unless that senator approves.

Seniority—The priority, precedence or status accorded members according to the length of their continuous service in a house or on a committee.

Seniority Loss—A type of punishment that reduces a member's seniority on his or her committees, including the loss of chairmanships. Party caucuses in both houses have occasionally imposed such punishment on their members, for example, for publicly supporting candidates of the other party.

Seniority Rule—The customary practice, rather than a rule, of assigning the chairmanship of a committee to the majority party member who has served on the committee for the longest continuous period of time.

Seniority System—A collection of long-standing customary practices under which members with longer continuous service than their colleagues in their house or on their committees receive various kinds of preferential treatment. Although some of the practices are no longer as rigidly observed as in the past, they still pervade the organization and procedures of Congress.

Sequestration—A procedure for canceling budgetary resources — that is, money available for obligation or spending — to enforce budget limitations established in law. Sequestered funds are no longer available for obligation or expenditure.

Sergeant at Arms—The officer in each house responsible for maintaining order, security and decorum in its wing of the Capitol, including the chamber and its galleries. Although elected by their respective houses, both sergeants at arms are invariably the candidates of the majority party.

Session—(1) The annual series of meetings of a Congress. Under the Constitution, Congress must assemble at least once a year at noon on Jan. 3 unless it appoints a different day by law. (2) The special meetings of Congress or of one house convened by the president, called a special session. (3) A house is said to be in session during the period of a day when it is meeting.

Severability (or Separability) Clause—Language stating that if any particular provisions of a measure are declared invalid by the courts the remaining provisions shall remain in effect.

Sine Die—Without fixing a day for a future meeting. An adjournment sine die signifies the end of an annual or special session of Congress.

Slip Law—The first official publication of a measure that has become law. It is published separately in unbound, single-sheet form or pamphlet form. A slip law usually is available two or three days after the date of the law's enactment.

Speaker—The presiding officer of the House of Representatives and the leader of its majority party. The Speaker is selected by the majority party and formally elected by the House at the beginning of each Congress. Although the Constitution does not require the Speaker to be a member of the House, in fact, all Speakers have been members.

Speaker Pro Tempore—A member of the House who is designated as the temporary presiding officer by the Speaker or elected by the House to that position during the Speaker's absence.

Speaker's Vote—The Speaker is not required to vote, and the Speaker's name is not called on a roll-call vote unless so requested.

Usually, the Speaker votes either to create a tie vote, and thereby defeat a proposal or to break a tie in favor of a proposal. Occasionally, the Speaker also votes to emphasize the importance of a matter.

Special Session—A session of Congress convened by the president, under his constitutional authority, after Congress has adjourned sine die at the end of a regular session. (See Adjournment Sine Die; Session.)

Spending Authority—The technical term for backdoor spending. The Congressional Budget Act of 1974 defines it as borrowing authority, contract authority and entitlement authority for which appropriation acts do not provide budget authority in advance. Under the Budget Act, legislation that provides new spending authority may not be considered unless it provides that the authority shall be effective only to the extent or in such amounts as provided in an appropriation act.

Spending Cap—The statutory limit for a fiscal year on the amount of new budget authority and outlays allowed for discretionary spending. The Budget Enforcement Act of 1997 requires a sequester if the cap is exceeded.

Split Referral—A measure divided into two or more parts, with each part referred to a different committee.

Sponsor—The principal proponent and introducer of a measure or an amendment.

Staff Director—The most frequently used title for the head of staff of a committee or subcommittee. On some committees, that person is called chief of staff, clerk, chief clerk, chief counsel, general counsel or executive director. The head of a committee's minority staff is usually called minority staff director.

Standing Committee—A permanent committee established by a House or Senate standing rule or standing order. The rule also describes the subject areas on which the committee may report bills and resolutions and conduct oversight. Most introduced measures must be referred to one or more standing committees according to their jurisdictions.

Standing Order—A continuing regulation or directive that has the force and effect of a rule, but is not incorporated into the standing rules. The Senate's numerous standing orders, like its standing rules, continue from Congress to Congress unless changed or the order states otherwise. The House uses relatively few standing orders, and those it adopts expire at the end of a session of Congress.

Standing Rules—The rules of the Senate that continue from one Congress to the next and the rules of the House of Representatives that it adopts at the beginning of each new Congress.

Standing Vote—An alternative and informal term for a division vote, during which members in favor of a proposal and then members opposed stand and are counted by the chair.

Star Print—A reprint of a bill, resolution, amendment or committee report correcting technical or substantive errors in a previous printing; so called because of the small black star that appears on the front page or cover.

State of the Union Message—A presidential message to Congress under the constitutional directive that the president shall "from time to time give to the Congress Information of the State of the Union, and recommend to their Consideration such Measures as he shall judge necessary and expedient." Customarily, the president sends an annual State of the Union message to Congress, usually late in January.

Statutes at Large—A chronological arrangement of the laws enacted in each session of Congress. Though indexed, the laws are not arranged by subject matter nor is there an indication of how they affect or change previously enacted laws. The volumes are numbered by Congress, and the laws are cited by their volume and page number. The Gramm-Rudman-Hollings Act, for example, appears as 99 Stat. 1037.

Straw Vote Prohibition—Under a House precedent, a member who has the floor during debate may not conduct a straw vote or otherwise ask for a show of support for a proposition. Only the chair may put a question to a vote.

Strike From the *Record*—Expunge objectionable remarks from the Congressional Record, after a member's words have been taken down on a point of order.

Subcommittee—A panel of committee members assigned a portion of the committee's jurisdiction or other functions. On legislative committees, subcommittees hold hearings, mark up legislation and report measures to their full committee for further action; they cannot report directly to the chamber. A subcommittee's party composition usually reflects the ratio on its parent committee.

Subpoena Power—The authority granted to committees by the rules of their respective houses to issue legal orders requiring individuals to appear and testify, or to produce documents pertinent to the committee's functions, or both. Persons who do not comply with subpoenas can be cited for contempt of Congress and prosecuted.

Subsidy—Generally, a payment or benefit made by the federal government for which no current repayment is required. Subsidy payments may be designed to support the conduct of an economic enterprise or activity, such as ship operations, or to support certain market prices, as in the case of farm subsidies.

Sunset Legislation—A term sometimes applied to laws authorizing the existence of agencies or programs that expire annually or at the end of some other specified period of time. One of the purposes of setting specific expiration dates for agencies and programs is to encourage the committees with jurisdiction over them to determine whether they should be continued or terminated.

Sunshine Rules—Rules requiring open committee hearings and business meetings, including markup sessions, in both houses, and also open conference committee meetings. However, all may be closed under certain circumstances and using certain procedures required by the rules.

Supermajority—A term sometimes used for a vote on a matter that requires approval by more than a simple majority of those members present and voting; also referred to as extraordinary majority.

Supplemental Appropriation Bill—A measure providing appropriations for use in the current fiscal year, in addition to those already provided in annual general appropriation bills. Supplemental appropriations are often for unforeseen emergencies.

Suspension of the Rules (House)—An expeditious procedure for passing relatively noncontroversial or emergency measures by a two-thirds vote of those members voting, a quorum being present.

Suspension of the Rules (Senate)—A procedure to set aside one or more of the Senate's rules; it is used infrequently, and then most often to suspend the rule banning legislative amendments to appropriation bills.

Task Force—A title sometimes given to a panel of members assigned to a special project, study or investigation. Ordinarily, these groups do not have authority to report measures to their respective houses.

Tax Expenditure—Loosely, a tax exemption or advantage, sometimes called an incentive or loophole; technically, a loss of governmental tax revenue attributable to some provision of federal tax laws that allows a special exclusion, exemption or deduction from gross income or that provides a special credit, preferential tax rate or deferral of tax liability.

Televised Proceedings—Television and radio coverage of the floor proceedings of the House of Representatives has been available since 1979 and of the Senate since 1986. They are broadcast over a coaxial cable system to all congressional offices and to some congressional agencies on channels reserved for that purpose. Coverage is also available free of charge to commercial and public television and radio broadcasters. The Cable-Satellite Public Affairs Network (C-SPAN) carries gavel-to-gavel coverage of both houses.

Teller Vote—A voting procedure, formerly used in the House, in which members cast their votes by passing through the center aisle to be counted, but not recorded by name, by a member from each party appointed by the chair. The House deleted the procedure from its rules in 1993, but during floor discussion of the deletion a leading member stated that a teller vote would still be available in the event of a breakdown of the electronic voting system.

Third-Degree Amendment—An amendment to a second-degree amendment. Both houses prohibit such amendments.

Third Reading—A required reading to a chamber of a bill or joint resolution by title only before the vote on passage. In modern practice, it has merely become a pro forma step.

Three-Day Rule—(1) In the House, a measure cannot be considered until the third calendar day on which the committee report has been available. (2) In the House, a conference report cannot be considered until the third calendar day on which its text has been available in the Congressional Record. (3) In the House, a general appropriation bill cannot be considered until the third calendar day on which printed hearings on the bill have been available. (4) In the Senate, when a committee votes to report a measure, a committee member is entitled to three calendar days within which to submit separate views for inclusion in the committee report. (In House committees, a member is entitled to two calendar days for this purpose, after the day on which the committee votes to report.) (5) In both houses, a majority of a committee's members may call a special meeting of the committee if its chairman fails to do so within three calendar days after three or more of the members, acting jointly, formally request such a meeting.

In calculating such periods, the House omits holiday and weekend days on which it does not meet. The Senate makes no such exclusion.

Tie Vote—When the votes for and against a proposition are equal, it loses. The president of the Senate may cast a vote only to break a tie. Because the Speaker is invariably a member of the House, the Speaker is entitled to vote but usually does not. The Speaker may choose to do so to break, or create, a tie vote.

Title—(1) A major subdivision of a bill or act, designated by a roman numeral and usually containing legislative provisions on the same general subject. Titles are sometimes divided into subtitles as well as sections. (2) The official name of a bill or act, also called a caption or long title. (3) Some bills also have short titles that appear in the sentence immediately following the enacting clause. (4) Popular titles are the unofficial names given to some bills or acts by common usage. For example, the Balanced Budget and Emergency Deficit Control Act of 1985 (short title) is almost invariably referred to as Gramm-Rudman (popular title). In other cases, significant legislation is popularly referred to by its title number (see definition (1) above). For example, the federal legislation that requires equality of funding for women's and men's sports in educational institutions that receive federal funds is popularly called Title IX.

Track System—An occasional Senate practice that expedites legislation by dividing a day's session into two or more specific time periods, commonly called tracks, each reserved for consideration of a different measure.

Transfer Payment—A federal government payment to which individuals or organizations are entitled under law and for which no goods or services are required in return. Payments include welfare and Social Security benefits, unemployment insurance, government pensions and veterans benefits.

Treaty—A formal document containing an agreement between two or more sovereign nations. The Constitution authorizes the president to make treaties, but the president must submit them to the Senate for its approval by a two-thirds vote of the senators present. Under the Senate's rules, that vote actually occurs on a resolution of ratification. Although the Constitution does not give the House a direct role in approving treaties, that body has sometimes insisted that a revenue treaty is an invasion of its prerogatives. In any case, the House may significantly affect the application of a treaty by its equal role in enacting legislation to implement the treaty.

Trust Funds—Special accounts in the Treasury that receive earmarked taxes or other kinds of revenue collections, such as user fees, and from which payments are made for special purposes or to recipients who meet the requirements of the trust funds as established by law. Of the more than 150 federal government trust funds, several finance major entitlement programs, such as Social Security, Medicare and retired federal employees' pensions. Others fund infrastructure construction and improvements, such as highways and airports.

Unanimous Consent—Without an objection by any member. A unanimous consent request asks permission, explicitly or implicitly, to set aside one or more rules. Both houses and their committees frequently use such requests to expedite their proceedings.

Uncontrollable Expenditures—A frequently used term for federal expenditures that are mandatory under existing law and therefore cannot be controlled by the president or Congress without a change in the existing law. Uncontrollable expenditures include spending required under entitlement programs and also fixed costs, such as interest on the public debt and outlays to pay for prior-year obligations. In recent years, uncontrollables have accounted for approximately three-quarters of federal spending in each fiscal year.

Unfunded Mandate—Generally, any provision in federal law or regulation that imposes a duty or obligation on a state or local government or private sector entity without providing the necessary funds to comply. The Unfunded Mandates Reform Act of 1995 amended the Congressional Budget Act of 1974 to provide a mechanism for the control of new unfunded mandates.

Union Calendar—A calendar of the House of Representatives for bills and resolutions favorably reported by committees that raise revenue or directly or indirectly appropriate money or property. In addition to appropriation bills, measures that authorize expenditures are also placed on this calendar. The calendar's full title is the Calendar of the Committee of the Whole House on the State of the Union.

Upper Body—A common reference to the Senate, but not used by members of the House.

U.S. Code—Popular title for the United States Code: Containing the General and Permanent Laws of the United States in Force on.... It is a consolidation and partial codification of the general and permanent laws of the United States arranged by subject under 50 titles. The first six titles deal with general or political subjects, the other forty-four with subjects ranging from agriculture to war, alphabetically arranged. A supplement is published after each session of Congress, and the entire Code is revised every six years.

User Fee—A fee charged to users of goods or services provided by the federal government. When Congress levies or authorizes such fees, it determines whether the revenues should go into the general collections of the Treasury or be available for expenditure by the agency that provides the goods or services.

Veto—The president's disapproval of a legislative measure passed by Congress. The president returns the measure to the house in which it originated without his signature but with a veto message stating his objections to it. When Congress is in session, the president must veto a bill within ten days, excluding Sundays, after the president has received it; otherwise it becomes law without his signature. The ten-day clock begins to run at midnight following his receipt of the bill. (See also Committee Veto; Item Veto; Line Item Veto Act of 1996; Override a Veto; Pocket Veto.)

Voice Vote—A method of voting in which members who favor a question answer aye in chorus, after which those opposed answer no in chorus, and the chair decides which position prevails.

Voting—Members vote in three ways on the floor: (1) by shouting "aye" or "no" on voice votes; (2) by standing for or against on division votes; and (3) on recorded votes (including the yeas and nays), by answering "aye" or "no" when their names are called or, in the House, by recording their votes through the electronic voting system.

War Powers Resolution of 1973—An act that requires the president "in every possible instance" to consult Congress before committing U.S. forces to ongoing or imminent hostilities. If the president commits them to a combat situation without congressional consultation, the president must notify Congress within forty-eight hours. Unless Congress declares war or otherwise authorizes the operation to continue, the forces must be withdrawn within sixty or ninety days, depending on certain conditions. No president has ever acknowledged the constitutionality of the resolution.

Well—The sunken, level, open space between members' seats and the podium at the front of each chamber. House members usually address their chamber from their party's lectern in the well on its side of the aisle. Senators usually speak at their assigned desks.

Whip—The majority or minority party member in each house who acts as assistant leader, helps plan and marshal support for party strategies, encourages party discipline and advises his or her leader on how colleagues intend to vote on the floor. In the Senate, the Republican whip's official title is assistant leader.

Yeas and Nays—A vote in which members usually respond "aye" or "no" (despite the official title of the vote) on a question when their names are called in alphabetical order. The Constitution requires the yeas and nays when a demand for it is supported by one-fifth of the members present, and it also requires an automatic yea-and-nay vote on overriding a veto. Senate precedents require the support of at least one-fifth of a quorum, a minimum of eleven members with the present membership of 100.

Congressional Information on the Internet

A huge array of congressional information is available for free at Internet sites operated by the federal government, colleges and universities and commercial firms. The sites offer the full text of bills introduced in the House and Senate, voting records, campaign finance information, transcripts of selected congressional hearings, investigative reports and much more.

THOMAS

The most important site for congressional information is THOMAS (*http://thomas.loc.gov*), which is named for Thomas Jefferson and operated by the Library of Congress. THOMAS' highlight is its databases containing the full text of all bills introduced in Congress since 1989, the full text of the *Congressional Record* since 1989 and the status and summary information for all bills introduced since 1973.

THOMAS also offers special links to bills that have received or are expected to receive floor action during the current week and newsworthy bills that are pending or that have recently been approved. Finally, THOMAS has selected committee reports, answers to frequently asked questions about accessing congressional information, publications titled *How Our Laws Are Made* and *Enactment of a Law* and links to lots of other congressional Web sites.

House of Representatives

The U.S. House of Representatives site (*http://www.house. gov*) offers the schedule of bills, resolutions and other legislative issues the House will consider in the current week. It also has updates about current proceedings on the House floor and a list of the next day's meeting of House committees. Other highlights include a database that helps users identify their representative, a directory of House members and committees, the House ethics manual, links to Web pages maintained by House members and committees, a calendar of congressional primary dates and candidate-filing deadlines for ballot access, the full text of all amendments to the Constitution that have been ratified and those that have been proposed but not ratified and lots of information about Washington, D.C., for visitors.

Another key House site is The Office of the Clerk On-line Information Center (*http://clerkweb.house.gov*), which has records of all roll-call votes taken since 1990. The votes are recorded by bill, so it is a lengthy process to compile a particular representative's voting record. The site also has lists of committee assignments, a telephone directory for members and committees, mailing label templates for members and committees, rules of the current Congress, election statistics from 1920 to the present, biographies of Speakers of the House, biographies of women who have served since 1917 and a virtual tour of the House Chamber.

One of the more interesting House sites is operated by the Subcommittee on Rules and Organization of the House Committee on Rules (*http://www.house.gov/rules/crs_reports. htm*). Its highlight is dozens of Congressional Research Service reports about the legislative process. Some of the available titles include *Legislative Research in Congressional Offices: A Primer, How to Follow Current Federal Legislation and Regulations; Investigative Oversight: An Introduction to the Law, Practice and Procedure of Congressional Inquiry;* and *Presidential Vetoes 1789 – Present: A Summary Overview.*

Senate

At least in the Internet world, the Senate is not as active as the House. Its main Web site (*http://www.senate.gov*) has records of all roll-call votes taken since 1989 (arranged by bill), brief descriptions of all bills and joint resolutions introduced in the Senate during the past week and a calendar of upcoming committee hearings. The site also provides the standing rules of the Senate, a directory of senators and their committee assignments, lists of nominations that the president has submitted to the Senate for approval, links to Web pages operated by senators and committees and a virtual tour of the Senate.

Information about the membership, jurisdiction and rules of each congressional committee is available at the U.S. Government Printing Office site (*http://www.access.gpo.gov/congress/ index.html*). It also has transcripts of selected congressional hearings, the full text of selected House and Senate reports and the House and Senate rules manuals.

General Reference

The U.S. General Accounting Office, the investigative arm of Congress, operates a site (*http://www.gao.gov*) that provides the full text of its reports from 1975 to the present. The reports cover a wide range of topics: aviation safety, combating terrorism, counternarcotics efforts in Mexico, defense contracting, electronic warfare, food assistance programs, Gulf War illness, health insurance, illegal aliens, information technology, long-term care, mass transit, Medicare, military readiness, money laundering, national parks, nuclear waste, organ donation and student loan defaults, among others.

The GAO Daybook is an excellent current awareness tool. This electronic mailing list distributes a daily list of reports and testimony released by the GAO. Subscriptions are available by sending an e-mail message to *majordomo@www.gao.gov*, and in the message area typing "subscribe daybook" (without the quotation marks).

Current budget and economic projections are provided at the Congressional Budget Office Web site (*http://www.cbo.gov*). The site also has reports about the economic and budget outlook for the next decade, the president's budget proposals, federal civilian employment, Social Security privatization, tax reform, water use conflicts in the West, marriage and the federal income tax and the role of foreign aid in development, among other topics. Other highlights include monthly budget updates, historical budget data, cost estimates for bills reported by congressional committees and transcripts of congressional testimony by CBO officials.

Campaign Finance

Several Internet sites provide detailed campaign finance data for congressional elections. The official site is operated by the Federal Election Commission (*http://www.fec.gov*), which regulates political spending. The site's highlight is its database of campaign reports filed from May 1996 to the present by House and presidential candidates, political action committees and political party committees. Senate reports are not included because they are filed with the Secretary of the Senate. The reports in the FEC's database are scanned images of paper reports filed with the commission.

The FEC site also has summary financial data for House and Senate candidates in the current election cycle, abstracts of court decisions pertaining to federal election law from 1976 to 1997, a graph showing the number of political action committees in existence each year from 1974 to the present and a directory of national and state agencies that are responsible for releasing information about campaign financing, candidates on the ballot, election results, lobbying and other issues. Another useful feature is a collection of brochures about federal election law, public funding of presidential elections, the ban on contributions by foreign nationals, independent expenditures supporting or opposing a candidate for federal office, contribution limits, filing a complaint, researching public records at the FEC and other topics. Finally, the site provides the FEC's legislative recommendations, its annual report, a report about its first twenty years in existence, the FEC's monthly newsletter, several reports about voter registration, election results for the most re-

cent presidential and congressional elections and campaign guides for corporations and labor organizations, congressional candidates and committees, political party committees and nonconnected committees.

The best online source for campaign finance data is Political Money Line (*http://www.tray.com*). The site's searchable databases provide extensive itemized information about receipts and expenditures by federal candidates and political action committees from 1980 to the present. The data, which are obtained from the FEC, are quite detailed. For example, for candidates contributions can be searched by Zip Code. The site also has lists of the top political action committees in various categories, lists of the top contributors from each state and much more.

Another interesting site is the American University Campaign Finance Website (*http://www1.soc.american.edu/campfin*), which is operated by the American University School of Communication. It provides electronic files from the FEC that have been reformatted in .dbf format so they can be used in database programs such as Paradox, Access and FoxPro. The files contain data on PAC, committee and individual contributions to individual congressional candidates.

More campaign finance data is available from the Center for Responsive Politics (*http://www.opensecrets.org*), a public interest organization. The center provides a list of all "soft money" donations to political parties of $100,000 or more in the current election cycle and data about "leadership" political action committees associated with individual politicians. Other databases at the site provide information about travel expenses that House members received from private sources for attending meetings and other events, activities of registered federal lobbyists and activities of foreign agents who are registered in the United States.

Index